Pro SharePoint 2003 Development Techniques

Nikander Bruggeman and
Margriet Bruggeman

Apress®

Pro SharePoint 2003 Development Techniques

Copyright © 2006 by Nikander Bruggeman and Margriet Bruggeman

ISBN-13 (paperback): 978-1-59059-761-3

ISBN-13 (electronic): 978-1-4302-0361-2

Printed and bound in the United States of America (POD)

Trademarked names may appear in this book. Rather than use a trademark symbol with every occurrence of a trademarked name, we use the names only in an editorial fashion and to the benefit of the trademark owner, with no intention of infringement of the trademark.

Lead Editor: Jonathan Hassell
Technical Reviewer: Scot Hillier
Editorial Board: Steve Anglin, Ewan Buckingham, Gary Cornell, Jason Gilmore, Jonathan Gennick,
    Jonathan Hassell, James Huddleston, Chris Mills, Matthew Moodie, Dominic Shakeshaft, Jim Sumser,
    Keir Thomas, Matt Wade
Project Manager: Tracy Brown Collins
Copy Edit Manager: Nicole Flores
Copy Editor: Jennifer Whipple
Assistant Production Director: Kari Brooks-Copony
Production Editor: Laura Cheu
Compositor: Susan Glinert Stevens
Proofreader: Dan Shaw
Indexer: Michael Brinkman
Artist: April Milne
Cover Designer: Kurt Krames
Manufacturing Director: Tom Debolski

Distributed to the book trade worldwide by Springer-Verlag New York, Inc., 233 Spring Street, 6th Floor, New York, NY 10013. Phone 1-800-SPRINGER, fax 201-348-4505, e-mail orders-ny@springer-sbm.com, or visit http://www.springeronline.com.

For information on translations, please contact Apress directly at 2855 Telegraph Avenue, Suite 600, Berkeley, CA 94705. Phone 510-549-5930, fax 510-549-5939, e-mail info@apress.com, or visit http://www.apress.com.

The information in this book is distributed on an "as is" basis, without warranty. Although every precaution has been taken in the preparation of this work, neither the author(s) nor Apress shall have any liability to any person or entity with respect to any loss or damage caused or alleged to be caused directly or indirectly by the information contained in this work.

The source code for this book is available to readers at http://www.apress.com in the Source Code/Download section.

Contents at a Glance

Contents

About the Authors

NIKANDER BRUGGEMAN started his career building web sites using HTML, CGI, and Perl. Later, when JavaScript 1.0 was released, he built numerous web sites based on LiveWire technology while working for a Netscape-oriented company. Nikander then moved to a company that specializes in Microsoft technology. Currently, Nikander is an independent consultant, specializing in building .NET applications using the latest Microsoft technology. His current work includes software design, development, consulting, and training, and he has worked for companies such as Universal Music, Arvato-Bertelsmann, Coca-Cola, Shell, Intel, and Sara Lee/DE. He was given the prestigious Most Valuable Professional (MVP) award from Microsoft for his work on the SharePoint Portal Server platform. Nikander has coauthored several other SharePoint books and has written numerous articles. He lives in the heart of Amsterdam, and when not developing software or writing about it, he loves to watch sports and movies. Nikander can be reached via `info@lcbridge.nl`.

MARGRIET BRUGGEMAN began her professional career as a quality assurance engineer. She then became a software developer, architect, consultant, and trainer. Margriet is an independent consultant specializing in building .NET applications using the latest Microsoft technology. She has worked for companies such as Interpay, Ericsson, Ford, Corus, Interpolis, and SNS Reaal. Margriet has written numerous articles, coauthored multiple SharePoint books, and was awarded the prestigious Most Valuable Professional (MVP) award from Microsoft for her work on the SharePoint Portal Server platform. Margriet is very fond of animals, and when not busy doing IT-related activities, she can be found near dogs, cats, horses, rabbits, birds, and other fuzzy creatures. Margriet can be reached via `info@lcbridge.nl`.

About the Technical Reviewer

SCOT HILLIER is an independent consultant and Microsoft Most Valuable Professional focused on creating solutions for information workers with SharePoint, Office, and related .NET technologies. He is the author of eight books on Microsoft technologies, including *Microsoft SharePoint: Building Office 2003 Solutions* and *Advanced Windows SharePoint Services*. Scot is also a former Microsoft regional director for Hartford, Connecticut. When not writing about technology, Scot can often be found presenting to audiences ranging from developers to C-level executives. Scot is a former naval submarine officer and a graduate of the Virginia Military Institute. Scot can be reached at scot@shillier.com.

Acknowledgments

When we reflect on the period in which we wrote this book, we both agree that it was a whole lot of work and a whole lot of fun. We did not have to do it all alone; so some thanks are in order. Firstly, we would like to thank everyone at Apress. Without their support, the book would not have been possible. Our special thanks go out to Jonathan Hassell, for his enthusiastic and quick responses, and Tracy Brown Collins, for bringing our project planning to the next level and speaking Dutch almost fluently. Nikander would like to thank his father and mother, Henk Bruggeman and Winie Bruggeman-Wuyster, for making him believe a lot can be accomplished if you truly want it. Margriet would like to thank her father, Adriaan van Vuuren, for his repeated offers of help that were much appreciated. Margriet deeply regrets that her mother, Maria van Vuuren-Licht, won't be able to see this book. We know you would have been so proud.

Introduction

SharePoint Products and Technologies 2003 has been around for a couple of years now. We like the product and have been working with SharePoint technology since the beta release of SharePoint Portal Server 2001. Lately, we had the feeling that there was room for a new book about SharePoint Products and Technologies 2003: a book that describes contemporary development techniques for doing SharePoint development. This book comes at a perfect time. It could not have been written one or two years earlier, because it describes brand-new technology; and in one or two more years SharePoint 2007 will hit the market and be slowly adopted by companies. The result of this thinking is the book you are holding in your hands.

What Does This Book Cover?

This book discusses different contemporary development techniques for doing SharePoint development. Every chapter is independent of the other chapters, so you can read the book from cover to cover or in any other order you see fit, according to your personal interest. The following sections describe the contents of each chapter.

Chapter 1: Incorporating .NET 2.0 in SharePoint

As the .NET 2.0 Framework is an important part of most technologies discussed in this book, we start with a discussion of the integration between SharePoint Products and Technologies 2003 and .NET Framework 2.0. This chapter discusses how to install .NET Framework 2.0 on Windows SharePoint Services server, creating SharePoint web parts via Visual Studio .NET 2005, enhancing development with the Guidance Automation Toolkit (GAT), learning how to run Windows SharePoint Services in combination with SQL Server 2005, and learning how to use .NET 2.0 controls in web parts.

Chapter 2: Using Ajax and Atlas in Web Parts

Ajax is a framework for communicating client-side with servers in an asynchronous manner. Atlas is a framework to build rich web applications on top of ASP.NET 2.0. This enhances the user interface experience significantly, getting much closer to a Windows Form application experience. In this chapter we show the reader how to use client-side JavaScript in web parts using .NET 2.0. This chapter discusses different types of server responses: plain text, HTML, XML, and JSON. This chapter also explains how to incorporate Ajax and Atlas into web parts.

Chapter 3: SQL Server 2005 Reporting Services

This chapter starts with a discussion of SQL Server 2005 Reporting Services. Then you will learn how to create a report using the Business Intelligence Development Studio. After that, you will learn which SharePoint Reporting web parts are available and how you should use them. This chapter takes a look at the architecture of Reporting extensions, taking a closer look at creating custom data extensions and delivering extensions. Finally, the chapter discusses what the SQL Server Report Pack for SharePoint Portal Server 2003 is and how you should use it.

Chapter 4: Windows Workflow Foundation

Creating workflows in SharePoint 2003 technology without the aid of third-party vendors has been quite difficult to do. Windows Workflow Foundation changes this. This chapter discusses what Windows Workflow Foundation is. Then it explains how to create workflows and custom activities using the Visual Studio 2005 Designer for Windows Workflow Foundation. The final part of the chapter is dedicated to showing you how to combine Windows Workflow Foundation and Windows SharePoint Services.

Chapter 5: Software Factories and Web Part Connections

In this chapter you will learn why software factories are an important contemporary trend in software architecture. The chapter teaches you how to build a domain-specific language for creating connectable web parts using the Visual Studio.NET 2005 DSL tools.

Chapter 6: Web Services for Remote Portlets

The Web Services for Remote Portlets (WSRP) protocol is a web services protocol for aggregating content and interactive web applications from remote sources. In this chapter, we discuss what WSRP is and how this specification can be of help in portal implementations. After that, we look deeper into the WSRP specification. Also, we explain how to configure a generic WSRP consumer web part in SharePoint and how to build WSRP producers.

Chapter 7: InfoPath

This chapter discusses the integration between SharePoint and InfoPath. It also discusses the integration between SharePoint, InfoPath, and BizTalk 2006. You will learn how to access data stored in a SharePoint list from within an InfoPath form and create and update InfoPath forms programmatically in a SharePoint form library.

Chapter 8: Impersonation and Elevation

Code is executed under a given identity. There are several techniques available to do this. This chapter provides a detailed discussion of the impersonation, elevation, and delegation techniques that are at your disposal.

Who Is This Book For?

This book is targeted to SharePoint Portal Server and Windows SharePoint Services developers who want to learn about the shape of the landscape of SharePoint 2003 development in 2006 and beyond, integrating a range of new .NET technologies that have already become or will soon become mainstream. The book will provide information and insight about contemporary development techniques that will help you in your daily activities as a SharePoint developer.

What Do You Need to Use This Book?

Each chapter discusses the requirements for testing the techniques and examples described in the chapter. In general, you will need to have access to Windows SharePoint Services, SharePoint Portal Server 2003, and Visual Studio .NET 2005.

Source Code

The code listings in this book can be downloaded from `http://www.lcbridge.nl/download`.

■ ■ ■

CHAPTER 1

Incorporating .NET 2.0 in SharePoint

Microsoft SharePoint Products and Technologies has been around for a couple of years now and has proven to be very useful for companies around the world that are implementing portal, team collaboration, or enterprise content management strategies.

The development landscape has changed considerably since SharePoint Products and Technologies was introduced in 2003, largely influenced by the release of Microsoft .NET Framework 2.0. This chapter discusses how to incorporate the exciting new features of .NET 2.0 into SharePoint Products and Technologies.

First, the chapter discusses the service packs for Office SharePoint Portal Server 2003 and Windows SharePoint Services, the two products that make up SharePoint Products and Technologies. We cover installation of these as well as ASP.NET 2.0 and how to use data stores.

This chapter also discusses how to create web parts with Visual Studio .NET 2005 and extend your development possibilities with its Guidance Automation Toolkit (GAT).

To finish this chapter we will show you how to incorporate the new ASP.NET 2.0 server controls within web parts.

SharePoint Products and Service Packs

SharePoint Products and Technologies is made up of two different products: Office SharePoint Portal Server 2003 and Windows SharePoint Services. At the end of 2005, Microsoft released Service Pack 2.0, two service packs for SharePoint Portal Server 2003 and Windows SharePoint Services. These two service packs contain four new enhancements. The following three enhancements apply to both SharePoint Portal Server and Windows SharePoint Services:

- *The ability to run on Microsoft Windows Server 64-bit versions.* SharePoint Portal Server and Windows SharePoint Services both support being run in Windows on Windows 64 (WOW 64) 32-bit emulation mode on 64-bit versions of Windows, although there are no performance improvements. However, other applications and the operating system itself might be able to take advantage of the 64-bit server functionality.

- *Use of SQL Server 2005*: Microsoft SQL Server 2005 includes features such as extended XML support and integrated Common Language Runtime (CLR) support. Windows SharePoint Services and SharePoint Portal Server 2003 do not take advantage of that new functionality. However, there are general benefits to be gained in upgrading to SQL Server 2005, such as better performance.

- *Improved extranet deployment options*: In Windows SharePoint Services and SharePoint Portal Server some of the hyperlinks within web pages and e-mail messages are absolute URLs. Earlier releases of Windows SharePoint Services generated those absolute URLs by using the protocol scheme, host, and port of the web request that Windows SharePoint Services received, or by using the base URL of the site, which could prevent Windows SharePoint Services from supporting certain advanced extranet scenarios where a reverse proxy server is deployed in front of the server running Windows SharePoint Services. This is solved by the new service packs.

The fourth enhancement, support for the Microsoft .NET Framework 2.0 Common Language Runtime and ASP.NET 2.0, only applies to Windows SharePoint Services. SharePoint Portal Server 2003 (with or without Service Pack 2.0) will not support .NET Framework 2.0. The only kind of support you have in SharePoint Portal Server 2003 for .NET Framework 2.0 is the ability to call .NET 2.0 web services and redisplay pages that are written in ASP.NET 2.0. Developing web parts in Visual Studio .NET 2005 is only possible for Windows SharePoint Services with Service Pack 2.0 installed.

The support in Windows SharePoint Services for ASP.NET 2.0 does not include integration with the ASP.NET 2.0 web part Framework. If you deploy a web part that is built in ASP.NET 2.0 to a Windows SharePoint Services server, it will function as a normal web form control.

Although Windows SharePoint Services with Service Pack 2.0 runs on the new Common Language Runtime, it is not redesigned to take advantage of the new features of ASP.NET 2.0. For example, there is no support for master pages in Windows SharePoint Services. On the other hand, the new class libraries found in ASP.NET 2.0 can be used within custom SharePoint web parts.

After applying Windows SharePoint Services Service Pack 2.0, the SharePoint worker process can run in ASP.NET 2.0 mode, but you can also choose to run in ASP.NET 1.0 mode. You will only be able to use the new features and the security and performance enhancements of ASP.NET 2.0 when Windows SharePoint Services runs in ASP.NET 2.0 mode. You can run ASP.NET 1.x and 2.0 at the same time on a server if you are using different Windows SharePoint Services virtual servers. Windows SharePoint Services itself has the same functionality, regardless of whether you are running on ASP.NET 2.0 or ASP.NET 1.x.

Installing Windows SharePoint Services and ASP.NET 2.0

In this section, we show you how to install Windows SharePoint Services Service Pack 2 and ASP.NET 2.0.

As a starting point, every SharePoint server will have ASP.NET 1.1 installed on it. However, it is possible to run ASP.NET 1.1 and ASP.NET 2.0 side by side on the same server. There is an important limitation: if you install ASP.NET 2.0 on a server, you cannot install SharePoint Portal Server 2003 on that machine anymore. As a consequence, upgrading to ASP.NET 2.0 is not an option for SharePoint Portal Server 2003, although it is an appealing option for Windows SharePoint Services. For Windows SharePoint Services installations, if you upgrade to ASP.NET 2.0 (and the .NET Framework 2.0, which is automatically upgraded when installing ASP.NET 2.0) you will be able to take advantage of the many improvements to the development framework and environment. Your code will also be able to take advantage of new security and performance enhancements.

In our experience the installation process works best if you start with a clean install of Windows Server 2003 R2. The R2 release is required; previous versions of Windows Server 2003 will not work. After installing Windows Server 2003 R2, the first thing to do is to install Internet Information Services (IIS). This can be done by going to Add or Remove Programs via the Control Panel and then choosing Add/Remove Windows Components. Make sure not to install FrontPage Server Extensions. Do not install ASP.NET at this time; otherwise the installation process will fail.

After installing IIS, you are ready to install ASP.NET 2.0. Go back to Add or Remove Programs and click Add/Remove Windows Components. Select Microsoft .NET Framework 2.0 and click Next to install.

The next step is to configure IIS for ASP.NET 2.0. Go to the Internet Information Services Manager by typing **inetmgr** at the command prompt and right-click the virtual server you want to configure, and then click Properties. In the Default Web Site Properties window go to the ASP.NET tab and choose the right ASP.NET version (version 2.0) from the drop-down list and click OK. Figure 1-1 shows the ASP.NET tab in the Default Web Site Properties window. Finally, restart IIS by typing **iisreset** at the command prompt.

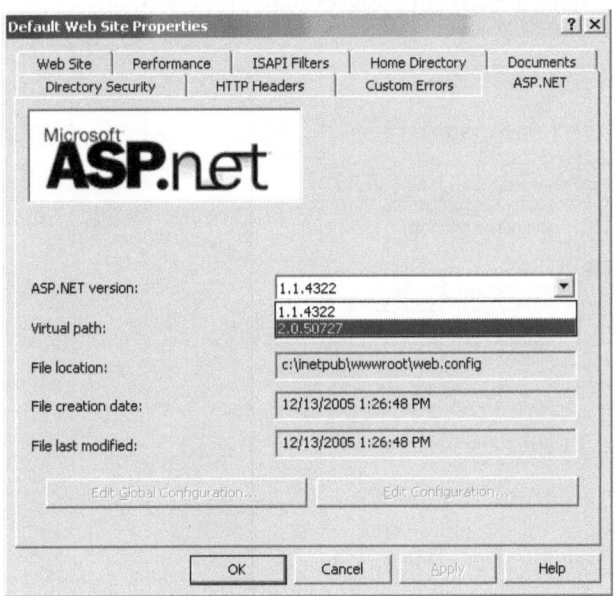

Figure 1-1. *The ASP.NET tab of the Default Web Site Properties window*

Data Stores

There are three possible data stores to choose from when installing Windows SharePoint Services: Windows Microsoft SQL Server 2000 Desktop Engine (WMSDE), which has limitations but is free; SQL Server 2000; or SQL Server 2005. WMSDE is a special version of the Microsoft SQL Server Desktop Engine (MSDE) and is designed to be used by Windows components. It is not limited in the same way the MSDE is. In it, the maximum size limit and current connections limit have been removed. Nevertheless, WMSDE is still more limited than SQL Server 2000 and it is certainly more limited than SQL Server 2005. WMSDE does not support full-text search, can be managed locally but not remotely, cannot be used in a web farm scenario, and does not include the SQL Enterprise Manager tool.

Installing SharePoint Services When Using WMSDE

If you want to use WMSDE as the data store for Windows SharePoint Services, follow these steps:

1. Go to Start ➤ Administrative Tools ➤ Manage Your Server and click Add or Remove a Role.

2. Click Next.

3. Select the SharePoint Services role, as shown in Figure 1-2, and follow the steps of the wizard.

This installation will also install Service Pack 2.0 of Windows SharePoint Services.

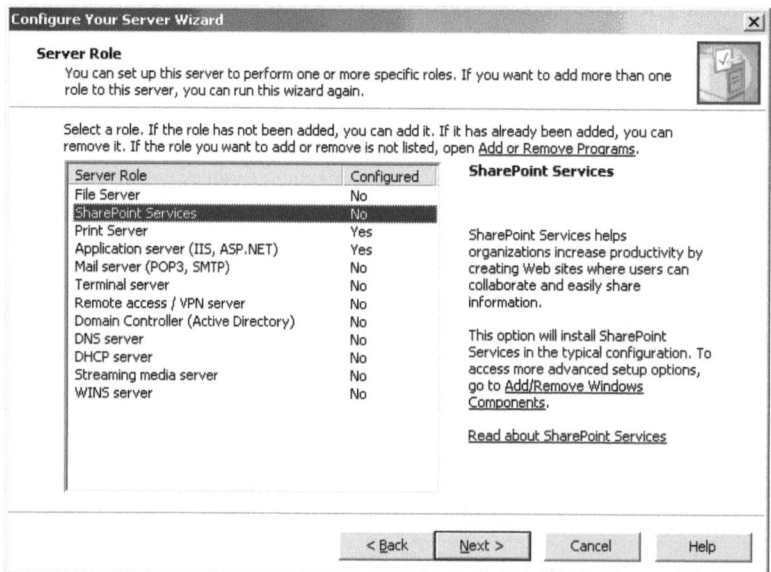

Figure 1-2. *Choose SharePoint Services in the Configure Your Server Wizard.*

Installing SharePoint Services When Using SQL Server 2000 or SQL Server 2005

When using SQL Server 2000 or 2005 as the data store, you have to install Windows SharePoint Services in a different way. Via Add/Remove Windows Components, select Windows SharePoint Services as shown in Figure 1-3. This installation already contains Service Pack 2.

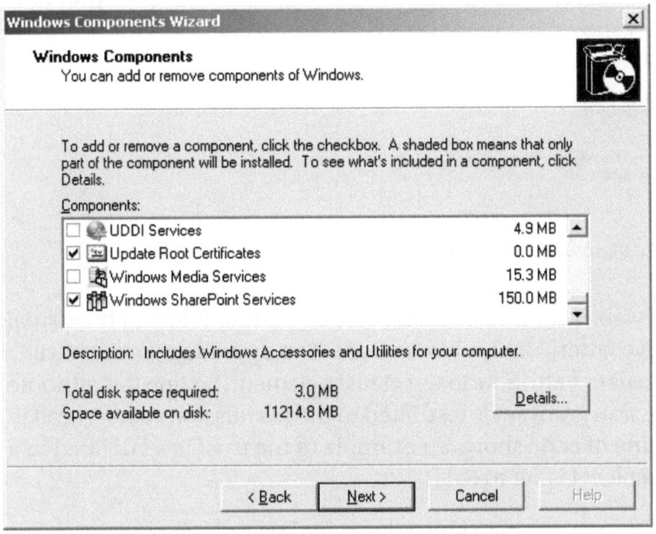

Figure 1-3. *Select SharePoint Services in the Windows Components Wizard.*

How to Configure ASP.NET 2.0

ASP.NET code runs at the trust level that is assigned to it. This trust level is determined by the code access security policy file specified in the web.config file. The Wss_minimaltrust.config file is an example of a code access security policy file, and it is the default policy file used in SharePoint Products and Technologies.

ASP.NET 2.0 implements a new security change that helps to lock down security for a virtual server in Internet Information Services 6.0. As a result of this security change, the permissions of web pages, web parts, and controls are limited to the intersection of the default ASP.NET permission set and the permission set currently granted by the trust level under which the code runs. The current trust level is defined in the web.config file of a SharePoint virtual server. Because this lockdown is incompatible with the security permission set required by Windows SharePoint Services, it must be disabled, which can be done via the web.config file of a SharePoint virtual server.

Another configuration requirement for ASP.NET 2.0 and Windows SharePoint Services is related to a new ASP.NET feature called *event validation*, which is responsible for monitoring callbacks to the ASP.NET infrastructure and making sure callback sources equal control targets. ASP.NET 2.0 event validation is not compatible with Windows SharePoint Services because some SharePoint pages use callbacks that are not associated to any particular control. This results in page execution errors, unless ASP.NET 2.0 event validation is turned off for any SharePoint-extended web application on a server.

The SharePoint stsadm.exe command line tool can be used to update the settings of the web.config file of a SharePoint virtual server so that ASP.NET 2.0 is compatible with Windows SharePoint Services. Use the following command:

```
stsadm -o upgrade -forceupgrade -url http://[MyVirtualServer]
```

When you use this command (which we will call the stsadm upgrade command from now on), you will see the pop-up window shown in Figure 1-4.

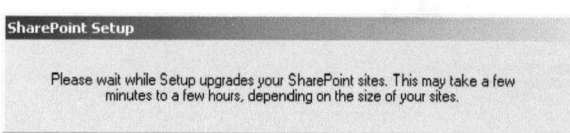

Figure 1-4. *Pop-up window when the* stsadm *command is running*

This command will update the web.config file that is located in the root folder of the virtual server. By default, this folder is [drive letter]:\inetpub\wwwroot. The upgrade operation will add the processRequestInApplicationTrust attribute to the <trust> element. Setting this attribute to false determines that the permission grant set is restricted to the permissions configured in the trust policy file. The following line of code shows an example of the trust level defined in a web.config file. In this case, the trust level is set to Full:

```
<trust level="Full" originUrl="" processRequestInApplicationTrust="false" />
```

The stsadm upgrade command will also add a namespaces section under the <pages> element. This section is new in .NET Framework 2.0. The <namespaces> element defines a collection of import directives to use during assembly precompilation. These are configured in the root web.config file. You can remove any of these namespaces from the collection by using the <remove> element in the web.config file for an application. You must remove the System.Web. UI.WebControls.WebParts namespace because it is the ASP.NET web part namespace and it conflicts with the SharePoint web part class, which has the following namespace: Microsoft. SharePoint.WebPartPages.WebPart. The following code listing demonstrates how to remove the Microsoft.SharePoint.WebPartPages.WebPart namespace:

```
<namespaces>
  <remove namespace="System.Web.UI.WebControls.WebParts" />
</namespaces>
```

Finally, the stsadm upgrade command will add an enableEventValidation attribute to the <pages> element, which turns event validation off. The following code listing demonstrates how to disable event validation:

```
<pages enableSessionState="false" enableViewState="true" enableViewStateMac="true" ➥
validateRequest="false" enableEventValidation="false">
```

When you have followed these steps, you can make your own SharePoint site using ASP.NET 2.0. Figure 1-5 shows you the first screen of a SharePoint site.

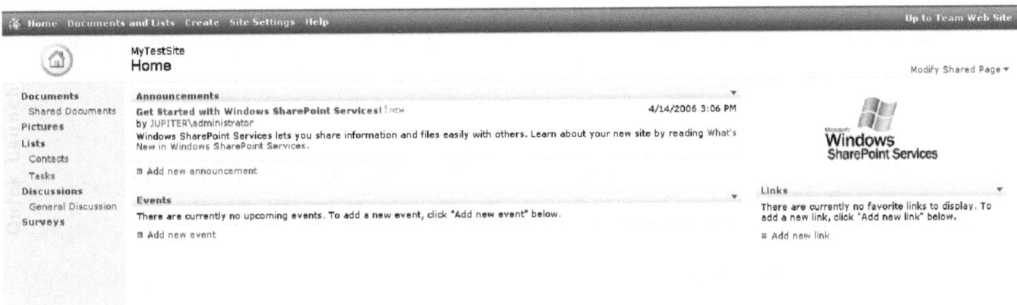

Figure 1-5. *The first screen of a default SharePoint site*

If you fail to run the stsadm and you browse to a Windows SharePoint Services site on a server with ASP.NET 2.0 installed on it, you will see the error that is shown in Figure 1-6.

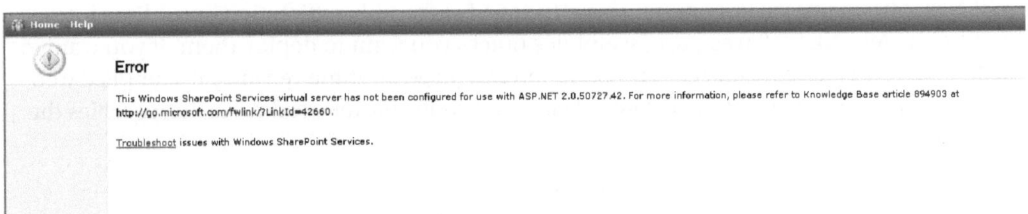

Figure 1-6. *Error when running SharePoint site in ASP.NET 2.0 without running the* stsadm *command*

If you want to go back to using ASP.NET 1.x instead of ASP.NET 2.0, you have to run the exact same stsadm command again to remove the elements and attributes from the web.config file. If you forget to do this and run your SharePoint site in ASP.NET 1.x, you will get an error, as shown in Figure 1-7.

Server Error in '/' Application.

Runtime Error

Description: An application error occurred on the server. The current custom error settings for this application prevent the details of the application error from being viewed.

Details: To enable the details of this specific error message to be viewable on the local server machine, please create a <customErrors> tag within a "web.config" configuration file located in the root directory of the current web application. This <customErrors> tag should then have its "mode" attribute set to "RemoteOnly". To enable the details to be viewable on remote machines, please set "mode" to "Off".

```
<!-- Web.Config Configuration File -->
<configuration>
    <system.web>
        <customErrors mode="RemoteOnly"/>
    </system.web>
</configuration>
```

Notes: The current error page you are seeing can be replaced by a custom error page by modifying the "defaultRedirect" attribute of the application's <customErrors> configuration tag to point to a custom error page URL.

```
<!-- Web.Config Configuration File -->
<configuration>
    <system.web>
        <customErrors mode="On" defaultRedirect="mycustompage.htm"/>
    </system.web>
</configuration>
```

Figure 1-7. *Error when running SharePoint site in ASP.NET 1.x without running the* stsadm *command*

Things to Remember

When your virtual server runs in ASP.NET 1.1 mode, you cannot call another assembly that is compiled in .NET 2.0. This is known as *upstreaming*. Downstreaming is possible; if your virtual server runs in ASP.NET 2.0, you can call another assembly that is compiled in .NET 1.x.

ASP.NET 2.0 web parts can be added to pages running in Windows SharePoint Services after Service Pack 2.0 is applied. They will not be treated as web parts; instead, they will be seen as standard web form controls. Out of the box, Windows SharePoint Services will not use any ASP.NET 2.0 constructs. It is not necessary to specify assembly redirection or runtime information for the ASP.NET 2.0 web part assemblies unless you want to deploy them. If you want to deploy web part packages that contain Common Language Runtime version 2.0–compiled web part assemblies, you will need to create a stsadm.exe.config file for stsadm.exe that specifies the following:

```xml
<?xml version="1.0" encoding="utf-8" ?>
<configuration>
  <startup>
    <supportedRuntime version="v2.0.50727" />
    <supportedRuntime version="v1.1.4322" />
  </startup>
</configuration>
```

This config file has to be placed next to stsadm.exe. The default location is [drive letter]:\ Program Files\Common Files\Microsoft Shared\web server extensions\60\BIN. If you do not create this config file, you will get the following error message: "Version 1.1 is not a compatible version."

Creating Web Parts via Visual Studio .NET 2005

After installing ASP.NET 2.0 and Windows SharePoint Services, you can start creating web parts. Start by opening Visual Studio .NET 2005 and create a project that is based on the class library project template.

First of all, you have to make sure that the dll that will be created when you compile your project will be placed in a bin folder under the root folder of your virtual server. If you do not have a bin folder under the root folder, you can create one yourself. By default, the location of the root folder will be [drive letter]\inetpub\wwwroot. Set the output path to the bin folder of the root folder of the SharePoint virtual server by right-clicking your project, choosing Properties, and clicking the Build tab. In the Output section, you will find the output path property, as shown in Figure 1-8.

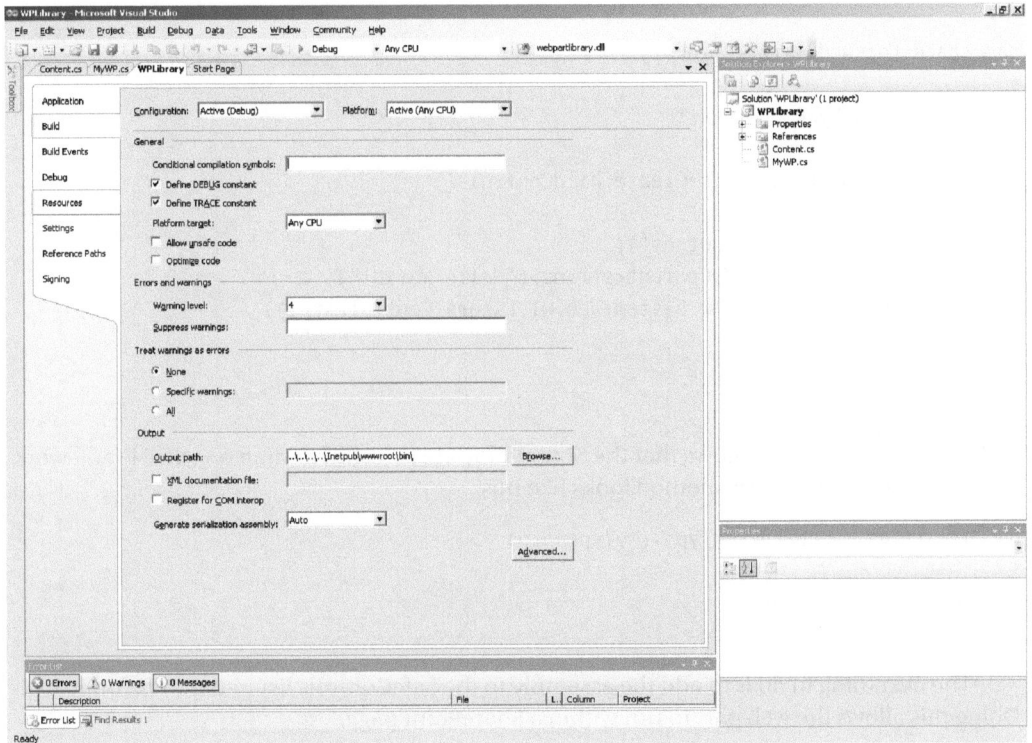

Figure 1-8. *Setting the output path property in Visual Studio .NET 2005*

Before starting to code the web part, you also have to add references in your project to the System.Web and the Microsoft.SharePoint dlls. By default, you can find the Microsoft.SharePoint.dll on the following location: [drive letter]:\Program Files\Common Files\Microsoft Shared\Web Server Extensions\60\ISAPI\.

The following code example shows a list of all the imported namespaces. It also shows that the web part inherits from the `Microsoft.SharePoint.WebPartPages.WebPart` class, the base class for all SharePoint web parts. To prove we are indeed using .NET Framework 2.0, we have overridden the `CreateChildControls()` method and used generics (a new feature of .NET Framework 2.0) to print a Hello World message to the page. The following code listing contains the entire code for a web part that uses .NET 2.0 generics to print a Hello World message to a SharePoint page:

```
using System;
using System.Collections.Generic;
using System.Text;
using System.Web.UI.HtmlControls;
using System.Web.UI.WebControls;
using Microsoft.SharePoint.WebPartPages;

namespace LoisAndClark.WPLibrary
{
  public class MyWP : WebPart
  {
    protected override void CreateChildControls()
    {
      Content obj = new Content();
      string str1 = obj.MyContent<string>("Hello World!");
      this.Controls.Add(new System.Web.UI.LiteralControl(str1));
    }
  }
}
```

The generic method shows that the SharePoint site is really running on .NET Framework 2.0. The code of the generic method looks like this:

```
public string MyContent<MyType>(MyType arg)
{
  return arg.ToString();
}
```

The next thing to do is to add the assembly to the SafeControls list in the web.config file. Doing this allows the web part to run within a SharePoint page.

```
<SafeControl Assembly="WPLibrary" Namespace="LoisandClark.WPLibrary" TypeName="*" ➥
Safe="True" />
```

There are two ways to import the web part in a SharePoint site: either you create a Description Web Part File (.dwp) file, or you browse to the web part gallery of your SharePoint site and upload the web part as a new web part. If the web part is not signed with a public key, the content of a .dwp file should look like this:

```
<?xml version="1.0" encoding="utf-8"?>
<WebPart xmlns="http://schemas.microsoft.com/WebPart/v2" >
  <Title>Title of Web Part</Title>
```

```
    <Description>Description of Web Part</Description>
    <Assembly>Assembly</Assembly>
    <TypeName>Namespace.Classname</TypeName>
</WebPart>
```

After creating a .dwp file you can browse to a SharePoint site, click Modify Shared Page ➤ Add Web Parts ➤ Import. Browse to the .dwp file that is located on your computer and click Import.

The other way to import a web part in a SharePoint site is via the Web Part Gallery. The Web Part Gallery is only available on the top-level site administration page, which means that if you add a web part there, it will be available on all the subsites. The way to get there is to click Site Settings ➤ Go to Site Administration ➤ Manage Web Part Gallery. You can also go to the Web Part Gallery page by entering the following URL: http://[MyServerName]/_catalogs/wp/Forms/AllItems.aspx. Then click New Web Part. This page will display all available web parts for this gallery, as shown in Figure 1-9.

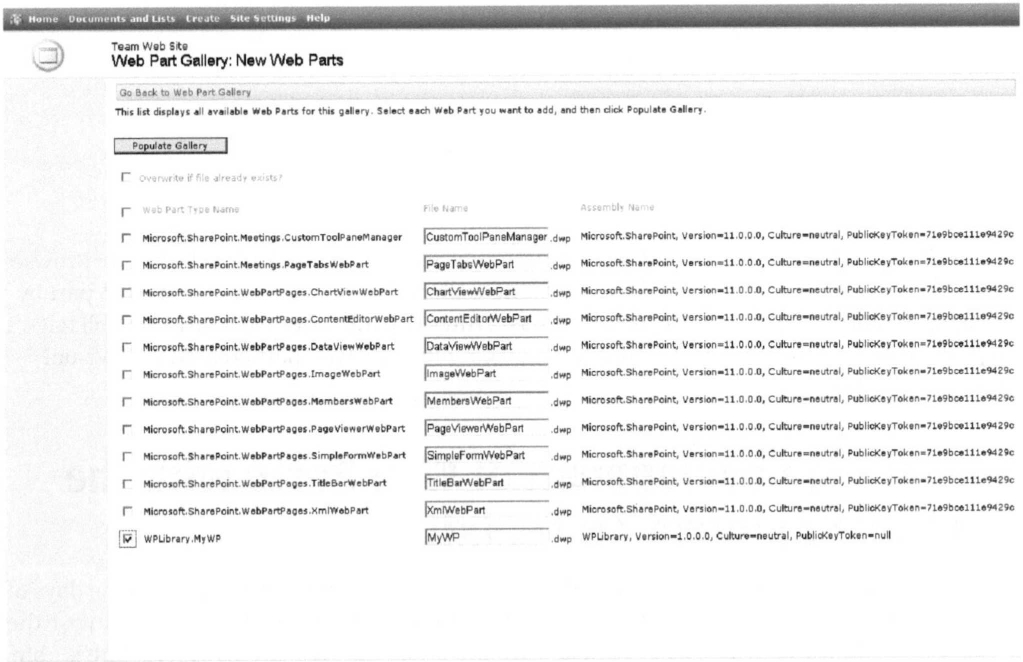

Figure 1-9. *The New Web Parts page of the Web Part Gallery*

Click the check box next to your web part and then click Populate Gallery. Notice that the MyWP web part (previously selected in Figure 1-9) is listed in the Web Part Gallery in the form of a reference to its web part description file (MyWP.dwp). This is shown in Figure 1-10. If the web part is not shown, open a command prompt and type **iisreset**. Then check again.

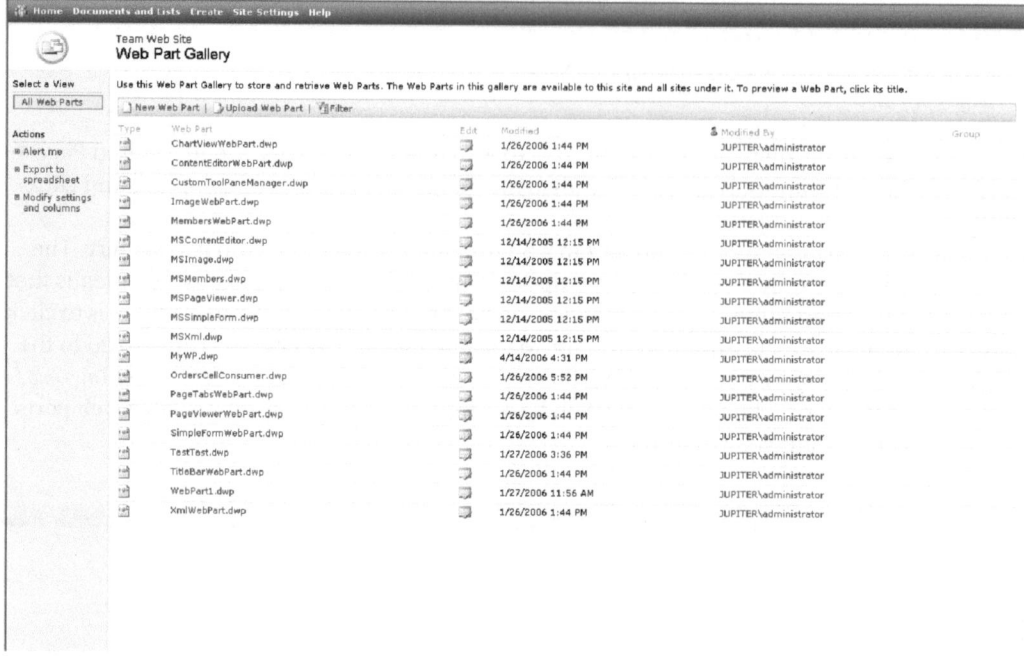

Figure 1-10. *The Web Part Gallery*

Go back to your SharePoint site and click Modify Shared Page ➤ Add Web Parts ➤ Browse. You will find your web part in the Team Web Site Gallery. Now you can add your web part by dragging and dropping it onto the web part page. After you add your web part, you will have a SharePoint site running on .NET Framework 2.0 containing a web part created with Visual Studio .NET 2005.

Enhancing Development of Web Parts with the Guidance Automation Toolkit

Creating a web part with Visual Studio .NET 2005 is more work than it used to be in the days of Visual Studio .NET 2003. If you create a web part with Visual Studio .NET 2003, you can use the web part template that can be downloaded from the Microsoft web site. This template is able to do the basic things needed to build web parts for you, thus saving you the effort of doing a boring bit of work. This is not the case with Visual Studio .NET 2005.

You can facilitate the development of web parts with the Guidance Automation Toolkit (GAT). The GAT is an extension to Visual Studio .NET 2005 that allows architects to automate the easy parts of development so that the developer can concentrate on the other parts. The GAT can be used to create assets that are developed in-house or by third parties, such as Microsoft. In the case of building a web part, the GAT can be used to build a package you can use as a template to start making web parts in Visual Studio .NET 2005. These packages are also known as *guidance packages*. We will show you how to use the GAT to create such a package.

Guidance Package Development

To help you with guidance package development, the GAT includes a Guidance Package Development Template. This template can be used to create a solution for guidance package development that includes the elements you need to create your own guidance package. The GAT is shipped with documentation that contains extensive information about the guidance package development process.

The web part library template can be downloaded from our web site: `http://www.lcbridge.nl/download`. The download is in the form of a Windows Installer file (.msi), which can be used to install a web part library template that can be used within Visual Studio .NET 2005.

In the previous section, we showed that you do not need a .dwp file to import a web part on a SharePoint site. However, if you want to strong-name your assembly you do need to create a .dwp file. Strong-named assemblies are explained later in this chapter in the "Installing and Using the Web Part Library Template" section.

We have created an item template that makes it possible to add a .dwp file to your web part library solution. If you want to use the web part library template, your computer needs to have the following software installed:

- Microsoft Windows SharePoint Services and Service Pack 2.0.

- Microsoft Visual Studio .NET 2005.

- Guidance Automation Extensions (GAX). This runtime component is required when running guidance packages. The Guidance Automation Extensions can be downloaded at `http://msdn.microsoft.com/vstudio/teamsystem/Workshop/gat/download.aspx`.

- Guidance Automation Toolkit. The GAT documentation says that you do not need GAT to use guidance packages, although in our experience this is not true. The current beta versions require it, even if you are not creating guidance packages but only using them.

Installing and Using the Web Part Library Template

In this section we show how to install and use the web part library template. Later on, we will discuss how to use GAT to create the web part library template itself and how to create a Windows Installer package for guidance packages. If you are only interested in using the web part library template to enhance the Visual Studio .NET 2005 web part development experience, this section contains all the information you need.

Download the WebPartLibrarySetup.msi file from our web site (`http://www.lcbridge.nl/download`). You can install the web part library template by double-clicking the Windows Installer Package. Close all instances of Visual Studio .NET 2005 before installing the package. The Windows Installer package will install all assemblies related to the web part library template in a folder dedicated to the guidance package. The Guidance Automation Extensions do not support assemblies in the Global Assembly Cache (GAC) and will not load assemblies located in there, even if the assembly is explicitly referenced in the guidance package. Double-click the .msi file to install the package. This will open a pop-up window with welcome text, as shown in Figure 1-11.

Note To create the Windows Installer package that is used to install the web part library template, we used the Technology Preview version of the Guidance Automation Toolkit because the official GAT was not released at the time of this writing.

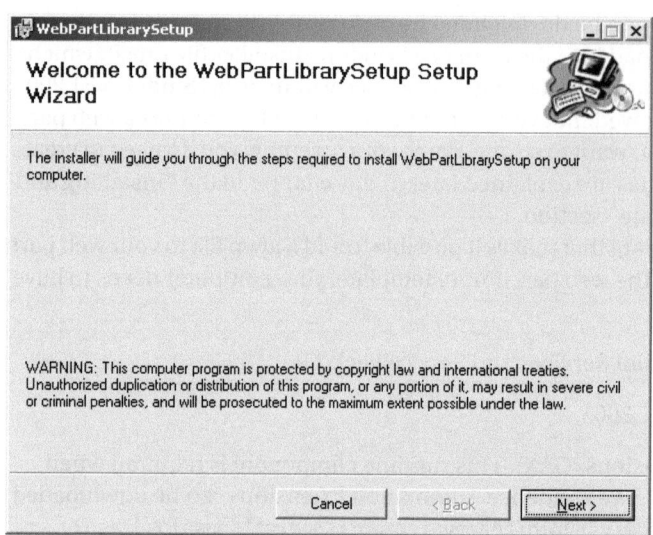

Figure 1-11. *First step of the setup of the web part library template*

Next, choose the folder where you want the template to be installed and click Next. See Figure 1-12.

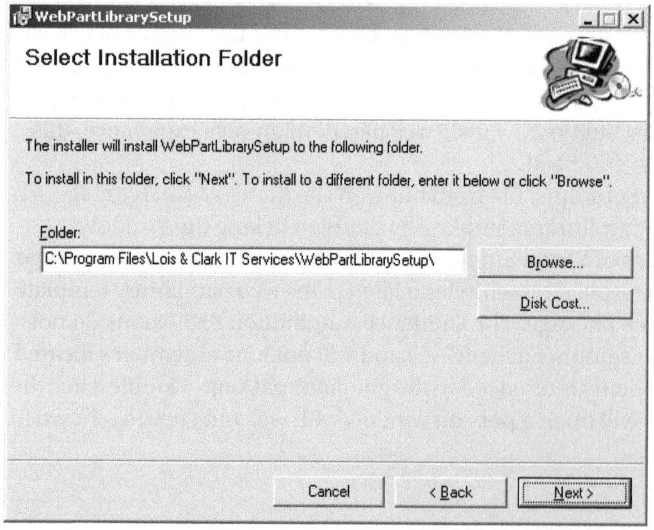

Figure 1-12. *Second step of the setup of the web part library template*

Click Next to start the installation, as shown in Figure 1-13.

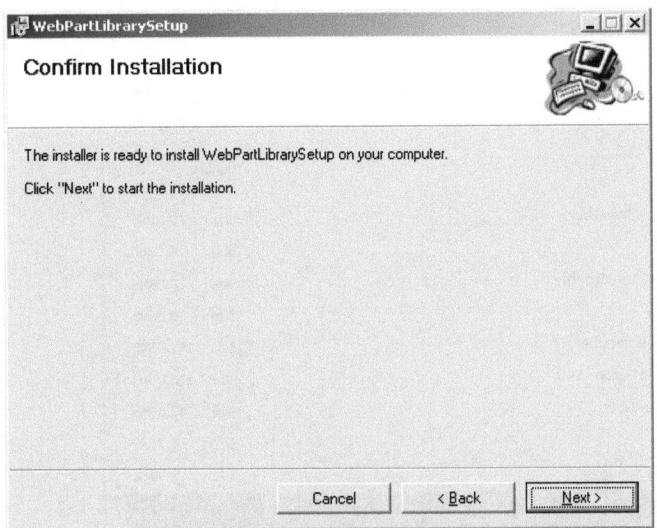

Figure 1-13. *Last step of the setup of the web part library template*

When the installation has succeeded, you will find the web part library template under Add and Remove Programs, as seen in Figure 1-14. This is the place where you can remove or repair the template. You cannot install two versions of the same guidance package at the same time. If you do attempt to install a guidance package with the same name as an existing guidance package, the Guidance Automation Extensions will throw an exception, informing you that you must uninstall the previous instance of the guidance package before installing the new one.

You will also find evidence of installing the web part library template in Visual Studio .NET 2005. Open Visual Studio .NET 2005 and choose File ➤ New ➤ Project. In the New Project window, you will see a new project type called Guidance Packages. Click Guidance Packages and underneath it you will find a package called WebPartLibrary. In the right window pane, you will see a template called WebPartLibrary Solution, as shown in Figure 1-15.

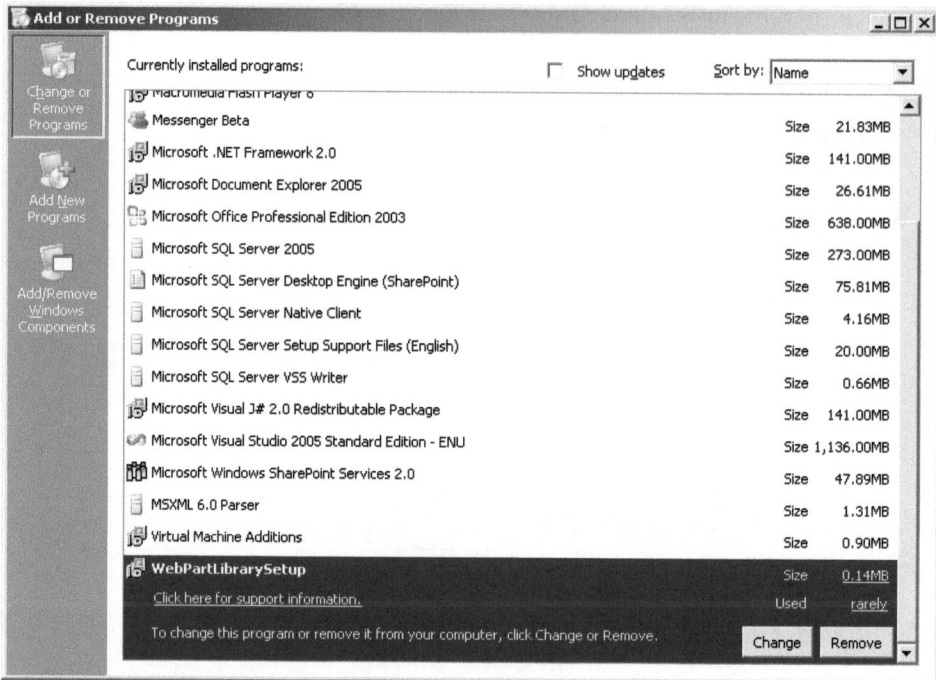

Figure 1-14. *The Add and Remove Programs window*

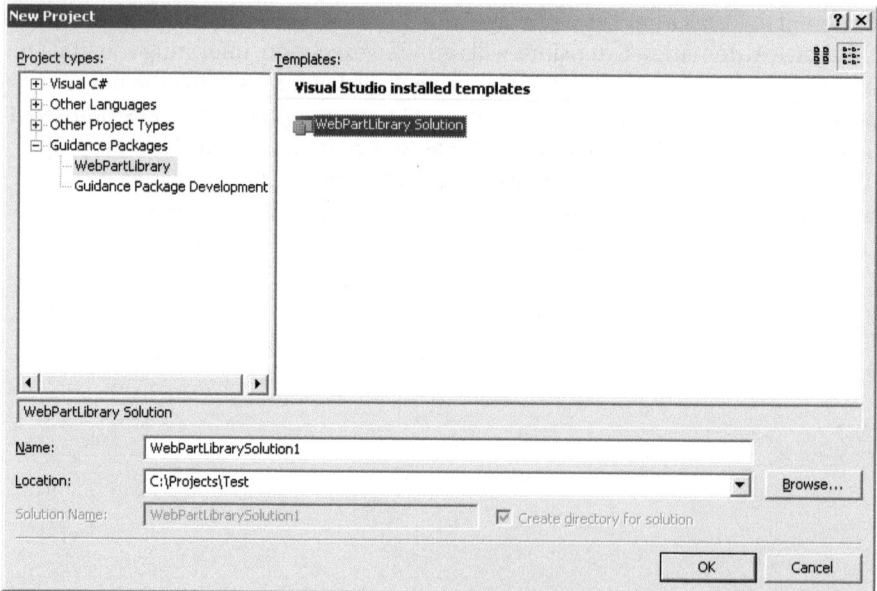

Figure 1-15. *Choose a project in Visual Studio .NET 2005.*

Click WebPartLibrary Solution, fill in a location and a descriptive name, and click OK. This will start a wizard page where you will fill in a project name and the name of the class that will be created initially. Then click Finish, as shown in Figure 1-16.

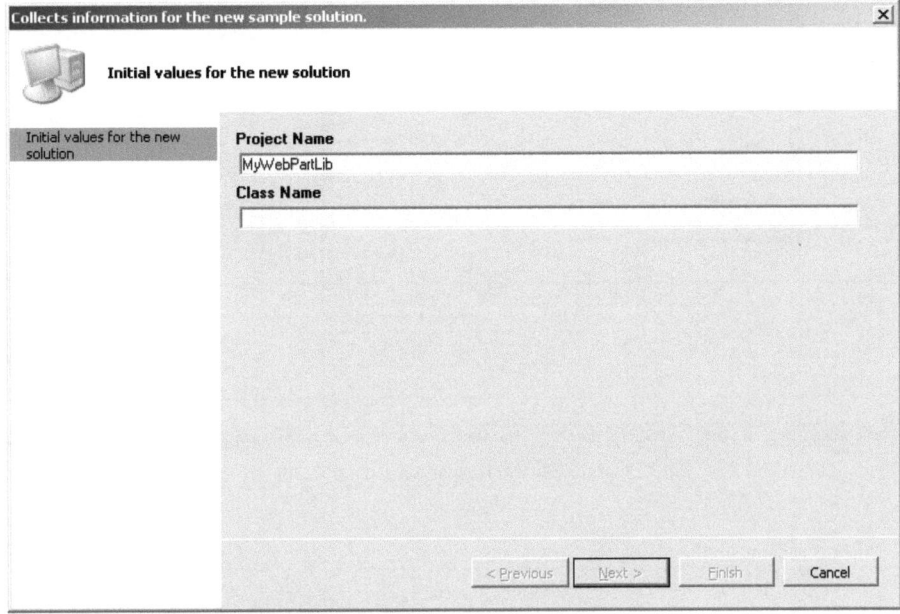

Figure 1-16. *Wizard page belonging to the project creation*

A couple of things will be created at this point:

- A solution containing a properties directory with an assembly.info file
- A references directory containing the following references:
  - System
  - System.Data
  - System.Web
  - System.Xml
  - Microsoft.SharePoint
- A class file called WebPart.cs

Figure 1-17 shows the new solution created with the help of the web part library template.

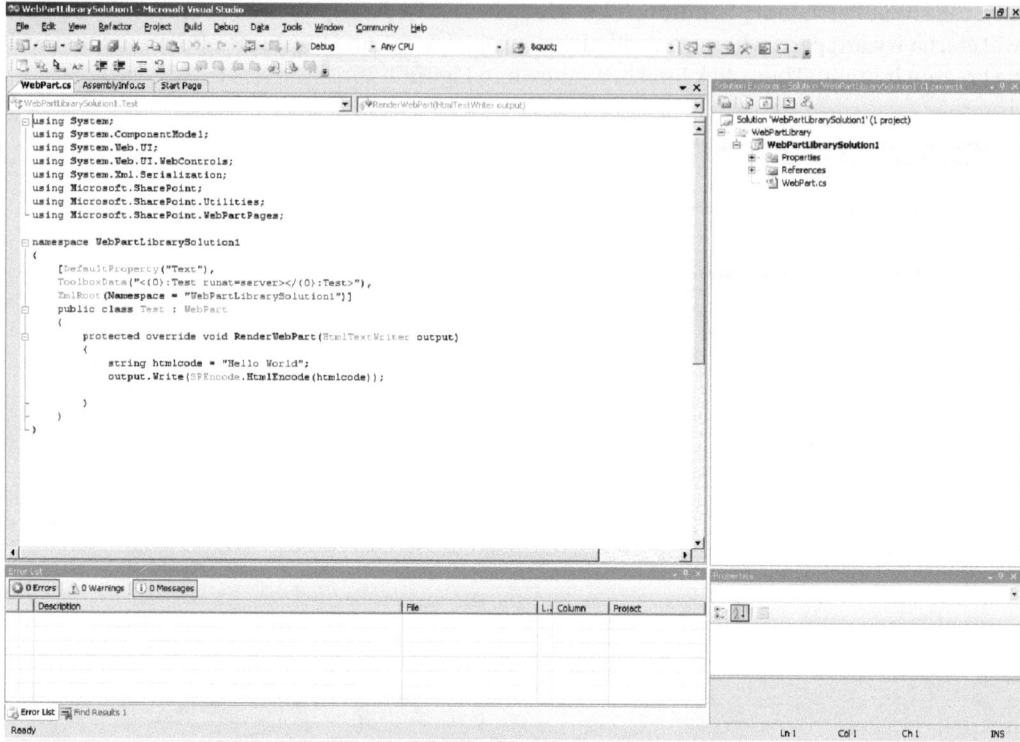

Figure 1-17. *Web part library template in Visual Studio*

The WebPart.cs class file contains the following code:

```
using System;
using System.ComponentModel;
using System.Web.UI;
using System.Web.UI.WebControls;
using System.Xml.Serialization;
using Microsoft.SharePoint;
using Microsoft.SharePoint.Utilities;
using Microsoft.SharePoint.WebPartPages;

namespace WebPartLibrarySolution1
{
  [DefaultProperty("Text"),
  ToolboxData("<{0}:Test runat=server></{0}:Test>"),
  XmlRoot(Namespace = "WebPartLibrarySolution1")]
  public class Test : WebPart
  {
    protected override void RenderWebPart(HtmlTextWriter output)
    {
```

```
        string htmlcode = "Hello World";
        output.Write(SPEncode.HtmlEncode(htmlcode));
    }
  }
}
```

The class itself inherits from the `Microsoft.SharePoint.WebPartPages.WebPart` class, which makes it a web part that is suitable to be used within a SharePoint site.

There are two things left to do. First, check if the output path of the project is changed to the bin directory of the root folder of the virtual server. If this is not the case, change the output path. This makes testing the web part considerably easier. Otherwise you would have to copy the web part dll manually each time you compile. By default, the root folder is [drive letter]\ inetpub\wwwroot. If the bin folder does not exist, you have to create one yourself. Secondly, as shown in the following code listing, you need to add your assembly to the SafeControls list of the web.config file, which is also located at the root of the virtual server:

```
<SafeControl Assembly="MyWebPartLib" Namespace="MyWebPartLib" TypeName="*" ➥
Safe="True" />
```

Here, we are using a partially qualified assembly name, which is great for creating code examples. We could have chosen to use fully qualified names, a practice that is recommended for production code. Those names include the following information: assembly name, version number, culture (which is always set to neutral for code assemblies), and the developer identity (a public key token).

Assemblies with fully qualified names are also known as *strong-named assemblies*. Strong-named assemblies make it easier to enforce security policies for assemblies, because you can assign security permissions based on developer identity. Another advantage is that strong names make creating unique assembly names easier, thus reducing chances for name conflicts. The content of a strong-named assembly cannot be tampered with after compilation, as strong-named assemblies contain a hash code representing the binary content of the assembly. This hash code is unique for every assembly, and the .NET CLR makes sure the hash code matches the assembly content during load time. If someone has tampered with your assembly after compilation, the hash code will not match the content and will not be loaded. A final advantage is that version policies are only applied to strong-named assemblies, not to assemblies with partially qualified names. Strong names are mandatory for assemblies that need to be installed in the GAC. The next code shows a SafeControl entry for a strong-named assembly:

```
<SafeControl Assembly="MyWebPartLib" Namespace="MyWebPartLib, ➥
Version=1.0.0.0, Culture=neutral, ➥
PublicKeyToken=71e9bce111e9429d" TypeName="*" ➥
Safe="True" />
```

If you want to register your web part on a SharePoint site via a web part description file, you can create one by right-clicking your project and choosing Add New Item. Under Categories, you will find a new category called WebPartLibrary. Click this category and choose the template called Web Part Dwp. Give the .dwp file a descriptive name and click Add. Figure 1-18 shows the Add New Item window.

You can also create a .dwp file by right-clicking your project and then choosing Web Part Dwp, as shown in Figure 1-19. This will open the Add New Item window as well.

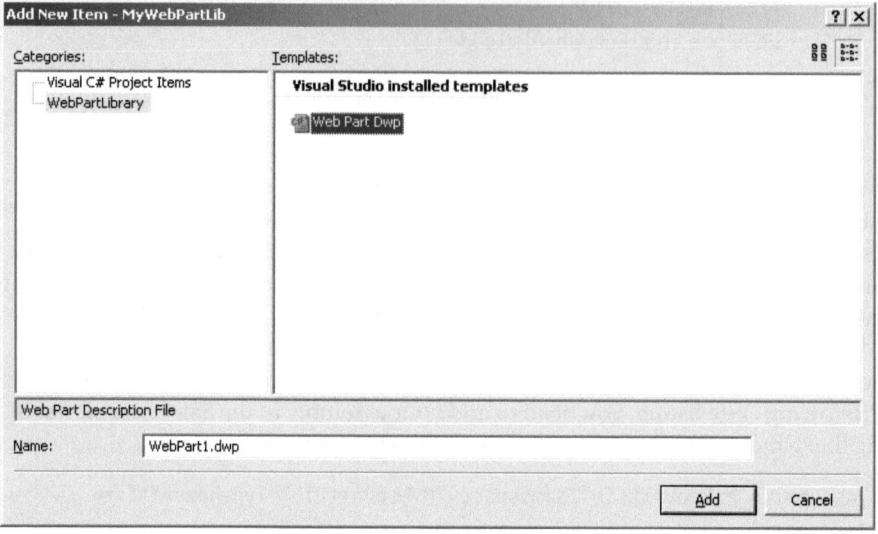

Figure 1-18. *The Add New Item window in Visual Studio .NET 2005*

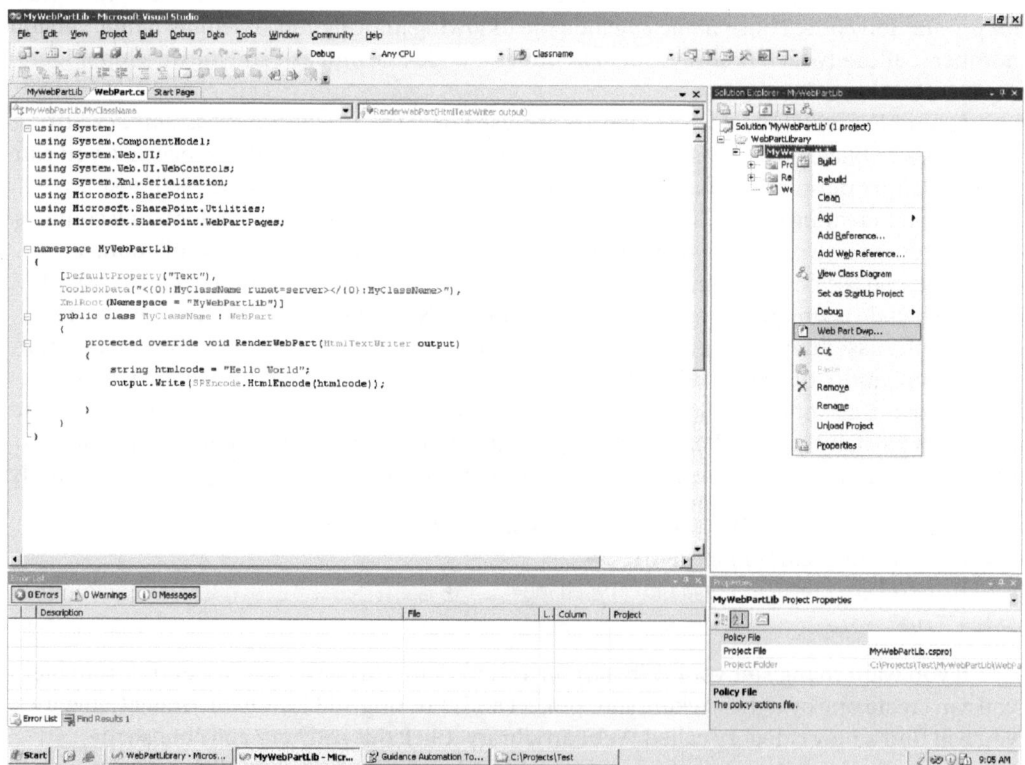

Figure 1-19. *Add a new web part .dwp file by right-clicking your project.*

This will start a wizard that collects information about the web part description file. The assembly name and namespace will have default values. You will only have to type the name of the class, a title for your web part, and a description. The title and description are shown on the SharePoint site page the web part is imported into. The wizard is shown in Figure 1-20.

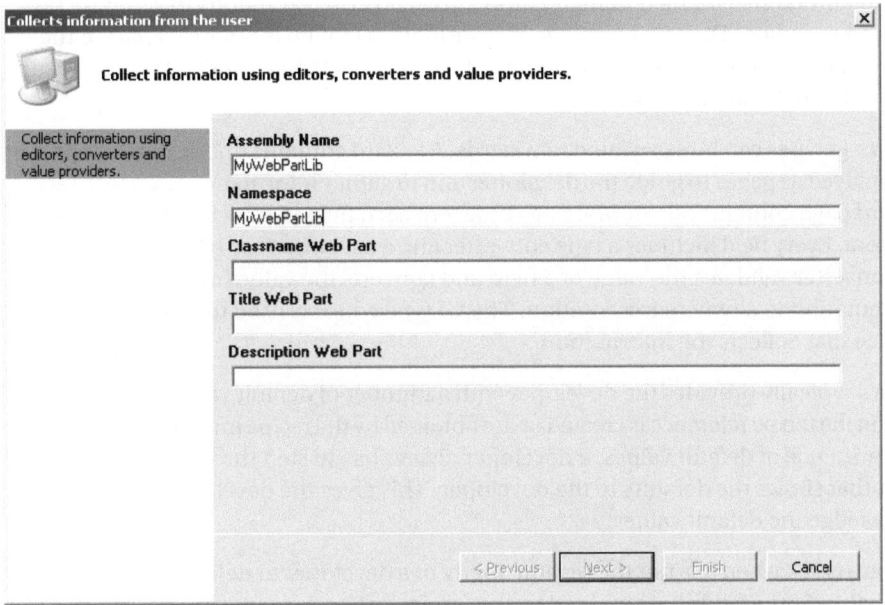

Figure 1-20. *The web part .dwp file wizard*

At this point, you have created your first web part via the web part library template. Now you can start adding your own code to the web part.

Guidance Automation Toolkit

In the previous section, you saw how to install the web part library template. If you want to create your own guidance packages, you will need to install the GAT. In this section, we discuss the general concepts you need to be aware of before you can start using the GAT. First you have to install the Guidance Automation Extensions, which can be downloaded at the Microsoft MSDN web site: http://msdn.microsoft.com/vstudio/teamsystem/workshop/gat/. Next, you should install the GAT itself. In this book we used the June 2006 Technology Preview version.

The GAT contains a couple of elements that work together to provide the automation functionality. The elements are recipes, actions, text template transformation templates, wizards, and Visual Studio templates, described in the following list:

- *Recipes*: Recipes automate a series of activities that are performed by a developer. Recipes are very suitable to automate repetitive actions.

- *Actions*: Actions are the most fine-grained parts of a recipe. Each action is an atomic unit of work. The order in which actions are executed is determined by the recipe definition. Actions are able to accept input via arguments gathered by a recipe or output received from another action that has already been run by the recipe.

- *Text template transformation templates (T4)*: T4 templates return a string that is inserted in the template output and contains a combination of text and *scriptlets*. Scriptlets are expressions written in VB.NET or C# that are interpreted when the text template transformation engine that is a part of the GAT runs a template. The outcome of a scriptlet is dynamic and is added to the template output. The text part of a template is always inserted unmodified in the template output. You can also use actions to generate text from a T4 template. The text template transformation engine is not just a part of the GAT; it is also included in the Domain Specific Language (DSL) Toolkit. We discuss the DSL Toolkit in detail in Chapter 5.

- *Wizards*: Recipes can be associated to wizards. A wizard contains one or more steps that are displayed as pages to guide the developer and to gather information used by a recipe. A wizard page contains one or more fields, where each field is associated to a recipe argument. Every field includes a type converter and a user interface (UI) type editor. The type converter validates the value of a field and converts the value from a user interface representation to a type representation. The UI type editor is used to render the user interface that collects the information.

  A wizard typically provides the developer with a number of default values that are either set when the recipe reference is created or are obtained by the recipe framework. Regardless of the presence of default values, a developer always has to step through the entire wizard that shows the defaults to the developer. This gives the developer a chance to acknowledge the default values.

  There are cases when it is not the responsibility of a developer to define or acknowledge a field value. Some fields are obtained by the framework or the wizard itself. This process is known as *value propagation*. Such fields are not shown in the wizard. If a field is required, the wizard framework will not allow access to later pages in the wizard via the wizard sidebar until all required fields contain data.

- *Visual Studio .NET templates*: In essence, a Visual Studio .NET template is nothing more than XML data that describes how to create Visual Studio solutions, projects, or items. Templates are unfolded by the Visual Studio template engine. Using the GAT, you can associate Visual Studio templates with recipes. This association means that when a template is unfolded, the wizard extension calls the recipe to let it collect parameter values, also known as *arguments*. The arguments are used to execute actions that may further transform solution items created by the template. Guidance packages can be managed via the Guidance Package Manager in Visual Studio .NET 2005. You can find the Guidance Package Manager via the Tools menu. Once a guidance package is installed and enabled for a particular solution, recipes can be executed to carry out the required tasks.

Creation of the Web Part Library Template

In this section, we explain how to use the GAT to create the web part library template that is discussed previously in the section "Installing and Using the Web Part Library Template." The GAT contains a predefined solution for developing a guidance package, which we will use to create a web part library template.

The first step for building a web part library template is to create a new folder in the Templates ➤ Solutions ➤ Projects folder. We will call this folder WebPartLibrary. This folder will contain the following files: WebPart.cs, WebPartLibrary.csproj, and a WebPartLibrary. vstemplate file. It will also contain a folder named Properties, and that folder will contain the assembly.info file.

The WebPartLibrary.vstemplate file is a Visual Studio template that looks identical to a normal Visual Studio template except that it contains additional information used by the recipe framework. The template includes a `<WizardExtension>` element that specifies a class in the recipe framework that implements template extensions for the GAT. The following XML shows the content of our WebPartLibrary Visual Studio template:

```
<VSTemplate Version="2.0.0" Type="Project" ➥
xmlns="http://schemas.microsoft.com/developer/vstemplate/2005">
  <TemplateData>
    <Name>WebPart Library Project</Name>
    <Description>WebPart class library project </Description>
    <Icon Package="{FAE04EC1-301F-11d3-BF4B-00C04F79EFBC}" ID="4547" />
    <ProjectType>CSharp</ProjectType>
    <SortOrder>20</SortOrder>
    <CreateNewFolder>false</CreateNewFolder>
    <DefaultName>ClassLibrary</DefaultName>
    <ProvideDefaultName>true</ProvideDefaultName>
  </TemplateData>
  <TemplateContent>
    <Project File="WebPartLibrary.csproj" ReplaceParameters="true">
      <ProjectItem ReplaceParameters="true">Properties\AssemblyInfo.cs</ProjectItem>
      <ProjectItem ReplaceParameters="true">WebPart.cs</ProjectItem>
    </Project>
  </TemplateContent>
  <WizardExtension>
    <Assembly>
      Microsoft.Practices.RecipeFramework.VisualStudio, Version=1.0.51206.0, ➥
      Culture=neutral, PublicKeyToken=b03f5f7f11d50a3a
    </Assembly>
    <FullClassName>
      Microsoft.Practices.RecipeFramework.VisualStudio.Templates.UnfoldTemplate
    </FullClassName>
  </WizardExtension>
</VSTemplate>
```

This XML is called a *solution template*. Solution templates are launched via the New command on the File menu.

The next file of the package is the WebPartLibrary.csproj file. This is a project template that contains a project description. The template unfolds to a project in an existing solution. The project template will include references to other assemblies and will be responsible for creating any class files, the project file (.csproj), and the assembly.info file. The following XML shows the project template that can be used to create the web part library project:

```xml
<Project DefaultTargets="Build" ➥
xmlns="http://schemas.microsoft.com/developer/msbuild/2003">
  <PropertyGroup>
    <Configuration Condition=" '$(Configuration)' == '' ">Debug</Configuration>
    <Platform Condition=" '$(Platform)' == '' ">AnyCPU</Platform>
    <ProductVersion>8.0.30703</ProductVersion>
    <SchemaVersion>2.0</SchemaVersion>
    <ProjectGuid>$guid1$</ProjectGuid>
    <OutputType>Library</OutputType>
    <AppDesignerFolder>Properties</AppDesignerFolder>
    <RootNamespace>$safeprojectname$</RootNamespace>
    <AssemblyName>$safeprojectname$</AssemblyName>
  </PropertyGroup>
  <PropertyGroup Condition=" '$(Configuration)|$(Platform)' == 'Debug|AnyCPU' ">
    <DebugSymbols>true</DebugSymbols>
    <DebugType>full</DebugType>
    <Optimize>false</Optimize>
    <OutputPath>\inetpub\wwwroot\bin\</OutputPath>
    <DefineConstants>DEBUG;TRACE</DefineConstants>
    <ErrorReport>prompt</ErrorReport>
    <WarningLevel>4</WarningLevel>
  </PropertyGroup>
  <PropertyGroup Condition=" '$(Configuration)|$(Platform)' == 'Release|AnyCPU' ">
    <DebugType>pdbonly</DebugType>
    <Optimize>true</Optimize>
    <OutputPath>\inetpub\wwwroot\bin\</OutputPath>
    <DefineConstants>TRACE</DefineConstants>
    <ErrorReport>prompt</ErrorReport>
    <WarningLevel>4</WarningLevel>
  </PropertyGroup>
  <ItemGroup>
    <Reference Include="System"/>
    <Reference Include="System.Data"/>
    <Reference Include="System.Xml"/>
    <Reference Include="System.Web"/>
    <Reference Include="Microsoft.SharePoint"/>
  </ItemGroup>
  <ItemGroup>
    <Compile Include="WebPart.cs" />
    <Compile Include="Properties\AssemblyInfo.cs" />
  </ItemGroup>
  <Import Project="$(MSBuildBinPath)\Microsoft.CSHARP.Targets" />
</Project>
```

The WebPart.cs file that is created by the project template looks like this:

```
using System;
using System.ComponentModel;
using System.Web.UI;
using System.Web.UI.WebControls;
using System.Xml.Serialization;
using Microsoft.SharePoint;
using Microsoft.SharePoint.Utilities;
using Microsoft.SharePoint.WebPartPages;

namespace $safeprojectname$
{
  [DefaultProperty("Text"),
  ToolboxData("<{0}:$ClassName$ runat=server></{0}:$ClassName$>"),
  XmlRoot(Namespace = "$safeprojectname$")]
    public class $ClassName$ : WebPart
    {
      protected override void RenderWebPart(HtmlTextWriter output)
      {
        string htmlcode = "Hello World";
        output.Write(SPEncode.HtmlEncode(htmlcode));
      }
    }
}
```

All arguments preceded by a $ will be replaced once the project is created. Some values are entered in the wizard by the developer, and some values will have dynamic values based on other values. For example, we have decided that the default namespace of a solution will be identical to the solution name. In the assembly.info file you will also find arguments that are preceded with $. You can look at the assembly.info code here:

```
using System.Reflection;
using System.Runtime.CompilerServices;
using System.Runtime.InteropServices;

[assembly: AssemblyTitle("$projectname$")]
[assembly: AssemblyDescription("")]
[assembly: AssemblyConfiguration("")]
[assembly: AssemblyCompany("$registeredorganization$")]
[assembly: AssemblyProduct("$projectname$")]
[assembly: AssemblyCopyright("Copyright © $registeredorganization$ $year$")]
[assembly: AssemblyTrademark("")]
[assembly: AssemblyCulture("")]
[assembly: Guid("$guid1$")]

[assembly: AssemblyVersion("1.0.0.0")]
[assembly: AssemblyFileVersion("1.0.0.0")]
```

The next thing to discuss is the item template. We have created a new item template in the Templates ➤ Items folder. Let us add an item template, which is responsible for making a .dwp file. You can see the item template XML here:

```xml
<VSTemplate Version="2.0.0" Type="Item" ➥
xmlns="http://schemas.microsoft.com/developer/vstemplate/2005">
  <TemplateData>
    <Name>Web Part Dwp</Name>
    <Description>Web Part Description File</Description>
    <Icon Package="{FAE04EC1-301F-11d3-BF4B-00C04F79EFBC}" ID="4515" />
    <ProjectType>CSharp</ProjectType>
    <SortOrder>10</SortOrder>
    <DefaultName>WebPart.dwp</DefaultName>
  </TemplateData>
  <TemplateContent>
    <ProjectItem ReplaceParameters="true">WebPart.dwp</ProjectItem>
  </TemplateContent>
  <WizardExtension>
    <Assembly>
      Microsoft.Practices.RecipeFramework.VisualStudio, Version=1.0.51206.0, ➥
      Culture=neutral, PublicKeyToken=b03f5f7f11d50a3a
    </Assembly>
    <FullClassName>
      Microsoft.Practices.RecipeFramework.VisualStudio.Templates.UnfoldTemplate
    </FullClassName>
  </WizardExtension>
  <WizardData>
    <Template xmlns=http://schemas.microsoft.com/pag/gax-template ➥
    SchemaVersion="1.0" Recipe="NewItemClass"/>
  </WizardData>
</VSTemplate>
```

The item template will be used when the developer wants to add a .dwp file to the project. The item template uses a recipe called NewItemClass that is discussed later in this section. The code for the WebPart.dwp file looks like this:

```xml
<?xml version="1.0" encoding="utf-8"?>
<WebPart xmlns="http://schemas.microsoft.com/WebPart/v2">
  <Title>$TitleWebPart$</Title>
  <Description>$DescriptionWebPart$</Description>
  <Assembly>$AssemblyName$</Assembly>
  <TypeName>$Namespace$.$ClassName$</TypeName>
</WebPart>
```

All arguments preceded by a $ will be replaced once the developer creates a new .dwp file.

Now you have seen the solution template, the project template, the item template, and all corresponding files. The last file that we have not discussed yet is WebPartLibrary.xml. You can find this file directly underneath the project in the Solution Explorer. This file contains the XML configuration code, consisting of all the recipes, actions, and wizards. The first part of the

WebPartLibrary.xml file contains a recipe called BindingRecipe. The `<Action>` element contains the item template called WebPartTemplate.vstemplate. The `<Arguments>` element contains all arguments that will be asked for in the first wizard page when you create the solution. The next code listing shows an example WebPartLibrary.xml file:

```
<Recipe Name="BindingRecipe">
  <Types>
    <TypeAlias Name="RefCreator" ➡
    Type="Microsoft.Practices.RecipeFramework.Library.Actions. ➡
    CreateUnboundReferenceAction, Microsoft.Practices.RecipeFramework.Library"/>
  </Types>
  <Caption>Creates unbound references to the guidance package</Caption>
  <Actions>
    <Action Name="CreateSampleUnboundItemTemplateRef" Type="RefCreator" ➡
    AssetName="Items\WebPartTemplate.vstemplate" ➡
    ReferenceType="WebPartLibrary.References.ClassLibraryReference, ➡
    WebPartLibrary" />
  </Actions>
</Recipe>
<Recipe Name="CreateSolution">
  <Caption>Collects information for the new sample solution.</Caption>
  <Arguments>
    <Argument Name="ProjectName">
      <Converter Type="Microsoft.Practices.RecipeFramework. ➡
      Library.Converters.NamespaceStringConverter, ➡
      Microsoft.Practices.RecipeFramework.Library"/>
    </Argument>
    <Argument Name="ClassName">
      <Converter Type="Microsoft.Practices.RecipeFramework. ➡
      Library.Converters.NamespaceStringConverter, ➡
      Microsoft.Practices.RecipeFramework.Library"/>
    </Argument>
  </Arguments>
  <GatheringServiceData>
    <Wizard xmlns=" ➡
    http://schemas.microsoft.com/pag/gax-wizards" ➡
    SchemaVersion="1.0">
      <Pages>
        <Page>
          <Title>Initial values for the new solution</Title>
          <Fields>
            <Field Label="Project Name" ValueName="ProjectName" />
            <Field Label="Class Name" ValueName="ClassName" />
          </Fields>
        </Page>
      </Pages>
    </Wizard>
  </GatheringServiceData>
</Recipe>
```

The next recipe that is important for the web part library template is called NewItemClass. This recipe contains all arguments that are collected by the wizard when you create a .dwp file. Some arguments have default values, such as assembly name and namespace.

```xml
<Recipe Name="NewItemClass" Recurrent="true">
  <xi:include href="TypeAlias.xml" xmlns:xi="http://www.w3.org/2001/XInclude" />
  <Caption>Collects information from the user</Caption>
  <Description></Description>
  <HostData>
    <Icon ID="1429"/>
    <CommandBar Name="Project" />
  </HostData>
  <Arguments>
    <Argument Name="CurrentProject" Type="EnvDTE.Project, EnvDTE, ➡
    Version=8.0.0.0, Culture=neutral, PublicKeyToken=b03f5f7f11d50a3a">
      <ValueProvider Type="Microsoft.Practices.RecipeFramework. ➡
      Library.ValueProviders.FirstSelectedProject, ➡
      Microsoft.Practices.RecipeFramework.Library" />
    </Argument>
    <Argument Name="Namespace">
      <Converter Type="Microsoft.Practices.RecipeFramework. ➡
      Library.Converters.NamespaceStringConverter, ➡
      Microsoft.Practices.RecipeFramework.Library"/>
      <ValueProvider Type="Evaluator" Expression= ➡
      "$(CurrentProject.Properties.Item('DefaultNamespace').Value)" />
    </Argument>
    <Argument Name="AssemblyName">
      <Converter Type="Microsoft.Practices.RecipeFramework. ➡
      Library.Converters.NamespaceStringConverter, ➡
      Microsoft.Practices.RecipeFramework.Library" />
      <ValueProvider Type="Evaluator" Expression="$(CurrentProject.Name)" />
    </Argument>
    <Argument Name="ClassName">
      <Converter Type="Microsoft.Practices.RecipeFramework. ➡
      Library.Converters.NamespaceStringConverter, ➡
      Microsoft.Practices.RecipeFramework.Library"/>
    </Argument>
    <Argument Name="TitleWebPart">
      <Converter Type="Microsoft.Practices.RecipeFramework. ➡
      Library.Converters.NamespaceStringConverter, ➡
      Microsoft.Practices.RecipeFramework.Library"/>
    </Argument>
    <Argument Name="DescriptionWebPart">
      <Converter Type="Microsoft.Practices.RecipeFramework. ➡
      Library.Converters.NamespaceStringConverter, ➡
      Microsoft.Practices.RecipeFramework.Library"/>
    </Argument>
  </Arguments>
</Arguments>
```

```xml
<GatheringServiceData>
  <Wizard xmlns="http://schemas.microsoft.com/pag/gax-wizards" SchemaVersion="1.0">
    <Pages>
      <Page>
        <Title>
          Collect information using editors, converters and value providers.
        </Title>
        <Fields>
          <Field ValueName="AssemblyName" Label="Assembly Name">
            <Tooltip></Tooltip>
          </Field>
          <Field ValueName="Namespace" Label="Namespace">
            <Tooltip></Tooltip>
          </Field>
          <Field ValueName="ClassName" Label="Classname Web Part">
            <Tooltip></Tooltip>
          </Field>
          <Field ValueName="TitleWebPart" Label="Title Web Part">
            <Tooltip></Tooltip>
          </Field>
          <Field ValueName="DescriptionWebPart" Label="Description Web Part">
            <Tooltip></Tooltip>
          </Field>
        </Fields>
      </Page>
    </Pages>
  </Wizard>
</GatheringServiceData>
</Recipe>
```

After customizing the code and making your own templates, build the project and register it. You can do this by right-clicking the project file and selecting Register Guidance Package. This launches a recipe that is associated with the guidance package. The recipe registers the package you are developing on your computer. Registration is a form of installation that you can perform without leaving the Visual Studio development environment. It is also possible to unregister the package. This will reverse the registration.

After registering the guidance package, you can open a new instance of Visual Studio to test the functionality of the package.

ASP.NET 2.0 Server Controls

In this section we will show you a couple of the ASP.NET 2.0 server controls used within a SharePoint web part. Using ASP.NET 2.0 server controls gives the developer great functionality for database access, calendars, text boxes, drop-down lists, and a lot of other common composite web functionality. Controls are very essential to the ASP.NET programming model. In ASP.NET there are nearly 60 new server controls.

The FileUpload Control

File upload is possible in ASP.NET 1.x, but you have to jump through some hoops to get everything working. For example, you have to add enctype="multipart/form-data" to the page's <form> element. The new ASP.NET 2.0 FileUpload server control makes the process of uploading files to the hosting server as simple as possible.

The FileUpLoad control displays a text box and a Browse button that allow users to select a file to upload to the server. The user specifies the file to upload by entering the fully qualified path to the file on the local computer (for example, C:\Temp\TestFile.txt) in the text box of the control. The user can also select the file by clicking the Browse button and then locating it in the Choose File dialog box. You need to hook up an event handler to a Submit button which calls the SaveAs() method of the FileUpLoad control. Via this method you can specify the location where the file will be saved. The file will not be uploaded to the server until the user presses the Submit button. The code used to create a SharePoint web part with the FileUpload control looks like this:

```
using System;
using System.Collections.Generic;
using System.Text;
using System.Web.UI.HtmlControls;
using System.Web.UI.WebControls;
using Microsoft.SharePoint.WebPartPages;

namespace LoisAndClark.WPLibrary
{
  public class MyWP : WebPart
  {
    FileUpload objFileUpload = new FileUpload();

    protected override void CreateChildControls()
    {
      this.Controls.Add(new System.Web.UI.LiteralControl ➡
      ("Select a file to upload:"));
      this.Controls.Add(objFileUpload);

      Button btnUpload = new Button();
      btnUpload.Text = "Save File";
      this.Load += new System.EventHandler(btnUpload_Click);
      this.Controls.Add(btnUpload);
    }

    private void btnUpload_Click(object sender, EventArgs e)
    {
      string strSavePath = @"c:\temp\";
      if (objFileUpload.HasFile)
      {
        string strFileName = objFileUpload.FileName;
        strSavePath += strFileName;
```

```
        objFileUpload.SaveAs(strSavePath);
      }
      else
      {
        // Let the user know that the file was not uploaded.
      }
    }
  }
}
```

Figure 1-21 shows how this web part looks on a SharePoint site.

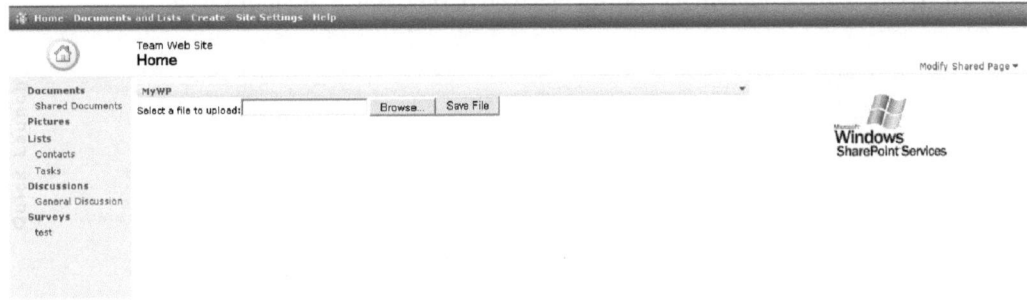

Figure 1-21. *The FileUpload control in a web part*

The BulletedList Control

Another new server control is the BulletedList control. This control, as the name says, displays a bulleted list of items in an *ordered* (<ol> HTML element) or *unordered* (<ul> HTML element) fashion. The BulletedList control has extra features such as data binding, support for custom images, and the option to choose bullet style. The bullet style lets you choose the style of the element that precedes the item. For example, you can choose to use numbers, squares, or circles. Child items can be rendered as plain text, hyperlinks, or buttons. The BulletedList control in the example uses a custom image that needs to be placed in a virtual directory on the server. The code looks like this:

```
using System;
using System.Collections.Generic;
using System.Text;
using System.Web.UI.HtmlControls;
using System.Web.UI.WebControls;
using Microsoft.SharePoint.WebPartPages;

namespace LoisAndClark.WPLibrary
{
  public class MyWP : WebPart
  {
    protected override void CreateChildControls()
    {
```

```
            BulletedList objBullist = new BulletedList();
            objBullist.BulletStyle = BulletStyle.CustomImage;
            objBullist.BulletImageUrl = @"/_layouts/images/favicon.gif";
            objBullist.Items.Add("One");
            objBullist.Items.Add("Two");
            objBullist.Items.Add("Three");
            objBullist.Items.Add("Four");
            this.Controls.Add(objBullist);
        }
    }
}
```

The result of the BulletedList control in a web part is shown in Figure 1-22.

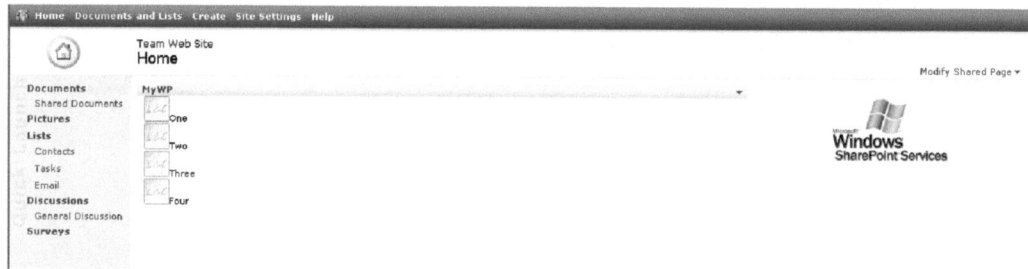

Figure 1-22. *The BulletedList control in a web part*

The Wizard Control

The Wizard server control enables you to build a sequence of steps that are displayed to the end user. You could use the Wizard control to either display or gather information in small steps. The Wizard control lets you define a group of views in which only one view at a time is active and is rendered to the client. Each view consists of four zones: sidebar, header, content, and navigation. The (optional) sidebar part contains an overview of all the steps in the wizard. The header contains the header information. The content part contains whichever control or controls you like. The navigation part consists of buttons to navigate through the steps in the wizard.

When you are constructing a step-by-step process that includes logic for every step taken, use the Wizard control to manage the entire process. The Wizard control navigation buttons fire server-side events whenever the user clicks one of the buttons. The navigation buttons help to navigate to other wizard views on the same page. Navigation can be linear and nonlinear; in other words, you can jump from one view to another or navigate randomly to whichever view you like. All the controls in a wizard view are part of the page so you can access them in code using their control IDs.

A wizard, represented by a Wizard object, consists of multiple steps that are each represented by a WizardStep control. WizardStep controls are added to a wizard via the Add() method of the WizardSteps property of the Wizard object. In this example, we have defined six different steps. Each step contains a text box. The state of the text boxes in the wizard is maintained automatically. The order of the steps is completely based upon the order in which they are added to the wizard. The `WizardSteps` property of a `Wizard` object contains a collection of steps. Changing the order of steps changes the order in which the end user sees them. Figure 1-23 shows the first step.

Figure 1-23. *Step 1 of the Wizard control in a web part*

The first step, the start step, always has one button called Next. The following steps will have two buttons, as seen in Figure 1-24.

Figure 1-24. *Step 2 of the Wizard control in a web part*

There are six steps in this example. The final step, step 6, will have a Previous and a Finish button, as you can see in Figure 1-25.

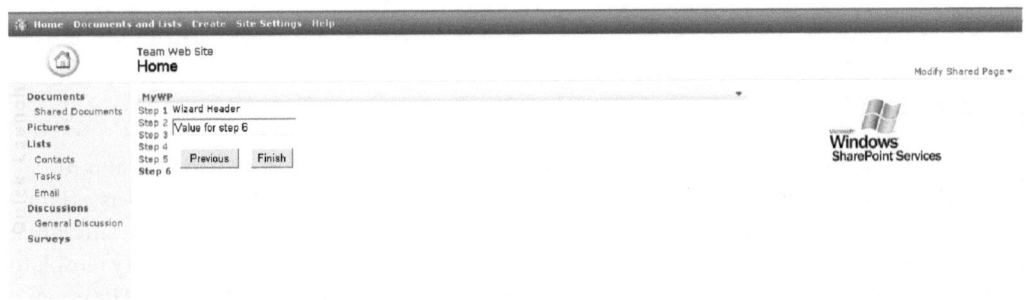

Figure 1-25. *The final step of the Wizard control in a web part*

This web part creates a very simple wizard; the Wizard control itself has a lot more options that we will not cover in this chapter. The code for the web part using the Wizard control looks like this:

```
using System;
using System.Collections.Generic;
using System.Text;
using System.Web.UI.HtmlControls;
using System.Web.UI.WebControls;
using Microsoft.SharePoint.WebPartPages;

namespace LoisAndClark.WPLibrary
{
  public class MyWP : WebPart
  {
    protected override void CreateChildControls()
    {
      Wizard objWizard = new Wizard();
      objWizard.HeaderText = "Wizard Header";

      for (int i = 1; i <= 6; i++)
      {
        WizardStepBase objStep = new WizardStep();
        objStep.ID = "Step" + i;
        objStep.Title = "Step " + i;
        TextBox objText = new TextBox();
        objText.ID = "Text" + i;
        objText.Text = "Value for step " + i;
        objStep.Controls.Add(objText);
        objWizard.WizardSteps.Add(objStep);
      }
      this.Controls.Add(objWizard);
    }
  }
}
```

Summary

This chapter explored the incorporation of the new features of ASP.NET 2.0 in SharePoint Products and Technologies 2003. We showed how to use SQL Server 2000 and 2005 as a data store and how to create web parts in Visual Studio .NET 2005. Then we discussed the Guidance Automation Toolkit to enhance the creation of web parts and created a web part library template guidance package. Finally, we showed you how to use a couple of the new ASP.NET 2.0 server controls within a web part.

CHAPTER 2

■■■

Using Ajax and Atlas in Web Parts

Ajax and Atlas deliver compelling web sites that are highly responsive and offer a great user interface experience. You may have heard this before, and the person who told you was not lying. Ajax makes it possible to perform asynchronous communication with a server. Atlas is a Microsoft implementation of Ajax. Another aspect of Atlas is that it makes creating advanced user interfaces using JavaScript a lot easier.

This chapter discusses what Ajax and Atlas are. It provides an overview of the more popular ASP.NET Ajax implementations. This chapter explains how to create Ajax server-side applications within the confines of a Windows SharePoint Services environment. This chapter also details how to deal with the client side of Ajax within SharePoint web parts and takes a look at server-side response types. From that point on, the chapter is dedicated solely to Atlas. We discuss several realistic examples where Atlas enhances the user interface experience within SharePoint web parts.

What Are Ajax and Atlas?

Ajax stands for Asynchronous JavaScript and XML and has been around for quite a long time. Ajax is a set of technologies that enables parts of a page to communicate directly to the server. If needed, communication can be performed asynchronously. Ajax uses a mixture of DHTML, JavaScript, and XMLHTTP to enrich the browser user interface experience.

Ajax-style applications really shine when you need to perform actions that take a long time to complete and you do not want to force the end user to wait. Typical examples are complex calculations, data retrieval over slow remote connections, retrieval of huge amounts of information, or data retrieval from multiple remote resources. Ajax is also great for server polling scenarios, where you continually refresh parts of a page with the latest information. Ajax's rich interaction comes close to that in Windows applications.

During the last year or so Ajax has become quite popular. One reason is because nowadays all popular browsers (such as Internet Explorer and Firefox) support a programmable document object model (DOM) and the latest versions of them offer the capability to communicate directly between client and server, without requiring a complete page postback.

Another reason has to do with the maturity level of Ajax-style development. In its infancy, Ajax-style development included a lot of manual work. The same was true for server-side web development. ASP.NET solved many of the complexities involved in developing the server side of web applications. Now, modern Ajax frameworks such as Atlas solve many of the complexities of the client side of web development.

The result of Ajax-style development is a new generation of web applications that are responsive and interactive and provide advanced user interfaces and are capable of processing data in real time.

Creating Ajax-style applications is not simple because you have to understand the different object models each browser has to offer. Browser compatibility issues can be a real hassle when doing client-side development. Another disadvantage is that a significant amount of the development work is spent in creating JavaScript script libraries. JavaScript is object-based instead of object-oriented and is type-unsafe. The JavaScript development experience does not compare to doing ASP.NET server-based development.

Atlas tries to solve these problems and is the logical next step in the evolution of Ajax-style applications. Atlas is a framework built on top of .NET 2.0 that allows developers to create Ajax-style applications combining client script libraries with the ASP.NET 2.0 server-based development framework. Atlas makes it easy to add rich client-side behavior to ASP.NET 2.0 web applications. Atlas offers a set of object-oriented application programming interfaces (APIs) making JavaScript development easier. Atlas offers cross-browser compatibility. Atlas can be programmed via a declarative model for client development without creating a line of code. The declarative model offers a development experience that is very similar to using ASP.NET server controls. Atlas offers web server controls that automatically emit all the client script needed for Atlas applications. Finally, Atlas offers integrated Visual Studio .NET 2005 development tools for client-side development, offering features such as debugging and statement completion.

The focus of Atlas is broader than Ajax. Ajax focuses on asynchronous communication with the server. Atlas is very capable of taking care of that, but Atlas goes a step further. Atlas tries to make client-side development easier, letting you create advanced user interfaces. The Atlas control toolkit (found at `http://atlas.asp.net`) offers a set of controls that are very easy to use and would require advanced JavaScript coding to implement yourself. At the time of this writing, the toolkit (version 1.0.60504.0) contained the following controls:

Cascading Drop-Down: This is a drop-down list that can be populated via web services.

Collapsible Panel: This control lets you create collapsible sections within a web page.

Confirm Button: This catches a button click and displays a new message window to the user.

DragPanel: This control lets you define page sections that can be dragged around the page.

Hover Menu: This control will let you associate a control with a pop-up panel to display additional content.

PopupControl: This control can be attached to any control to open a pop-up window that displays additional content.

Reorder List: This implements a bulleted databound list with items that can be reordered interactively.

Text Box Watermark: This can be attached to an ASP.NET text box control to get watermark behavior. This lets you display a default message in a text box (for example, Type First Name Here) that goes away once the user has typed some text into the text box.

Toggle Button: This can be attached to the ASP.NET check box control to enable the use of custom images to show the state of the check box.

This chapter focuses on the Ajax part of Atlas, not on the Atlas controls. Nevertheless, we want to whet your appetite for using the Atlas controls a little bit by showing some screenshots of them. Figure 2-1 shows the DragPanel control.

DragPanel
Drag Me
"Atlas" includes:
Client script libraries that provide a complete solution for creating client-based Web applications. The client script libraries support object-oriented development, cross-browser compatibility, asynchronous calls to Web services, and behaviors and components for creating a full-featured UI.
Web server controls that provide a declarative way to emit markup and client script for "Atlas" features.
Web services, such as
Drag

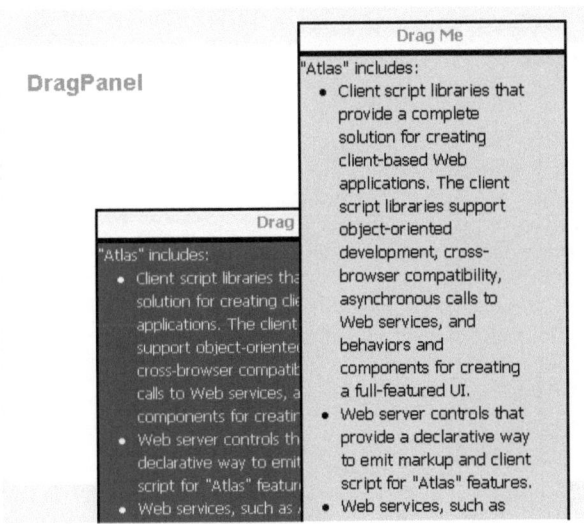

Figure 2-1. *The DragPanel control*

Figure 2-2 shows the Hover Menu control.

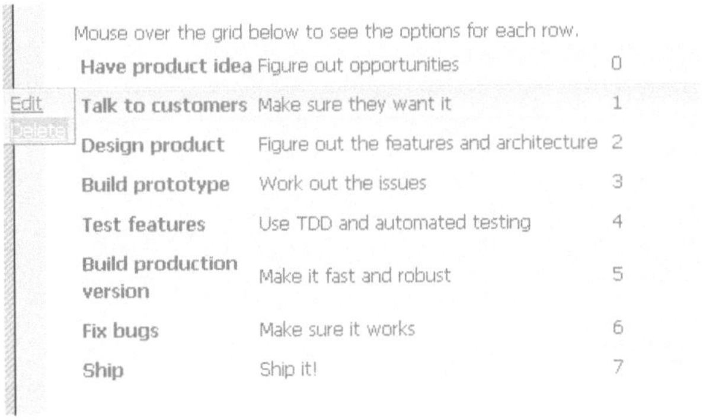

Mouse over the grid below to see the options for each row.
Have product idea Figure out opportunities 0
Edit
Delete
Talk to customers Make sure they want it 1
Design product Figure out the features and architecture 2
Build prototype Work out the issues 3
Test features Use TDD and automated testing 4
Build production version Make it fast and robust 5
Fix bugs Make sure it works 6
Ship Ship it! 7

Figure 2-2. *The Hover Menu control*

Figure 2-3 shows the PopupControl.

Figure 2-3. *The PopupControl*

Figure 2-4 shows the Reorder List control.

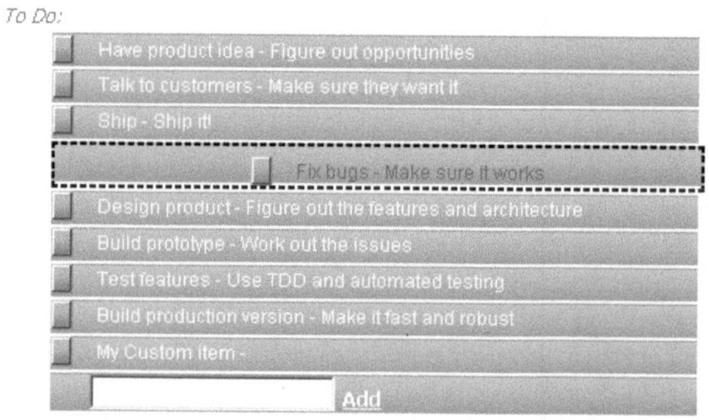

Figure 2-4. *The Reorder List control*

Figure 2-5 shows the Text Box Watermark control.

Figure 2-5. *The Text Box Watermark control*

Figure 2-6 shows the Toggle Button control.

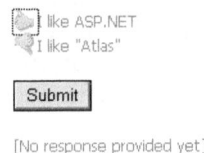

Submit

[No response provided yet]

Figure 2-6. *The Toggle Button control*

Ajax Frameworks for ASP.NET

As a testament to the popularity of Ajax, if you search for it on the Internet, you will probably find a couple dozen Ajax implementations. There are Ajax frameworks written in JavaScript, C++, Java, ColdFusion, Lisp, Perl, PHP, Python, and the list goes on. Even if you limit the search to .NET frameworks, you will find more than ten of them. The following list provides an overview of the well-known Ajax frameworks that are targeted toward ASP.NET:

Atlas: The first Ajax framework for ASP.NET is Atlas. Atlas is created by Microsoft. Atlas integrates an extensive set of client script libraries with the rich, server-based development platform of ASP.NET 2.0. At the time of this writing Atlas was not released officially; it was still in the Community Technology Preview (CTP) phase. Atlas only supports ASP.NET 2.0. More information can be found at http://atlas.asp.net.

ComfortASP.NET: Internally, ComfortASP.NET uses a mixture of DHTML, JavaScript, and XMLHTTP. The developer only implements pure server-side ASP.NET. ComfortASP.NET supports ASP.NET 1.1 and ASP.NET 2.0. ComfortASP.NET reduces HTML traffic. More information can be found at http://www.comfortasp.de/.

MagicAjax.NET: MagicAjax.NET is an open source framework that lets you put Ajax-enabled controls on a web page within an Ajax panel. MagicAjax.NET does not require you to write any JavaScript. MagicAjax.NET supports ASP.NET 1.1 and ASP.NET 2.0. More information can be found at http://www.magicajax.net.

ZumiPage: ZumiPage is a commercial framework that requires no code changes to existing projects. ZumiPage supports ASP.NET 1.1 and ASP.NET 2.0. More information can be found at http://www.zumipage.com.

Outpost: Outpost is a free framework that gets the HTML of page controls that were changed and transports the changes automatically to the client in a hidden postback. Outpost supports ASP.NET 1.1 and ASP.NET 2.0. More information can be found at http://csharpedge.blogspot.com.

FastPage: FastPage is a commercial framework that is easy to use, install, and configure. FastPage supports ASP.NET 1.1 and ASP.NET 2.0. More information can be found at http://fastpage.more.at.

As you can see, when it comes to choosing an Ajax framework for .NET you have plenty of choices. With the Atlas framework being an exception, all frameworks offer support for ASP.NET 1.1 as well as ASP.NET 2.0. Atlas only offers support for ASP.NET 2.0. Most of the frameworks are free.

When choosing a framework we prefer not to focus on the current features of a framework, per se. We are also interested in where the framework will be two or three years from now. We expect Atlas will become the primary framework for .NET developers who are doing Ajax-style development in ASP.NET 2.0 applications. As a result, in this chapter we have chosen to focus on Atlas and ignore the other .NET Ajax implementations.

Creating Web Services in Windows SharePoint Services

If you want to incorporate Ajax into your SharePoint applications, it is very likely that the Ajax client side communicates with a server side implemented using web services. Since this chapter discusses Atlas, a framework that uses .NET 2.0, we will only focus on Windows SharePoint Services (with Service Pack 2.0). As you learned in Chapter 1 there is no support in SharePoint Portal Server 2003 for .NET 2.0.

In this section, we show how to create .NET 2.0 web services on Windows SharePoint Services servers. We have to warn you though: the process of creating web services on a SharePoint server is neither easy nor fun.

After installing Windows SharePoint Services on a server, all HTTP requests are intercepted by the SharePoint ISAPI filter (stsfilter.dll) and handled by Windows SharePoint Services. ISAPI filters, or Internet Server API filters, are tightly integrated with the web server. ISAPI filters can intercept HTTP requests before ASP.NET or Windows SharePoint Services gets the chance to handle such requests. As a result, if you do not take any steps and create a web service on a Windows SharePoint Services server, a web service request will be intercepted by SharePoint and will fail miserably. To avoid this, you should decide which virtual directory name you want to use for your web service and create an unmanaged path for this, thus telling Windows SharePoint Services not to intercept the request to the virtual folder and let IIS handle the request instead.

The following steps describe how to add an unmanaged path for a test web service that we will call AskMe:

1. Go to Start ➤ All Programs ➤ Administrative Tools ➤ SharePoint Central Administration.

2. On the Windows SharePoint Services Central Administration page, in the Virtual Server Configuration section, click Configure Virtual Server Settings.

3. Click Default Web Site.

4. In the Virtual Server Management section, click Define Managed Paths.

5. In the Add a New Path section, enter the following value for Path: **AskMe**. Select the Excluded Path radio button. Click OK.

Before you can use Visual Studio .NET 2005 to create a web service, you need to do some manual work. First, using Windows Explorer, you need to create a destination folder for your web service. Then you need to create a new virtual directory in Internet Information Services Manager for this folder. The following steps describe how to create a virtual directory in Internet Information Services 6.0 for a test web service called AskMe that is created later on:

1. Open Windows Explorer.

2. Create a folder called AskMe in [drive letter]:\inetpub\wwwroot.

3. Choose Start ➤ Run. Type **inetmgr** and click OK.

4. Expand the Local Computer node.

5. Expand the Web Sites node.

6. Expand the Default Web Site node.

7. Locate the AskMe folder, right-click it and choose Properties.

8. On the AskMe Properties page, click Create.

9. Click OK.

Now you can use Visual Studio .NET 2005 to create the AskMe web service. In the next steps, you will create a web service called AskMe and add a class to it called Mediator:

1. Open Visual Studio .NET 2005.

2. Choose File ➤ New ➤ Web Site.

3. On the New Web Site screen, click ASP.NET Web Service.

4. Make sure Location is set to HTTP.

5. Set the URL to http://localhost/AskMe.

6. Click OK.

7. Right-click Service.asmx ➤ Delete ➤ OK.

8. Right-click the http://localhostAskMe/ project ➤ Add New Item.

9. On the Add New Item – http://localhost/AskMe/ screen, choose the following item template: Web Service.

10. Enter the name **Mediator.asmx**.

11. Make sure the Place Code in Separate File check box is checked.

12. Click Add.

By default a HelloWorld() method is added to Mediator.asmx. This is the method we will use to validate whether the AskMe web service works. You can precompile the AskMe web service if you want, but in ASP.NET 2.0 there is no longer a need to compile your code and put the assembly into the bin folder. The actual code for Mediator.asmx is placed in a code-behind class called Mediator.cs. The Mediator.cs class is located in the App_Code folder. If you open a browser and navigate to http://localhost/askme/mediator.asmx you can see that the AskMe web service works as expected.

If all you want to do is create a general web service, you are finished. If you want to create a web service that will run in a given SharePoint context, things will get more painful. Web services that need to run in a given SharePoint context are stored in a virtual folder called _vti_bin. This is a virtual directory in IIS that is mapped to the [drive letter]:\Program Files\ Common Files\Microsoft Shared\web server extensions\60\ISAPI folder. The name of the _vti_bin folder originates from a company called Vermeer Technologies Incorporated, which was acquired by Microsoft in the beginning of 1996. Vermeer Technologies was responsible for creating the original version of FrontPage. The _vti_bin folder is a special Common Gateway Interface (CGI)–like folder that contains server-side functionality that needs to be available within the entire virtual server. On a SharePoint server, the _vti_bin folder is the place where the default SharePoint web service files are stored.

Note The influence of the old Vermeer Technologies Inc. on SharePoint technology does not stop with the folder name. SharePoint uses a customized version of FrontPage Server Extensions. This is why FrontPage can be used to adjust SharePoint sites. This is also why you should never install FrontPage Server Extensions on a SharePoint server.

If you reference a web service in the context of a given SharePoint site, the web service will have access to this context. For example, suppose you create the Mediator.asmx file within the AskMe web service and add it to _vti_bin. Its URL would be http://localhost/_vti_bin/ Mediator.asmx. If you create a SharePoint site called Atlas, you can reference Mediator.asmx within the context of the SharePoint site via the following URL: http://localhost/atlas/ _vti_bin/Mediator.asmx. We will look at this in more detail later.

Since our web service only supports a method that returns a greeting to the world, it will not help us much to test whether the web service runs successfully within a given SharePoint context. In the next step, remove the HelloWorld() method and replace it with a GetCurrentSiteName() method that returns the name of the SharePoint site in which the context of the AskMe web service runs. In order to do that you need to set a reference to Microsoft.Share-Point.dll, which is located in [drive letter]:\Program Files\Common Files\Microsoft Shared\ web server extensions\60\ISAPI. Import the Microsoft.SharePoint.WebControls namespace. Add the following code to the GetCurrentSiteName() method:

```
return SPControl.GetContextWeb(Context).Name;.
```

The complete code listing looks like this:

```
using System;
using System.Web;
using System.Collections;
using System.Web.Services;
using System.Web.Services.Protocols;
using Microsoft.SharePoint.WebControls;

[WebService(Namespace = "http://tempuri.org/")]
[WebServiceBinding(ConformsTo = WsiProfiles.BasicProfile1_1)]
public class Mediator : System.Web.Services.WebService
{
```

```
public Mediator ()
{
}

[WebMethod]
public string GetCurrentSiteName()
{
  return SPControl.GetContextWeb(Context).Name;
}
}
```

At this point, we have created the AskMe web service in a separate virtual folder. Now you will see how to create a web service that can be run within a SharePoint context. In the first part of the process, you will need to create a static discovery (.disco) and a Web Services Description Language (.wsdl) file using the disco.exe tool. The DISCO protocol is used to discover web services located on a particular domain. A .disco file contains a list of web services and points to their WSDL files. WSDL is a language designed to describe a web service and all its methods. The following procedure explains how to create .disco and .wsdl files for the MediatorService web service:

1. Open a Visual Studio 2005 command prompt.

2. Navigate to the web service folder [drive letter]:\inetpub\wwwroot\AskMe.

3. Run the following command: `disco http://localhost/askme/mediator.asmx`.

As a result, three new files will be created in the AskMe folder: mediator.disco, mediator.wsdl, and results.discomap. Results.discomap contains references to the .wsdl and .disco files and can be used to generate web service proxy classes via the WSDL tool. In this example, we will use Visual Studio .NET 2005 to locate the AskMe web service and create a web service proxy class. Because of this, the results.discomap file is irrelevant in this example.

The two files that are important in the example are mediator.disco and mediator.wsdl. The `Microsoft.SharePoint` namespace needs to be registered within both of the files. To do this, open the mediator.disco and mediator.wsdl files in any text editor. In both files, locate the following line: `<?xml version="1.0" encoding="utf-8"?>`. Replace this line with the following lines of code:

```
<%@ Page Language="C#" Inherits="System.Web.UI.Page"%>
<%@ Assembly Name="Microsoft.SharePoint, Version=11.0.0.0, ➥
   Culture=neutral, PublicKeyToken=71e9bce111e9429c" %>
<%@ Import Namespace="Microsoft.SharePoint.Utilities" %>
<%@ Import Namespace="Microsoft.SharePoint" %>
<% Response.ContentType="text/xml"; %>
```

The page directives indicate that the .disco and .wsdl files are not XML anymore. XML parsers will not be able to handle these directives. However, the ASP.NET engine will be able to recognize the page directives, so you need to rename both files to .aspx pages. Rename the mediator.disco file to Mediatordisco.aspx and save the mediator.wsdl file as Mediatorwsdl.aspx. Now you need to add support for service virtualization to the Mediatordisco.aspx and

Mediatorwsdl.aspx. This means that it needs to be possible to change the end point address of the web service at runtime. Instead of using a static address, the address of the web service depends on the context of a request. First, open Mediatordisco.aspx and locate the following line:

```
<contractRef ref="http://localhost/askme/mediator.asmx?wsdl" ➡
docRef="http://localhost/askme/mediator.asmx" ➡
xmlns="http://schemas.xmlsoap.org/disco/scl/" />
```

Replace this line with the following:

```
<contractRef ref=<% SPEncode.WriteHtmlEncodeWithQuote(Response, ➡
SPWeb.OriginalBaseUrl(Request) + "?wsdl", '"'); %> ➡
docRef=<% SPEncode.WriteHtmlEncodeWithQuote(Response, ➡
SPWeb.OriginalBaseUrl(Request), '"'); %> ➡
xmlns="http://schemas.xmlsoap.org/disco/scl/" />
```

Then locate the following line:

```
<soap address="http://localhost/askme/mediator.asmx" xmlns:q1= ➡
"http://tempuri.org/" binding="q1:MediatorSoap" ➡
xmlns="http://schemas.xmlsoap.org/disco/soap/" />
```

Replace the line with the following:

```
<soap address=<% SPEncode.WriteHtmlEncodeWithQuote(Response, ➡
SPWeb.OriginalBaseUrl(Request), '"'); %> xmlns:q1= ➡
"http://tempuri.org/" binding="q1: MediatorSoap" ➡
xmlns="http://schemas.xmlsoap.org/disco/soap/" />
```

Now open Mediatorwsdl.aspx, and toward the end of the file, locate the line

```
<soap:address location="http://localhost/askme/mediator.asmx" />
```

and replace it with

```
<soap:address location=<% SPEncode.WriteHtmlEncodeWithQuote( ➡
Response, SPWeb.OriginalBaseUrl(Request), '"'); %> />
```

Find the following line:

```
<soap12:address location="http://localhost/askme/mediator.asmx" />
```

Replace the line with this:

```
<soap12:address location=<% SPEncode.WriteHtmlEncodeWithQuote( ➡
Response, SPWeb.OriginalBaseUrl(Request), '"'); %> />
```

At this point, you have successfully added service virtualization. Move the Mediatordisco.aspx and Mediatorwsdl.aspx pages to the _vti_bin folder ([drive letter]:\Program Files\Common Files\ Microsoft Shared\web server extensions\60\ISAPI), because this is the folder where all SharePoint web services are stored. By the way, if you do not move these files, you will not be able to compile the AskMe web service anymore. Follow these steps to copy the files to the _vti_bin folder:

1. Copy Mediator.asmx to the _vti_bin folder.

2. Copy the App_Code and App_Data folders to the _vti_bin folder.

Because the AskMe web service is written in .NET 2.0 and uses the Microsoft.SharePoint assembly, the web.config file of the _vti_bin folder needs to contain a reference to the SharePoint dll. Add the following XML below the `<system.web>` element of the web.config file in the _vti_bin folder:

```
<compilation debug="false">
  <assemblies>
    <add assembly="Microsoft.SharePoint, Version=11.0.0.0, ➥
    Culture=neutral, PublicKeyToken=71E9BCE111E9429C"/>
  </assemblies>
</compilation>
```

The complete web.config file should resemble the following code listing:

```
<configuration>
  <system.web>
    <compilation debug="false">
      <assemblies>
        <add assembly="Microsoft.SharePoint, Version=11.0.0.0, ➥
        Culture=neutral, PublicKeyToken=71E9BCE111E9429C"/>
      </assemblies>
    </compilation>
    <webServices>
      <protocols>
        <remove name="HttpGet" />
        <remove name="HttpPost" />
        <remove name="HttpPostLocalhost" />
        <add name="Documentation" />
      </protocols>
    </webServices>
    <customErrors mode="On"/>
    <trust level="Full" originUrl="" />
  </system.web>
</configuration>
```

If you include the AskMe.Mediator.asmx file in the list of default Windows SharePoint Services web services, it will be easier to reference the web service via Visual Studio .NET 2005. You can do this by opening spdisco.aspx (also located in the _vti_bin folder) and adding the following lines within the `<discovery>` element:

```
<contractRef ref=<% SPEncode.WriteHtmlEncodeWithQuote(Response, spWeb.Url + ➥
"/_vti_bin/Mediator.asmx?wsdl", '"'); %> docRef=<% ➥
SPEncode.WriteHtmlEncodeWithQuote(Response, spWeb.Url + ➥
"/_vti_bin/Mediator.asmx", '"'); %> xmlns="http://schemas.xmlsoap.org/disco/scl/" />
```

```
<soap address=<% SPEncode.WriteHtmlEncodeWithQuote(Response, spWeb.Url + ➡
"/_vti_bin/Mediator.asmx", '"'); %> ➡
xmlns:q1="http://schemas.microsoft.com/sharepoint/soap/directory/" ➡
binding="q1:MediatorSoap" xmlns="http://schemas.xmlsoap.org/disco/soap/" />
```

If you open a browser and go to http://localhost/_vti_bin/mediator.asmx?WSDL, you should see a valid web service description file. Now you can add a reference to the web service from within a web part library project and access the SharePoint context from within a web part in this library.

1. From within Visual Studio .NET 2005, right-click your project, then choose Add Web Reference.

2. Click the Web Services on the Local Machine link.

3. Locate the Mediator web service and click it.

4. Change the web reference name to MediatorService and click Add Reference.

Note In order to complete these steps, you must create a web part and open it in Visual Studio .NET 2005. If you are not sure how to do this, refer to Chapter 1.

Now you need to create an instance of the MediatorService web service and set the current security credentials that are used for web service client authentication. If you do not set the security credentials correctly, you will get an "HTTP status 401: Unauthorized" error. You can set the correct SharePoint context via the Url property of the MediatorService web service. You can assign the following static value: http://localhost/atlas/_vti_bin/mediator.asmx. This ensures the MediatorService web service is run within the context of the Atlas SharePoint site. You can also set this property dynamically by using the Url property of the current SharePoint site. The following code example uses the latter approach:

```
string strValue = String.Empty;
SPWeb objSite = SPControl.GetContextWeb(Context);
strValue = objSite.Url + "/_vti_bin/mediator.asmx";
MediatorService.Mediator objMediator = new MediatorService.Mediator();
objMediator.Credentials = CredentialCache.DefaultCredentials;
objMediator.Url = strValue;
strValue = objMediator.GetCurrentSiteName();
```

Figure 2-7 shows that the web service returns the SharePoint site name from the current context. As we promised, creating web services on a Windows SharePoint Services server can be quite painful.

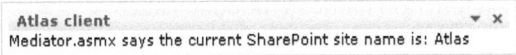

Figure 2-7. *Web service returns SharePoint site name from current context*

JavaScript in Web Parts

Web services are an important part of Ajax-style development. We have already taken an in-depth look at creating web services on a Windows SharePoint Services server. The other important part of Ajax is JavaScript. In this section, we will look in detail at JavaScript development within SharePoint web parts. A working understanding of the concepts in this section is essential for understanding the rest of this chapter.

The Content Editor Web Part

The easiest way to add JavaScript to a SharePoint page is probably via the content editor web part. The content editor web part can be used to add formatted text, tables, hyperlinks, and images to a web part page. You can also add JavaScript by typing it straight into the Content Editor Web Part Text Entry window, as shown in the next example:

1. Go to a SharePoint page ➤ Modify Shared Page ➤ Add Web Parts ➤ Browse.

2. Locate the content editor web part and drag it to the page.

3. Click the Open the Tool Pane link.

4. Click the Source Editor… button.

5. Type the following JavaScript code in the Text Entry – Web Page Dialog window: **<script>alert("hi!");</script>**.

6. Click Save.

Web Part Tokens

The SharePoint web part framework contains several web part tokens that are used to aid client-side development when creating web parts. The tokens we like to use most are the _WPR_ and _WPQ_ tokens.

When rendered, the _WPR_ token is replaced with the path to the web part resources folder of the SharePoint site containing the web part. The web part resources folder is a predefined folder that can be found on the following location: [drive letter]:\inetpub\wwwroot\wpresources. The web part resources folder is meant to store web part resources such as images or JavaScript libraries. If you use the _WPR_ token on a SharePoint site called Atlas, the token will be replaced with the following value: `http://myserver/Atlas/wpresources/Atlas`.

The _WPQ_ token is used to create names that are unique per web part. For example, if you create a JavaScript function called `DoSometing()` there is always the possibility that another web part could create a JavaScript function with the same name. If you place the same web part on a page multiple times, you have the guarantee that you will get name conflicts. To prevent this type of problem, append the _WPQ_ token to a function name. A function called DoSomething_WPQ_() will be rendered to something like DoSomethingWPQ1().

The following lines of code demonstrate the use of web part tokens and can be added to a web part:

```
string strValue = "WPQ: " + ReplaceTokens("_WPQ_") +
" WPR " + ReplaceTokens("_WPR_");
```

Figure 2-8 shows the result of a web part containing this line of code. The other available web part tokens are _LogonUser_ and _WPID_. The _LogonUser_ token specifies the domain\user name for the currently logged-on user. The _WPID_ token specifies the control ID of the web part.

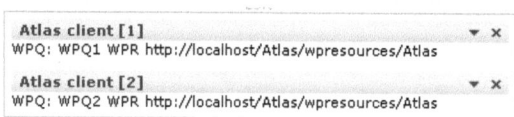

Figure 2-8. *The web part tokens*

Rendering JavaScript Within a Web Part

When rendering JavaScript within a This section shows how to use JavaScript within web parts. web part you should register an event handler for the PreRender event in the web part constructor and render the JavaScript within the PreRender event handler. This ensures the web part framework loads the JavaScript before the web part is rendered to the web part page.

The ClientScriptManager class, which is new in ASP.NET 2.0, can be used to manage client-side scripts. You can obtain an instance of the ClientScriptManager class via the ClientScript property of the Page object that is always available within a web part. Use the ClientScriptManager instance to add JavaScript to the page. You can use the IsClientScriptBlockRegistered() method of the ClientScriptManager class to add a JavaScript library (a .js file) to the page. The best place to store the JavaScript library is the web part resources folder. The following code shows how to register a JavaScript library on a web page:

```
if (!Page.ClientScript.IsClientScriptIncludeRegistered ("MyKey1"))
{
  Page.ClientScript.RegisterClientScriptInclude("MyKey1", ➥
  "/wpresources/customlib.js");
}
```

As you can see, a unique key is used to check whether the JavaScript library is already added to the page. Do not use the _WPQ_ token as a key. The _WPQ_ token is used to create names that are guaranteed to be unique within a page. The key used here ensures no duplicate registrations take place on a single page.

You can also render dynamic pieces of JavaScript code to a page. Use the RegisterClientScriptBlock() method of the ClientScriptManager class to do this. The following code shows an example of this:

```
if (!Page.ClientScript.IsClientScriptBlockRegistered("MyKey2"))
{
  Page.ClientScript.RegisterClientScriptBlock(typeof(string), "MyKey2", ➥
  "alert('test');", true);
}
```

Note Generally, we prefer to use JavaScript libraries instead of dynamic pieces of JavaScript code. This makes it much easier to write and change JavaScript code. A disadvantage is that you cannot work with web part tokens in JavaScript libraries, so you need to take this into consideration when developing web parts. This development style may become a problem when you want to use the same web part on the same SharePoint page more than once. This chapter shows examples of these approaches in the sections "JavaScript On-Demand Loading" and "Building a Performance Counter Web Part."

The complete code for a web part registering JavaScript on a page is shown here:

```
using System;
using System.Collections.Generic;
using System.Text;
using System.Web.UI;
using System.Web.UI.HtmlControls;
using System.Web.UI.WebControls;
using Microsoft.SharePoint;
using Microsoft.SharePoint.WebPartPages;

namespace LoisAndClark.Atlas
{
  public class AtlasClient : WebPart
  {
    public AtlasClient ()
    {
      PreRender += new EventHandler(AtlasClient_PreRender);
    }

    void AtlasClient_PreRender(object sender, EventArgs e)
    {
      if (!Page.ClientScript.IsClientScriptIncludeRegistered ("MyKey1"))
      {
        Page.ClientScript.RegisterClientScriptInclude("MyKey1", ➥
        "/wpresources/customlib.js");
      }
```

```
    if (!Page.ClientScript.IsClientScriptBlockRegistered("MyKey2"))
    {
      Page.ClientScript.RegisterClientScriptBlock(typeof(string), ➥
      "MyKey2", "alert('test');", true);
    }
  }

  protected override void CreateChildControls()
  {
    try
    {
      // … do stuff…
    }
    catch (Exception err)
    {
      Controls.Add(new LiteralControl(err.Message));
    }
  }
 }
}
```

JavaScript On-Demand Loading

Ajax-style applications rely heavily on the use of JavaScript. If you add your JavaScript functions to JavaScript script libraries, the end user will have to wait until all script libraries have been loaded. This could take a while, as the complexity of the Ajax application increases, thus defeating the primary purpose of Ajax, namely, to create a great user interface experience. In this section we discuss JavaScript on-demand loading, a technique where JavaScript libraries are loaded as needed.

Note The on-demand approach is applied to the .NET Framework as well. The .NET Common Language Runtime (CLR) loads assemblies as needed (on-demand loading), and Intermediate Language (IL) within an assembly is compiled as needed (just-in-time compilation).

Alas, JavaScript on-demand loading is something that is not done automatically for you. In its simplest form, the JavaScript on-demand approach consists of a piece of JavaScript code calling a web service. The web service does not return a normal response but instead returns a piece of JavaScript code that is executed via the JavaScript eval() function. The following code shows an example:

```
var strJsCode = CallWebService(); // web service returns "alert('hi');";
eval(strJsCode); // This line is equivalent to: alert('hi');
```

Note The `eval()` JavaScript function is built into the JavaScript language and evaluates a string and parses it on the fly. In SharePoint Portal Server 2001 the `eval()` function was the core of the web part rendering process. All server-side code in web parts (either VBScript or JavaScript) was retrieved from the web part XML and parsed by the `eval()` function when the web part was rendered.

The second solution for JavaScript on-demand loading is more sophisticated and more complex to implement. In this approach, a JavaScript function knows which JavaScript library it needs and loads the required library on demand, waits until the JavaScript library is loaded, and then calls a function within the newly loaded library.

In the following example, you should create a new JavaScript library called ondemand.js. Add the JavaScript library to the web part resources folder ([drive letter]:\inetpub\wwwroot\wpresources). The entire content of the ondemand.js JavaScript library looks like this:

```
function OnDemandHello()
{
  alert('on demand hi!');
}
```

We will show how to load this library on demand from another script library that we will call customlib.js. The customlib.js JavaScript library is registered on the page from within a web part via the `RegisterClientScriptInclude()` method that is described in the section "Rendering JavaScript Within a Web Part." Suppose the customlib.js library contains a function called `CustomLibHello()` that wants to call the `OnDemandHello()` function in the ondemand.js library. The `CustomLibHello()` function calls a function that adds the ondemand.js script library to the page dynamically, like so:

```
var objHeadElement = document.getElementsByTagName('head')[0];
var objScriptLibrary = document.createElement('script');
objScriptLibrary.id = 'OnDemandScript';
objScriptLibrary.type = 'text/javascript';
objScriptLibrary.src = '/wpresources/ondemand.js';
objHeadElement.appendChild(objScriptLibrary);
```

The JavaScript within the ondemand.js script library will not be loaded immediately, so you will have to check explicitly whether the function that you want to call is already available. You can use the following code:

```
if (self.OnDemandHello)
{
  // OnDemandHello is available.
}
```

If the `OnDemandHello()` function is not available, you should use the `setTimeout()` function that is a part of the JavaScript language to try again later after *x* number of milliseconds. The following code listing shows how to implement JavaScript on demand for the `OnDemandHello()` function in the customlib.js JavaScript library:

```
function CustomLibHello()
{
  LoadOnDemand();
}

function LoadOnDemand()
{
  ensureUploadScriptIsLoaded();
  if (self.OnDemandHello == null )
  {
    alert('not yet loaded');
    setTimeout("LoadOnDemand();",2000);
  }
  else
  {
    alert('loaded');
    OnDemandHello();
  }
}

function ensureUploadScriptIsLoaded()
{
  if (self.OnDemandHello)
  {
    // OnDemandHello() is already loaded.
    return;
  }

  var objHeadElement = document.getElementsByTagName('head')[0];
  var objScriptLibrary = document.createElement('script');
  objScriptLibrary.id = 'OnDemandScript';
  objScriptLibrary.type = 'text/javascript';
  objScriptLibrary.src = '/wpresources/ondemand.js';
  objHeadElement.appendChild(objScriptLibrary);
}
```

Debugging JavaScript

Although JavaScript is not a very advanced language, you can use Visual Studio .NET 2005
and enjoy a rich debugging experience. If you want to debug JavaScript code, you need to do
the following:

1. Go to your browser and click Tools ➤ Internet Options ➤ Advanced ➤ Uncheck Disable
   Script Debugging (Internet Explorer).

2. Close the browser and start it again.

Now you can debug JavaScript as shown in Figure 2-9.

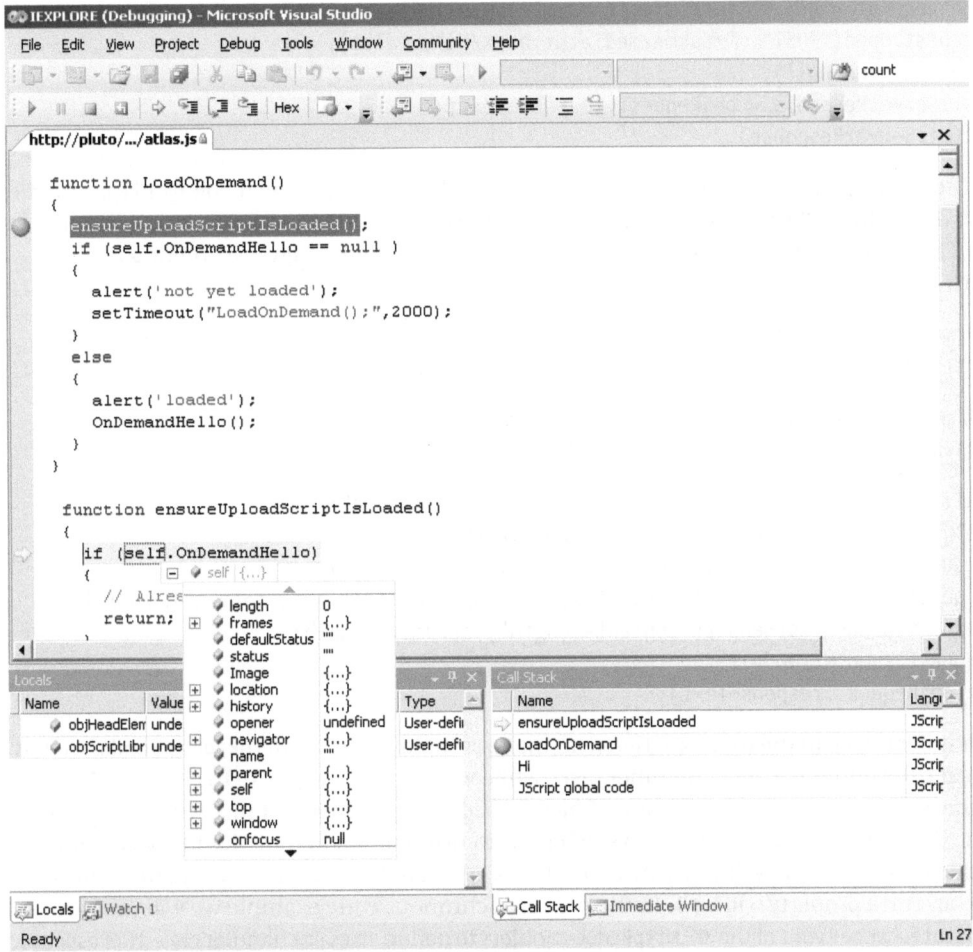

Figure 2-9. *Debugging JavaScript using Visual Studio .NET 2005*

Remote Calls Prior to Atlas

In this section we discuss how to use client-side JavaScript to communicate with web services without using Atlas. If you start using Atlas you probably will not use these techniques anymore, but if we take a moment to discuss the older techniques for doing asynchronous communication with the server side it will help you understand Atlas better.

Retrieving Data via XMLHttpRequest

Microsoft implemented the XMLHttpRequest object for the first time in Internet Explorer 5. The purpose of the XMLHttpRequest object is to let clients retrieve and convert XML from the server and use the client-side Document Object Model to do something useful with this data. The following JavaScript code calls a web service method Hi() defined within Mediator.asmx:

```
var objRequest = new ActiveXObject("Msxml2.XMLHTTP");
objRequest.open("POST", "/askme/mediator.asmx/Hi", false);
objRequest.send(null);
var strServerResponse = objRequest.responseText;
alert(strServerResponse);
```

The false option that is passed as an argument to the open() method of the XMLHttpRequest object makes the call *synchronous*, meaning that the code will wait until a response comes back. The send() method completes the request. The Hi() method gives a greeting to all its clients, and its response looks like this:

```
<?xml version="1.0" encoding="utf-8" ?>
<string xmlns="http://tempuri.org/">Hi all!</string>
```

If needed, you can also pass arguments to a web service. The following code example shows how to pass two arguments to a web service method called Hi2():

```
var strBody = "strFirstArg=MyFirst&strSecondArg=MySecond";
var objRequest = new ActiveXObject("Msxml2.XMLHTTP");
objRequest.open("POST", "/askme/mediator.asmx/Hi2", false);
objRequest.setRequestHeader("Content-Type", "application/x-www-form-urlencoded");
objRequest.setRequestHeader("Content-Length", strBody.length);
objRequest.send(strBody);
alert(objRequest.responseText);
```

It is beneficial to the user experience to make asynchronous XMLHttpRequest calls, so that the user can continue to work on other tasks while waiting for a response to come back. You can check if the response is ready by calling the readystate property of the XMLHttpRequest object. The readystate property always reflects the current point in the call's lifecycle. Initially, upon creation, the state value is 0. After a call it is 1. When the response is back, the value of the readystate property will be 4. In the next asynchronous code example we will use the readystatechange event of the XMLHttpRequest object to define an event handler called OnResponse. The event handler will be called multiple times (once per call state) during the call lifecycle. In the OnResponse event handler we will check the readystate property to see when the response is ready, as shown in the following code:

```
objRequest = new ActiveXObject("Msxml2.XMLHTTP");
objRequest.open("POST", "/askme/mediator.asmx/Hi", true);
objRequest.onreadystatechange = OnResponse;
objRequest.send(null);

function OnResponse()
{
  if ( _objRequest.readyState != 4 )
  {
    alert('not ready yet');
    return;
  }
```

```
  // Error checking
  if ( _objRequest.status != 200 )
  {
    alert("unexpected status!");
  }

  var strResponse = _objRequest.responseText;
  alert(strResponse);
}
```

You can use the abort() method of the XMLHttpRequest object to abort a remote call, like this: _objRequest.abort();. The following code shows a technique that aborts a remote call after five seconds have passed:

```
function MyRemoteCall()
{
  objRequest = new ActiveXObject("Msxml2.XMLHTTP");
  objRequest.open("POST", "/askme/mediator.asmx/Hi", true);
  objRequest.onreadystatechange = OnResponse;
  objRequest.send(null);
  setTimeout("Abort()", 5000);
}

function Abort()
{
  objRequest.abort();
  alert("abort");
}

function OnResponse()
{
  if ( _objRequest.readyState != 4 )
  {
    //alert('not ready yet');
    return;
  }

  if ( _objRequest.status != 200 )
  {
    alert("unexpected status!");
  }

  var strResponse = _objRequest.responseText;
  alert(strResponse);
}

MyRemoteCall();
```

In the previous example you saw how to use the `responseText` property of the `XMLHttpRequest` object to retrieve the response as a string. You can also retrieve the response as XML directly using the `responseXML` property, like so:

```
var xmlResponse = _objRequest.responseXML;
alert(xmlResponse.innerXml);
```

Web Service Behavior

`XMLHttpRequest` is the first step in the evolution of Ajax-style application development. The `XMLHttpRequest` object makes communicating with web services via JavaScript possible but not easy. The next step in the evolution of building Ajax applications is the WebService behavior that can be downloaded from the MSDN web site (`http://msdn.microsoft.com/archive/default.asp?url=/archive/en-us/samples/internet/behaviors/library/webservice/default.asp`). Behaviors are a way of programmatically packaging actions and associating those actions to page elements. The WebService behavior enables client-side script to invoke remote methods exposed by web services or other web services that support Simple Object Access Protocol (SOAP) and WSDL. The WebService behavior is a simple, lightweight component that encapsulates the capability to invoke remote methods using SOAP. The behavior is implemented as an HTML component (HTC) file.

Note If you want to use the WebService behavior within a web part, you need to download it and preferably store it in the web part resources folder.

If you have a choice, we do not recommend using the WebService behavior, because Atlas is even more developer-friendly and the WebService behavior is not supported anymore. Having said that, the next code example shows how to use the WebService behavior. In the code example, the behavior is attached to a page element, a `<div>` with the following ID: service. The `useService()` function of the WebService behavior ties the web service to a friendly name that can be used later to call the web service. You can call the web service asynchronously by specifying an event handler that we will call `OnGetNameResult`.

```
<html>
<body onload="InitRemoteCall();">
<div id="service" style="behavior:url(webservice.htc)"></div>

<script>
function InitRemoteCall()
{
  service.useService("http://pluto/AskMe/Mediator.asmx?WSDL","Mediator");
  var intId = service.Mediator.callService(OnGetNameResult, "GetCurrentSiteName");
}
```

```
function OnGetNameResult(objResult)
{
  if ( objResult.error )
  {
    alert(objResult.errorDetail.string + " " + ➥
    objResult.errorDetail.code + " " + objResult.errorDetail.raw);
  }
  else
  {
    alert(objResult.value);
  }
}
</script>
</body>
</html>
```

The previous example shows how to call the GetCurrentSiteName() web service method without passing any arguments to it. If you want to call a web service via the WebService behavior and pass multiple arguments to the web service, you can do it like this:

```
var intId = service.HelloService.callService(OnGetNameResult, ➥
"GetCurrentSiteName", "arg1", "arg2");
```

■ **Note** To ensure that the useService() method works correctly, it should be placed inside a handler for the onload event, so that the first attempt to call a method in the behavior only occurs after the page has been downloaded and parsed. Web services referenced by the useServer() method need to reside on the same domain as the web server.

Web Service Message Types

At this point you have seen how to create a web service on a Windows SharePoint Services server. You have also seen how to call web services via client-side JavaScript using the XMLHttpRequest object and the WebService behavior. This section is dedicated to discussing the types of responses that can be given by web services.

Plain Text

If a web service just needs to return simple data, a plain text response will be sufficient. If the web service returns a single value, the JavaScript code would use an XMLHttpRequest object to issue a request and store the result in a variable. Calling a web service via XMLHttpRequest is discussed in a previous section, "Retrieving Data via XMLHttpRequest." The part of the code that assigns the web service response to a JavaScript variable would look something like this:

```
var strResponse = _objRequest.responseText;
```

Plain text is very suitable for simple data structures as well. Suppose a web service response contains name, city, and country information. The web service could return this information in plain text like this: MyName|MyCity|MyCountry. The advantage is that this format contains a minimal amount of information with only very little overhead. This is only for simple data structures. If you want to pass complex data structures you are better off using XML or JavaScript Object Notation (JSON) formats. The section "JSON Messages" later in this chapter discusses JSON in detail. The following code shows an example of accepting a simple data structure in plain text format:

```
// web service response looks like this: MyName|MyCity|MyCountry
var arrResult = objRequest.responseText.split('|');
var strName = arrResult[0];
var strCity = arrResult[1];
var strCountry = arrResult[2];
```

HTML Response

Web service responses can also contain HTML. Now we are entering the domain of Web Services for Remote Portlets (WSRP). We have dedicated Chapter 6 to WSRP, so we will not discuss the ins and outs of returning HTML via a web service here.

The next line of code contains a short code example that shows how to use an HTML response and update the contents of a page dynamically using DHTML:

```
document.getElementById('MyDisplay').innerHTML = strHtmlResponse;
```

XML Message

All web service responses are wrapped in XML (SOAP), whether the response itself is plain text, HTML, XML, or JSON. You can choose to work with XML directly in JavaScript. Let's say we have a web service with a web service method called Hi() that returns the following response (plain text wrapped in XML):

```
<?xml version="1.0" encoding="utf-8" ?>
<string xmlns="http://tempuri.org/">Hi</string>
```

Using the responseText property of the XMLHttpRequest object returns the value Hi (in plain text). You can access the XML of the response by using the responseXML property of the XMLHttpRequest object. XML can be used to transfer complex data structures and is very flexible. In addition, you can use XML schemas to define the format of an XML message in an unambiguous manner. The following example shows how to work with XML using JavaScript:

```
var objXmlDom = objRequest.responseXML;
alert(objXmlDom.documentElement.firstChild);
```

JSON Messages

JSON (pronounced *Jason*) is a serialization format created in 2002 as (supposedly) a cleaner and lighter alternative to XML. It is possible to express simple as well as complex types in JSON. JSON is based on a subset of the JavaScript programming language and is very easy to parse and generate in a JavaScript programming environment. This makes JSON a well-suited, lightweight data-interchange format for browser-server communication. If you want to learn more about JSON, visit http://www.json.org/.

A JSON representation of a string type is a collection of zero or more characters wrapped in double quotes. This means the JSON representation of the name William Bender looks like this: "William Bender". A JSON representation can be converted to a JavaScript (simple or complex) type using the JavaScript eval() function. You could also dynamically generate a new function that handles the conversion using the Function() JavaScript function. Both approaches are shown here:

```
var strJSON = "\"William Bender\"";
var strResult = eval(strJSON);
strResult = new Function("return " + strJSON);
```

The JSON representation of a number is identical to the number itself. The JSON representation of the number 7 is 7. This is shown here:

```
var strJSON = "7";
var intResult = eval(strJSON);
```

The JSON representation of a Boolean is either true or false. This is shown here:

```
var strJSON = "true";
var blnResult = eval(strJSON);
if ( blnResult )
{
  alert(blnResult);
}
```

An array is an ordered collection of values. The JSON representation of an array begins with a left bracket ([) and ends with a right bracket (]). Values are separated by a comma (,). The JSON representation of a number array looks like this: [1, 2, 3]. This is shown here:

```
var strJSON = "[1, 2, 3]";
var arrResult = eval(strJSON);
alert(arrResult[0]);
```

The JSON representation of a string array looks like this: ["Bob", "Sue"]. This is shown here:

```
var strJSON = "[\"Bob\", \"Sue\"]";
var arrResult = eval(strJSON);
alert(arrResult[1]);
```

Objects are unordered sets of name-value pairs. JSON representations of objects are enclosed by curly braces ({}). Each name is followed by a colon (:). Name-value pairs are separated by commas (,). Look at the following definition of a JavaScript object called Person containing Name and Age properties:

```
function Person(strName, strAge)
{
  this.Name = strName;
  this.Age = strAge;
}
```

The JSON representation of the Person object looks like this: {"Name":"Jack","Age":47}. Although you are able to use the eval() function to convert this JSON string representation to a JavaScript object containing Name and Age properties, this is less simple than converting JSON representations to simple types. Instead we recommend you use a JSON parser to do the conversion for you.

Another argument for using a JSON parser is that the eval() function compiles and executes any JavaScript code. This makes you vulnerable for script injection attacks. A good JSON parser will offer safeguards against this sort of attack and thus will be safer.

If you want to use a JSON parser, you can download one at http://www.json.org/json.js. The parser consists of only 120 lines of code including comments and is very easy to use. Add the JSON parser to the web part resources folder ([drive letter]:\inetpub\wwwroot\wpresources) and register the JavaScript library containing the JSON parser with the web part page. In an earlier section, called "JavaScript in Web Parts," we explain how to register JavaScript libraries from within a web part with web part pages.

The following example shows how to convert the following JSON object representation {"Name":"Jack","Age":47} to a JavaScript object using the parseJSON() function. The parseJSON() function is defined within the JSON parser library:

```
var strJSON = "{\"Name\":\"Jack\",\"Age\":47}";
var objPerson = strJSON.parseJSON();
alert(objPerson.Name + " " + objPerson.Age);
```

Note It is possible to create complex object hierarchies via JSON because nested types are allowed.

It is easy to retrieve the JSON representation of a JavaScript type via the toJSONString() function that is defined within the JSON parser library. This is shown in the following code:

```
function Person(strName, strAge)
{
  this.Name = strName;
  this.Age = strAge;
}

var objPerson = new Person("Jason", 47);
var strPerson = objPerson.toJSONString();
alert(strPerson);
```

At first look, JSON seems to be less verbose than XML. However, you should not take this for granted. We have seen complex structures where the differences between XML and JSON representations were minimal. If you care a lot about the size of data, you should consider ZIP-encoding the data before sending it to the browser. After ZIP-encoding the data, we have seen examples where the zipped XML object representation actually is smaller than the zipped JSON representation. We would advise you to experiment first if you want to claim the JSON representation is the smallest.

In our opinion the size of a JSON message probably will not be the deciding factor when it comes to choosing a message format. A disadvantage of JSON compared to XML is that you cannot describe the structure of a JSON message the way you can describe XML messages using schemas. We also believe JSON has the disadvantage of being less readable compared to XML object representations. The big advantage of JSON is that JSON is a representation of JavaScript types built into the JavaScript programming language that requires very little coding and processing.

Installing Atlas

If you want to install Atlas, go to `http://atlas.asp.net`, click the Download link, and choose the latest Atlas release. After download is complete, installation is easy; just click the Atlas.msi file and follow the Atlas Setup Wizard. After installation, start Visual Studio .NET 2005. Choose File ➤ New ➤ Web Site. Under the My Templates section, you should see a new entry for the Atlas Web Site template. Choose this template if you want to create a new Atlas-enabled web site.

All requests for ASP.NET pages on a SharePoint extended web site are handled by the SharePointHandlerFactory. This can be verified by opening the web.config file of the root web folder [drive letter]:\inetpub\wwwroot\web.config and looking at the `<httpHandlers>` element. You will find a handler that links the SharePointHandlerFactory to *.aspx pages. Because of this, you will need to create an unmanaged path for any Atlas-enabled web site before creating it. The section "Creating Web Services in Windows SharePoint Services" earlier in this chapter describes how to create unmanaged paths.

■ Note At the time of this writing, Atlas was not released officially. The examples in this book are created using the April 2006 Community Technology Preview (CTP) build.

Building a Performance Counter Web Part

It has been quite a tour to get to the point where we can build our first Atlas web part. We will be honest with you: although Atlas is quite easy to use in itself, in the current release the integration with SharePoint Products and Technologies 2003 is difficult. Using Atlas technology in web parts is very powerful and offers a great user interface experience for end users. However, the way things are now, using Atlas within SharePoint web parts is not very developer-friendly. At least not when compared to the developer friendliness offered by Atlas without SharePoint.

In the next example, we will show how to build a SharePoint web part that uses Atlas to show server performance counters. The web part will continue updating the performance counter by polling a web service that returns performance information.

In our example we have chosen to use the following performance counters: Processor/% Processor Time, Web Service/Total Bytes Sent, and Web Service/Bytes Received/sec. We have chosen these counters randomly—our only criterion being that the performance counter values need to change often. When implementing a performance counter web part for an enterprise, you will probably be more interested in other performance counters than the ones we have chosen. For example, you could create a web part that displays the key performance counters used by the Microsoft IT staff to monitor the performance of SharePoint Products and Technologies. A detailed overview of those performance counters can be found on the following web site: http://www.microsoft.com/technet/itsolutions/msit/infowork/spsperfnote.mspx.

The following code listing shows how to retrieve the value for the Processor Time performance counter. In order to try out the code, you need to import the System.Diagnostics namespace. As an important side note, the first call to the NextValue() method of the PerformanceCounter class always results in zero. Normally, you would create a static member containing an instance of the PerformanceCounter class, or store the instance in the ASP.NET Session object. In our implementation we take a shortcut and call the NextValue() method twice with a two-second interval between two calls. This way we can retrieve a realistic indicator of current processor usage, instead of a zero.

```
PerformanceCounter objCounter = new PerformanceCounter();
objCounter.CategoryName = "Processor";
objCounter.CounterName = "% Processor Time";
objCounter.InstanceName = "_Total";
objCounter.MachineName = ".";  // current computer
objCounter.ReadOnly = true;

int intCurrentCpuUsage = Convert.ToInt32(objCounter.NextValue());
Thread.Sleep(2000);

return objCounter.NextValue();
```

The easiest way to retrieve performance counter names, category names, and instance names is via the Visual Studio Server Explorer. Open Visual Studio .NET 2005 and choose View ➤ Server Explorer. Within the Server Explorer, expand Servers ➤ [server name] ➤ Performance Counters ➤ [category name] ➤ [counter name]. Then choose the instance name you are interested in.

Note You can use the Extensible Performance Counter List (Exctrlst.exe) tool to enable or disable performance categories. This tool can be downloaded from the Microsoft web site (http://www.microsoft.com).

The first step you should do to create the performance counter web part is to create a new Atlas-enabled virtual directory and add a web service that returns values of various performance counters, as shown in the following steps:

1. Choose Start ➤ Administrative Tools ➤ SharePoint Central Administration.

2. On the Windows SharePoint Services Central Administration page, click Configure Virtual Server Settings.

3. Click Default Web Site.

4. On the Windows SharePoint Services Virtual Server Settings page, locate the Virtual Server Management section and click Define Managed Paths.

5. On the Windows SharePoint Services Define Managed Paths page, locate the Add a New Path section and enter the following path value: **askme2**.

6. Set the Type value to Excluded Path.

7. Click OK.

8. Open Windows Explorer and navigate to [drive letter]:\inetpub\wwwroot.

9. Create a new folder and call it AskMe2.

10. Choose Start ➤ Run, and type **inetmgr**.

11. In Internet Information Services Manager, expand the [server name] (local computer) node ➤ Web Sites ➤ Default Web Site.

12. Right-click the AskMe2 folder and choose Properties.

13. On the AskMe2 Properties window click Create.

14. Click OK.

15. Open Visual Studio .NET 2005.

16. Choose File ➤ New ➤ Web Site.

17. Choose the Atlas Web Site template. Make sure the Location type value is set to HTTP. Set the location to the following value: http://localhost/askme2.

At this point, you have created an Atlas web site called AskMe2. Using the following steps, add a web service to this project called PerformanceService. This will be the service that returns a couple of performance counter values. The PerformanceService web service will contain three methods: GetProcessorTime(), GetCounter2(), and GetCounter3().

1. Right-click the AskMe2 project and choose Add New Item ➤ Web Service.

2. Choose the following name: PerformanceService.asmx. Make sure the Place Code in Separate File check box is not checked.

3. Click Add.

Now clear PerformanceService.asmx and add the following code to it:

```
<%@ WebService Language="C#" Class="LoisAndClark.PerformanceService" %>

using System;
using System.Web;
using System.Web.Services;
using System.Web.Services.Protocols;
using System.Diagnostics;
using System.Threading;
```

```csharp
namespace LoisAndClark
{
  [WebService(Namespace = "http://tempuri.org/")]
  [WebServiceBinding(ConformsTo = WsiProfiles.BasicProfile1_1)]
  public class PerformanceService : System.Web.Services.WebService
  {
    [WebMethod]
    public float GetProcessorTime()
    {
      PerformanceCounter objCounter = new PerformanceCounter();
      objCounter.CategoryName = "Processor";
      objCounter.CounterName = "% Processor Time";
      objCounter.InstanceName = "_Total";
      objCounter.MachineName = ".";
      objCounter.ReadOnly = true;

      int intCurrentCpuUsage = Convert.ToInt32(objCounter.NextValue());
      Thread.Sleep(2000);

      return objCounter.NextValue();
    }

    [WebMethod]
    public float GetCounter2()
    {
      PerformanceCounter objCounter = new PerformanceCounter();
      objCounter.CategoryName = "Web Service";
      objCounter.CounterName = "Total Bytes Sent";
      objCounter.InstanceName = "_Total";
      objCounter.MachineName = ".";
      objCounter.ReadOnly = true;

      float fltPagesPerSecond = objCounter.NextValue();
      Thread.Sleep(2000);

      return objCounter.NextValue();
    }

    [WebMethod]
    public float GetCounter3()
    {
      PerformanceCounter objCounter = new PerformanceCounter();
      objCounter.CategoryName = "Web Service";
      objCounter.CounterName = "Bytes Received/sec";
      objCounter.InstanceName = "_Total";
      objCounter.MachineName = ".";
      objCounter.ReadOnly = true;
```

```
      float fltCurrentCpuUsage = objCounter.NextValue();
      Thread.Sleep(2000);

      return objCounter.NextValue();
    }
  }
}
```

Now that you have created a web service, you will also need a test client. In the next step, you will add an .ASPX page to the AskMe2 project that uses Atlas to call the PerformanceService web service. Click Add New Item ➤ Web Form, call the page PerformanceTest.aspx and make sure the check box Place Code in Separate File is not checked.

There is nothing special about the page yet. You have to add some parts to it to make the page an Atlas-enabled client. First you need to add the Atlas script manager to the HTML header of the PerformanceTest.aspx page. In the following example the Atlas script manager is used to add a reference to the PerformanceService web service:

```
<head>
  <atlas:ScriptManager runat="server" ID="scriptManager">
    <services>
      <atlas:servicereference path="~/PerformanceService.asmx" />
    </services>
  </atlas:ScriptManager>
</head>
```

The Atlas script manager is the brains of an Atlas-enabled ASP.NET page. The script manager offers functionality for developers and orchestrates partial page refreshes and incremental updates. The set of responsibilities of the Atlas script manager will become even more extensive in the future. The script manager renders all client-side registrations for the Atlas script library.

Unfortunately the script manager does not work the way we want it to in SharePoint 2003 environments. The settings in the web.config file of an Atlas web site are not compatible with the settings in SharePoint web.config files. The script manager is only useful in environments where the server-side application is Atlas-enabled. The current April 2006 CTP release of Atlas rules out SharePoint 2003 environments. The result of this is that in SharePoint environments you have to do without the Atlas script manager and you need to add the required client-side registrations manually. The client-side registrations will need to refer to an Atlas-enabled server-side application.

The easiest way to get all required client-side registrations is to create an Atlas test client within an Atlas web site, run it, view the HTML source of the page, and copy all required client registrations and modify them a bit so that all path settings are correct when the client registrations are used within a SharePoint web part. That is the reason we are creating PerformanceTest.aspx in the first place: to be able to copy all client registrations.

The next interesting bit of the PerformanceTest.aspx page is a JavaScript function called GetPerfCounter(). It seems that this function is able to call the PerformanceService web service directly by calling LoisAndClark.PerformanceService.GetProcessorTime(). In reality this function calls a JavaScript proxy created by the Atlas framework. The proxy calls the actual PerformanceService web service asynchronously. As an argument to the JavaScript proxy, you will need to pass the name of the function (in this case OnRequestComplete()) that will handle the web service response. The web service response will be passed as an argument to the event handler, as shown in the following code:

```
function GetPerfCounter()
{
  LoisAndClark.PerformanceService.GetProcessorTime(OnRequestComplete);
}

function OnRequestComplete(strResult)
{
  var objDisplay = document.getElementById("Results");
  objDisplay.innerHTML = strResult;
}
```

The following code listing shows the complete code for PerformanceTest.aspx:

```
<html>
<head>
  <atlas:ScriptManager runat="server" ID="scriptManager">
    <services>
      <atlas:servicereference path="~/PerformanceService.asmx" />
    </services>
  </atlas:ScriptManager>
</head>
<body>

  <form id="Form1" runat="server">
    <input id="GetPerformanceCounter" type="button" ➡
      value="Get Performance Counter" onclick="GetPerfCounter()" />
  </form>

  <span id="Results"></span>

  <script type="text/javascript">
  function GetPerfCounter()
  {
    LoisAndClark.PerformanceService.GetProcessorTime(OnRequestComplete);
  }

  function OnRequestComplete(strResult)
  {
    var objDisplay = document.getElementById("Results");
    objDisplay.innerHTML = strResult;
  }
  </script>
</body>
</html>
```

Right-click PerformanceTest.aspx ➤ Set As Start Page. Press F5 to start the web application. You will see a pop-up window asking whether you would like to enable debugging. Choose Modify the Web.config to enable debugging and click OK. If you click the Get Performance Counter button, you will see how the PerformanceService web service is called via Atlas from the client-side application. The result is shown in Figure 2-10.

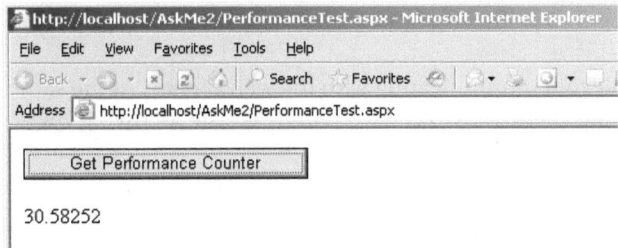

Figure 2-10. *The Get Performance Counter*

Do not close the browser yet. Right-click PerformanceTest.aspx ➤ View Source. Find the `<script>` element containing a reference to WebResource.axd and copy it. You will need this reference later when you are building an Atlas-enabled SharePoint web part. On our page the reference looks like this:

```
<script src="/AskMe2/WebResource.axd?d=.➥
5MnscVmDoRfTQHbUT78DAeo4k9kVhBNNCTePiOwYHKpkHlsY_ ➥
gNJdrrZSZi7tkaKScFHpxh6vPlHMTHYMxZSGouO_ ➥
nG8uJtGDDMaIBI2QbgFSuXTY9hFUsyILWwrYTL5rhvel_aBr- ➥
Kk2X39Tk63g2&amp;t=632827805195841856" type="text/javascript"></script>
```

The `src` attribute of the `<script>` element refers to an HTTP handler called WebResource.axd. This HTTP handler enables ASP.NET pages to load embedded resources from .NET assemblies. Examples of such embedded resources are client scripts, images, and data files. In this case, the reference to WebResource.axd will cause the server to generate the Atlas client library (written in JavaScript). The `d` argument in the URL refers to an encrypted identifier that uniquely identifies the requested web resource. The `t` argument is the time stamp for the requested assembly and is used for caching purposes. The `t` argument is optional.

If you continue looking through the HTML source of the rendered PerformanceTest.aspx page, you will find an interesting part that adds a reference to the Atlas globalization handler:

```
<script src="/AskMe2/atlasglob.axd" type="text/javascript"></script>
```

The Atlas globalization handler is an HTTP handler that determines the culture of the user, for settings such as language, decimal digits, currency symbols, date-time format, and names of the month, and sets the client-side `Sys.CultureInfo` object accordingly. `Sys.CultureInfo` is a part of the Atlas runtime located in the Atlas.js JavaScript library and handles everything related to culture settings. The final interesting part of the HTML source of the rendered PerformanceTest.aspx page adds a reference to the PerformanceService web service JavaScript proxy:

```
<script type="text/xml-script">
  <page xmlns:script="http://schemas.microsoft.com/xml-script/2005">
    <references>
      <add src="/AskMe2/PerformanceService.asmx/js" />
    </references>
    <components />
  </page>
</script>
```

The JavaScript proxy is responsible for communicating with the web service. At the same time, the proxy makes it very easy for the client-side to call web services. The following code shows an example of a JavaScript proxy:

```
Type.registerNamespace('LoisAndClark');
LoisAndClark.PerformanceService = new function()
{
  this.path = "http://pluto/AskMe2/PerformanceService.asmx";
  this.appPath = "http://pluto/AskMe2/";
  var cm =Sys.Net.ServiceMethod.createProxyMethod;
  cm(this,"GetProcessorTime");
  cm(this,"GetCounter2");
  cm(this,"GetCounter3");
}
```

Now that we have identified the important parts of an Atlas client, you are ready to incorporate Atlas in a web part. As the first step, create a new web part. If you are unsure how to do this, refer to Chapter 1. Create a new JavaScript library called atlas.js and place it in the web part resources folder. Specify an event handler for the PreRender event in the web part constructor and use the PreRender event handler to register the atlas.js JavaScript library in it.

In the next part, you will add the required client registrations to the web part. If it were possible to use the script manager within SharePoint 2003 environments, this would be quite easy. All you would need to do is add the following code to the CreateChildControls() method of your web part:

```
ScriptManager objManager = new ScriptManager();
objManager.ID = "scriptManager";
objManager.RegisterScriptReference("/Ask2/GreetingService.asmx");
```

This code works for normal Atlas-enabled web sites, and it will even work for SharePoint 2007 installations that are Atlas-enabled. Using the script manager does not work within SharePoint 2003 environments because of settings in web.config files of Atlas web sites that are not compatible with the settings in SharePoint 2003 web.config files. The only reason we show the previous code is so you can see that adding client registrations in normal Atlas solutions is easy to do. Adding client registrations in SharePoint 2003 environments is harder than we would like. In such situations you will need to add all client registrations manually. Basically, using Atlas itself is not difficult; using Atlas in an officially unsupported environment such as SharePoint 2003 makes it more complex. To us, the benefits of using Atlas technology in SharePoint 2003 are compelling enough to jump through the extra hoops.

The ScriptManager class is located in the Microsoft.Web.UI namespace (located in the Microsoft.Web.Atlas assembly). Alas, since you cannot use the ScriptManager class you will need to add all client registrations manually. Override the web part CreateChildControls() method and add the following code to it:

```
// Watch out: replace d parameter value with your own identifier retrieved from
// the source of PerformanceTest.aspx!
string strSrc1 = "<script src=\"/AskMe2/WebResource.axd?d=5Mnsc...1856\" ➡
type=\"text/javascript\"></script>";
Controls.Add(new LiteralControl(strSrc1));

string strSrc2 = "<script src=\"/AskMe2/atlasglob.axd\" ➡
type=\"text/javascript\"></script>";
Controls.Add(new LiteralControl(strSrc2));

string strSrc3 = "<script type=\"text/xml-script\"> \n"
  + "<page xmlns:script=\"http://schemas.microsoft.com/xml-script/2005\"> \n"
  + "<references> \n"
  + "<add src=\"/AskMe2/PerformanceService.asmx/js\" /> \n"
  + "</references> \n"
  + "<components /> \n"
  + "</page></script> \n";
Controls.Add(new LiteralControl(strSrc3));

string strDisplay = "<div id=\"ProcessorTimeDisplay\">Display 1</div> \n";
Controls.Add(new LiteralControl(strDisplay));

strDisplay = "<div id=\"Counter2Display\">Display 2</div> \n";
Controls.Add(new LiteralControl(strDisplay));

strDisplay = "<div id=\"Counter3Display\">Display 3</div> \n";
Controls.Add(new LiteralControl(strDisplay));
```

■**Note** The d parameter passed to WebResource.axd is an encrypted identifier that uniquely identifies the requested web resource. The value of this parameter needs to be copied from the HTML source of the PerformanceTest.aspx test page created earlier.

The complete code listing for the PerformanceCounter web part looks like this:

```
using System;
using System.Collections.Generic;
using System.Text;
using System.Web.UI;
using System.Web.UI.HtmlControls;
using System.Web.UI.WebControls;
```

```
using Microsoft.SharePoint;
using Microsoft.SharePoint.WebPartPages;
using Microsoft.Web.UI;

namespace LoisAndClark.PerformanceCounterWebPart
{
  public class PerformanceCounterWebPart : WebPart
  {
    public PerformanceCounterWebPart ()
    {
      PreRender += new EventHandler(PerformanceCounterWebPart_PreRender);
    }

    void PerformanceCounterWebPart_PreRender(object sender, EventArgs e)
    {
      if (!Page.ClientScript.IsClientScriptBlockRegistered("Atlas"))
      {
        Page.ClientScript.RegisterClientScriptInclude("Atlas", ➥
        "/wpresources/atlas.js");
      }
    }

    protected override void CreateChildControls()
    {
      try
      {
        // Watch out: replace d parameter value with your own
        // identifier retrieved from the source of PerformanceTest.aspx!
        string strSrc1 = "<script
        src=\"/AskMe2/WebResource.axd?d= 5MnscVmD...\" ➥
        type=\"text/javascript\"></script>";
        Controls.Add(new LiteralControl(strSrc1));

        string strSrc2 = "<script src=\"/AskMe2/atlasglob.axd\" ➥
        type=\"text/javascript\"></script>";
        Controls.Add(new LiteralControl(strSrc2));

        string strSrc3 = "<script type=\"text/xml-script\"> \n"
        + "<page xmlns:script=\"http://schemas.microsoft.com/xml-script/2005\"> \n"
        + "<references> \n"
        + "<add src=\"/AskMe2/PerformanceService.asmx/js\" /> \n"
        + "</references> \n"
        + "<components /> \n"
        + "</page></script> \n";
        Controls.Add(new LiteralControl(strSrc3));
```

```
      string strDisplay = "<div id=\"ProcessorTimeDisplay\">Display 1</div> \n";
      Controls.Add(new LiteralControl(strDisplay));

      strDisplay = "<div id=\"Counter2Display\">Display 2</div> \n";
      Controls.Add(new LiteralControl(strDisplay));

      strDisplay = "<div id=\"Counter3Display\">Display 3</div> \n";
      Controls.Add(new LiteralControl(strDisplay));
    }
    catch (Exception err)
    {
      Controls.Add(new LiteralControl(err.Message));
    }
   }
  }
}
```

The atlas.js JavaScript library calls the PerformanceService web service and defines several JavaScript handlers for the web service responses. The following line of code shows how to call the GetProcessorTime() method of the PerformanceService web service and define a JavaScript handler called OnProcessorTimeResponse that handles the web service response:

```
LoisAndClark.PerformanceService.GetProcessorTime(OnProcessorTimeResponse);
```

We have built a mechanism around the Atlas web service calls to make sure web service calls are made when the client-side application is ready to do this. The complete code for Atlas.js looks like this:

```
var intTimeOut = 5000;

function GetProcessorTime()
{
  LoisAndClark.PerformanceService.GetProcessorTime(OnProcessorTimeResponse);
}

function GetCounter2()
{
  LoisAndClark.PerformanceService.GetCounter2(OnCounter2Response);
}

function GetCounter3()
{
  LoisAndClark.PerformanceService.GetCounter3(OnCounter3Response);
}

function OnProcessorTimeResponse(objResult)
{
```

```
      var objDisplay = document.getElementById("ProcessorTimeDisplay");
      objDisplay.innerHTML = "Processor time: " + objResult;
      setTimeout("GetCounter3()", intTimeOut);
}

function OnCounter2Response(objResult)
{
      var objDisplay = document.getElementById("Counter2Display");
      objDisplay.innerHTML = "Counter 2: " + objResult;
      setTimeout("GetProcessorTime()", intTimeOut);
}

function OnCounter3Response(objResult)
{
      var objDisplay = document.getElementById("Counter3Display");
      objDisplay.innerHTML = "Counter 3: " + objResult;
      setTimeout("GetProcessorTime()", intTimeOut);
}

function Init()
{
   try
   {
      if ( LoisAndClark != null )
      {
         GetProcessorTime();
         GetCounter2();
         GetCounter3();
      }
   }
   catch (err)
   {
      setTimeout("Init()", 1000);
   }
}

Init();
```

Note By default you cannot call a normal web service via Atlas. If you wish to access a web service, it needs to support the generation of Atlas client script proxies. You can do this by registering the Microsoft.Web.Services.ScriptHandlerFactory assembly to handle all web service requests. The Documentation section of the web site http://atlas.asp.net describes how to do this, should you feel the need to do so. You can also take a look at the web.config file of an Atlas web site and copy the missing sections to the web service web.config file.

The performance counter web part can be seen in action in Figure 2-11.

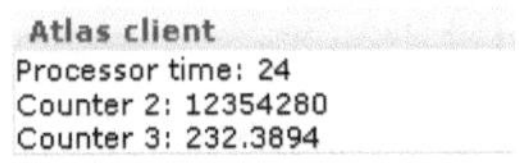

Atlas client
Processor time: 24
Counter 2: 12354280
Counter 3: 232.3894

Figure 2-11. *Performance counter web part*

Building a Company Contact Web Part Using Atlas and JSON

In the next example we show you how to build a company contact web part using Atlas and JSON. If you want to be able to test the example, you should create a custom SharePoint list that contains a default title, company name, contact person, city, and country, and call this list ContactInfo (set the column types of all columns to a single line of text). Figure 2-12 shows the ContactInfo list.

Figure 2-12. *Company contact list*

The idea of the company contact web part is that if you type the name of the company and click the AutoFill button, the web part will call a web service that retrieves the rest of the form information for you from the ContactInfo SharePoint list. The web service will return the data in JSON format, so the client-side application of the web part needs to be able to deal with that.

In the next step, you will create the server-side of the company contact application. Add a new web service to the AskMe2 project; make sure the Place Code in Separate File check box is not checked, and name the web service ContactService.asmx. The following code will loop through every item in the ContactInfo SharePoint list:

```
SPSite objSites = new SPSite(strUrl);
SPWeb objSite = objSites.OpenWeb();
SPList objContactList = objSite.Lists["ContactInfo"];

foreach (SPListItem objItem in objContactList.Items)
{

}
```

The ContactService web service returns a JSON message containing all contact informa-tion. The ContactService web service will return a JSON message that looks like this:

```
{"ContactPerson":"[value]", "City":"[value]", "Country":"[value]"}
```

The following code listing shows the complete implementation of the ContactService web service. Make sure to add a reference to the Microsoft.SharePoint assembly:

```
<%@ WebService Language="C#" Class="LoisAndClark.ContactService" %>
using System;
using System.Web;
using System.Collections;
using System.Web.Services;
using System.Web.Services.Protocols;
using Microsoft.SharePoint;

namespace LoisAndClark.CompanyContact
{
  [WebService(Namespace = "http://tempuri.org/")]
  [WebServiceBinding(ConformsTo = WsiProfiles.BasicProfile1_1)]
  public class ContactService : System.Web.Services.WebService
  {
    public ContactService()
    {
    }

    [WebMethod]
    public string GetContactInfo(string strCompanyName)
    {
      string strResponse = "\"ContactPerson\":\"{0}\", \"City\":\"{1}\", ➡
      \"Country\":\"{2}\"";
      string strUrl = "http://pluto/Atlas/";

      try
      {
        SPSite objSites = new SPSite(strUrl);
        SPWeb objSite = objSites.OpenWeb();
        SPList objContactList = objSite.Lists["ContactInfo"];
        foreach (SPListItem objItem in objContactList.Items)
        {
          string strName = objItem["CompanyName"].ToString();
          if (strName == strCompanyName)
          {
            string strContact = objItem["ContactPerson"].ToString();
            string strCity = objItem["City"].ToString();
            string strCountry = objItem["Country"].ToString();
```

```
            strResponse = "{" + String.Format(strResponse, strContact, ➥
            strCity, strCountry) + "}";
            break;
        }
      }
      return strResponse;
    }
    catch (Exception err)
    {
      throw;
    }
  }
 }
}
```

The web part code looks very much like the previous example in the "Building a Performance Counter Web Part" section of this chapter. Because the web service returns a JSON response, you need to add a reference to json.js, the JavaScript library that facilitates working with JSON. The JSON script library is discussed in further detail in the section "JSON Messages." You also need to register atlas.js, the custom JavaScript library that contains the logic that calls the web service and processes the response. Then you need to add the required client registrations, and add fields for company name, contact person, city, and country to the web part. If you enter a value for the company name, the example shows how to use Atlas to autofill the other fields. The complete code listing for the CompanyContactClient web part looks like this:

```
using System;
using System.Web.UI;
using Microsoft.SharePoint.WebPartPages;

namespace LoisAndClark.CompanyContact
{
  public class CompanyContactClient : WebPart
  {
    public CompanyContactClient ()
    {
      PreRender += new EventHandler(CompanyContactClient _PreRender);
    }

    void CompanyContactClient_PreRender(object sender, EventArgs e)
    {
      if (!Page.ClientScript.IsClientScriptBlockRegistered("JSON"))
      {
        Page.ClientScript.RegisterClientScriptInclude("JSON", ➥
        "/wpresources/json.js");
      }

      if (!Page.ClientScript.IsClientScriptBlockRegistered("Atlas"))
      {
```

```
            Page.ClientScript.RegisterClientScriptInclude("Atlas", "/wpresources/atlas.js");
        }
    }

    protected override void CreateChildControls()
    {
      // Watch out: replace d parameter value with your own
      // identifier retrieved from the source of PerformanceTest.aspx!
      string strSrc1 = "<script src=\"/AskMe2/WebResource.axd?d=5Mn…1856\" ➥
      type=\"text/javascript\"></script>";
      Controls.Add(new LiteralControl(strSrc1));

      string strSrc2 = "<script src=\"/AskMe2/atlasglob.axd\" ➥
      type=\"text/javascript\"></script>";
      Controls.Add(new LiteralControl(strSrc2));

      string strSrc3 = "<script type=\"text/xml-script\"> \n"
        + "<page xmlns:script=\"http://schemas.microsoft.com/xml-script/2005\"> \n"
        + "<references>\n"
        + "<add src=\"/AskMe2/ContactService.asmx/js\" />\n"
        + "</references>\n"
        + "<components />\n"
        + "</page></script> \n";
      Controls.Add(new LiteralControl(strSrc3));

      string strCompanyName = "Name:     <input ➥
      id=\"CompanyName\" type=\"text\" />";
      Controls.Add(new LiteralControl(strCompanyName));

      string strAutoFill = "<input id=\"AutoFill\" type=\"button\" ➥
      value=\"AutoFill...\" ➥
      onclick=\"AutoFillRequest();\" /><br/>";
      Controls.Add(new LiteralControl(strAutoFill));

      string strContactPerson = "Contact:   ➥
      <input id=\"ContactPerson\" type=\"text\" /><br/>";
      Controls.Add(new LiteralControl(strContactPerson));

      string strCity = "City:        ➥
      <input id=\"City\" type=\"text\" /><br/>";
      Controls.Add(new LiteralControl(strCity));

      string strCountry = "Country: <input id=\"Country\" type=\"text\" /><br/>";
      Controls.Add(new LiteralControl(strCountry));
    }
  }
}
```

The final part of the company contact Atlas solution is the content of the atlas.js JavaScript library. It contains a function called AutoFillRequest() that calls the ContactService web service. A callback function called OnAutoFillResponse() converts the web service response to a JavaScript object and uses the object to set the values of the contact person, city, and country fields. The content of the atlas.js JavaScript library looks like this:

```
function AutoFillRequest()
{
  var objCompanyName = document.getElementById("CompanyName");
  LoisAndClark.ContactService.GetContactInfo(objCompanyName.value, ➥
  OnAutoFillResponse)
}

function OnAutoFillResponse(strResult)
{
  var objContact = strResult.parseJSON();

  var objContactPerson = document.getElementById("ContactPerson");
  objContactPerson.value = objContact.ContactPerson;

  var objCity = document.getElementById("City");
  objCity.value = objContact.City;

  var objCountry = document.getElementById("Country");
  objCountry.value = objContact.Country;
}
```

Figure 2-13 shows the company contact web part with a name typed in by the end user. In Figure 2-14 the AutoFill has filled in the rest of the fields.

Figure 2-13. *The user types in a name in the company contact web part.*

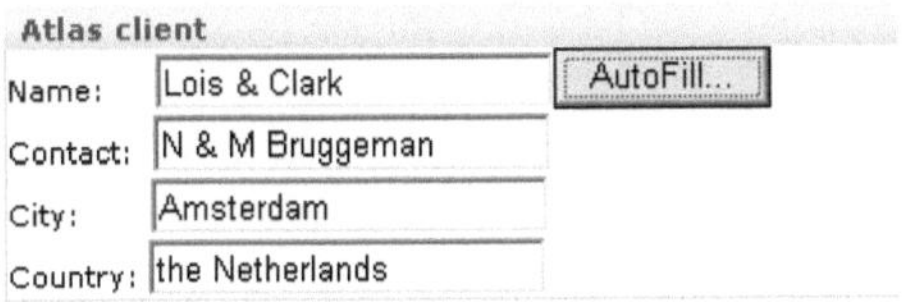

Figure 2-14. *AutoFill fills in the rest of the fields.*

Building an Autocompletion Web Part

Our example shows how to use Atlas to enhance the user interface in a powerful way. We will create an autocompletion web part using the Atlas autoComplete behavior. We will use Atlas to call a web service that retrieves all SharePoint lists within a SharePoint site starting with what is typed into a text box. Figure 2-15, Figure 2-16, and Figure 2-17 show how the Atlas autoComplete behavior works.

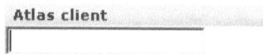

Figure 2-15. *The text box in the web part*

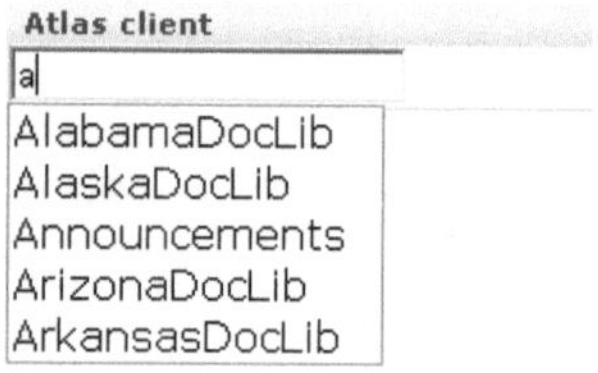

Figure 2-16. *The SharePoint lists returned by the web service*

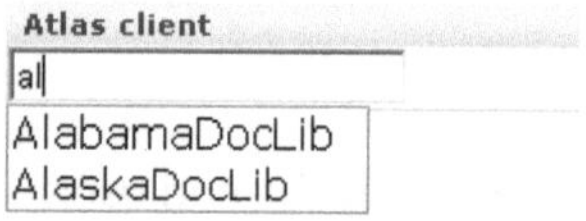

Figure 2-17. *The SharePoint lists narrowed down after more letters are typed in*

Add another web service to the AskMe2 project you created previously and call it DocLibExtenderService.asmx. Do not place the code in a separate file. The DocLibExtenderService web service retrieves all SharePoint lists from a given SharePoint site, like this:

```
SPSite objSites = new SPSite(strUrl);
SPWeb objSite = objSites.OpenWeb();
SPListCollection objLists = objSite.Lists;

foreach (SPList objList in objLists)
{
    ...
}
```

Atlas autocompletion web services return string arrays containing all results starting with a given prefix. Because of this, we want to add all lists to a data structure that makes it easy to sort and filter. We have chosen to use the ADO.NET DataView to do this. The following code shows how to filter and sort document libraries via a DataView.

```
DataTable dtLists = new DataTable();
dtLists.Columns.Add("ListName", typeof(string));

… code that retrieves all SharePoint lists…

foreach (SPList objList in objLists)
{
  DataRow drList = dtLists.NewRow();
  drList["ListName"] = objList.Title;
  dtLists.Rows.Add(drList);
}

_dvLists = dtLists.DefaultView;
_dvLists.Sort = "listname ASC";

string strFilter = "listname LIKE 'A%'";
_dvLists.RowFilter = strFilter;
```

The Atlas autocompletion web service interface is very strict. Not only does it require a given signature, the parameter names have to match exactly, otherwise the autocompletion web service will not work. Although this limits the usefulness of Atlas autocompletion web services, they are so powerful that it pays to work around this limitation. The Atlas autocompletion web service interface looks like this:

```
public string[] MyMethodName(string prefixText, int count)
```

The only variable part of this interface is the method name. You are not allowed to change the signature or parameter names. The return type needs to be some type of string array, although there is some flexibility here. In the implementation of the MyMethodName(), a string array is returned. As another example, a generic List collection (List<string>) would work too. The prefixText argument contains the prefix of any match found by the autocompletion service. The count argument limits the maximum number of results. By the way, our example autocompletion wizard does not implement a maximum result limit and ignores the count argument. The complete code listing for the autocompletion wizard looks like this:

```
<%@ WebService Language="C#" Class="LoisAndClark.DocLibExtenderService" %>

using System;
using System.Web;
using System.Web.Services;
using System.Web.Services.Protocols;
using Microsoft.SharePoint;
using System.Collections;
using System.Data;
using System.Diagnostics;
```

```
namespace LoisAndClark
{
  [WebService(Namespace = "http://tempuri.org/")]
  [WebServiceBinding(ConformsTo = WsiProfiles.BasicProfile1_1)]
  public class DocLibExtenderService : System.Web.Services.WebService
  {
    static DataView _dvLists = null;

    private void InitLists(string strUrl)
    {
      if (_dvLists == null)
        {
          DataTable dtLists = new DataTable();
          dtLists.Columns.Add("ListName", typeof(string));

          SPSite objSites = new SPSite(strUrl);
          SPWeb objSite = objSites.OpenWeb();
          SPListCollection objLists = objSite.Lists;

          foreach (SPList objList in objLists)
            {
              DataRow drList = dtLists.NewRow();
              drList["ListName"] = objList.Title;
              dtLists.Rows.Add(drList);
            }

          _dvLists = dtLists.DefaultView;
          _dvLists.Sort = "listname ASC";
        }
    }

    //Note: it is very important to use the correct names for the arguments!
    [WebMethod]
    public string[] GetLists(string prefixText, int count)
    {
      string strReturn = String.Empty;

      try
        {
          string strUrl = "http://pluto/Atlas/";
          InitLists(strUrl);
          string strFilter = String.Format("listname LIKE '{0}%'", prefixText);
          _dvLists.RowFilter = strFilter;

          string[] arrLists = new string[_dvLists.Count];
          for (int i = 0; i < _dvLists.Count; i++)
            {
```

```
        arrLists[i] = _dvLists[i]["ListName"].ToString();
      }

      return arrLists;
    }
    catch (Exception err)
    {
      Trace.Write(err.Message);
      throw;
    }
  }
 }
}
```

You have completed the server-side part of the autocompletion example. Incorporating the autocompletion web service on the client is made very easy, thanks to the Atlas declarative model. In the previous examples, you wrote some, but not much, JavaScript code to tie everything together. One of the main goals of Atlas is to make client-side development easier. That is why Atlas offers a declarative model for client development that requires no code at all. This declarative model is very similar to using ASP.NET server controls.

Using the Atlas declarative model, you can tie the DocLibExtender web service to a text box called ListsTextBox. As the end user starts typing in the ListsTextBox text box, Atlas calls the GetLists() method of the web service and shows the web service response in a <div> element called MyDisplay. The DocLibExtender web service is called as soon as the user types in a minimum number of keys in the ListsTextBox text box, which equals the value of the minimumPrefixLength attribute of the <autoComplete> behavior. The maximum number of items that the client wants to retrieve equals the completionSetCount attribute of the <autoComplete> behavior, although it's up to the service to do something with this maximum or not. You can also specify the completion interval, which is the time it takes between service calls. The declarative code looks like this:

```
<script type="text/xml-script">
  <page xmlns:script="http://schemas.microsoft.com/xml-script/2005">
    <components>
      <textBox id="ListsTextBox">
        <behaviors>
          <autoComplete
            completionList="MyDisplay"
            serviceURL="DocLibExtenderService.asmx"
            serviceMethod="GetLists"
            minimumPrefixLength="1"
            completionSetCount="15"
            completionInterval="500" />
        </behaviors>
      </textBox>
    </components>
  </page>
</script>
```

Finally, you have to create a web part that adds the declarative code to the page. The complete code listing looks like this:

```
using System;
using System.Web.UI;
using Microsoft.SharePoint.WebPartPages;

namespace LoisAndClark.AutoCompletion
{
  public class AutoCompletionClient : WebPart
  {
    protected override void CreateChildControls()
    {
      string strSrc1 = "<script src=\"/AskMe2/WebResource.axd?d=5Mnsc[…]856\" ➥
        type=\"text/javascript\"></script>";
      Controls.Add(new LiteralControl(strSrc1));

      string strSrc2 = "<script src=\"/AskMe2/atlasglob.axd\" ➥
        type=\"text/javascript\"></script>";
      Controls.Add(new LiteralControl(strSrc2));

      string strSrc3 = "<script type=\"text/xml-script\"> \n"
        + "<page xmlns:script=\"http://schemas.microsoft.com/xml-script/2005\"> \n"
        + "<components> \n"
        + "<textBox id=\"ListsTextBox\"> \n"
        + "<behaviors> \n"
        + "<autoComplete  \n"
        + "completionList=\"MyDisplay\"  \n"
        + "serviceURL=\"/AskMe2/DocLibExtenderService.asmx\"  \n"
        + "serviceMethod=\"GetLists\"  \n"
        + "minimumPrefixLength=\"1\"  \n"
        + "completionSetCount=\"15\"  \n"
        + "completionInterval=\"500\" /> \n"
        + "</behaviors> \n"
        + "</textBox> \n"
        + "</components> \n"
        + "</page></script> \n";
      Controls.Add(new LiteralControl(strSrc3));

      string strKey = "<input id=\"ListsTextBox\" type=\"text\" />";
      Controls.Add(new LiteralControl(strKey));
    }
  }
}
```

Client-Side Connectable Web Parts and Atlas

The SharePoint web part infrastructure allows web parts to exchange information at runtime. This mechanism is called *web part connections*. Connectable web parts can communicate client-side and server-side. Client-side connectable web parts and Atlas match together really well. In this section, we will build two connectable web parts that offer a master-detail view. We do not provide detailed information about creating connectable web parts here. If you want to learn more about the connected web part infrastructure, refer to Chapter 5.

We will use the ContactService web service created previously in the section "Building a Company Contact Web Part."

The provider web part is a standard connectable web part that does not need to know anything about Atlas. The complete code for the provider web part looks like this:

```
using System;
using System.ComponentModel;
using System.Web.UI;
using Microsoft.SharePoint.WebPartPages;
using System.Xml.Serialization;
using System.Web.UI.WebControls;
using System.Security;
using Microsoft.SharePoint.Utilities;
using Microsoft.SharePoint.WebPartPages.Communication;

namespace LoisAndClark.Connectable
{
  public class ProviderPart : WebPart, ICellProvider
  {
    public event CellProviderInitEventHandler CellProviderInit;
    public event CellReadyEventHandler CellReady;

    private bool _blnConnected = false;
    private string _strConnectedWebPartTitle = string.Empty;
    private string _strRegistrationErrorMsg = "An error has occurred trying ➡
    to register your connection interfaces.";
    private bool _blnRegistrationErrorOccurred = false;
    private string _strNotConnectedMsg = "NOT CONNECTED. To use this Web ➡
    Part, connect it to a client-side Cell Consumer Web Part.";

    public override void EnsureInterfaces()
    {
      try
      {
        RegisterInterface("MyCellProviderInterface_WPQ_",
          InterfaceTypes.ICellProvider,
          WebPart.UnlimitedConnections,
          ConnectionRunAt.Client,
```

```
          this,
          "CellProviderInterface_WPQ_",
          "Provide Cell To",
          "Provides a single value to a cell consumer Web Part.");
    }
    catch (SecurityException err)
    {
      blnRegistrationErrorOccurred = true;
    }
}

public override ConnectionRunAt CanRunAt()
{
  return ConnectionRunAt.Client;
}

public override void PartCommunicationConnect(
  string strInterfaceName,
  WebPart objConnectedPart,
  string strConnectedInterfaceName,
  ConnectionRunAt enumRunAt)
{
  if (strInterfaceName == "MyCellProviderInterface_WPQ_")
  {
    blnConnected = true;
    strConnectedWebPartTitle = SPEncode.HtmlEncode(objConnectedPart.Title);
  }
}

public void CellConsumerInit(object objSender, CellConsumerInitEventArgs ➥
objCellConsumerInitEventArgs)
{
}

protected override void RenderWebPart(HtmlTextWriter output)
{
  if (_blnRegistrationErrorOccurred)
  {
    output.Write(_strRegistrationErrorMsg);
    return;
  }

  if (_blnConnected)
  {
    output.Write(ReplaceTokens("<P>\n"
```

```
+ "    Company name: \n"
+ "    <INPUT TYPE=\"text\" ID=\"CompanyName_WPQ_\"/>\n"
+ "    <INPUT TYPE=\"button\" ID=\"CellButton_WPQ_\" ➥
onclick=\"CellButtonClick_WPQ_()\" VALUE=\"AutoFill\"/><br/>\n"
+ "</P>\n"

+ "<SCRIPT LANGUAGE=\"JavaScript\">\n"
+ "<!-- \n"
+ "    var CellProviderInterface_WPQ_ = new Provider_WPQ_();\n"

+ "    function Provider_WPQ_()\n"
+ "    {\n"
+ "        this.PartCommunicationInit = myInit;\n"
+ "        this.PartCommunicationMain = myMain;\n"
+ "        this.CellConsumerInit = myCellConsumerInit;\n"

+ "        function myInit()\n"
+ "        {\n"
+ "            var cellProviderInitEventArgs = new Object();\n"
+ "            cellProviderInitEventArgs.FieldName = \"ProvideCell\";\n"
+ "            cellProviderInitEventArgs.FieldDisplayName = \"Provide ➥
Cell\";\n"

+ "            WPSC.RaiseConnectionEvent(\"MyCellProviderInterface_WPQ_ ➥
\", \"CellProviderInit\", cellProviderInitEventArgs);\n"
+ "        }\n"

+ "        function myMain()\n"
+ "        {\n"
+ "            var cellReadyEventArgs = new Object();\n"
+ "            cellReadyEventArgs.Cell = null;\n"

+ "            WPSC.RaiseConnectionEvent(\"MyCellProviderInterface_WPQ_ ➥
\", \"CellReady\", cellReadyEventArgs);\n"
+ "        }\n"

+ "        function myCellConsumerInit(sender, cellConsumerInitEventArgs)\n"
+ "        {\n"
+ "            document.all(\"ConnectedField_WPQ_\").innerText = ➥
cellConsumerInitEventArgs.FieldDisplayName;\n"
+ "        }\n"
+ "    }\n"

+ "    function CellButtonClick_WPQ_()\n"
+ "    {\n"
+ "        var cellReadyEventArgs = new Object();\n"
+ "        cellReadyEventArgs.Cell = ➥
document.all(\"CompanyName_WPQ_\").value;\n"
```

```
        + "        WPSC.RaiseConnectionEvent(\"MyCellProviderInterface_WPQ_\", ➥
        \"CellReady\", cellReadyEventArgs);\n"
        + "   }\n"
        + "//-->\n"
        + "</SCRIPT>\n"));
    }
    else
    {
      output.Write(_strNotConnectedMsg);
    }
  }
}
}
```

In the consumer web part you need to add some additional client-side code. First you need to retrieve the cell value that is provided by the provider web part. Then pass this value as an argument to the JavaScript function that calls the ContactService web service. This function specifies an event handler JavaScript function that handles the ContactService response and updates the user interface. Since the response is in JSON format, you can use the parseJSON() function defined in the JSON script library (json.js) to convert the information to a JavaScript object. The JavaScript code that needs to be added to the consumer web part looks like this:

```
function myCellReady(sender, cellReadyEventArgs)
{
  if(cellReadyEventArgs.Cell != null)
  {
    AutoFillRequestWPQ1(cellReadyEventArgs.Cell);
  }
}

function AutoFillRequestWPQ1(strCompanyName)
{
  LoisAndClark.ContactService.GetContactInfo(strCompanyName, ➥
  OnAutoFillResponseWPQ1)
}

function OnAutoFillResponseWPQ1(strResult)
{
  var objContact = strResult.parseJSON();
  var objContactPerson = document.getElementById("ContactPerson");
  objContactPerson.innerHTML = objContact.ContactPerson;
  var objCity = document.getElementById("City");
  objCity.innerHTML = objContact.City;
  var objCountry = document.getElementById("Country");
  objCountry.innerHTML = objContact.Country;
}
```

The complete code for the consumer web part looks like this:

```
using System;
using System.ComponentModel;
using System.Web.UI;
using Microsoft.SharePoint.WebPartPages;
using System.Xml.Serialization;
using System.Web.UI.WebControls;
using System.Security;
using Microsoft.SharePoint.Utilities;
using Microsoft.SharePoint.WebPartPages.Communication;

namespace LoisAndClark.Connectable
{
  public class ConsumerPart : WebPart
  {
    public event CellConsumerInitEventHandler CellConsumerInit;

    private bool _blnConnected = false;
    private string _strConnectedWebPartTitle = string.Empty;
    private string _strRegistrationErrorMsg = "An error has occurred trying to ➥
    register your connection interfaces.";
    private bool _blnRegistrationErrorOccurred = false;
    private string _strNotConnectedMsg = "NOT CONNECTED. To use this Web Part, ➥
    connect it to a client-side Cell Provider Web Part.";

    public ConsumerPart()
    {
      PreRender += new EventHandler(ClientPart_PreRender);
    }

    void ClientPart_PreRender(object sender, EventArgs e)
    {
      if (!Page.ClientScript.IsClientScriptBlockRegistered("JSON"))
      {
        Page.ClientScript.RegisterClientScriptInclude("JSON", ➥
        "/wpresources/json.js");
      }
    }

    public override void EnsureInterfaces()
    {
      try
      {
        RegisterInterface("MyCellConsumerInterface_WPQ_",
          InterfaceTypes.ICellConsumer,
          WebPart.LimitOneConnection,
          ConnectionRunAt.Client,
          this,
```

```
          "CellConsumerInterface_WPQ_",
          "Consume Cell From",
          "Consume a single value from another Web Part.");
    }
    catch (SecurityException err)
    {
      blnRegistrationErrorOccurred = true;
    }
}

public override ConnectionRunAt CanRunAt()
{
    return ConnectionRunAt.Client;
}

public override void PartCommunicationConnect(string strInterfaceName,
    WebPart objConnectedPart,
    string strConnectedInterfaceName,
    ConnectionRunAt enumRunAt)
{
    if (strInterfaceName == "MyCellConsumerInterface_WPQ_")
    {
      blnConnected = true;
      strConnectedWebPartTitle = SPEncode.HtmlEncode(objConnectedPart.Title);
    }
}

public void CellProviderInit(object objSender, ➥
CellProviderInitEventArgs objCellProviderInitEventArgs)
{
}

public void CellReady(object sender, CellReadyEventArgs cellReadyEventArgs)
{
}

protected override void RenderWebPart(HtmlTextWriter output)
{
    if (_blnRegistrationErrorOccurred)
    {
      output.Write(_strRegistrationErrorMsg);
      return;
    }
```

```
if (_blnConnected)
{
 output.Write(ReplaceTokens(
 "<script src=\"/AskMe2/WebResource.axd?d=5M… 195841856\" ➥
 type=\"text/javascript\"></script>"
 + "<script src=\"/AskMe2/atlasglob.axd\" type=\"text/javascript\"></script>"
 + "<script type=\"text/xml-script\"> \n"
 + "<page xmlns:script=\"http://schemas.microsoft.com/xml-script/2005\"> \n"
 + "<references>\n"
 + "<add src=\"/AskMe2/ContactService.asmx/js\" />\n"
 + "</references>\n"
 + "<components />\n"
 + "</page></script> \n"
 + "<P>\n"
 + "<div id=\"ContactPerson\">Contact person placeholder</div>"
 + "<div id=\"City\">City placeholder</div>"
 + "<div id=\"Country\">Country placeholder</div>"

 + "<SCRIPT LANGUAGE='JavaScript'>\n"
 + "<!-- \n"

 + "function AutoFillRequest_WPQ_(strCompanyName)\n"
 + "{ \n"
 + "LoisAndClark.ContactService.GetContactInfo(strCompanyName, ➥
 OnAutoFillResponse_WPQ_)\n"
 + "}\n"

 + "function OnAutoFillResponse_WPQ_(strResult)\n"
 + "{\n"
 + "var objContact = strResult.parseJSON();\n"

 + "var objContactPerson = document.getElementById(\"ContactPerson\");\n"
 + "objContactPerson.innerHTML = objContact.ContactPerson;\n"

 + "var objCity = document.getElementById(\"City\");\n"
 + "objCity.innerHTML = objContact.City;\n"

 + "var objCountry = document.getElementById(\"Country\");\n"
 + "objCountry.innerHTML = objContact.Country;\n"
 + "}\n"

 + "var CellConsumerInterface_WPQ_ = new Consumer_WPQ_();\n"

 + "function Consumer_WPQ_()\n"
 + "{\n"
 + "this.PartCommunicationInit = myInit;\n"
 + "this.CellProviderInit = myCellProviderInit;\n"
```

```
          + "this.CellReady = myCellReady;\n"
          + "this.GetInitEventArgs = myGetInitEventArgs;\n"

          + "function myInit()\n"
          + "{\n"
          + "var cellConsumerInitEventArgs = new Object();\n"
          + "cellConsumerInitEventArgs.FieldName = \"ConsumerCellName\";\n"
          + "cellConsumerInitEventArgs.FieldDisplayName = \"Consume Cell\";\n"

          + "WPSC.RaiseConnectionEvent(\"MyCellConsumerInterface_WPQ_\", ➥
          \"CellConsumerInit\", cellConsumerInitEventArgs);\n"
          + "}\n"

          + "function myCellProviderInit(sender, cellProviderInitEventArgs)\n"
          + "{\n"
          + "document.all(\"ConnectedField_WPQ_\").innerText = ➥
          cellProviderInitEventArgs.FieldDisplayName;\n"
          + "}\n"

          + "function myCellReady(sender, cellReadyEventArgs)\n"
          + "{\n"
          + "if(cellReadyEventArgs.Cell != null)\n"
          + "{\n"
          + "AutoFillRequest_WPQ_(cellReadyEventArgs.Cell);\n"
          + "}\n"
          + "}\n"

          + "function myGetInitEventArgs()\n"
          + "{\n"
          + "var cellConsumerInitEventArgs = new Object();\n"
          + "cellConsumerInitEventArgs.FieldName = \"Consume Cell\";\n"
          + "cellConsumerInitEventArgs.FieldDisplayName = \"Consume Cell\";\n"

          + "return(cellConsumerInitEventArgs);\n"
          + "}\n"
          + "}\n"
          + "//-->\n"
          + "</SCRIPT>\n"));
      }
      else
      {
        output.Write(_strNotConnectedMsg);
      }
    }
  }
}
```

Figure 2-18 shows a SharePoint page after importing both the consumer and provider web parts.

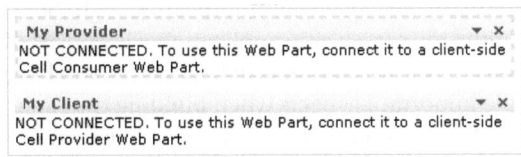

Figure 2-18. *Unconnected provider and consumer web parts*

The consumer and provider web parts are still unconnected to each other. Next, you will connect the provider web part to the consumer web part:

1. Click the Web Part Menu arrow of the My Provider Web Part ➤ Modify Shared Web Part.

2. Again click the Web Part Menu arrow of the My Provider Web Part ➤ Connections ➤ Provide Cell To ➤ My Client.

3. Now the provider and consumer web parts should look like Figure 2-19.

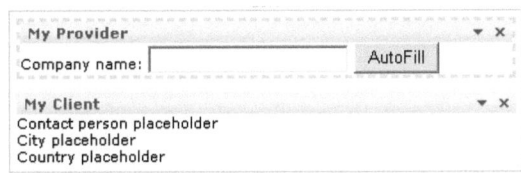

Figure 2-19. *Connected consumer and provider web parts*

If you enter a value in the company name text box and click the AutoFill button in the My Provider web part, this value will be propagated to the My Client web part. The My Client web part will use the value to call the ContactService web service via Atlas. The ContactService web service looks in the ContactInfo SharePoint list to see if it can find the contact information that matches the company name. Once the contact information is returned, the My Client web part updates the user interface. All of the processing is handled client-side. The result is seen in Figure 2-20.

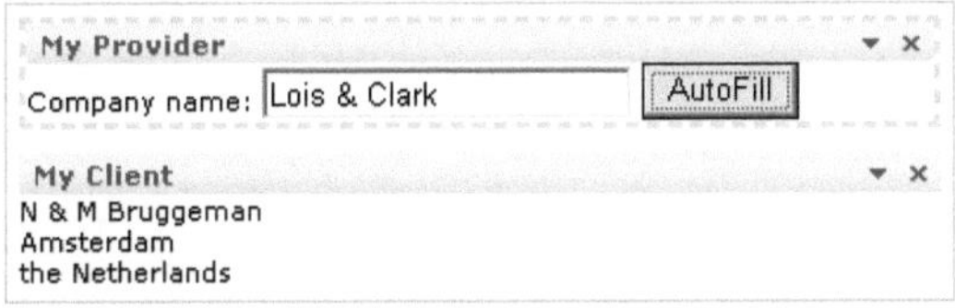

Figure 2-20. *Client-side connectable web parts and Atlas*

Summary

This chapter discussed what Ajax and Atlas are. We looked at some of the more popular Ajax implementations for .NET. Ajax-style applications rely heavily on communication with the server-side application. Nowadays, most of the time the server-side application will consist of web services. It is not easy to run web services on a Windows SharePoint Services server, but you have learned how to do it. There are multiple important aspects when building the client-side of Ajax-style applications. Within Ajax-style development, you can choose between various types of server responses: plain text, HTML, XML and JSON. We showed you examples of all these message types and discussed their benefits and disadvantages.

Atlas is an Ajax implementation, and this chapter explained how to use it. We discussed how to install Atlas and how to use it within web parts. We detailed information about creating a performance counter web part that uses Atlas to provide up-to-date information about performance counters that run on the server. We also explained how to create a web part that shows company contact information that is stored in a SharePoint list. The company contact information is retrieved using Atlas in a JSON message format. Finally, the chapter detailed how to use Atlas autocompletion in a web part and how to use Atlas within connectable web parts.

■■■

CHAPTER 3

SQL Server 2005 Reporting Services

Business intelligence is all about having comprehensive knowledge of all of the factors that affect your business. *Business intelligence* can be described as the process that transforms data to information, thus providing in-depth knowledge about customers, competitors, business partners, economic environment, or internal operations. Such knowledge helps companies gain a competitive edge, so it should come as no surprise that as of late, business intelligence is a very popular topic.

Microsoft's Business Intelligence suite supports all facets of decision-making. It consists of such products as SQL Server Analysis Services, Office Business Scorecard Manager, and SQL Server Reporting Services. This chapter only focuses on SQL Server 2005 Reporting Services—which provides web reporting on a variety of data sources, published reports, and subscriptions—in relationship to SharePoint 2003. We discuss the basics of Reporting Services and show you how to create a simple report using Business Intelligence Development Studio. Then we show you how to view a report via the Report Manager and how to use the SharePoint reporting web parts. We also cover reporting extensions and the SQL Server Report Pack for SharePoint Portal Server.

Introducing Reporting Services

The intention of this section is to get you acquainted and comfortable with SQL Server 2005 Reporting Services. As Reporting Services is quite a large topic, we will start with a general overview. Later in the chapter, we will cover detailed topics regarding the combination of Reporting Services and SharePoint 2003.

Reporting Services is a middle-tier server that runs under Internet Information Services (IIS) and allows you to build a reporting environment on top of an existing web server infrastructure. With Reporting Services it is possible to retrieve data from any available data server for any data source type that has a Microsoft .NET Framework–managed data provider, OLE DB provider, or ODBC data source. The Reporting Services product consists of three main components: databases, report server, and client applications. The Reporting Services architecture is shown in Figure 3-1.

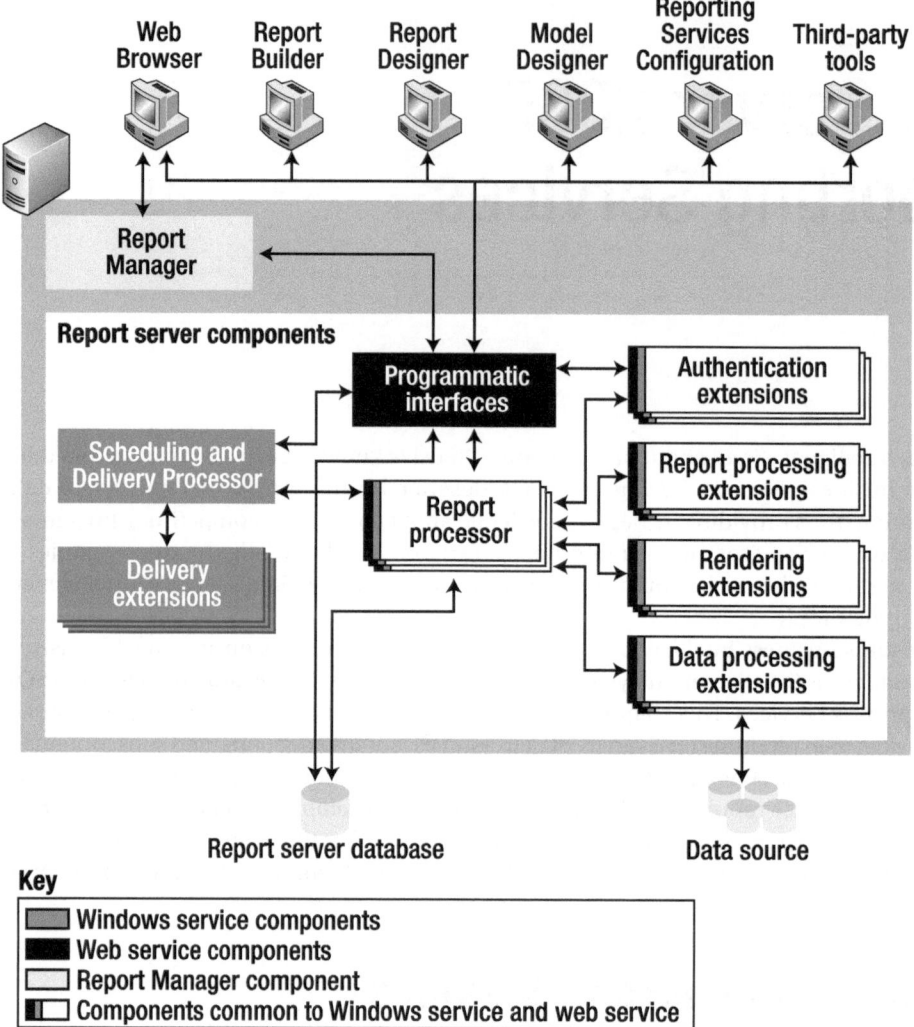

Figure 3-1. *Reporting Services architecture*

When you install Reporting Services, the following databases are created: report server and ReportServerTempDB. The report server database is the primary database that is used to store all information about reports. The ReportServerTempDB database contains cached copies of reports that are used to improve performance.

The report server is the most important component in the SQL Server Reporting Services architecture. It is responsible for responding to every client request to render a report or to perform a management request. The report server consists of two parts: a Windows service and a web service. This way the report server provides an optimized and parallel processing infrastructure for processing and rendering reports. The report server Windows service provides initialization, scheduling and delivery services, as well as server maintenance. Clients can access report servers via the report server web service layer. It performs end-to-end processing for reports that run on demand. It also provides the primary programmatic interface for applications that integrate with a report server, for example Report Manager, Report Builder, and SQL Server Management Studio.

The report server can be divided into two subcomponents: report processors and extensions. Report processors support the integrity of the reporting system and cannot be modified; you can think of them as the hub of the report server. Extensions are also processors, but they perform very specific functions. Extensions will be discussed later, in the section "Reporting Services Extensions."

The following client applications are part of Reporting Services: Report Manager, Business Intelligence Development Studio, and command-line utilities. We will cover Report Manager and Business Intelligence Development Studio in more detail later in the "Building a Report" and "Viewing a Report" sections of this chapter. First we will discuss the command-line utilities.

Reporting Services is shipped with three command-line utilities:

Rsconfig.exe: This tool is used to configure and manage a report server connection to the report server database.

Rskeymgmt.exe: This tool is an encryption key management tool. You can use it to back up, apply, create, and delete symmetric keys. You can also use this tool to attach a report server instance to a shared report server database.

Rs.exe: This tool is a script host that you can use to perform scripted operations. Use this tool to run Microsoft Visual Basic .NET scripts that copy data between report server databases, publish reports, create items in a report server database, and more.

Note If you want to learn more about the Rsconfig, Rskeymgmt, and Rs command-line tools, SQL Server 2005 Books Online (Start ➤ All Programs ➤ Microsoft SQL Server 2005 ➤ Documentation and Tutorials ➤ SQL Server Books Online) contains a complete overview of the arguments that are available for these tools and explains in detail how to use the Reporting Services tools.

Building a Report

It is possible to create interactive, tabular, or free-form reports that retrieve data as soon as a user opens the report. You can also create reports at scheduled time intervals. In this section, we will show you how to build a simple report. Our server configuration consists of one server with SQL Server 2005 and Reporting Services installed on it, and another server with Windows SharePoint Services and .NET Framework 2.0 installed on it. The Windows SharePoint Services server uses the SQL Server 2005 database of the first server as its data store.

The first thing we are going to do is build a report project; this is done via Business Intelligence Development Studio. Business Intelligence Development Studio is the environment that you will use to develop reports and report models in SQL Server 2005 Reporting Services. Business Intelligence Development Studio is a Visual Studio 2005 environment with enhancements that are specific to SQL Server 2005 business intelligence solutions. When you install Reporting Services, the following project templates are made available in Business Intelligence Development Studio:

Report Model Project: This is used as a starting point for building your own report model. A *report model* is a simplified view of a database and is used by the Report Builder. This project type is not relevant for this chapter.

Report Server Project: This is used as a starting point for building your own report.

Report Server Project Wizard: This is used as a starting point for building your own report with the help of the Report Wizard.

In this section, we will describe how to create a report project using the AdventureWorks database. The AdventureWorks database is a sample database that is shipped with SQL Server 2005. This is the database that is used in sample projects and code examples that are included in SQL Server 2005 Books Online. The AdventureWorks database is not installed by default in SQL Server 2005.

The AdventureWorks sample database can be downloaded from the MSDN web site via the Code Samples page (`http://msdn.microsoft.com/sql/downloads/samples/`). The AdventureWorks sample database is provided for three different processor types; you should download a file called AdventureWorksDB.msi for the processor type most appropriate for you.

The next steps describe how to install the AdventureWorks database:

1. Double-click the msi file to start installation. This starts the AdventureWorksDB – InstallShield Wizard. Follow the steps in this wizard to install the AdventureWorks database. The wizard installs the required AdventureWorks data (MDF) file that contains the AdventureWorks data and objects such as tables, indexes, stored procedures, and views.

2. Open Microsoft SQL Server Management Studio.

3. Right-click Databases ➤ Attach. This opens the Attach Databases window.

4. Click the Add... button.

5. Select the AdventureWorks_Data.mdf file. By default it should be located at the following location: c:\Program Files\Microsoft SQL Server\MSSQL.1\MSSQL\Data.

6. Click OK twice.

After following these steps, the AdventureWorks database should appear in the Object Explorer window of Microsoft SQL Server Management Studio. Now you are ready to build a report using the AdventureWorks sample database.

You can open Business Intelligence Development Studio via All Programs ➤ Microsoft SQL Server 2005 ➤ SQL Server Business Intelligence Development Studio. The following steps will show you how to create a report project:

1. Open Business Intelligence Development Studio and click File ➤ New ➤ Project. This will open the New Project dialog box.

2. Choose Business Intelligence Projects in the Project Types list, and choose Report Server Project Wizard in the Templates list.

3. Give the project a name and choose the location where you want to create the project. Finally click OK. This will create a report project.

4. After creating the report project, the Report Wizard will be opened. The next step is to create a report definition file.

5. Click Next on the first page; this opens the Select the Data Source page. On this page, you need to define a data source that you want to use for your report. In our example we will make use of the AdventureWorks database.

6. Give the data source the following name: AdventureWorks.

7. Select the following type of data source: Microsoft SQL Server.

8. Specify the following connection string (replace [server] with your server name):

   ```
   Data source=[server]; initial catalog=AdventureWorks
   ```

9. Click Next; this opens the Design the Query page. This page specifies the query that retrieves the data for the report. You can do this manually by typing the query directly in the text box, or you can use the Query Builder. Type the following query and click Next:

   ```
   SELECT AddressID, AddressLine1, AddressLine2, City, StateProvinceID,
   PostalCode, rowguid, ModifiedDate
   FROM Person.Address
   ```

10. On the Select the Report Type page, you can choose if you want a tabular report or a matrix type of report. We stick to the default, the tabular one, and click Next.

11. On the Design the Table page, you can choose how to group the data in the table. Click Next. Figure 3-2 shows the Design the Table page.

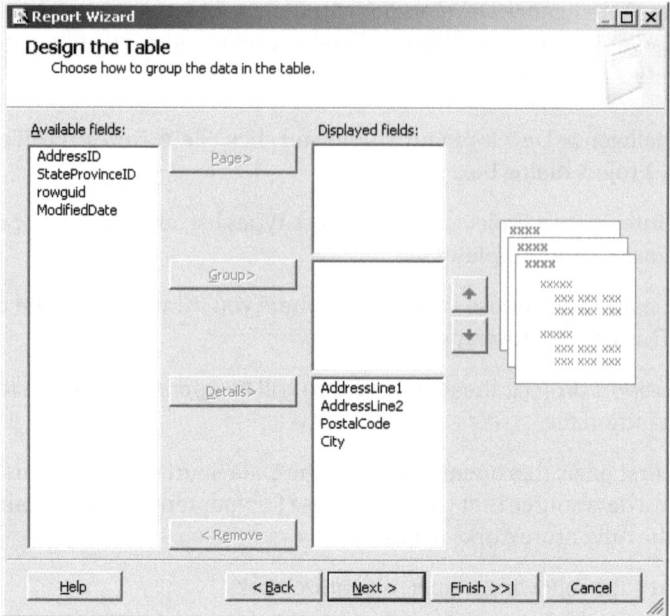

Figure 3-2. *The Design the Table page in the Report Wizard*

12. On the Choose the Table Style page, you can choose which table style you would like to use. There are six standard themes you can choose from. Click Next.

13. The Choose the Deployment Location of the Report Wizard allows you to specify the location where the report is deployed. Accept the default settings and click Next.

14. The last page of the wizard offers you the chance to enter a descriptive name for the report and add a summary to it. Before you click Finish, notice the check box that allows you to preview the report.

Figure 3-3 shows Business Intelligence Development Studio with a preview of the report that we have created.

The report that we created is opened in the Report Designer in Business Intelligence Development Studio. Report Designer is a graphical tool for creating reports. There are three tabs available for building the report query, designing the report layout, and viewing a rendered version of the report:

1. On the Data tab, you generate the query that provides data to the report.

2. On the Layout tab, you arrange and format the look of the report.

3. On the Preview tab, you render the report to see what the actual report will look like when it is saved to the report server.

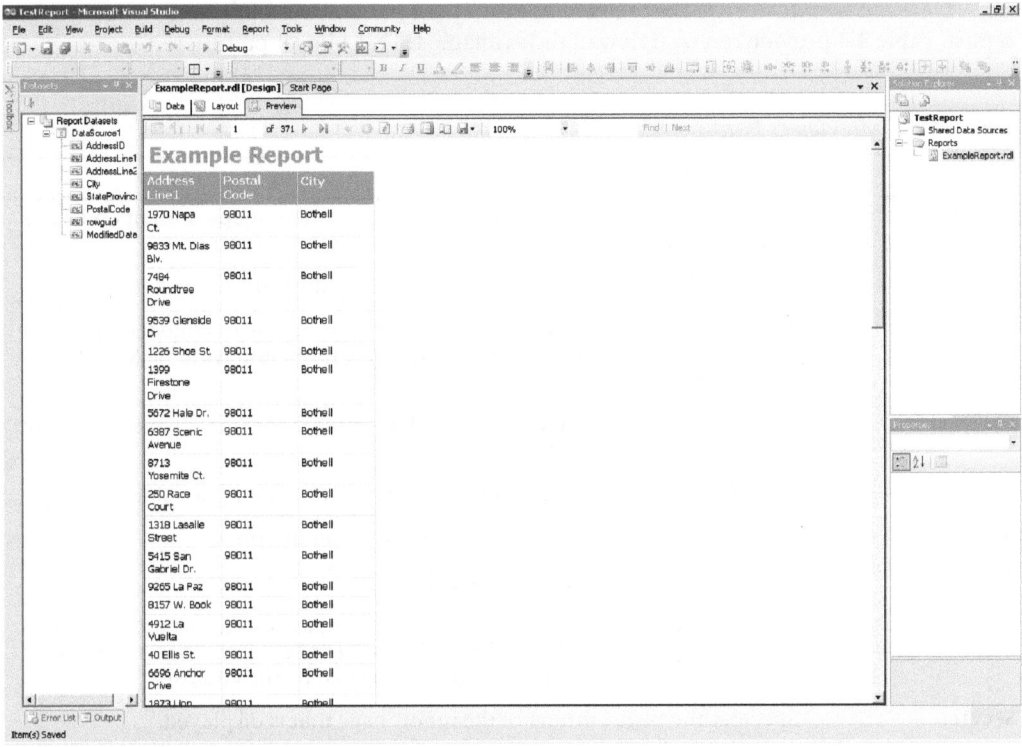

Figure 3-3. *Business Intelligence Development Studio*

Viewing a Report

There are different ways that you can run and view a report. If you want to view reports that are published to a report server, you can choose between the use of Report Manager, SharePoint web parts, or a browser. When you open a report located in the report server, it will be rendered as HTML in an HTML viewer. This HTML viewer provides page navigation and other functionality that is useful for working with a report.

You can also directly open a report located on a report server in a browser by typing the URL of the report in the browser. The first part of a report URL specifies the report location; it includes the name of the web server, the name of the report server virtual directory, and the fully qualified name of the report. A *fully qualified name* includes the path to the report and concludes with the name of the report itself. The second part of a report URL specifies parameters. URL access parameters are used to configure the look and feel of a report. There are several types of parameters.

Report parameters are passed to a report. They can refer to anything you like, such as a customer ID. Report parameters can be used as variables in a report or as values for filtering report queries.

HTML viewer parameters are prefixed by `rc:`. These parameters indicate how to render a report. Table 3-1 provides an overview of the available HTML viewer parameters.

Table 3-1. *HTML Viewer Parameters*

Name	Description
DocMap	Shows or hides a report document map. Document maps present end users with an integrated navigation pane when a report is rendered.
DocMapID	Specifies the document map ID to scroll to in the report.
EndFind	Specifies the last page that is to be searched for the text defined in the search. This parameter is typically used in conjunction with the `StartFind` parameter.
FallbackPage	Specifies the page number to display if a search (`FindString`) or a document map selection (`DocMapID`) fails.
FindString	Specifies the text to search for in the report. By default, this value is empty.
GetImage	Gets a particular icon for the HTML viewer user interface.
Icon	Gets the icon for a rendering extension.
Parameters	Shows or hides the parameters area of the toolbar. You can set this parameter to `true`, `false`, or `Collapsed`. If the value is set to `Collapsed`, the parameter area will not be displayed, but it can be toggled by the end user.
Section	Specifies the page number of the report page that is displayed.
StartFind	Specifies the first page that is to be searched for the text defined in the search. This parameter is typically used in conjunction with the `EndFind` parameter.
Stylesheet	Specifies a style sheet that is to be applied to the HTML viewer.
Toolbar	Shows or hides the toolbar. If you omit this parameter, the toolbar will be displayed.
Zoom	Sets the report zoom value to either an integer percentage or a string constant (such as `Page Width` and `Whole Page`).

Device information settings can be used to influence the report server rendering process. You do not need to provide device information settings per se, as all device information settings have default values. Table 3-2 provides an overview of the device information settings for rendering in HTML format. All device information settings commands are prefixed by `rc:`.

Table 3-2. *Device Information Settings Commands*

Name	Description
BookmarkID	Specifies the report section (bookmark) to jump to.
HTMLFragment	Indicates whether an HTML fragment should be created (omitting `<HTML>` and `<BODY>` tags) instead of a full HTML document.
JavaScript	Indicates whether the report supports JavaScript.

Table 3-2. *Device Information Settings Commands*

Name	Description
LinkTarget	Specifies the target for hyperlinks in the report.
ReplacementRoot	Specifies the path used for prefixing the value of the href attribute of the <A> tag in the report. By default, the report server provides the value for this path.
StreamRoot	Specifies the path used for prefixing the value of the src attribute of the <IMG> tag in the report. By default, the report server provides the value for this path.
StyleStream	Indicates whether styles and scripts are created as a separate stream. By default this value is false and styles and scripts are created as parts of the document.
Type	Specifies the short name of the browser type, for example IE5, as defined in browscap.ini.

■**Note** The browscap.ini file lists the features a browser supports. When a browser connects to a web server, it will automatically send an HTTP User Agent header. This HTTP User Agent Header is an ASCII string that will identify the browser and its version number. The BrowserType object compares the header to entries in the Browscap.ini file. This way you can determine the capabilities of the client browser on the server-side application.

Report server command parameters are prefixed by rs:. They are targeted toward the report server and are used to define the type of request being made. Table 3-3 provides an overview of the report server commands.

Table 3-3. *Report Server Commands*

Name	Description
Command	Sets the type of request being made. Supported values are GetDataSourceContents, GetResourceContents, ListChildren, and Render. GetDataSourceContents shows the properties of a given shared data source as XML. GetResourceContents renders a resource and displays it in an HTML page. ListChildren displays children of the item passed to the URL within a generic item-navigation page. Render renders the specified report.
Format	Specifies the format in which to render the report. Examples of valid values are: HTML4.0, EXCEL, CSV, PDF, and XML.
ParameterLanguage	Provides a language for the parameters passed in a URL. Culture information is passed in the form of values consisting of a language and a region part. Valid examples of such values are en-US and nl-NL.
Snapshot	Renders a report based on a report history snapshot.

Credential parameters can be used to supply username (prefixed by dsu:) and password (prefixed by dsp:) information to the report server. The credentials are used to connect to a data source. Table 3-4 provides an overview of the credential parameters.

Table 3-4. *Credential Parameters*

Name	Description
dsu	Username that is used to access the data source
dsp	Password that is used to access the data source

To conclude this section, the following code shows an example report URL:

http://[server]/ReportServer/Pages/ReportViewer.aspx?%2fReport2&rs:Command=Render.

Figure 3-4 shows a report that is opened directly in the browser.

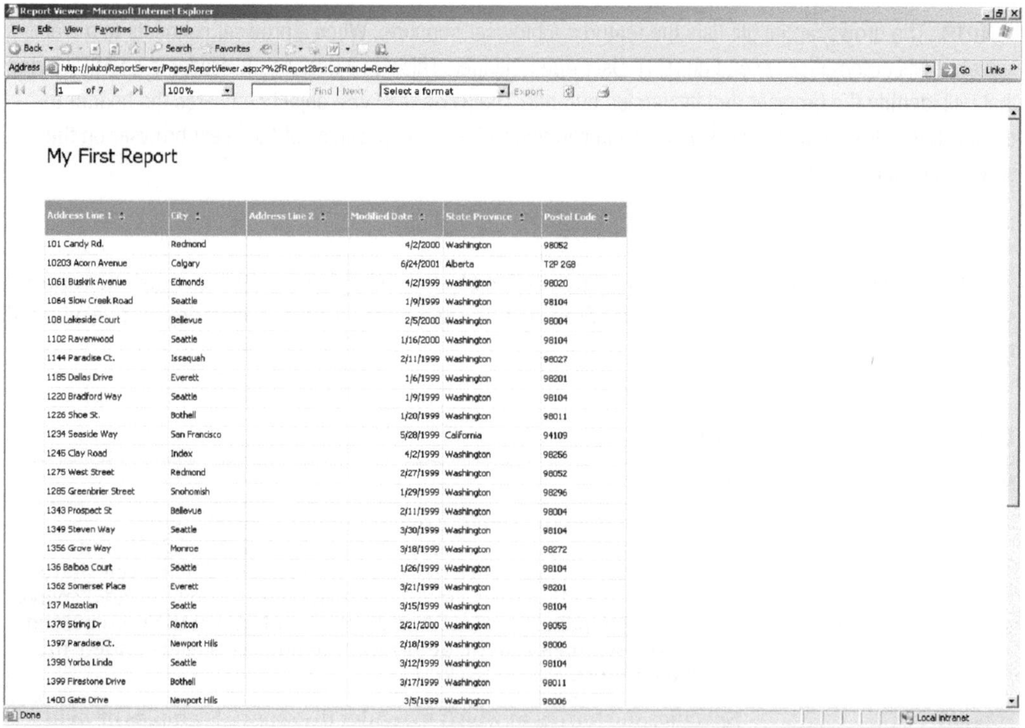

Figure 3-4. *Report opened via the browser*

Report Manager

The Report Manager installed with Reporting Services is a web-based tool to access and manage reports via Internet Explorer 6.0 and higher. You can administer a report server over an HTTP connection via Report Manager.

The customization options of Report Manager are very limited; you can modify the application title on the Site Settings page and that's it. If you find that Report Manager does not meet your needs, you can develop a custom report viewer or configure SharePoint Web parts to explore and view reports from within a SharePoint site.

The ability to perform a task in Report Manager depends on user role assignments. A user who is assigned to a role that has full permissions has access to the complete set of application menus and pages available for managing a report server. A user assigned to a role that has permissions to view and run reports sees only the menus and pages that support those activities. Each user can have different role assignments for different report servers. Each user can also have different permissions for the various reports and folders that are stored on a single report server.

You can use Report Manager to perform the following tasks:

- To view reports, search for reports, and subscribe to reports.

- To create and maintain a folder hierarchy to store items on the report server.

- To configure site properties.

- To configure role-based security to determine access to items and operations.

- To configure report execution properties, report history, and report parameters.

- To create report models that connect to and retrieve data from a Microsoft SQL Server Analysis Services data source or from a SQL Server relational data source.

- To create shared schedules and shared data sources to make schedules and data source connections more manageable.

- To create data-driven subscriptions that roll out reports to a large recipient list.

- To create linked reports to reuse and repurpose an existing report in different ways.

- To use Report Builder, a report design tool to create and modify model-driven ad hoc reports.

By default, the Report Manager URL is `http://[server]/reports`. Figure 3-5 shows the Report Manager.

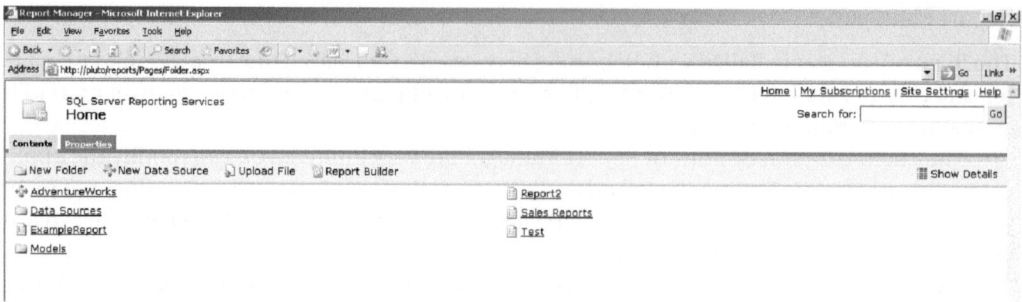

Figure 3-5. *The Report Manager*

SharePoint Reporting Web Parts

SQL Server 2005 Reporting Services provides a set of SharePoint web parts that make it easy for you to integrate reports into a SharePoint site. This can either be a SharePoint Portal Server site or a Windows SharePoint Services site. The web parts are optimized to run within a SharePoint environment; however, they can also be run as stand-alone components within ASP.NET pages. The web parts cannot be customized. The following web parts are provided:

- Report Explorer

- Report Viewer

The Report Explorer web part can be used to show available reports on a report server. This web part lets you browse the report server folder hierarchy and you can view a report. You can also create or edit a subscription to a report. The subscription feature allows you to receive reports via e-mail.

The Report Viewer web part is used to view and navigate multipage reports as well as export reports to supported formats. Using web part connections, this web part can be connected to the Report Explorer web part to enable display of the selected report within the web part page. Figure 3-6 shows the reporting web parts on a SharePoint site.

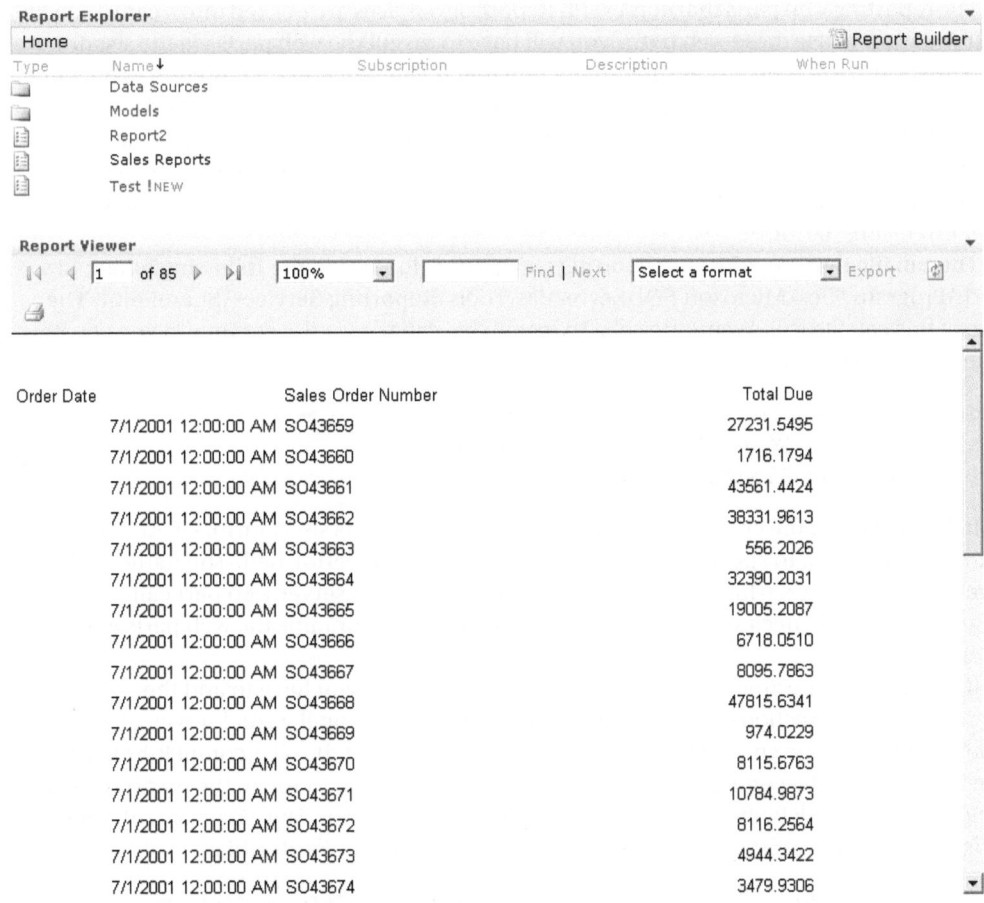

Figure 3-6. *Reporting web parts*

Installing Reporting Web Parts

If you want to use the reporting web parts, you must take notice of the following requirements:

- Install Windows SharePoint Services using at least Service Pack 1.0. It is also possible to use these web parts with SharePoint Portal Server 2003, with no service packs required.

■**Note** If you have installed .NET Framework 2.0 on the SharePoint server, you cannot install SharePoint Portal Server on the same machine. More information about this topic can be found in Chapter 1.

- Include Report Manager when installing Reporting Services.

- Add the Reporting Services virtual directories to the Windows SharePoint Services list of exclusions (unmanaged paths). You do not have to do this when you are running SQL Server on a different server.

The reporting web parts that come with Reporting Services are packed into a cabinet (.cab) file. If you want to use these web parts, you will have to install the web parts via the stsadm.exe tool. The stsadm.exe tool is a command-line tool that is a part of every SharePoint installation. The tool offers a complete set of operations and you can use it from the command line or from within a batch file. Stsadm.exe must be run on the server itself. If you want to use the tool, you must be a member of the local administrators group on the server. You can find the stsadm.exe tool in the following folder: [drive letter]:\Program Files\Common Files\Microsoft Shared\web server extensions\60\bin\.

The cab file that contains the reporting web parts is located in the following folder: [drive letter]:\Program Files\Microsoft SQL Server\90\Tools\Reporting Services\SharePoint. The name of this cab file is RSWebParts.cab. To install this cab file via the command line you have to run the following line of code:

```
stsadm.exe -o addwppack -filename "[drive letter]:\Program ➥
Files\Microsoft SQL Server\90\Tools\Reporting ➥
Services\SharePoint\RSWebParts.cab"
```

Instead of using the operations parameter, we have used its short form, -o. After the -o parameter, you need to specify which operation needs to be performed. The name of the operation is addwppack, which adds a web part package to your server web part gallery. The filename parameter specifies the path to the cabinet file that contains the web parts and all its associated files.

If you are running SharePoint on multiple virtual servers, you have to add the control to the <SafeControls> section of the web.config file for each additional virtual server. Stsadm.exe automatically adds the control to the <SafeControls> section of the web.config for the virtual server specified on the command line. The web.config file can be found in the root directory of the virtual server; by default, this is [drive letter]:\Inetpub\wwwroot. The <SafeControl> element that is added to the <SafeControls> section of the web.config looks like this:

```
<SafeControl Assembly="RSWebParts, Version=8.0.242.0, Culture=neutral, ➥
PublicKeyToken= 89845dcd8080cc91" Namespace= ➥
"Microsoft.ReportingServices.SharePoint.UI.WebParts" TypeName="*" Safe="True" />
```

Using Reporting Web Parts

Once you have installed the reporting web parts via the stsadm.exe command line tool, you can add them to a web part page via the SharePoint user interface. To add the web part to a SharePoint site, you must at least have web designer rights, so you are able to customize pages in the SharePoint site.

Go to your SharePoint site and click Modify Shared Page. Go to Add Web Parts and click Browse. Select the Virtual Server Gallery. From the web part list select the Report Explorer web part or the Report Viewer web part, and drag it to the zone where you want the web part to be placed. Figure 3-7 shows the Virtual Server Gallery that contains the Report Explorer and Report Viewer web parts.

Figure 3-7. *The Virtual Server Gallery containing the reporting web parts*

After placing the reporting web parts onto your SharePoint site, you need to configure the web parts. You can do this by clicking the Web Part Menu of the web part and choosing Modify Shared Web part. This will open the Report Explorer task pane, as shown in Figure 3-8.

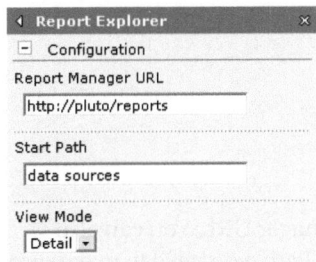

Figure 3-8. *Configuration of the Report Explorer web part*

In the Report Explorer task pane, you have to configure a couple of things. First of all, you need to configure the Report Manager URL. This is the URL that you use to go to the Report Manager in the browser (by default, http://[server]/reports). The Start Path is optional; this can be a specific folder that is shown in the Report Manager. In Figure 3-8 we are using the data sources folder. The View Mode has two settings: Detail or List. Detail view includes metadata about the items and folders shown in the web part, such as type and subscription information. It is also possible to sort items based on metadata columns. Figure 3-9 shows the Report Explorer web part in Detail View Mode. When you click a report shown in the Report Explorer web part, the report is opened in a new window.

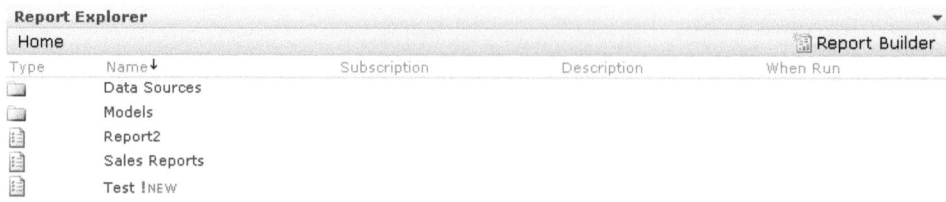

Figure 3-9. *The Report Explorer web part*

The Report Viewer web part can be configured by clicking the Web Part Menu of the web part and choosing Modify Shared Web Part. Figure 3-10 shows what the Report Viewer task pane looks like.

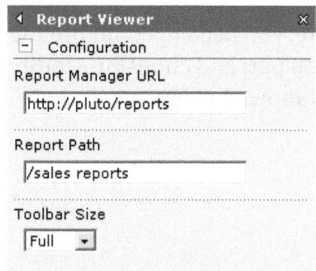

Figure 3-10. *Configuration of the Report Viewer web part*

In the Report Viewer task pane, you can enter the Report Manager URL. You can also specify a Report Path, which is optional. If you do specify a Report Path, you need to make sure the Report Path starts with a forward slash followed by the name of the report you would like to see. There are three modes for the Toolbar Size: None, Small, and Full. The None mode will not show any kind of toolbar in the web part; the web part will only show the report. The Small mode shows the paginating part of the toolbar. The name of the Full mode says it all: in this mode the web part shows everything. Figure 3-11 shows the Report Viewer web part with the Full mode toolbar selected.

When you specify the Report Path for the Report Viewer web part and the Start Path for the Report Explorer web part, you have configured two reporting web parts that work alone. It is possible to connect the two web parts, in which case the Report Path and the Start Path properties should not be filled in. This way, once you select a report in the Report Explorer web part, it will be shown in the Report Viewer web part. Follow the next steps to connect the reporting web parts:

1. Go to the Report Explorer web part and click the Web Part Menu of the web part and choose Modify Shared Web Part.

2. Again, click the Web Part Menu of the Report Explorer web part and point to Connections, point to Show Report In, and click Report Viewer.

3. Click a report in the Report Explorer web part and notice that it is opened in the Report Viewer web part.

Figure 3-11. *The Report Viewer web part*

Reporting Services Extensions

SQL Server 2005 Reporting Services is designed with extensibility in mind. A managed code Application Programming Interface (API) is available so that you can easily develop, install, and manage extensions consumed by many Reporting Services components. Reporting Services can be extended in various ways:

Data processing extensions: Data processing extensions make it possible to consume custom data and include this data into reports using the report server and Report Designer.

Delivery extensions: Delivery extensions make it possible to extend the range of mechanisms that can be used to send report notifications to end users and to extend the subscription management pages of Report Manager to support subscriptions of custom delivery extension types.

Security extensions: Security extensions are used by report server for authenticating and authorizing users and groups to the server. The default security mechanism that is used by report server is Windows authentication. You can create custom security models using Security extensions, for example, you could create a security model based on forms-based authentication. A single Reporting Services installation only allows you to use one security extension at a time.

Rendering extensions: Rendering extensions are responsible for transforming data and layout information into a specific format. By default, Reporting Services includes six rendering extensions: HTML, Excel, CSV, Image, PDF, and XML. Using the Rendering API, you can create support for other formats as well.

Report processing extensions: Report processing extensions are responsible for processing report items. Using the processing API, you can create support for the processing of custom report items. By default, report server is able to process tables, charts, matrices, lists, text boxes, and images.

Every report server installation requires the presence of one or more security extensions, data processing extensions, and rendering extensions. Delivery and custom report processing extensions are optional and only need to be present if you want to support report distribution or custom controls.

The Reporting Services Extension Library contains all the types that make up Reporting Services. This library can be used to access reporting services and to extend Reporting Services components. Table 3-5 shows the namespaces that are available within the Reporting Services Extension Library.

Table 3-5. *Namespaces Reporting Services Extension Library*

Name	Description
Microsoft.ReportingServices.DataProcessing	All types located in this namespace allow you to build custom components that extend the data processing capabilities of Reporting Services.
Microsoft.ReportingServices.Interfaces	All types located in this namespace allow you to create and send custom notifications via your own delivery extensions. This namespace also contains all types related to Reporting Services security extensions.
Microsoft.ReportingServices.ReportRendering	All types located in this namespace allow you to extend the default rendering capabilities of Reporting Services. Custom rendering extensions can be built using the types in this namespace in conjunction with the types that can be found in the Microsoft.ReportingServices.Interfaces namespace.

Data Processing Extension Example

Data processing extensions allow you to connect to a data source and retrieve data. For example, the data processing extension for SQL Server, which is included with Reporting Services, can be used to connect to a SQL Server database and retrieve data from this database. The data processing extensions that are included with Reporting Services use a common set of interfaces that indicate the kind of functionality that needs to be implemented by each data processing extension.

If you want to add a custom data processing extension, you need to implement the complete set, or in some scenarios a *subset*, of the interfaces described in the Reporting Services data processing API, as shown in Figure 3-12.

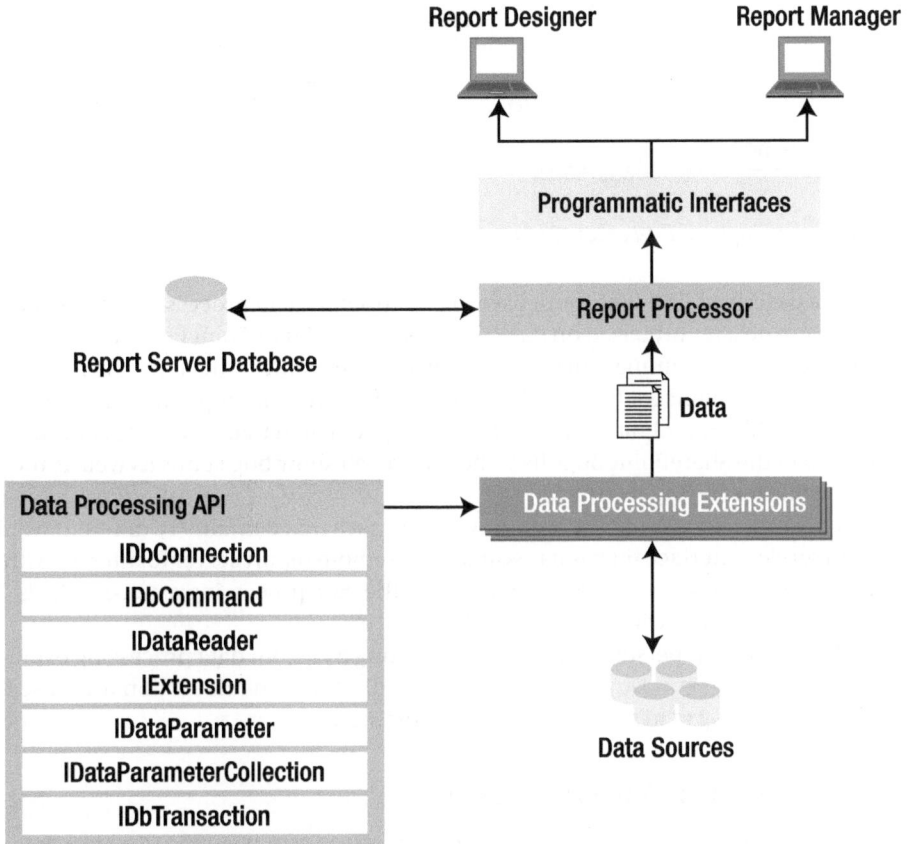

Figure 3-12. *Report server architecture*

The first thing that happens when a report server processes data via data extensions is the creation of a connection object. Report server makes sure the correct connection string and current client credentials are included. The command text of the report is used to create a command object. In the process, the data processing extension may include code that parses the command text and creates any parameters for the command. Once the command object and any parameters are processed, a data reader is generated that returns a result set and enables the report server to associate the report data with the report layout. Figure 3-13 shows this process.

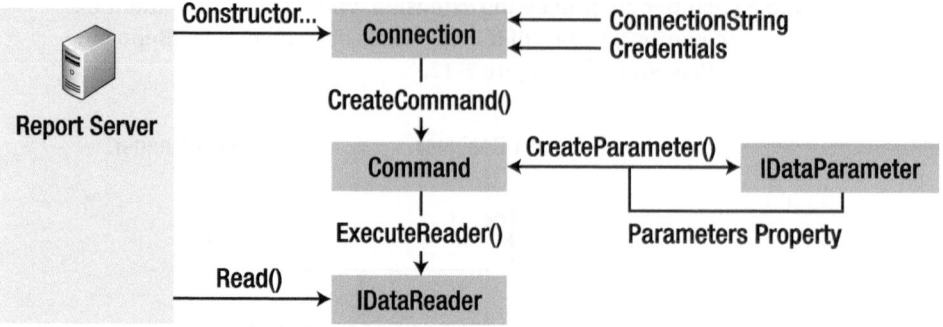

Figure 3-13. *Data processing via data extensions*

In the example described in this section, we will create a new data processing extension that will be used to create a report based on data retrieved from a SharePoint list. We will use a SharePoint list that contains a summary of bugs. Such lists can become rather long and it might not be so easy for a project manager to get a clear picture of the current bug status. To solve this, we are going to build a SharePoint list data processing extension that creates a report that is based on the data in the SharePoint Bugs list. The report will show bug status as well as the developers responsible for solving the bugs.

Windows SharePoint Services offers a web service interface that contains 16 different web services. This web service interface makes it possible for a remote report server to interact with SharePoint. We will use the Lists web service for creating the data processing extension. This web service can be used to work with lists and list data.

As far as we know, the first person to write about creating a custom data processing extension for SharePoint lists was Teun Duynstee. The example discussed in this section was based on the code found on his blog at http://www.teuntostring.net.

Developing a Custom Data Extension

The first thing you need to do to create a custom data processing extension is to create a new Visual C# class library. The next steps will show you how to do this:

1. Go to Start ➤ All Programs ➤ Microsoft Visual Studio 2005 ➤ Microsoft Visual Studio 2005. This will open the Visual Studio development environment.

2. Go to File ➤ New ➤ Project. This will open the New Project dialog box.

3. Select Visual C# in the Project Types list and select Class Library in the Templates list. Enter the following name for the project: SharePointListExtension.

The next thing to do is to add a reference to the Microsoft.ReportingServices.Interfaces assembly that can be found at the following location: [drive letter]:\Program Files\Microsoft SQL Server\MSSQL.3\Reporting Services\ReportServer\bin. Follow the next steps to add this reference:

1. Right-click References in the Solution Explorer and choose Add Reference.

2. In the Add Reference dialog box click the Browse tab and browse to the following location: [drive letter]:\Program Files\Microsoft SQL Server\MSSQL.3\Reporting Services\ReportServer\bin.

3. Click the Microsoft.ReportingServices.Interfaces.dll file and click OK.

We are going to add another reference, but this time it will be a web reference. We will refer to the Windows SharePoint Services Lists web service. Follow the next steps to add the web reference:

1. Right-click References in the Solution Explorer and choose Add Web Reference.

2. In the Add Web Reference dialog box type the following URL: http://[server]/_vti_bin/Lists.asmx and click the Go button.

3. Call the web reference WssLists and click Add Reference.

The first class we are going to create is a connection class, which we will simply call Connection. The Connection class implements the IDbConnection and IDbConnectionExtension interfaces. This class is responsible for managing the connection to a SharePoint list and is the starting point for users of the data processing extension.

The IDbConnection interface supports the IExtension interface, which means that implementing the IDbConnection interface in a connection class implicitly means supporting the IExtension interface as well. We will discuss the IExtension interface a little bit later; first, we will take a closer look at the IDbConnection interface.

Our class will contain two constructors. The first constructor does nothing and accepts no parameters. The second constructor accepts a String parameter containing the connection string to the SharePoint list and sets the ConnectionString property, which is a part of the IDbConnection interface. The second constructor looks like this:

```
public Connection(string strConnection)
{
  ConnectionString = strConnection;
}
```

If you want to support the IDbConnection interface, you have to implement the following methods:

BeginTransaction(): This method begins a database transaction. In our connection class this method is not supported and will always throw a NotSupportedException error.

```
public IDbTransaction BeginTransaction()
{
  throw new NotSupportedException();
}
```

CreateCommand(): This method creates and returns a Command object associated with the connection. We will discuss the Command class later on.

```
public IDbCommand CreateCommand()
{
  return new Command(this);
}
```

Close(): This method is intended to close the connection to a database. In our example it is a simple method, because we do not have a real database connection that needs to be opened and closed. Here the method just indicates the current connection state is closed:

```
public void Close()
{
  _objConnState = System.Data.ConnectionState.Closed;
}
```

Open(): This method is intended to open a database connection using the settings specified in the ConnectionString property of the provider-specific Connection object. The same that is true for the Close() method is true for the Open() method; as we do not have a real database connection, the method just indicates the current connection state is open:

```
public void Open()
{
  _objConnState = System.Data.ConnectionState.Open;
}
```

We also have to implement the following properties from the IDbConnection interface:

ConnectionString: This property gets or sets the string used to open a database. The format of the connection string expected by the SharePoint list connection class is a name/value pair that looks like this: data source=http://[myserver]. The set part of the ConnectionString property knows how to add the name/value pair to a HybridDictionary collection called _objConn:

```
public string ConnectionString
{
  get { return _strConn; }
  set
  {
    _strConn = value;
    _objConn.Add(_strConn.Substring(0, _strConn.IndexOf("=")).ToLower(),➥
    _strConn.Substring(_strConn.IndexOf("=") + 1));
  }
}
```

ConnectionTimeout: This property returns the maximum time to wait for trying to establish a connection. If the time-out period has expired, the attempt is terminated and an error is generated. In this example, this property is not supported and will therefore always return 0 (zero).

```
public int ConnectionTimeout
{
  get { return 0; }
  set { }
}
```

The IExtension interface enables a class to implement the localized name of the extension (a friendly name, such as SharePointListExtension) that will be displayed in the user interface and to process extension-specific configuration information stored in the Reporting Services configuration file. The LocalizedName property and the SetConfiguration() method of the IExtension interface are implemented in the Connection class.

We have also implemented the IDbConnectionExtension interface to extend our Connection class to include support for credentials in Reporting Services. The following properties are implemented:

IntegratedSecurity: This property indicates whether the connection should use integrated security rather than supply a username and password. With this property you enable the integrated security check box and the username and password text boxes of the Data Source dialog in the Report Designer. This way credentials can be stored and retrieved by the Report Designer for data sources that support authentication. The credentials are stored securely and are used when rendering reports in preview mode.

UserName: This property gets or sets the username that is used when connecting to the database.

Impersonate: This property sets the username of the user that is impersonated while queries are executed. This property is ignored by the report server if impersonation is not supported by the data provider.

Password: This property gets or sets the password to use when connecting to the database.

The complete code listing for the Connection class looks like this:

```
using System;
using d = System.Data;
using System.Collections.Specialized;
using System.Security.Permissions;
using System.Security.Principal;
using Microsoft.ReportingServices.DataProcessing;
using Microsoft.ReportingServices.Interfaces;

namespace LoisandClark.SharePointListExtension
{
  public class Connection : IDbConnection, IDbConnectionExtension
  {
    private string _strConn;
    private string _strLocName = "SharePoint";
    private string _strImpersonate;
    private string _strUsername;
    private string _strPassword;
```

```csharp
private bool _blnSecurity;
private HybridDictionary _objConn = new HybridDictionary();
private d.ConnectionState _objConnState = d.ConnectionState.Closed;

public Connection()
{ }

public Connection(string strConnection)
{
  ConnectionString = strConnection;
}

public string ConnectionString
{
  get { return _strConn; }
  set
  {
    _strConn = value;
    _objConn.Add(_strConn.Substring(0, _strConn.IndexOf("=")).ToLower(), ➥
    _strConn.Substring(_strConn.IndexOf("=") + 1));
  }
}

public IDbTransaction BeginTransaction()
{
  throw new NotSupportedException();
}

public void Open()
{
  _objConnState = d.ConnectionState.Open;
}

public void Close()
{
  _objConnState = d.ConnectionState.Closed;
}

public IDbCommand CreateCommand()
{
  return new Command(this);
}

public string LocalizedName
{
  get { return _strLocName; }
  set { _strLocName = value; }
}
```

```
}

public void SetConfiguration(string configuration)
{ }

public void Dispose()
{ }

public int ConnectionTimeout
{
  get { return 0; }
  set { }
}

public string strDataSourcePath
{
  get
  {
    if (_objConn.Contains("data source"))
    {
      string strUrl = (string)_objConn["data source"];
      if (!strUrl.EndsWith("/"))
      {
        strUrl = strUrl + "/";
      }
      return strUrl;
    }
    return "";
  }
}

public d.ConnectionState State
{
  get { return _objConnState; }
}

public bool IntegratedSecurity
{
  get { return _blnSecurity; }
  set { _blnSecurity = value; }
}

public string UserName
{
  get { return _strUsername; }
  set { _strUsername = value; }
}
```

```
    public string Password
    {
      get { return _strPassword; }
      set { _strPassword = value; }
    }

    public string Impersonate
    {
      set { _strImpersonate = value; }
    }


  }
}
```

The next class you need to create is a Command class. A Command class formulates a request and passes it on to the data source. Command requests can take many different syntactical forms, including text and XML. If results are returned, a Command object always returns results as a DataReader object. To create a Command class, you will have to implement the IDbCommand interface. The IDbCommand interface contains the following methods:

Cancel(): This method attempts to cancel the execution of an object implementing the IDbCommand interface. Our Command class will not support this operation; it will throw a NotSupportedException.

CreateParameter(). This method creates a new instance of an object implementing the IDataParameter interface. In this example we will not use parameters; the operation will return null instead.

ExecuteReader(): This method executes a command request (the contents of the CommandText property) against the Connection object and builds a response object that supports the IDataReader interface. The ExecuteReader() method is overloaded and includes an implementation that takes a CommandBehavior enumeration as an argument. The default ExecuteReader() method accepts no parameters and calls the overload passing CommandBehavior.SingleResult as its single argument. The overloaded method calls a custom GetDataTableFromWSS() method. This method does not belong to any of the interfaces that are a part of the Data Processing API; it is just used for clarity and we will get back to this method in a moment. ExecuteReader() methods of data processing extensions need to support the ability to handle schema-only requests. Schema-only requests are specified using the CommandBehavior.SchemaOnly command behavior enumeration value. A response to such requests contains type and name information about fields or columns but does not include actual data:

```
public IDataReader ExecuteReader()
{
  return ExecuteReader(CommandBehavior.SingleResult);
}
```

```
public IDataReader ExecuteReader(CommandBehavior behavior)
{
  d.DataTable objDataTable = GetDataTableFromWSS((behavior == ➥
  CommandBehavior.SchemaOnly));
  return new DataReader(this._objConn, objDataTable, _objDataParameters);
}
```

The IDbCommand interface contains the following properties:

CommandText: This property gets or sets the text command to run against the data source. We will use this property to specify which SharePoint list we want to use. Therefore, instead of using a SQL query, we will use the name of a SharePoint list:

```
public string CommandText
{
  get { return _strText; }
  set { _strText = value; }
}
```

CommandTimeout: This property gets or sets the maximum wait time before terminating the attempt to execute a command and generating an error. We have specified the wait time for our solution to be 60 seconds:

```
public int CommandTimeout
{
  get { return 60 * 1000; }
  set { }
}
```

CommandType: This property indicates or specifies how the CommandText property should be interpreted, for example as text:

```
public CommandType CommandType
{
  get { return _objCmdType; }
  set
  {
    if (value != CommandType.Text)
    {
      throw new NotSupportedException();
    }
    _objCmdType = value;
  }
}
```

Parameters: This property gets the IDataParameterCollection. In this example, we will do nothing with parameters, so this property will return an empty collection.

Transaction: This property gets or sets the transaction context in which the Command object of a SQL Server Reporting Services data provider executes. In this example we will not support transactions. The Transaction property returns null.

We promised to pay some attention to the GetDataTableFromWSS() method that gets called by the ExecuteReader() method of the Command class. This method is the core of the code for our custom data extension. We will discuss parts of the method and show the entire method in the complete code listing of the Command class.

The first part of the GetDataTableFromWSS() method sets up a proxy object that is able to call the SharePoint web service, as shown in the following code:

```
WssLists.Lists objLists = new WssLists.Lists();
objLists.Url = _objConn.strDataSourcePath + "_vti_bin/Lists.asmx";
objLists.Credentials = GetCredential(_objConn);
objLists.PreAuthenticate = true;
objLists.Timeout = this.CommandTimeout;
```

The next part of the code calls the GetListCollection() method. This method returns an XmlNode containing the entire list collection node. The method looks for the Name attribute because it contains a GUID (Globally Unique Identifier) that identifies SharePoint lists. We are going to use this GUID when calling the web service later, as shown in this code listing:

```
XmlNode ListCollectionNode = objLists.GetListCollection();
XmlElement xmlElem = (XmlElement)ListCollectionNode. ➥
SelectSingleNode(String.Format("wss:List[@Title='{0}']", ➥
this.CommandText), NameSpaceManager);
if (xmlElem == null)
{
  throw new ArgumentException(String.Format(" ➥
  List {0} does not exist in site {1}", this.CommandText, ➥
  _objConn.strDataSourcePath));
}

string strTechListName = xmlElem.GetAttribute("Name");
XmlNode xmlNode = objLists.GetList(strTechListName);
```

For each column in the SharePoint list, we will add a new column to our DataTable with an identical name. In SharePoint, each column has two names—one called Name and another called DisplayName. Upon column creation, these two names are always the same. Later, the DisplayName can be changed by end users. The SharePoint user interface displays the DisplayName of the column. Having taken this into account, it is better to use the DisplayName of the column as the ColumnName in our DataTable. The Name of the SharePoint column is added to a hybrid dictionary. This way we can always look up which Name belongs to a given ColumnName, as shown in this code listing:

```
StringBuilder objStringBuilder = new StringBuilder();
HybridDictionary objDictionary = new HybridDictionary();
d.DataTable objResult = new d.DataTable("list");
foreach (XmlElement xmlField in xmlNode.SelectNodes(" ➥
wss:Fields/wss:Field", NameSpaceManager))
{
  string strName = xmlField.GetAttribute("Name");
  string strDisplayName = xmlField.GetAttribute("DisplayName");
```

```
  if (objResult.Columns.Contains(strDisplayName))
  {
    strDisplayName = strDisplayName + " (" + strName + ")";
  }
  objResult.Columns.Add(strDisplayName, TypeFromField(xmlField));
  objStringBuilder.AppendFormat("<FieldRef Name=\"{0}\"/>", strName);
  objDictionary.Add(strDisplayName, strName);
}

if (blnSchema)
{
  return objResult;
}

XmlElement fields = xmlNode.OwnerDocument.CreateElement("ViewFields");
fields.InnerXml = objStringBuilder.ToString();
```

In the following code, we will load the data into the DataTable by making use of the GetListsItems() method of the SharePoint web service:

```
XmlNode ItemsNode = objLists.GetListItems(strTechListName, "", null, ➡
fields, "1000000", null);
System.Text.RegularExpressions.Regex CheckLookup = ➡
new System.Text.RegularExpressions.Regex("^\\d+;#");

foreach (XmlElement Item in ItemsNode.SelectNodes(" ➡
rs:data/z:row", NameSpaceManager))
{
  d.DataRow newRow = objResult.NewRow();
  foreach (d.DataColumn col in objResult.Columns)
  {
    if (Item.HasAttribute("ows_" + (string) objDictionary[col.ColumnName]))
    {
      string val = Item.GetAttribute("ows_" + ➡
      (string)objDictionary[col.ColumnName]);
      if (CheckLookup.IsMatch((string)val))
      {
        string valString = val as String;
        val = valString.Substring(valString.IndexOf("#") + 1);
      }
      newRow[col] = val;
    }
  }
  objResult.Rows.Add(newRow);
}
return objResult;
}
```

The complete code listing for the Command class can be downloaded from our web site at http://www.lcbridge.nl/download/.

The next class to discuss is the DataReader class. If you want to create a DataReader class you have to implement the IDataReader interface. The DataReader implementation must provide two basic capabilities: forward-only access over the result sets obtained by executing a command, and access to the column types, names, and values within each row. You can use the Read() method of the DataReader object to obtain a row from the results of the query.

The complete code listing for the DataReader class looks like this:

```csharp
using System;
using System.Collections;
using d = System.Data;
using System.Diagnostics;
using System.Globalization;
using System.IO;
using System.Security;
using System.Security.Permissions;
using System.Security.Principal;
using Microsoft.ReportingServices.DataProcessing;

namespace LoisandClark.SharePointListExtension
{
  public class DataReader : IDataReader
  {
    private Connection _objConn = null;
    private d.DataTable _objDataTable;
    private DataParameterCollection _objDataParameters = null;
    IEnumerator enumTable = null;

    internal DataReader()
    { }

    internal DataReader(Connection objConn, d.DataTable objDataTable)
    {
      _objConn = objConn;
      _objDataTable = objDataTable;
    }

    internal DataReader(Connection objConn, d.DataTable objDataTable, ➥
      DataParameterCollection objParameters) ➥
      : this(objConn, objDataTable)
    {
      _objDataParameters = objParameters;
    }
```

```csharp
public bool Read()
{
  if (enumTable == null)
  {
    enumTable = _objDataTable.Rows.GetEnumerator();
  }
  return enumTable.MoveNext();
}

protected d.DataRow CurrentRow
{
  get { return (d.DataRow)enumTable.Current; }
}

public int FieldCount
{
  get { return _objDataTable.Columns.Count; }
}

public string GetName(int i)
{
  return _objDataTable.Columns[i].ColumnName;
}

public Type GetFieldType(int i)
{
  return _objDataTable.Columns[i].DataType;
}

public Object GetValue(int i)
{
  return CurrentRow[i];
}

public int GetOrdinal(string strName)
{
  foreach (d.DataColumn objColumn in _objDataTable.Columns)
  {
    if (objColumn.ColumnName == strName)
    {
      return objColumn.Ordinal;
    }
  }
  throw new IndexOutOfRangeException(" ➡
  There is no field with the name " + strName);
}
```

```
    public void Dispose()
    {
      _objDataTable.Dispose();
    }
  }
}
```

The DataParametercollection class implements the ArrayList and the IDataParameterCollection interfaces. The IDataParameterCollection interface contains the Add() method; with this method you can populate the IDataParameterCollection class. The following code listing shows the DataParameterCollection class:

```
using System;
using System.Collections;
using System.Globalization;
using Microsoft.ReportingServices.DataProcessing;

namespace LoisandClark.SharePointListExtension
{
  public class DataParameterCollection : ArrayList, IDataParameterCollection
  {
    public object this[string index]
    {
      get { return this[IndexOf(index)]; }
      set { this[IndexOf(index)] = value; }
    }

    public override int Add(object value)
    {
      return Add((IDataParameter)value);
    }

    int IDataParameterCollection.Add(IDataParameter parameter)
    {
      if (parameter.ParameterName != null)
      {
        return base.Add(parameter);
      }
      else
      {
        throw new ArgumentException("parameter must be named");
      }
    }
  }
}
```

Deployment of a Custom Data Extension

The deployment of a custom data extension is simple. You need to make sure the custom data extension is accessible to the report server and the Report Designer. You can do this by copying the extension to the appropriate directories and adding entries to the appropriate Reporting Services configuration files:

1. Copy your assembly to the bin directory of the report server where you want to use your custom extension. The default location is [drive letter]:\Program Files\Microsoft SQL Server\MSSQL.3\Reporting Services\ReportServer\bin.

2. Copy your assembly to the Report Designer directory. The default location is [drive letter]:\Program Files\Microsoft Visual Studio 8\Common7\IDE\PrivateAssemblies.

3. The name of the report server configuration file is RSReportServer.config and is located at [drive letter]:\Program Files\Microsoft SQL Server\MSSQL.3\ Reporting Services\ReportServer. Open the RSReportServer.config file in a text editor. Go to the <Data> section and add the following entry:

```
<Extension Name="SPS" ➡
Type="LoisandClark.SharepointListExtension.Connection, ➡
LoisandClark.SharepointListExtension"/>
```

4. The name of the Report Designer configuration file is RSReportDesigner.config and is located at [drive letter]:\Program Files\Microsoft Visual Studio 8\Common7\IDE\ PrivateAssemblies. Open the RSReportServer.config file in a text editor. Go to the <Data> section and add the following entry:

```
<Extension Name="SPS" ➡
Type="LoisandClark.SharepointListExtension.Connection, ➡
LoisandClark.SharepointListExtension"/>
```

The value of the Name attribute is the unique name of the data processing extension. The value of the Type attribute is a comma-separated list that includes an entry for the fully qualified namespace of the Connection class including the class name itself, followed by the name of your assembly (do not include the extension .dll). By default, data processing extensions are visible. To hide an extension from user interfaces such as Report Manager, add a Visible attribute to the <Extension> element, and set it to false.

The last thing you need to do is to add a code group for your custom assembly. Follow the next steps to add a code group for the report server and the Report Designer:

1. For the report server you will have to add a code group to the rssrvpolicy.config file located in [drive letter]:\Program Files\Microsoft SQL Server\MSSQL.3\ Reporting Services\ReportServer. The following code is a valid code group for our custom data extension:

```xml
<CodeGroup class="UnionCodeGroup"
  version="1"
  PermissionSetName="FullTrust"
  Name="LCExtensionCodeGroup"
  Description="Code group for my data processing extension">
  <IMembershipCondition class="UrlMembershipCondition"
    version="1"
    Url="C:\Program Files\Microsoft SQL Server\MSSQL.3\Reporting
    Services\ReportServer\bin\LoisandClark.SharepointListExtension.dll"
  />
</CodeGroup>
```

Note A *permission* allows code to perform a specific operation. A *permission set* is a collection of permissions. .NET provides seven predefined permission sets; one of them is called FullTrust. The FullTrust permission set is the most liberal of all named permission sets and allows code to perform all operations. A code group specifies which permission set applies to a .NET assembly based on origin-based evidence (.NET examines where the assembly is coming from) or content-based evidence (.NET looks at the actual content of an assembly). The .NET Common Language Runtime (CLR) evaluates which code groups apply to a given assembly, and based on this information the CLR determines which permissions are granted to an assembly. The code group in the previous listing associates the assembly SharePointListExtension.dll to the FullTrust permission set.

2. For the Report Designer you can add a code group to the rspreviewpolicy.config file located in [drive letter]:\Program Files\Microsoft Visual Studio 8\Common7\IDE\ PrivateAssemblies:

```xml
<CodeGroup class="UnionCodeGroup"
  version="1"
  PermissionSetName="FullTrust"
  Name="LCExtensionCodeGroup"
  Description="Code group for my data processing extension">
  <IMembershipCondition class="UrlMembershipCondition"
    version="1"
    Url="C:\Program Files\Microsoft Visual Studio 8\Common7\IDE\ ➥
    PrivateAssemblies\LoisandClark.SharepointListExtension.dll"
  />
</CodeGroup>
```

Using the Custom Data Extension

Now that you have created a custom data extension, you are probably interested to learn how you can use it as well. Let's create a report that is based on a custom Bugs SharePoint list. This list contains the bugs our testers have discovered and assigned to developers. Figure 3-14 shows our sample Bugs SharePoint list.

Bugs

New Item | Filter

Title	Priority	Code	Description	Developer
Portal crash ! NEW	Must	001	Portal crash	Erhardt Guenther
Search exception ! NEW	Must	002	Search exception	Merrick Ordinsky
Unauthorized access ! NEW	Must	003	Unauthorized access	Merrick Ordinsky
Wrong CSS stylesheet ! NEW	Should	004	Wrong CSS stylesheet	Erhardt Guenther
Unsecure code ! NEW	Should	005	Unsecure code	Erhardt Guenther
Navigation failure ! NEW	Could	006	Navigation failure	Erhardt Guenther
Incorrect web part ! NEW	Should	007	Incorrect web part	Merrick Ordinsky
Failed to open data source ! NEW	Must	008	Failed to open data source	Merrick Ordinsky
Wrong contactperson name ! NEW	Could	009	Wrong contactperson name	Erhardt Guenther
Incorrect company address ! NEW	Would	010	Incorrect company address	Deofilio Harbinger
Broken link ! NEW	Could	011	Broken link	Deofilio Harbinger
Small spelling mistake ! NEW	Would	012	Small spelling mistake	Deofilio Harbinger
Slow performance ! NEW	Could	013	Slow performance	Merrick Ordinsky
Error in Netscape browser ! NEW	Would	014	Error in Netscape browser	Merrick Ordinsky

Figure 3-14. *Bugs SharePoint list*

We are going to use our new SharePoint list data extension to create a report via Reporting Services.

Open SQL Server Business Intelligence Development Studio by clicking Start ➤ All Programs ➤ Microsoft SQL Server 2005 and choose SQL Server Business Intelligence Development Studio.

Click File ➤ New Project and choose Business Intelligence Projects in the Project types list. In the Templates list choose Report Server Project Wizard, give your project a descriptive name, and click OK. We will call our report project BugsReportProject. Figure 3-15 shows the New Project dialog window.

Once you have clicked OK, a report project will be created and the Report Wizard will be started. On the first page of the Report Wizard, you have to select the data source you are going to use. In the Type drop-down list, choose our custom SharePoint data extension and specify the connection string. Figure 3-16 shows the Select the Data Source page from the Report Wizard.

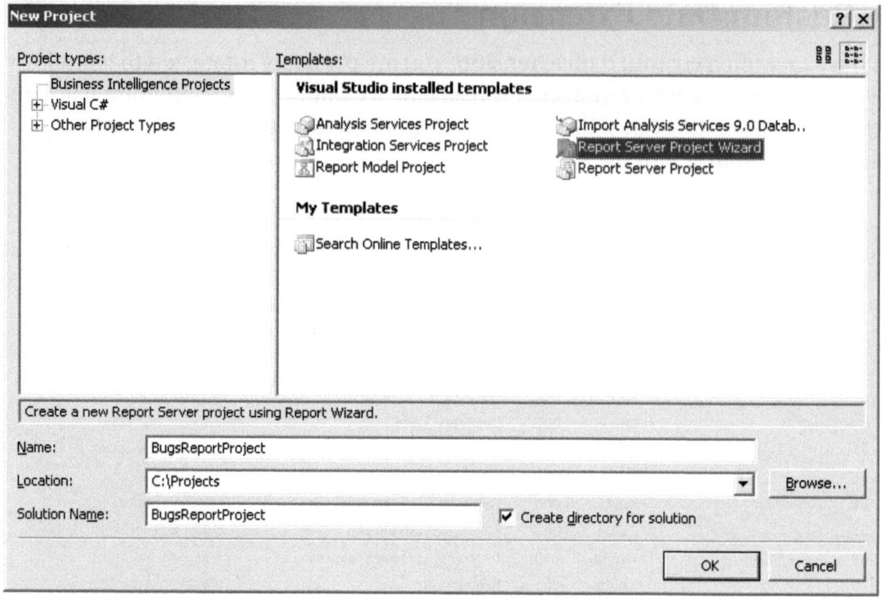

Figure 3-15. *New Project dialog window*

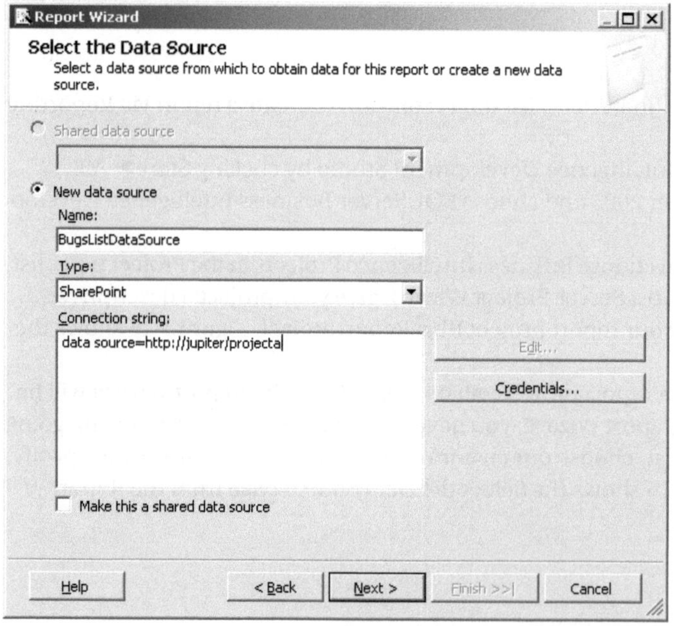

Figure 3-16. *Select the Data Source page in the Report Wizard*

If you want to use a specific username and password, you have to click the Credentials button. This opens a Data Source Credentials dialog box that lets you specify whether you want to use Windows Authentication, no credentials, or a specific username and password, as shown in Figure 3-17. Choose to specify a username and password, click OK, and click Next in the Report Wizard.

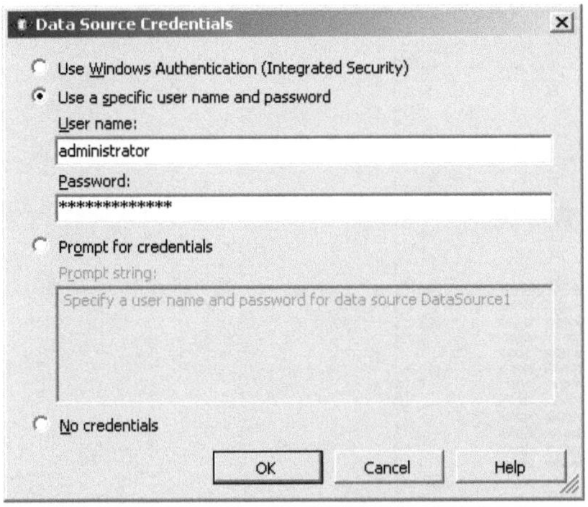

Figure 3-17. *Data Source Credentials page in the Report Wizard*

The next page of the Report Wizard is the Design the Query page. This page gives you the opportunity to use the query designer to build a query. You will not need a query designer for our extension, since all you have to do is add the name of the SharePoint list you want to use for the report. In our example, this will be the Bugs list. Figure 3-18 shows the Design the Query page of the Report Wizard. When you are done, click Next to go to the next page.

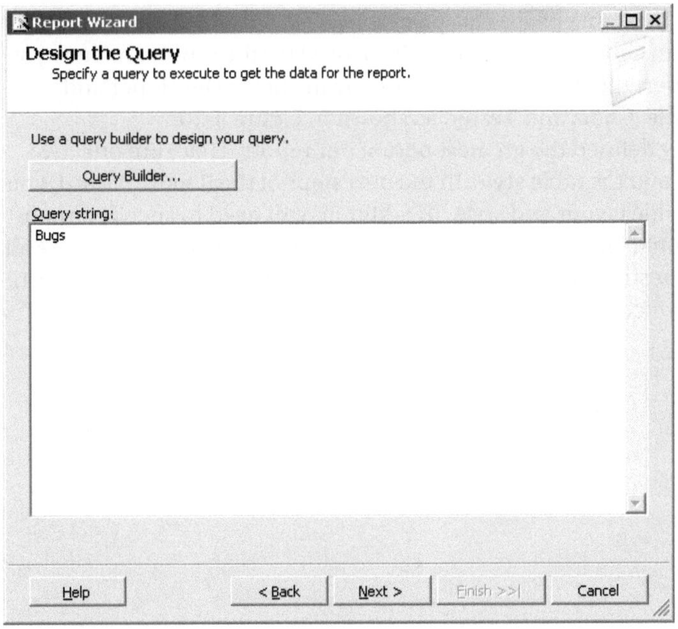

Figure 3-18. *Design the Query page*

The next page is the Select the Report Type page. This page will let you choose between a tabular report and a matrix report, as shown in Figure 3-19. We will choose the tabular report type and click Next.

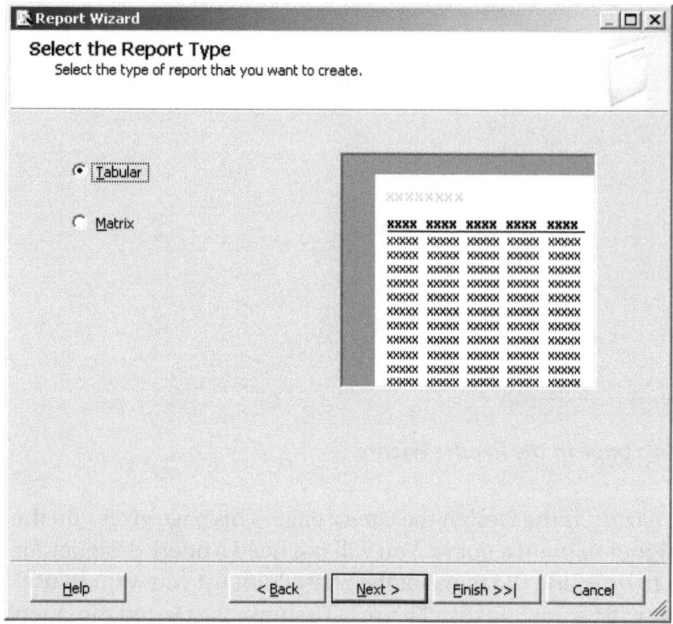

Figure 3-19. *Select the Report Type page*

The next page is the Design the Table page. This page shows all available fields from the Bugs SharePoint list. Here you can choose which fields will be used for the report and how you want to use them. We want a report that groups information by the fields Developer and Priority and shows the details Title, Code, and Tester, as shown in Figure 3-20.

At this point we have already defined the greatest part of our report. There are only two things left to do: the table layout and the table style. In the next steps of the Report Wizard, you will get the chance to choose a table layout and style. In addition, you need to specify a report server URL and the name you would like to give to your freshly made report. These steps are all very simple; therefore, we will not show them. When you are done and have created a report, you can be proud of the result, which will resemble Figure 3-21.

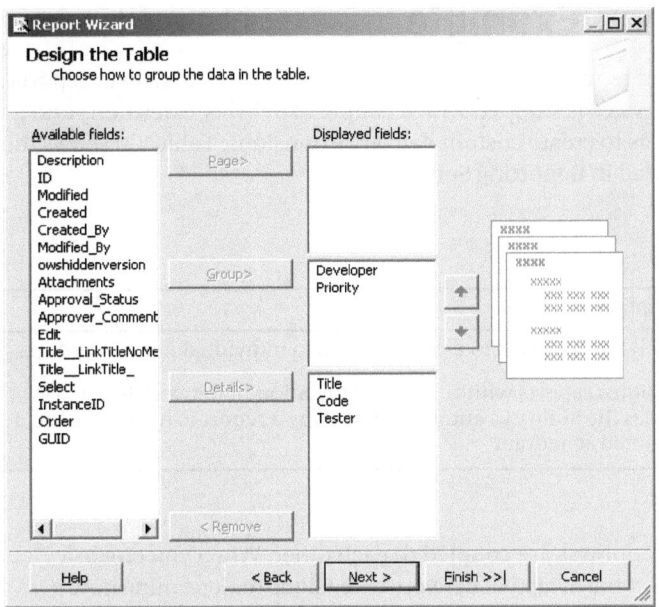

Figure 3-20. *Design the Table page*

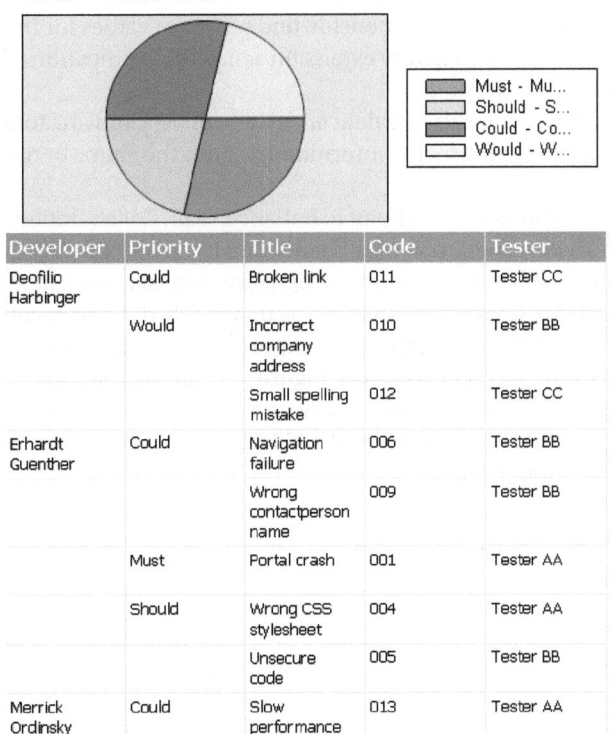

Figure 3-21. *Bugs report made with the SharePoint list data extension*

Delivering Extension Example

After having created and published reports, you can use Reporting Services to deliver reports to various locations. Reporting Services is shipped with a couple of delivery extensions and a delivery API that enables developers to create custom delivery extensions. Table 3-6 shows the delivery extensions that are included in Reporting Services.

Table 3-6. *Delivery Extensions*

Name	Description
Report Server E-Mail	Uses an SMTP server to e-mail reports to individual users or groups.
Report Server File Share	Distributes reports within your organization to network file shares. Provides the ability to automatically copy a report to a file share on a designated schedule.

Delivery extensions and subscriptions are coupled to each other. When you create a subscription, you can choose one of the available delivery extensions to determine how a report is delivered.

In Reporting Services, subscriptions are stored in the report server database. When events occur, Reporting Services matches the event against subscriptions contained in the report server database. For each subscription tied to the event, the report server creates a notification. For data-driven subscriptions, a notification is created for each recipient. Once a notification is created, the report server invokes a particular delivery extension and passes in values for the extension settings specified in the notification. The delivery extension sends the notification to the user as specified by the selected delivery extension.

Delivery extensions implement the Reporting Services delivery extension API and are able to receive notifications from the report server and provide information about the status of the notification.

The MSDN article "Deliver SQL Server Reports to SharePoint to Enhance Team Collaboration" by Ed Hild explains how to create a custom delivery extension for SharePoint. It can be found at the following location: http://msdn.microsoft.com/msdnmag/issues/06/03/ReportingServices/. In this chapter we will not discuss how to create delivery extensions, as this article does an excellent job of that. It explains how people subscribe to weekly status reports that are delivered to a SharePoint document library via a custom delivery extension. Figure 3-22 shows the New Subscription page of the Report Manager, which allows you to choose a method of delivery. In this example we have chosen to use the custom delivery method SPS Library Delivery, which is able to deliver reports to SharePoint document libraries.

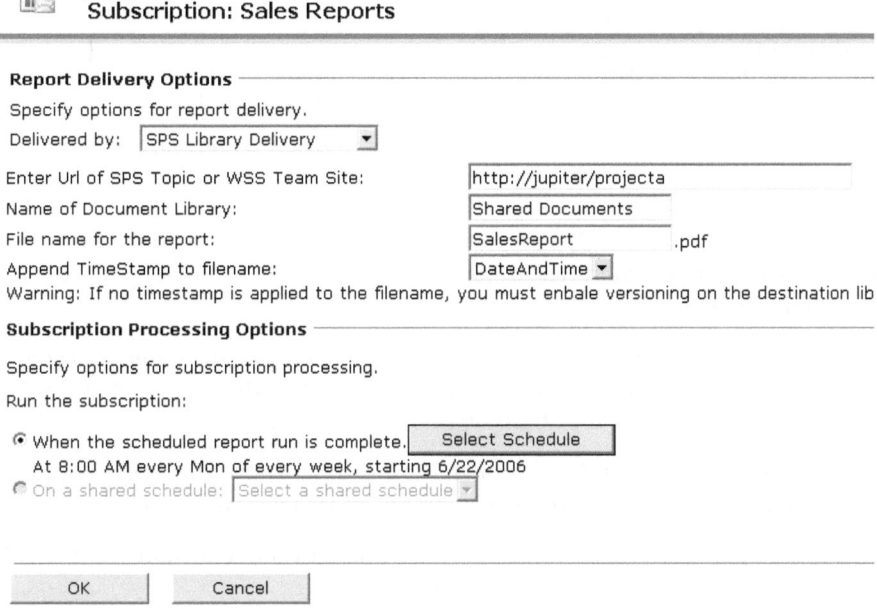

Figure 3-22. *New Subscription page in the Report Manager*

SQL Server Report Pack for SharePoint Portal Server 2003

You can download a SQL Server Report Pack that contains eight reports from the Microsoft web site for SharePoint Portal Server 2003. In this section we will use the Report Pack in combination with SQL Server 2005 Reporting Services, although it works with SQL Server 2000 as well.

The eight reports included in the Report Pack work with a sample database that contains information extracted from a SharePoint Portal Server 2003 server. This database can be populated with data extracted from your own SharePoint Portal Server environment using the included Data Extraction Program (DEP). The DEP will read the current SharePoint Portal Server data and uses the SharePoint object model to do so.

Another interesting possibility is the parsing of the Windows SharePoint Services log files. The easiest way to parse IIS log files is to install and use the Log Parser, which adds the data to the database. Table 3-7 shows the download links.

Table 3-7. *Download Links for SQL Server Report Pack*

Tool	Link
SQL Server Report Pack for SharePoint Portal Server 2003	http://www.microsoft.com/downloads/ details.aspx?familyid=49159368-544B-4B09-8EED-4844B4E33D3D&displaylang=en#Requirements
Log Parser 2.2	http://www.microsoft.com/technet/scriptcenter/tools/ logparser/default.mspx

You can also use the sample reports as templates for designing new reports. The Report Pack includes the following reports:

Storage Report: This report shows a listing of the virtual servers and the number of collections, sites, areas, lists, files, and sizes they have. The report also shows a size distribution and storage usage chart, and the top 20 sites based on their size.

Storage Trend Report: This report shows four charts illustrating the virtual server storage trend, site collection growth trend, area growth trend, and list growth trend.

Site Trend Report: This report shows hit counts for virtual servers, collections, areas, and lists. It also shows the top 20 sites based on hit counts.

Comprehensive Site Collections Report: This report shows the list of site collections, the site collection owners, the configurable characteristics about collection owners, and the date the collection was last accessed.

Detailed Site Collection Report: This report shows the top 20 accessed pages (based on hit count) for a site collection.

Detailed Page Report: This report shows which users have access to a page, when users last accessed a page, the referrer URLs, and the total number of hits per user. In addition, the report shows two charts illustrating user distribution and referrer distribution.

Best Bet Keyword: This report shows the top 20, the top 10, the bottom 10, or the bottom 20 keywords used for searching. This report also shows which keywords have best bets associated to them.

Search Terms: This report shows the top 20, the top 10, the bottom 10, or the bottom 20 search terms used for searching. In addition, the report shows which search terms match with a defined keyword. Figure 3-23 is taken from the Report Pack documentation and shows a sample report.

To be able to run the Report Pack, your system must meet the following requirements:

- SQL Server 2000 SP3a or later. In this section, we use SQL Server 2005.

- SQL Server 2000 Reporting Services SP1 or SQL Server 2005 Reporting Services.

- Internet Information Server Log Parser utility.

- SharePoint Portal Server 2003.

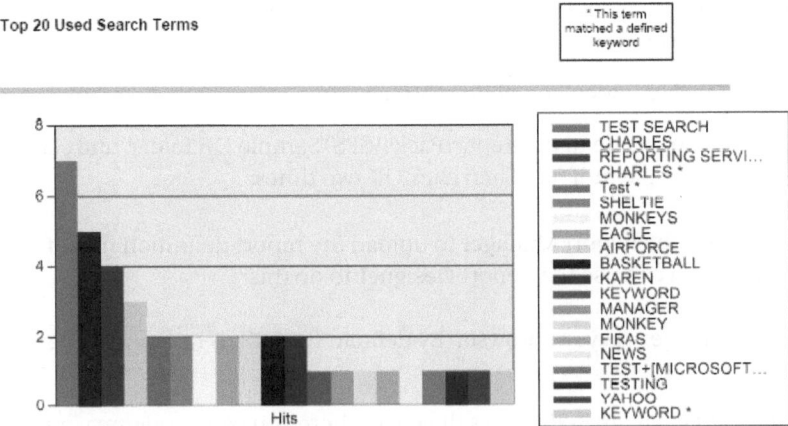

Figure 3-23. *Sample report of top 20 search terms*

To install the Report Pack files to your hard drive, double-click the installation file that you downloaded (SQLReportPackSPS.msi). The default location of the Report Pack files is [drive letter]:\Program Files\Report packs\SPS. The installation wizard offers the opportunity to specify what parts of the Report Pack you want to install, as shown in Figure 3-24.

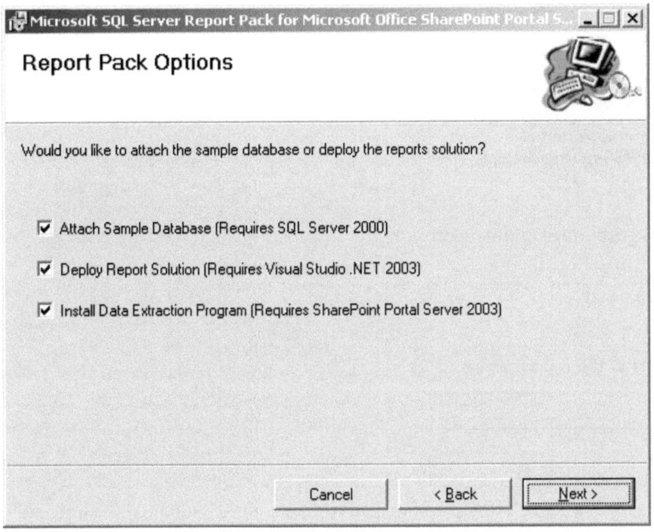

Figure 3-24. *The Report Pack installation wizard*

When you are using SQL Server 2005, as we did, you can choose to attach the sample database via the installation wizard. Be careful not to do this, as it will not work properly. The wizard will create a new database, but it will not fill the database with test data. Instead, you should attach the database by making use of the SQL Server Management Studio. Follow the next steps to attach the database:

1. Open the SQL Server Management Studio via Start ➤ All Programs ➤ Microsoft SQL Server 2005 ➤ SQL Server Management Studio.

2. Right-click the Databases folder, and choose Attach.

3. Click the Add button, navigate to the ReportPacks\SPS\Sample DB folder, and select the dbSPSReportingSample.mdf file. Then click OK two times.

Next, we are going to use the Report Manager to upload the report definition files of the Report Pack. Alternatively, you can use the Report Designer to do this:

1. Go to the Report Manager via your browser. By default, the URL is http://[server]/reports.

2. Click New Data Source. Figure 3-25 shows the page where you can configure your new data source.

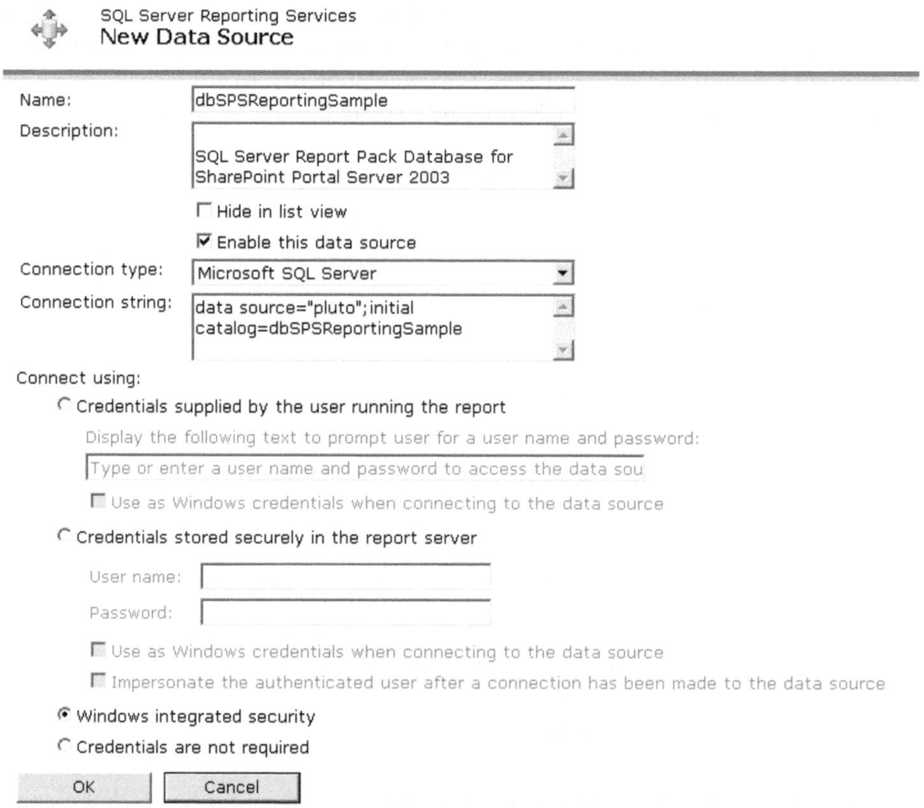

Figure 3-25. *New Data Source page in the Report Manager*

3. Enter a value for the Name field—for example, dbSPSReportingSample.

4. Enter a value for the Description field. This field is optional.

5. Check the check box Enable This Datasource.

6. Select the value Microsoft SQL Server in the Connection Type drop-down list.

7. The value for the connection string field is the following:

```
data source="[sqlserver]";initial catalog=dbSPSReportingSample
```

8. Select the Windows NT Integrated Security radio button.

9. Click OK to save the data source.

To add a sample report to the Report Manager, follow the next steps:

1. Click Upload File in the Report Manager. This will open the Upload File page, as shown in Figure 3-26. Click the Browse button to go to the folder with the sample report files. By default this will be the [drive letter]:\Program Files\Report Packs\SPS\Report Definition Files folder.

Figure 3-26. *Upload File page in the Report Manager*

2. Choose a report to upload and click Open.

3. Click OK to open the report file.

4. Click the name of the report to open it.

The last thing that we are going to show is how to load the database with our own Share-Point data. First we are going to create and configure the reporting and staging databases that we are going to need. The purpose of the staging database is to hold the latest data temporarily until it can be placed into the reporting database. The reporting database contains the stored procedures that are used to place the data from the staging database into the reporting database.

1. Open the SQL Server Management Studio. Go to Start ➤ All Program ➤ Microsoft SQL Server 2005, and click SQL Server Management Studio.

2. In the Object Explorer, right-click the name of your server and choose New Query.

3. Open the dbSPSReportingStaging.sql to create the staging database. By default this file is located at [drive letter]:\Program Files\Report Packs\SPS\SQL Scripts. You have to modify line 6 of this file and enter the correct path of the SQL Server DATA Directory. By default, this is [drive letter]:\Program Files\Microsoft SQL Server\MSSQL.1\MSSQL\Data. Click Execute on the SQL Editor toolbar to execute the query.

4. Open the dbSPSReporting.sql to create the staging database. By default this file is located at [drive letter]:\Program Files\Report Packs\SPS\SQL Scripts. You have to modify line 6 of this file and enter the correct path of the SQL Server DATA Directory. By default this is [drive letter]:\Program Files\Microsoft SQL Server\MSSQL.1\MSSQL\Data. Click Execute on the SQL Editor toolbar to execute the query.

5. In the Object Explorer select Databases. Right-click, and choose refresh.

6. Right-click the dbSPSReporting database in the Object Explorer and choose New Query. Run the Load_Dims_Null.sql, DateGenerator_dim.sql, and time_dim.sql to populate the dim tables of the reporting database with their default values.

To make use of the Data Extraction Program you will need to modify its configuration file. The name of this configuration file is RPDataExtraction.exe.config and it is located by default at [drive letter]:\Program Files\Report Packs\SPS\Data Extraction. Open the configuration file with a text editor, such as Notepad. The RPDataExtraction.exe.config looks like this:

```xml
<?xml version="1.0" encoding="utf-8"?>
<configuration>
  <!-- IMPORTANT:  All keys are required unless they are noted as optional -->
  <appSettings>
    <!-- This is the path to the WSS logs -->
    <add key="WSSPath" value="WSS"/>
    <!-- This is the path to the IIS logs -->
    <add key="IISPath" value="IIS"/>
    <!-- This is the path to the Log Parser application -->
    <add key="LogParserPath" ➥
      value="C:\Program Files\Log Parser 2.2\LogParser.exe" />
    <!-- This is the ip address or hostname of
      the SQL server used for reporting -->
    <add key="DatabaseServer" value="pluto" />
    <!-- This is the name of the Staging Database -->
    <add key="StagingDatabase" value="dbSPSReportingStaging" />
    <!-- This is the name of the Reporting Database -->
    <add key="ReportingDatabase" value=" dbSPSReporting" />
    <!-- This is the search term used to filter
      search crawl hits from the WSS logs -->
    <add key="SearchAgent" value="MS Search 4.0 Robot" />
    <!-- This is the key of the first property
      to extract from the site owner's user profile -->
    <add key="Property1" value="Title" />
```

```
    <!-- This is the key of the second property
      to extract from the site owner's user profile -->
    <add key="Property2" value="WorkEmail" />
    <!-- This is the key of the third property to extract
      from the site owner's user profile -->
    <add key="Property3" value="WorkPhone" />
    <!-- This is the url to the portal site
      (optional, used to get user profile data for wss sites) -->
    <add key="MainPortalURL" value="http://pluto:85/" />
    <!-- This tells the application whether to pause
      before closing on an application error (optional) -->
    <add key="PauseOnError" value="false" />
    <!-- This tells the application whether to pause
      before closing (optional) -->
    <add key="PauseOnComplete" value="false" />
    <!-- This is the path to the application's log file (optional) -->
    <add key="LogFilePath" value="RPDataExtraction.log" />
  </appSettings>
</configuration>
```

The basic keys you have to configure are WSSPath, IISPath, LogParserPath, DatabaseServer, StagingDatabase, and ReportingDatabase. You have to pay attention to the first two keys in the configuration file: the WSSPath and IISPath keys that refer to the paths of the WSS and IIS logs. You have to create specific directories for these two logs on the same server where you want to run the Data Extraction Program. These paths can be relative or absolute. If a relative path is chosen, it assumes the path where the Data Extraction Program is installed as its base. An example is [drive letter]:\Program Files\Report Packs\SPS\Data Extraction.

Next you should install the IIS Log Parser. Double-click the installation file (LogParser.msi) and follow the instructions. We are going to use the Data Extraction Program that extracts data from SharePoint Portal Server 2003. This program will also parse the Windows SharePoint Services and IIS logs to populate the reporting database.

If you want to have data for the Site Trend Report, you have to turn on usage analysis logging. Follow the next steps to do this:

1. Go to your portal and click Site Settings.

2. Under General Settings, click Go to SharePoint Portal Server Central Administration.

3. Under Component Configuration, click Configure Usage Analysis Processing.

4. Select Enable Logging and click OK, as shown in Figure 3-27.

If you want to analyze the IIS and WSS log files, you should copy them to the directories specified in the Data Extraction Program configuration file. There are two ways to do this: manually or via a sample batch file called copylogs.bat. If you want to use the copylogs.bat file, you have to modify the paths in the batch file to suit the conditions on your server. By default, the copylogs.bat file is located at [drive letter]:\Program Files\Report Packs\SPS\Data Extraction. The copylogs.bat file contains documentation explaining how to modify the batch file.

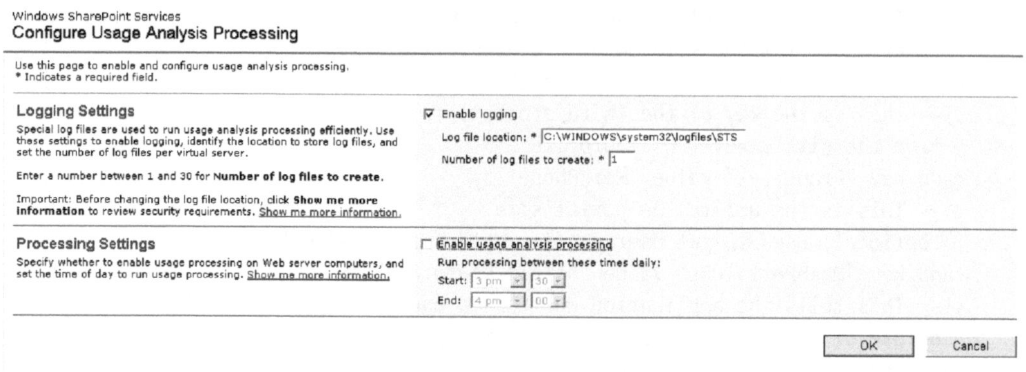

Figure 3-27. *Configure Usage Analysis Processing page in SharePoint*

If you want to copy the log files manually, you need to copy the IIS log files from their original location. By default, this is [drive letter]:\WINDOWS\system32\LogFiles. Copy the log files to the path specified in the Data Extraction Program configuration file, for example, [drive letter]:\ Program Files\Report Packs\SPS\Data Extraction\IIS. Under the IIS folder, you need to create subfolders for each front-end web server in the SharePoint server farm. Name each subfolder after the machine name of the front-end web server. Underneath each machine name, create a subfolder for each IIS Website identifier. Such names start with W3SVC, for example, W3SVC87257621.

You also have to copy the WSS log files to a path that is defined in the configuration file of the Data Extraction Program. By default, the WSS log files are located at [drive letter]:\ WINDOWS\system32\LogFiles\STS. You can change this location via the Configure Usage Analysis Processing page of SharePoint central administration (see Figure 3-27). In the WSS log destination location, create a subfolder for every machine on each front-end web server in the SharePoint server farm.

After copying the logs, you can either choose to manually execute the Data Extraction Program to collect data or you can schedule data collection by defining a scheduled task using the Scheduled Tasks folder in the Control Panel. In our opinion, it is best to create a scheduled task that runs the Data Extraction Program every day during off-hours.

Note Because of a bug in the SQL Server Report Pack, you will probably receive the following error during the execution of the Data Extraction Program: System.Data.SqlClient.SqlException. Microsoft has released a Knowledge Base article that explains how to fix this. You can find this article, "Bug: You Receive a System. Data.SqlClient.SqlException Error Message When You Run the Data Extraction Program Tool (Rpdataextraction.exe), at the following link: http://support.microsoft.com/?kbid=906508.

Summary

In this chapter you learned what SQL Server 2005 Reporting Services is. You learned how to create a report using Business Intelligence Development Studio, and you learned which SharePoint Reporting web parts are available and how you should use them. We looked in detail at the architecture of reporting extensions, taking a closer look at creating custom data extensions and delivering extensions. Finally, we discussed what the SQL Server Report Pack for SharePoint Portal Server 2003 is and how you should use it.

CHAPTER 4

■■■

Windows Workflow Foundation

Windows Workflow Foundation enables developers to create workflow-enabled applications. Out of the box, SharePoint 2003 does not contain extensive workflow capabilities. Windows Workflow Foundation can help to fill this gap by making it easy for developers to create their own workflows.

In this chapter we discuss what Windows Workflow Foundation is and how you can create a workflow using the Visual Studio 2005 Designer for Windows Workflow Foundation. After that, we will create a workflow and a custom activity to get you familiar with the technology. Finally, we explain how to create a custom workflow and use it in a Windows SharePoint Services 2003 environment.

Getting to Know Windows Workflow Foundation

Windows Workflow Foundation is a part of .NET Framework 3.0 (code named WinFX). It is a new framework for building workflow-enabled applications in a visual manner, by creating a graphical model representing a workflow.

Note Building applications by creating a graphical model is also known as *model-driven development*. Windows Workflow Foundation implements a domain-specific language for creating workflows. If you want to learn more about domain-specific languages, refer to Chapter 5.

Windows Workflow Foundation contains an in-process workflow engine and tools to create workflows and is available for several different platforms: Windows Vista, Windows XP, and any member of the Windows Server 2003 family as part of the .NET Framework 3.0 Runtime Components. The Windows Vista operating system will be released at the end of 2006 and will be shipped with .NET Framework 3.0.

Windows Workflow Foundation is one of the three key technologies that make up .NET Framework 3.0; the other two technologies are Windows Presentation Foundation (WPF) and Windows Communication Foundation (WCF). WPF is a new presentation framework for Windows. It contains features that make it easier to create user interfaces and work with 2D and 3D drawing, fixed and adaptive documents, vector graphics, raster graphics, animation, data binding, audio, and video.

WCF is a new framework for building connected systems that combines and unifies previous connection systems, such as web services, Web Services Enhancements, .NET remoting, .NET Enterprise Services, and System.Messaging.

With Windows Workflow Foundation it is possible to support all kinds of workflow scenarios, such as business application workflows or document-centric workflows. Later in the chapter in section "Creating Workflows for SharePoint 2003," we will discuss the creation of document-centric workflows for SharePoint environments using Windows Workflow Foundation.

Creating a workflow graphically instead of writing code has many benefits. It is easier to understand workflows than code because workflows are a visual representation of the process. Because of this, it is easy to convey the meaning of a workflow to the customer. Another advantage is that changes to the workflow can be implemented via configuration instead of via code. This makes visually created workflows a lot easier to manage than workflows created in code. In the following sections, we will delve deeper into the concepts related to Windows Workflow Foundation.

Activities

We will start with taking a look at the basic structure of a workflow. A workflow consists of a set of activities that form a model to describe a real-world problem. Activities are the building blocks of a workflow; every single step within a workflow requires an activity. Windows Workflow Foundation utilizes three different kinds of activities:

Simple activity. A simple activity represents a simple action in its most basic form. An example of such a simple activity is the DelayActivity.

Composite activity. A composite activity is an activity that aggregates one or more child activities within a single activity. An example of such a composite activity is the IfElse activity.

Rule activity. A rule activity drives the flow of a workflow. The rule activity is also called a *data-driven activity.* An example of this type of activity is the EventDriven activity.

Out of the box, the Windows Workflow Foundation framework contains a default set of activities that provide functionality for the creation of workflows that contain control flow, conditions, event handling, and state management, and are able to communicate with other applications and services. Table 4-1 shows the activities that are included out of the box in Windows Workflow Foundation.

Table 4-1. *Out of the Box Activities*

Name	Description
CallExternalMethodActivity	This activity is able to communicate with a local service and is often used in conjunction with the HandleExternalEvent activity.
CodeActivity	This activity lets you add custom logic to a workflow in the form of code written using VB.NET or C#.

Table 4-1. *Out of the Box Activities (Continued)*

Name	Description
CompensateActivity	If possible, this activity lets you undo actions that are already performed once an error occurs during workflow execution. If it is not possible to undo a given action, this activity can be used to call code that starts some kind of compensating action that responds to the workflow failure.
CompensationHandlerActivity	This activity aggregates one or more compensating activities. This activity is typically used in conjunction with CompensateActivity and TransactionScope activities.
ConditionedActivityGroup	This activity lets you aggregate one or more child activities that are executed conditionally. The child activities can be executed based on some kind of condition that applies to the ConditionedActivityGroup activity itself; it is also possible that a child activity is executed based on a condition that only applies to the child.
DelayActivity	This activity lets you incorporate delays into workflows that are based on time-out intervals.
EventDrivenActivity	This activity aggregates one or more activities that handle a specific event.
EventHandlersActivity	This activity allows you to associate events to response handlers.
EventHandlingScopeActivity	This activity aggregates child activities and decides if event handling is supported when those child activities are executed.
FaultHandlerActivity	This activity provides an exception-handling mechanism within workflows.
FaultHandlersActivity	This activity aggregates multiple child activities of type FaultHandlerActivity, thus providing an exception-handling mechanism within workflows.
HandleExternalEventActivity	This activity is able to communicate with a local service by handling an event that is raised by such a service and is often used in conjunction with the CallExternalMethod activity.
IfElseActivity	This activity supports the ability to add decisioning mechanisms to a workflow. Such activities test for a condition and perform activities that are a part of the first branch that matches the conditions.
IfElseBranchActivity	This activity represents a specific branch of an IfElseActivity activity.
InvokeWebServiceActivity	This activity allows you to add Web service communication within a workflow.
InvokeWorkflowActivity	This activity allows you to invoke another workflow within your workflow.
ListenActivity	This activity is a composite activity that aggregates child activities of the EventDriven activity type.
ParallelActivity	This activity can be used to add parallel processing power (multithreading) to your workflows. This activity allows you to add two or more child Sequence activities that are executed concurrently by the ParallelActivity activity.

Table 4-1. *Out of the Box Activities (Continued)*

Name	Description
PolicyActivity	This activity represents a collection of rules. Each rule within the collection consists of conditions and resulting actions.
ReplicatorActivity	This activity lets you create single child activities.
SequenceActivity	This activity lets you link multiple activities together that are to be executed sequentially.
SetStateActivity	This activity lets you specify a transition to a new state if you are creating a workflow that contains multiple states.
StateActivity	This activity lets you represent each separate state in a state machine type of workflow.
StateFinalizationActivity	This activity aggregates child activities that are executed whenever a StateActivity activity is finished executing.
StateInitializationActivity	This activity aggregates child activities that are executed upon entering a StateActivity activity.
SuspendActivity	This activity lets you temporarily suspend the operation of a workflow. You might want to do this if there is some kind of event or error condition that requires special attention.
SynchronizationScopeActivity	This activity aggregates activities that are executed sequentially in a synchronized domain.
TerminateActivity	This activity allows you to end workflow execution immediately. You might want to do this if an irrecoverable error condition occurs.
ThrowActivity	This activity is part of a larger exception-management framework that allows you to implement an error-handling mechanism in your workflows. This activity allows you to throw exceptions to signal unexpected conditions in your workflow.
TransactionScopeActivity	This activity allows you to implement an error-handling mechanism in your workflows.
WebServiceFaultActivity	This activity is used to represent errors that occur during communication with a Web service, thus allowing you to model such events.
WebServiceInputActivity	This activity is able to receive data from a web service. This activity is essential if you want to implement web service communication into your workflows.
WebServiceOutputActivity	This activity is able to respond to a web service request made during the interaction between a workflow and a web service to a workflow. This activity is essential if you want to implement two-way interaction between web services and workflows.
WhileActivity	This activity adds conditional logic to your workflows that enable a workflow to loop until a given condition is met.

If you design a workflow, you can choose to make use of one of the activities belonging to this default set or you can create your own activities. Developers are free to create their own custom activity libraries and use them in other workflows.

Activities can be sequential, in which case the order of workflow actions is specified at design time. Alternatively, activities can be event-driven. In such scenarios the order of workflow actions is determined at run time in response to external events. Each activity contains the following logic/data:

- Metadata responsible for describing design time properties of the activity.

- Instance data describing the activity run-time state.

- Activity behavior in the form of programmed execution logic.

- Validation logic that can be used to validate activity metadata. This is optional.

Figure 4-1 shows a basic workflow that consists of several activities and uses custom activity libraries.

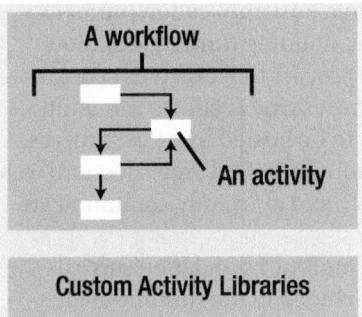

Figure 4-1. *Workflow with activities*

Components

Windows Workflow Foundation provides services as well as a framework and consists of the following components (see Figure 4-2):

Base activity library: This library contains all activities that are available out of the box. Activities are essential building blocks for creating custom workflows and are discussed in the previous section, "Activities."

Runtime engine: The workflow runtime engine is able to interpret and execute workflows created using Windows Workflow Foundation. The runtime engine is also responsible for keeping track of workflow state.

Runtime services: The Windows Workflow Foundation workflow runtime engine that hosts workflows can be hosted by different host applications. SharePoint is an example of such a host. This is a very flexible system, which is made possible via the workflow runtime services. The workflow runtime services are also responsible for handling any communication between the host application and the workflow.

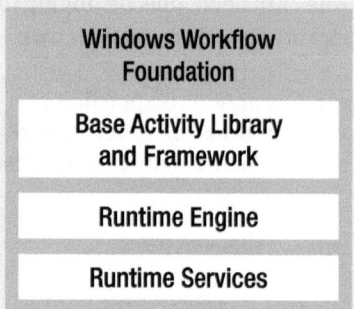

Figure 4-2. *Windows Workflow Foundation*

Windows Workflow Foundation is shipped with a couple important tools that facilitate workflow creation: a visual designer and a debugger. Both of them are integrated into Visual Studio 2005 and are discussed later in this chapter, in the sections "Visual Studio 2005 Designer for Windows Workflow Foundation" and "Debugging a Workflow."

The workflow runtime engine is hosted in-process within a host application (never as a stand-alone process) and is responsible for creating and maintaining running workflow instances. Per application domain (in .NET, the fundamental process that executes code) there can be only one workflow runtime engine. A workflow runtime engine is able to run multiple workflow instances concurrently. The runtime engine needs to be hosted by a host process, such as console applications, Windows form-based applications, ASP.NET web sites, and web services. Because a workflow is hosted in-process, it can easily and efficiently communicate with its host application.

The workflow runtime engine utilizes many Windows Workflow Foundation services when a workflow instance runs. The following services are included in the runtime engine:

- Execution

- Tracking

- State management

- Scheduler

- Rules

Besides the runtime engine itself, Windows Workflow Foundation contains multiple runtime services. Runtime services are pluggable, so applications can provide these services in unique ways within their execution environment. Table 4-2 shows an overview of the runtime services that are provided out of the box with Windows Workflow Foundation.

Table 4-2. *Runtime Services*

Name	Description
Persistence	The persistence service is responsible for saving and loading state data to and from a persistent data store, such as a SQL Server database. Some workflows, called *persistent workflows,* need to be able to survive system reboots or run for a long period of time. Building such workflows is made easier by the Windows Workflow Foundation runtime services persistence service.
Communication	The communication service is responsible for handling the communication between a workflow and other applications, services, or workflows.
Timer	The timer service handles activities within workflows that are time-related. The DelayActivity, discussed previously in the section "Activities," is an excellent example of such an activity.
Tracking	The tracking service facilitates in the tracking and monitoring of the execution flow of workflows. The tracking service also enables you to persist this information to a data store, such as a log file or a SQL Server database.
Transaction	The transaction service facilitates the incorporation of transactions within custom workflows.
Threading	The threading service facilitates the inclusion of multithreaded operations within custom workflows.

Workflow Styles

Windows Workflow Foundation supports two styles of workflow: sequential and state machine workflows. Before you start creating a workflow project, it is important to figure out what style of workflow you want to use.

The *sequential* workflow style is used for repetitive operations such as designing a set of activities that must always be performed in the same order. The workflow follows the sequence until the last activity is completed, and the workflow always remains in control of what happens next. Such workflows are not necessarily entirely deterministic; you can use branching logic such as IfElse activities or Parallel activities and let the exact sequence of events vary. For example, imagine you are creating a workflow that describes the process of installing software. This is a typical scenario where you always follow the steps one by one and in the same order. Therefore you can represent this process using a sequential workflow. Figure 4-3 shows an example sequential workflow.

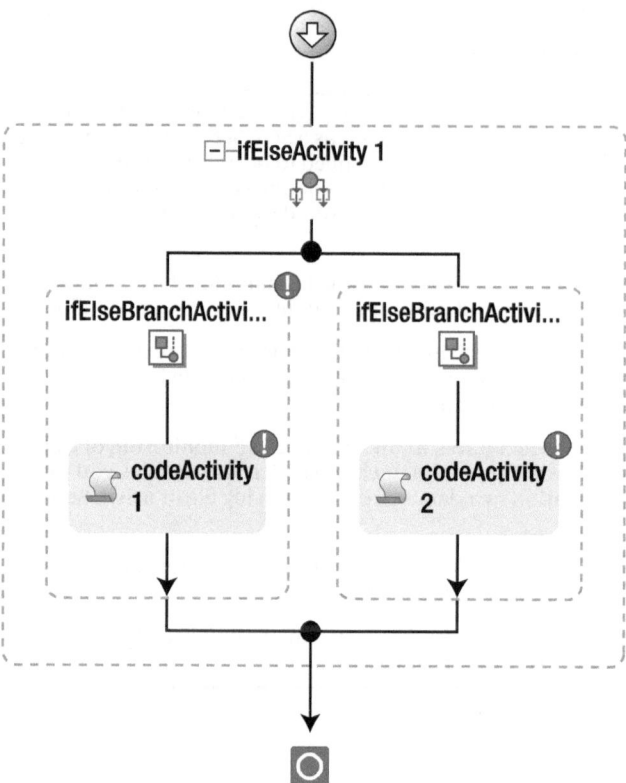

Figure 4-3. *Sequential workflow*

The *state machine* workflow style is used when you want to model your workflow as a state machine. State machine workflows are made up of different states, one of those being the starting state, which always is the state that is entered once the workflow process begins. Each state can receive a certain set of events. Based on these events, the workflow can transition from one state to another state. In state machine workflows, the end-user is always in control. That is why this type of workflow is also known as *human-oriented workflow*. It is not required to define a final state, but if you do happen to have a final state in a workflow and the transition is made to this state, the workflow will end.

An example of a state machine workflow is an online shop where one of the states of the workflow process describes the situation where the customer can submit an order and wait for approval of the credit card data. Another state in the workflow process describes the situation where the customer, for the time being, is satisfied with selecting a couple of products and wants to place the order at a later time. Therefore, each customer finds himself in one of the states in the workflow process and goes to another state depending on his choices. Figure 4-4 shows a state machine workflow.

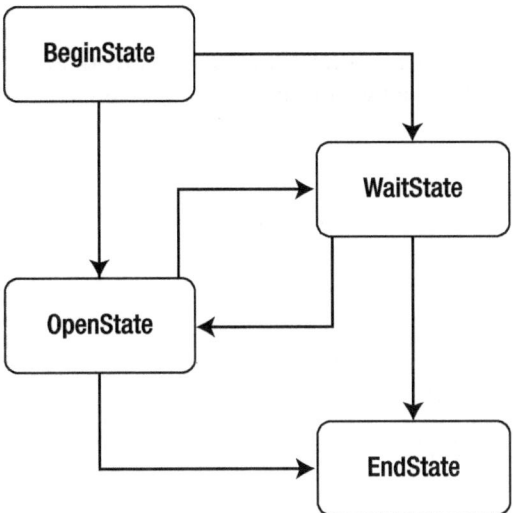

Figure 4-4. *State machine workflow*

Installing Windows Workflow Foundation

Before we can get into the details of creating workflows using Windows Workflow Foundation, we will first discuss the installation process. To install Windows Workflow Foundation, you will need a server with Windows Vista, Windows Server 2003 SP1, or Windows XP SP2, and the RTM Release of Visual Studio 2005 or Visual Studio 2005 Express Edition.

You must first install the WinFX Runtime Components. At the time this book was written, the latest release of the WinFX Runtime Components was the February 2006 Community Technology Preview (CTP). The WinFX Runtime Components February 2006 CTP makes Windows Presentation Foundation, Windows Communication Foundation, and Windows Workflow Foundation available for Windows XP and Windows Server 2003. This way, developers are able to experiment with the early builds of these technologies and will get used to the development experience.

You can download the WinFX Runtime Components February 2006 CTP at http://www.microsoft.com/downloads. You can choose to either download only the download file (winfxsetup.exe) or the entire package (winfxrc.exe). You will need an Internet connection when you use the download file for installation; if you want to install WinFX when you are not online, you should use the entire package for installation instead.

After installing the WinFX Runtime Components, you need to install the Visual Studio 2005 Extensions for Windows Workflow Foundation Beta 2. Visual Studio 2005 Extensions for Windows Workflow Foundation Beta 2 provides support to developers for building Windows Workflow Foundation applications and is used in combination with .NET Framework 2.0 and WinFX Runtime Components.

You can download the Visual Studio 2005 Extensions for Windows Workflow Foundation Beta 2_2(EN).exe at http://www.microsoft.com/downloads. When you install the Visual Studio 2005 Extensions, you can choose to install the following components (see Figure 4-5):

- Windows Workflow SDK.

- Visual Studio 2005 Designer for Windows Workflow Foundation. Windows Workflow Foundation will be automatically installed if it is not yet installed on the server.

- Windows Workflow Foundation Debugger.

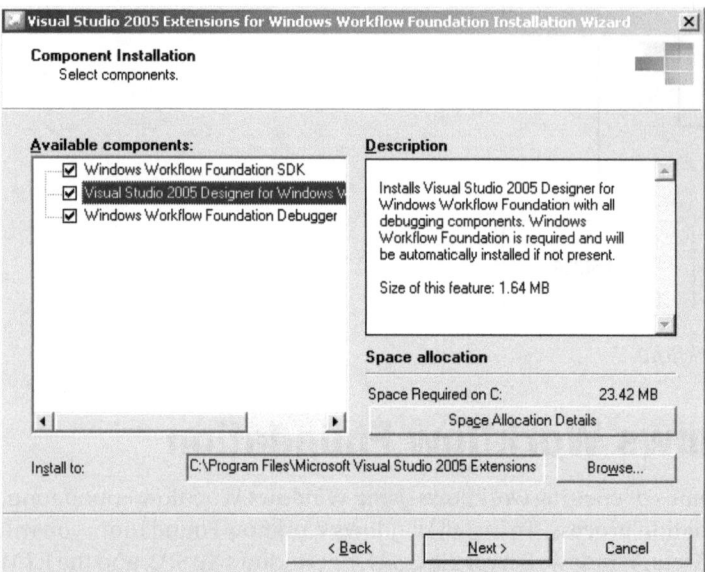

Figure 4-5. *The Visual Studio 2005 Extensions for Windows Workflow Foundation Installation Wizard*

Visual Studio 2005 Designer for Windows Workflow Foundation

After you install Visual Studio 2005 Extensions for Windows Workflow Foundation, a new project type will appear on the Project Types pane of the Visual Studio .NET File New dialog window. This new project type is called Workflow (see Figure 4-6).

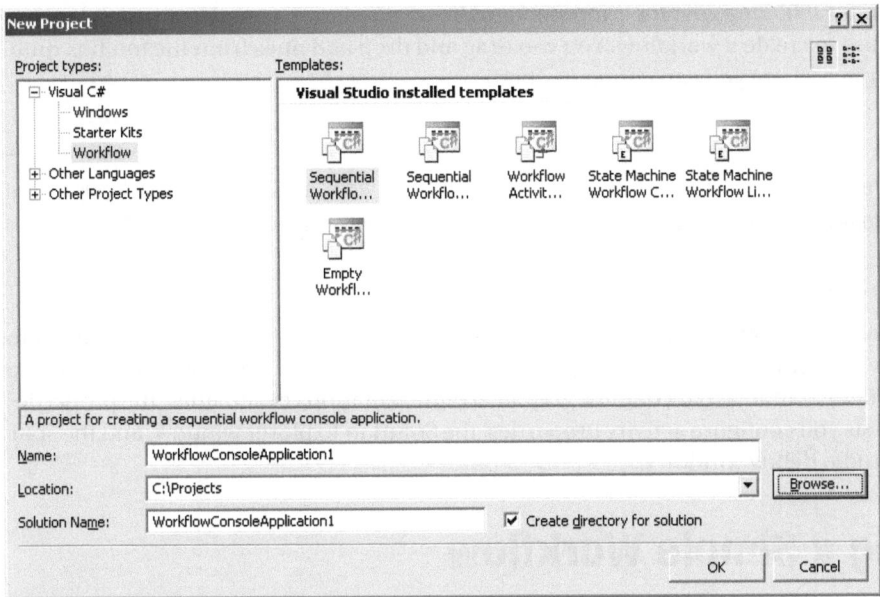

Figure 4-6. *The File New dialog window*

The Project Types section contains the following Visual Studio .NET 2005 project templates:

Sequential Workflow Console Application: This project is a starting point for creating sequential workflows hosted by a console host application.

Sequential Workflow Library: This project is a starting point for creating your own sequential workflows in the form of a library (.dll).

Workflow Activity Library: This project is a starting point for creating your own activities that can be reused later as building blocks in a workflow.

State Machine Workflow Console Application: This project is a starting point for creating state machine workflows hosted by a console host application.

State Machine Workflow Library: This project is a starting point for creating your own state machine workflow in the form of a library (.dll).

Empty Workflow Project: This project is an unconfigured workflow project that can include multiple workflows and/or activities.

Visual Studio 2005 Designer for Windows Workflow Foundation contains a visual designer that you can use to create a workflow. You can drag and drop activities from the toolbox onto the design surface where you can configure them.

■**Note** You are now looking at a domain-specific language (DSL) at work. A DSL is a concept closely related to software factories. If you want to find out more about software factories and DSLs, refer to Chapter 5.

The Visual Studio 2005 Designer for Windows Workflow Foundation should be familiar to experienced Visual Studio users. Besides the design surface, there are other windows available such as the toolbox window that contains graphical representations of activities, the properties window that lets you configure activity properties, the Solution Explorer window, and the standard Visual Studio debug windows.

Creating a Simple Workflow

To get you up and running, this section explains how to create a workflow. The first workflow you are going to create is going to be very simple. You will create a workflow that asks for your name and says hello. This simple workflow uses conditional execution to determine whether your name is Bob. If it is, the workflow will recognize you; if it is not, the workflow will think of you as a stranger. The first thing you need to do is to create a new workflow project by following these steps:

1. Click Start ➤ All Programs ➤ Microsoft Visual Studio 2005 ➤ Microsoft Visual Studio 2005, to open Visual Studio 2005.

2. Click File ➤ New ➤ Project and select the Workflows project type, then choose the following template: Sequential Workflow Console Application.

3. Give the workflow the following name: HelloWorkflow. Then click OK.

We have chosen to create a sequential workflow console application because this template generates a workflow scheme that is hosted within a console application, which makes it easy to test our workflow. Since workflows cannot be executed directly, you will need some kind of host to test a workflow.

You can pass parameters to a workflow. Those parameters are mapped to workflow properties whose names have to be identical to the parameter names. Under the cover, workflows are represented by classes that inherit from the activity base class located in the System.Workflow.ComponentModel namespace; so parameters are eventually mapped to class properties.

The default view selected in the workflow project is the workflow design view of a default workflow item that is called workflow1.cs. On the left side of your Visual Studio editor, in the design view, you will see the Toolbox that contains activities related to this type of workflow. Follow these steps to create the example workflow:

1. Drag a CodeActivity from the Toolbox onto the design view.

2. Select the CodeActivity, and in the Properties window, select the Name property and give the CodeActivity the following name: question.

3. Drag an IfElseActivity from the toolbox onto the design view directly below the CodeActivity.

4. Select the IfElseActivity, and in the Properties window, select the Name property and give the IfElseActivity the following name: decideGreeting.

5. Select the left IfElseBranchActivity and in the Properties window, select the Name property and give the IfElseBranchActivity the following name: bobBranch.

6. Select the right IfElseBranchActivity and in the Properties window, select the Name property and give the IfElseBranchActivity the following name: strangerBranch.

7. Drag a CodeActivity from the Toolbox onto the design view below the left IfElseBranchActivity (bobBranch).

8. Select the CodeActivity, and in the Properties window select the Name property and give the CodeActivity the following name: HelloBob.

9. Drag a CodeActivity from the Toolbox onto the design view below the right IfElseBranchActivity (strangerBranch).

10. Select the CodeActivity and in the Properties window, select the Name property and give the CodeActivity the following name: HelloStranger.

Figure 4-7 shows the sequential workflow you have just made. You will notice the presence of several exclamation signs in the workflow. This means that there is some additional information required to make these activities work.

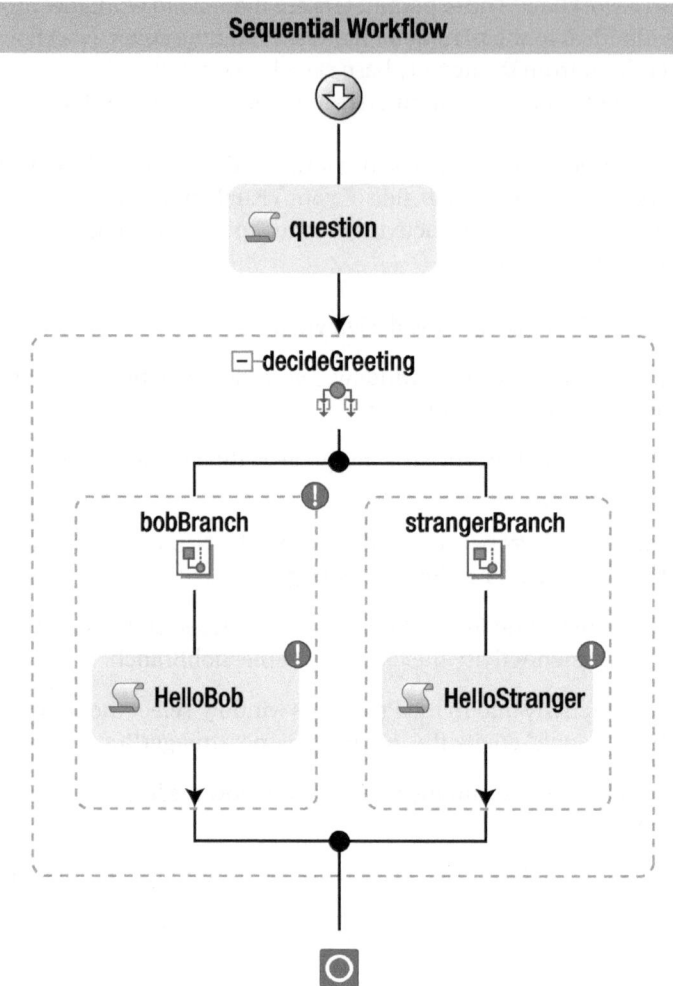

Figure 4-7. *Sequential workflow example*

Next we are going to add a parameter to the workflow. We can do this by going to the code view of workflow1.cs, right-clicking workflow1.cs, and selecting View Code. You must add the following code:

```
string strFirstname;

public string Firstname
{
  get { return strFirstname; }
  set { strFirstname = value; }
}
```

We are going back to the design view of our workflow to add some code to the CodeActivity shapes:

1. Double-click the question CodeActivity.

2. Add the following code:

```
Console.WriteLine("Hi, what is your name?");
Firstname = Console.ReadLine();
```

3. Go back to the design view of the workflow and double-click the HelloBob CodeActivity.

4. Add the following code:

```
Console.WriteLine("Hello Bob");
Console.ReadLine();
```

5. Go back to the design view of the workflow and double-click the HelloStranger CodeActivity.

6. Add the following code:

```
Console.WriteLine("Hello Stranger");
Console.ReadLine();
```

The last thing you need to do is to add code to the bobBranch activity. Follow the next steps:

1. Select the bobBranch activity and go to the Properties window.

2. Select System.Workflow.Activities.Rules.RuleConditionReference in the `Condition` property.

3. Expand the `Condition` property and give the `ConditionName` property the following name: Bob

4. Click the button in the `Expression` property value; this will open the Rule Condition Editor window (see Figure 4-8).

5. Add the following code: `this.Firstname == "bob"` and click OK.

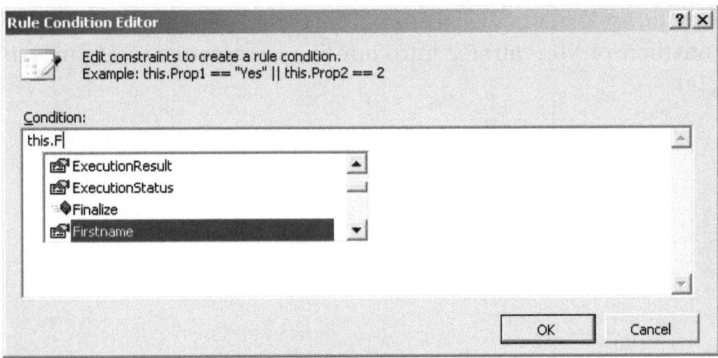

Figure 4-8. *Rule Condition Editor window*

If you want to run the workflow, just hit the F5 button.

Debugging a Workflow

When creating workflows there will come a time when the workflow does not act as expected, so you need to pay attention to workflow debugging techniques. Debugging a workflow works in much the same way as debugging programs that are written in other Visual Studio programming languages. It is possible to debug a workflow by attaching to a process, as shown in these steps:

1. Select Debug on the Menu bar in Visual Studio and click Attach to Process.

2. Select which process you want to attach to in the Attach to Process dialog window and click Attach.

3. Place breakpoints and run the workflow.

You can also debug a workflow by setting a breakpoint and hitting the F5 button. If you have a workflow dll and a workflow host application located in different Visual Studio projects, you must set the workflow dll project as the startup project when you want to debug the workflow using the F5 button. In such situations, you must also set the path to the host application in the workflow dll project's `Start external program` property.

You can place breakpoints in the code or in the design view. If you want to set a breakpoint in design view, you need to select the activity where you want to set a breakpoint, and then set the breakpoint by pressing F9 (see Figure 4-9).

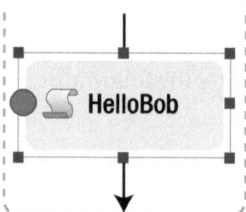

Figure 4-9. *Setting a breakpoint in the design view*

As the code reaches the breakpoint, Visual Studio .NET 2005 shows the activity containing the breakpoint and from there on you can step into code like you are used to. Figure 4-10 shows the breakpoint being hit.

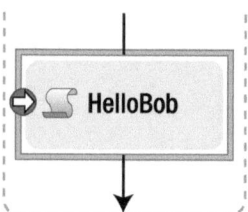

Figure 4-10. *Hitting a breakpoint in the design view*

Creating an Activity

To get familiar with every aspect of Windows Workflow Foundation, we are also going to create a simple activity. We will create an activity that will show a string in a message box. Follow these steps to create a custom activity:

1. Click File ➤ New ➤ Project and the New Project dialog window will open.

2. Choose to create a Workflow Activity Library and give it the following name: TestActivity. Click OK.

An *activity* is a class that ultimately inherits from the `System.Workflow.ComponentModel.Activity` base class. You can create an activity based on other existing activities by inheriting from a built-in activity, a custom activity, or an activity created by a third-party vendor. If you want to build an activity that is completely new, you need to inherit from the activity base class directly.

In the example described in this section, we are going to create a new activity that is a direct child of the base activity class. By default, the activity class that is made when you create a Workflow Activity Library project inherits from the `SequenceActivity` class. To change this, go to the code view of `Activity1.cs` and change the base class of `activity1` to `Activity`.

After compilation of the Workflow Activity Library project, an activity becomes available automatically on the toolbox, so users can drag and drop your activity onto the design view of a workflow. It is useful for an activity to have dependency properties. Dependency properties bind their values to relevant data that includes other properties in other activities that use this custom activity. Follow these steps to insert a dependency property.

1. Go to the code view of your activity class.

2. Right-click in the class and choose Insert Snippet.

3. Choose Workflow and press Tab.

4. Choose DependencyProperty – Property and press Tab (see Figure 4-11).

Figure 4-11. *Inserting the DependencyProperty – Property code snippet*

The following code listing shows the result of inserting this code snippet:

```
public static DependencyProperty MyPropertyProperty = ➥
    System.Workflow.ComponentModel.DependencyProperty.Register("MyProperty", ➥
    typeof(string), typeof(MyTestActivity));

[Description("This is the description which appears in the Property Browser")]
[Category("This is the category which will be displayed in the Property Browser")]
[Browsable(true)]
```

```
[DesignerSerializationVisibility(DesignerSerializationVisibility.Visible)]
public string MyProperty
{
  get
  {
    return ((string)(base.GetValue(MyTestActivity.MyPropertyProperty)));
  }
  set
  {
    base.SetValue(MyTestActivity.MyPropertyProperty, value);
  }
}
```

This code creates a static instance of the DependencyProperty type and defines a property (this time a member type, not a static type) that uses the DependencyProperty static instance as a key for retrieving the runtime value of the MyProperty property.

You need to give the static member the following name: MessageProperty. The name of the actual property (the member type) will be Message. You also need to change the [Description] and [Category] attributes of the property. The value of these attributes will be displayed in the Property Browser. Use the tab button to tab through the code snippet and customize the code so it is equal to the following code listing:

```
public static DependencyProperty MessageProperty = ➥
  System.Workflow.ComponentModel.DependencyProperty.Register("Message", ➥
  typeof(string), typeof(MyTestActivity));

[Description("Message")]
[Category("Parameters")]
[Browsable(true)]
[DesignerSerializationVisibility(DesignerSerializationVisibility.Visible)]
public string Message
{
  get
  {
    return ((string)(base.GetValue(MyTestActivity.MessageProperty)));
  }
  set
  {
    base.SetValue(MyTestActivity.MessageProperty, value);
  }
}
```

Lastly, you need to add an Execute() method. This method is a mediator that manages the core tasks of the workflow:

```
protected override ActivityExecutionStatus Execute ➥
  (ActivityExecutionContext executionContext)
{
  System.Windows.Forms.MessageBox.Show(Message);
  return ActivityExecutionStatus.Closed;
}
```

You can find the new custom activity on the Toolbox of the workflow solution used to develop the new activity (see Figure 4-12).

Figure 4-12. *Custom activity in Toolbox*

If you want to reuse this activity in another project, follow these steps:

1. Right-click in the Toolbox area and select Choose Items.

2. In the Choose Toolbox Items dialog window, click the Activities tab and click Browse.

3. Browse to your activity assembly and click Open.

4. Your activity will be mentioned in the list of activities and you can check the activity to include it on the Toolbox (see Figure 4-13).

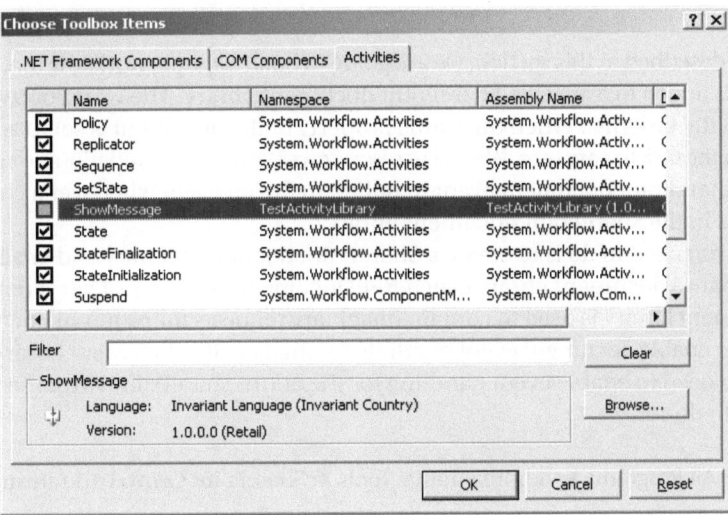

Figure 4-13. *Choose Toolbox Items dialog window*

Creating Workflows for SharePoint 2003

SharePoint 2003 is a huge improvement over SharePoint 2001. This does not mean to say that everybody was happy with SharePoint 2003 at first; people who just looked at the out-of-the-box workflow capabilities in SharePoint 2003 were disappointed. They were like taking a step back, compared to SharePoint 2001. But even 2001's workflow capabilities were not that great. The general perception was and is that the workflow capabilities of SharePoint 2003 are not satisfactory in most cases, a gap which has been filled by a range of third-party vendors.

It is possible to create your own custom workflows. SharePoint 2003 is shipped with the Event Sink API that allows you to make use of the SharePoint event model and provides custom handlers for the various events that fire because of some user action. Developers can create managed code assemblies that define handlers for these events and then bind the handlers to document libraries. The event handlers can call into the SharePoint object model to access the configuration and content databases directly. Event handlers can also be used to invoke external services; in such cases SharePoint can be used to display the information retrieved from other systems. The SharePoint Event Sink API offers an excellent opportunity to create advanced workflows using Windows Workflow Foundation.

Note You need to be aware that you can only use Windows Workflow Foundation in combination with Windows SharePoint Services 2003 environments, not in SharePoint Portal Server 2003 environments. This is caused by the fact that Windows Workflow Foundation requires the presence of .NET Framework 2.0, which is not supported in SharePoint Portal Server 2003 environments. If you want more information about this topic, refer to Chapter 1.

In the example described in this section, we are going to build a simple workflow that starts when a document is added to a specific SharePoint document library. The workflow will then create a new task in the tasks list. When the status property of the document is set to approved, the workflow will set the task to complete. We will use Windows Workflow Foundation to create the workflow and use SharePoint document event handling to fire an event whenever a change is made to documents in the SharePoint document library.

The first thing you need to do is to create a SharePoint document library and enable it for event handling. Create a document library called RFPDocuments. This is just a test name that indicates the document library is used to contain imaginary requests for proposal documents. You will also need to enable document event handling for this specific document library. If you want to do this, you need to enable event handling for the entire SharePoint virtual server. Follow these steps to do so:

1. Click Start ➤ All Programs ➤ Administrative Tools ➤ SharePoint Central Administration.

2. Click Configure Virtual Server Settings in the Virtual Server Configuration section.

3. Click the name of the virtual server you want to configure—in our case that will be Default Web Site.

4. Click Virtual Server General Settings in the Virtual Server Management section.

5. At the bottom of the Virtual Server General Settings page, go to the Event Handlers
   section and click On (see Figure 4-14). Click OK.

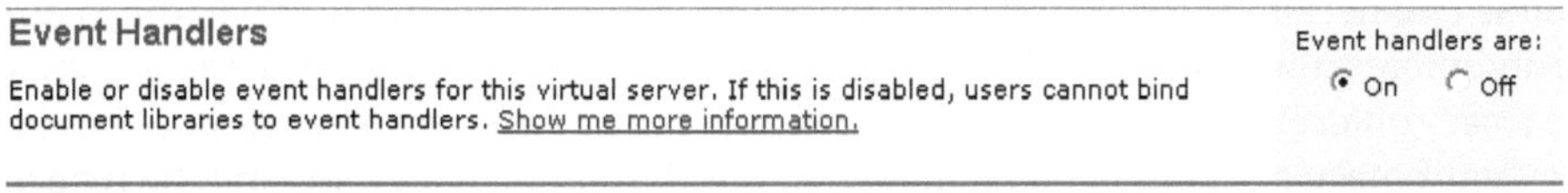

Event Handlers   Event handlers are:

Enable or disable event handlers for this virtual server. If this is disabled, users cannot bind   ⊙ On   ○ Off
document libraries to event handlers. Show me more information.

Figure 4-14. *The Event Handlers section on the Virtual Server General Settings page*

Next, create your own document event handler. Follow these steps:

1. Open Visual Studio 2005 and create a new class library by clicking File ➤ New ➤ Project.
   Choose to create a C# Class Library and give it the following name: MyWorkflowSolution.

2. Add a reference to the Microsoft.SharePoint assembly that can be found at [drive letter]:\
   Program Files\Common Files\Microsoft Shared\web server extensions\60\ISAPI.
   Right-click References in the Solution Explorer and choose Add Reference. Browse to
   the Microsoft.SharePoint assembly and click OK.

3. Add a reference to the System.Workflow.Runtime assembly that is located at
   [drive letter]:\Program Files\Reference Assemblies\Microsoft\WinFx\v3.0. Right-click
   References in the Solution Explorer and choose Add Reference. Browse to the
   System.Workflow.Runtime assembly and click OK.

4. Right-click the `class1.cs` and choose Rename. Give the class the following name:
   `RFPEvent.cs`.

The `RFPEvent` class has to implement the IListEventSink interface to be able to respond to
events within a SharePoint document library. The IListEventSink interface contains the
`OnEvent()` event handler. The `OnEvent()` event handler contains one parameter, a `Microsoft.`
`SharePoint.SPListEvent`. This method responds to one of the following changes that occur to
a document in a document library:

Checked in: A document is checked in to a document library.

Checked out: A document is checked out from a document library.

Check out cancelled: A check out is cancelled and changes made to the checked out document are undone.

Copied: A document in a document library is copied.

Deleted: A document is deleted from a document library.

Edited: An existing document or the value of a custom column in the library is edited.

Moved: A document is moved in a document library.

Renamed: A document is renamed in a document library.

Uploaded: A new document is saved to a document library.

The following code block contains the code for your `RFPEvent` class. The `OnEvent()` event handler checks which SharePoint list event has taken place. In the case of an `Update` or an `Insert` event, it creates an instance of the `WorkflowRuntime` type that represents the workflow runtime engine, and starts your custom workflow. The `CreateWorkflow()` method contains two arguments; the first one is the type of workflow to create, and the second argument is a `Dictionary` object that can contain any parameter of any data type. You will add the SharePoint `listEvent` object, containing metadata about the SharePoint list event, and the type of event that has taken place (`Insert` or `Delete`) to this dictionary, because you will use them later in your workflow code:

```
using System;
using System.Collections.Generic;
using System.Text;
using Microsoft.SharePoint;
using System.Workflow.Runtime;

namespace LoisandClark.MyWorkflowSolution
{
  public class RFPEvent : IListEventSink
  {
    public void OnEvent(SPListEvent listEvent)
    {
      if (listEvent.Type == SPListEventType.Insert || ➥
      listEvent.Type == SPListEventType.Update)
      {
        Dictionary<string, object> objParameters = new Dictionary<string, object>();
        objParameters.Add("ListEvent", listEvent);
        objParameters.Add("ListEventType", listEvent.Type);
        WorkflowRuntime wfRuntime = new WorkflowRuntime();
        WorkflowInstance wfInstance = ➥
        wfRuntime.CreateWorkflow(typeof(SPSWorkflow.RFPWorkflow), objParameters);
        wfInstance.Start();
      }
    }
  }
}
```

The next step is to strong name the assembly and install it in the Global Assembly Cache. You can do this by following these steps:

■**Note** Chapter 1 contains more information about strong names.

---

1. Right-click your project and choose Properties.

2. Click the Signing tab at the left.

3. Choose <New…> in the drop-down list at Choose a String Name Key File.

4. A Choose String Name Key dialog box will open and you can give the key file a name and click OK.

5. Build the solution by clicking Build in the toolbar and choose Build Solution.

6. To install your solution in the Global Assembly Cache, you have to drag the dll of your assembly to the [drive letter]:\Windows\Assembly directory via Windows Explorer.

Now you are ready to bind document event handling to a specific document library—in this example to the RFPDocuments document library:

1. Go to your document library and click Modify Settings and Columns.

2. Click Change Advanced Settings in the General Settings section. This option is not available if you have not enabled event handling for your virtual server.

3. On the Advanced Settings page, you can define an event handler for your document library that will fire when a change is made to an item in that document library (see Figure 4-15). Only users with full permissions for a document library can add event handlers. In the Assembly Name text box, type the string name for the assembly containing the event handler class. In this example, this is the following name: `LoisandClark.MyWorkflowSolution, version=1.0.0.0, Culture=Neutral, PublicKeyToken=40709448e24dfe41`.

Note If you are re-creating this solution on your own computer, the public key token will be different from the one listed here. Locate the MyWorkflowSolution assembly in the Global Assembly Cache (the [drive letter]:\windows\assembly directory) and click Properties to determine the correct public key token.

In the Class Name text box, type the full class name for the event handler; in this example the name is `LoisandClark.SPSWorkflow.RFPEvent`. In the Properties text box, you can type any text you want. You can retrieve that text via the `SinkData` property of the `SPListEvent` object. In this example we will not use properties for document event handling.

4. Reset Internet Information Server by typing `iisreset` at a command prompt.

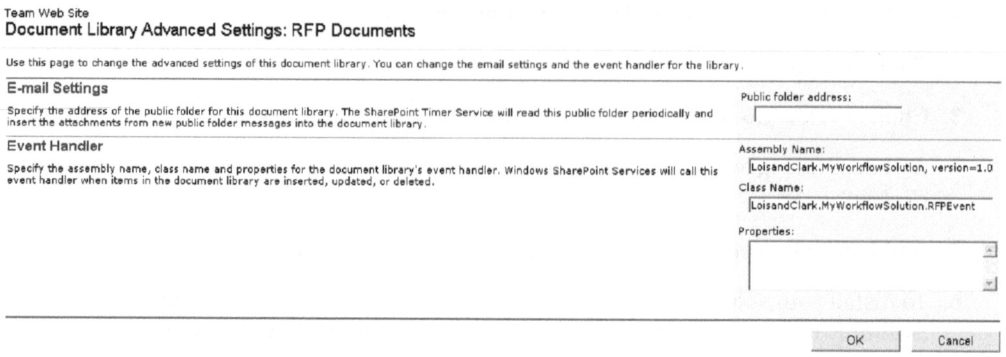

Team Web Site
Document Library Advanced Settings: RFP Documents

Use this page to change the advanced settings of this document library. You can change the email settings and the event handler for the library.

E-mail Settings

Specify the address of the public folder for this document library. The SharePoint Timer Service will read this public folder periodically and insert the attachments from new public folder messages into the document library.

Public folder address:

Event Handler

Specify the assembly name, class name and properties for the document library's event handler. Windows SharePoint Services will call this event handler when items in the document library are inserted, updated, or deleted.

Assembly Name:
LoisandClark.MyWorkflowSolution, version=1.0

Class Name:
LoisandClark.MyWorkflowSolution.RFPEvent

Properties:

OK   Cancel

Figure 4-15. *Advanced Settings page of a document library*

> **Note** If you want to learn more about document event handling, you can download the Windows SharePoint Services Toolkit: Document Library Event Handler at `http://www.microsoft.com/downloads`. This Document Library Event Handler Toolkit contains an introduction to the Windows SharePoint Services list events feature for document libraries. It also contains a sample solution that shows how to handle list events for document libraries.

The next thing to do is to make your custom workflow. You are going to make a simple sequential workflow. In this example, you are going to add the workflow to your MyWorkflowSolution instead of creating a new workflow solution. Follow these steps to make the workflow:

1. Right-click on your project and choose Add ➤ New Item.

2. In the Add New Item dialog window choose Sequential Workflow (code); give the workflow class the following name: `RFPWorkflow.cs`.

3. Click Add.

On the design view of our RFPWorkflow, we are going to create a workflow that will create a task when a document is inserted into the RFPDocument document library. The workflow will update the task status when the document is updated. Follow the next steps to create RFPWorkflow:

1. Drag a CodeActivity from the Toolbox onto the design view.

2. Select the CodeActivity, and in the Properties window, select the Name property and give the CodeActivity the following name: initValues.

3. Drag an IfElseActivity from the toolbox onto the design view directly below the CodeActivity.

4. Select the IfElseActivity, and in the Properties window select the Name property and give the IfElseActivity the following name: Status.

5. Select the left IfElseBranchActivity, and in the Properties window select the Name property, and give the IfElseBranchActivity the following name: CreateBranch.

6. Select the right IfElseBranchActivity, and in the Properties window select the Name property, and give the IfElseBranchActivity the following name: UpdateBranch.

7. Drag a CodeActivity from the Toolbox onto the design view below the left IfElseBranchActivity (CreateBranch).

8. Select the CodeActivity, and in the Properties window select the Name property and give the CodeActivity the following name: CreateTask.

9. Drag a CodeActivity from the Toolbox onto the design view below the right IfElseBranchActivity (UpdateBranch).

10. Select the CodeActivity, and in the Properties window select the Name property, and give the CodeActivity the following name: UpdateTask.

Right-click somewhere in the design view and choose View Code. This will bring up the code view of our RFPWorkflow class. Add the following using directives:

```
using System.Runtime.InteropServices;
using System.Security.Principal;
using Microsoft.SharePoint;
```

Add two properties called ListEvent and ListEventType. These names must be identical to the names given to the parameters added to the workflow dictionary in the RFPEvent class. Parameters added to a workflow dictionary are mapped automatically to class properties. If the names of the class properties are not identical to the names of the workflow dictionary you will not be able to retrieve the parameters.

```
public SPListEvent ListEvent
{
  get { return objListEvent; }
  set { objListEvent = value; }
}

public SPListEventType ListEventType
{
  get { return objListEventType; }
  set { objListEventType = value; }
}
```

We are going to add code to the CodeActivity shapes. Double-click the initValues CodeActivity and add the code displayed in the next code listing. This code will initialize two variables that are used in the CreateTask and UpdateTask CodeActivity shapes. The first variable, objSite, will contain the result of the call to the OpenWeb() method of the Site object that returns the SharePoint site where the document event has taken place.

The second variable, objFile, will contain the result of the call to the GetFile() method of the objSite object that returns a file object that is located at the specified URL. The file object represents the inserted or updated document in the RFPDocuments document library. The UrlAfter property of the SPListEvent class returns the new site-relative URL of the document after the event occurs. We are using the UrlAfter property instead of the UrlBefore property because we are interested in the document name after the document is inserted (or updated) into the document library.

The last five lines of code are related to impersonating another user account that has sufficient permissions for interacting with SharePoint. We are not going to explain the impersonation code in this chapter. Refer to Chapter 8 if you want detailed information on this subject.

```
private void initValues_ExecuteCode(object sender, EventArgs e)
{
  objSite = ListEvent.Site.OpenWeb();
  objFile = objSite.GetFile(ListEvent.UrlAfter);

  WindowsIdentity objOrgIdentity = WindowsIdentity.GetCurrent();
  bool blnReturn = LogonUser([username], [domain], [password], ➥
  LogonTypes.Interactive, LogonProviders.Default, out objToken);
  WindowsIdentity objIdentity = new WindowsIdentity(objToken);
  objUserContext = objIdentity.Impersonate();
}
```

Double-click the CreateTask CodeActivity and add the code displayed in the next code listing. This code will create a task when a document is inserted into your document library:

```
private void CreateTask_ExecuteCode(object sender, EventArgs e)
{
  try
  {
    string strTitle = objFile.Title;
    SPListItemCollection objListItems = objSite.Lists["Tasks"].Items;
    SPListItem objTask = objListItems.Add();
    objTask["Title"] = "Document to Review: " + strTitle;
    objTask["Assigned To"] = objSite.Users[@"jupiter\administrator"];
    objTask["Status"] = "In Process";
    objTask.Update();
  }
  catch (Exception err)
  {
    // error handling
  }
  finally
  {
    objUserContext.Undo();
    CloseHandle(objToken);
  }
}
```

Double-click the UpdateTask CodeActivity and add the code displayed in the next code listing. This code will update the task that is related to the document updated in the document library. The task status will be set to Complete. The finally block contains some code that reverts the impersonated account back to the original identity:

```
private void UpdateTask_ExecuteCode(object sender, EventArgs e)
{
  try
  {
    string strTitle = objFile.Title;
    SPList objTaskList = objSite.Lists["Tasks"];
    SPListItemCollection objTaskListItems = objTaskList.Items;
    foreach (SPListItem objTask in objTaskListItems)
    {
      if (objTask["Title"].ToString() == "Document to Review: " + strTitle)
      {
        objTask["Status"] = "Complete";
        objTask.Update();
      }
    }
  }
  catch (Exception err)
  {
    // error handling
  }
  finally
  {
    objUserContext.Undo();
    CloseHandle(objToken);
  }
}
```

The complete code of the RFPWorkflow class is shown in the next code listing. We have not discussed the code that is related to impersonation. If you want more information about this topic, refer to Chapter 8.

```
using System;
using System.ComponentModel;
using System.ComponentModel.Design;
using System.Collections;
using System.Drawing;
using System.Workflow.ComponentModel.Compiler;
using System.Workflow.ComponentModel.Serialization;
using System.Workflow.ComponentModel;
using System.Workflow.ComponentModel.Design;
using System.Workflow.Runtime;
using System.Workflow.Activities;
using System.Workflow.Activities.Rules;
```

```csharp
using System.Runtime.InteropServices;
using System.Security.Principal;
using Microsoft.SharePoint;

namespace LoisandClark.SPSWorkflow
{
  public sealed partial class RFPWorkflow : SequentialWorkflowActivity
  {
    public RFPWorkflow()
    {
      InitializeComponent();
    }

    SPListEvent objListEvent;
    SPListEventType objListEventType;
    SPWeb objSite;
    SPFile objFile;
    WindowsImpersonationContext objUserContext;
    IntPtr objToken;

    private void initValues_ExecuteCode(object sender, EventArgs e)
    {
      objSite = ListEvent.Site.OpenWeb();
      objFile = objSite.GetFile(ListEvent.UrlAfter);
      WindowsIdentity objOrgIdentity = WindowsIdentity.GetCurrent();
      bool blnReturn = LogonUser([username], [domain], [password], ➡
      LogonTypes.Interactive, LogonProviders.Default, out objToken);
      WindowsIdentity objIdentity = new WindowsIdentity(objToken);
      objUserContext = objIdentity.Impersonate();
    }

    private void CreateTask_ExecuteCode(object sender, EventArgs e)
    {
      try
      {
        string strTitle = objFile.Title;
        SPListItemCollection objListItems = objSite.Lists["Tasks"].Items;
        SPListItem objTask = objListItems.Add();
        objTask["Title"] = "Document to Review: " + strTitle;
        objTask["Assigned To"] = objSite.Users[@"jupiter\administrator"];
        objTask["Status"] = "In Process";
        objTask.Update();
      }
      catch (Exception err)
      {
        // error handling
      }
```

```
    finally
    {
      objUserContext.Undo();
      CloseHandle(objToken);
    }
}

private void UpdateTask_ExecuteCode(object sender, EventArgs e)
{
    try
    {
      string strTitle = objFile.Title;
      SPList objTaskList = objSite.Lists["Tasks"];
      SPListItemCollection objTaskListItems = objTaskList.Items;
      foreach (SPListItem objTask in objTaskListItems)
      {
        if (objTask["Title"].ToString() == "Document to Review: " + strTitle)
        {
          objTask["Status"] = "Complete";
          objTask.Update();
        }
      }
    }
    catch (Exception err)
    {
      // error handling
    }
    finally
    {
      objUserContext.Undo();
      CloseHandle(objToken);
    }
}

[DllImport("advapi32.dll", SetLastError = true)]
static extern bool LogonUser(
string principal,
string authority,
string password,
LogonTypes logonType,
LogonProviders logonProvider,
out IntPtr token);

[DllImport("kernel32.dll", SetLastError = true)]
static extern bool CloseHandle(IntPtr handle);
```

```
enum LogonTypes : uint
{
  Interactive = 2,
  Network,
  Batch,
  Service,
  NetworkCleartext = 8,
  NewCredentials
}

enum LogonProviders : uint
{
  Default = 0, // default
  WinNT35,
  WinNT40, // uses NTLM
  WinNT50 // negotiates Kerberos or NTLM
}

public SPListEvent ListEvent
{
  get { return objListEvent; }
  set { objListEvent = value; }
}

public SPListEventType ListEventType
{
  get { return objListEventType; }
  set { objListEventType = value; }
}
  }
}
```

Before you can deploy your workflow, there is one last thing to do in the design view of the RFPWorkflow. You need to add some code to the CreateBranchActivity. This code will check whether the ListEventType property is equal to the SPListEventType.Insert enumeration value. The SPListEventType.Insert enumeration is a list that contains an overview of all valid list event types. The reason you want to do this is to add a new task when the SPListEventType enumeration value is equal to Insert, or if you want to update a task when the SPListEventType enumeration value is equal to Update.

1. Select the CreateBranchActivity and choose System.Workflow.Activities.Rules. RuleConditionReference in the Condition property in the Properties window.

2. Expand the Condition property and give the ConditionName property the following name: CreateStatus.

3. Click the button in the Expression property value; this will open the Rule Condition Editor window and add the following code:

```
this.ListEventType == Microsoft.SharePoint.SPListEventType.Insert
```

4. Click OK.

Figure 4-16 shows what your RFPWorkflow workflow should look like.

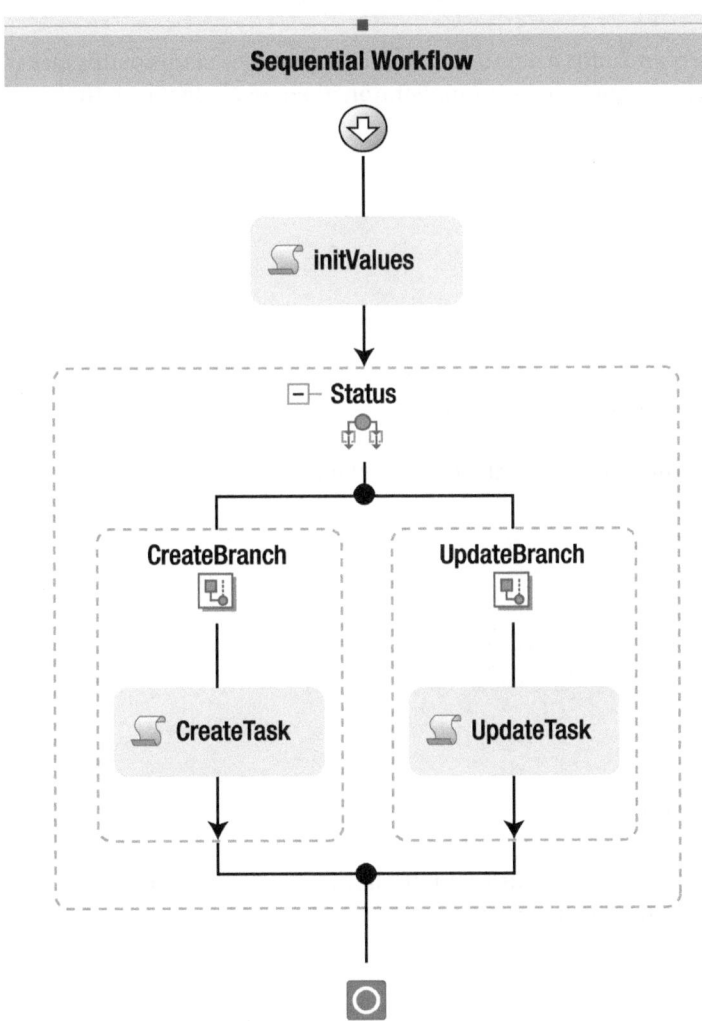

Figure 4-16. *RFPWorkflow design view*

With the RFPWorkflow workflow set up and running, you can test it by inserting a new document into the RFPDocuments document library. This is shown in Figure 4-17.

Figure 4-17. *RFPDocuments document library with a new document inserted*

The workflow process starts and adds a new task to the Tasks list. The status of this task is set to In Process and the task is assigned to the administrator, as shown in Figure 4-18.

Figure 4-18. *New task in the Tasks list with status In Process*

When you update the document, the task will be updated too, and its status will be set to Complete, as shown in Figure 4-19.

Figure 4-19. *Updated task with status Complete*

Although this is a very simple workflow, this example clarifies how to use Windows Workflow Foundation in combination with SharePoint.

Summary

In this chapter we discussed what Windows Workflow Foundation is. We showed how to create a workflow by using the Visual Studio 2005 Designer for Windows Workflow Foundation and how to create custom activities. We also explained how to use Windows Workflow Foundation in combination with Windows SharePoint Services 2003.

CHAPTER 5

Software Factories and Web Part Connections

The notion of software factories is one of the most important contemporary trends in software architecture. The main promise of software factories is the industrialization of software development, thus increasing productivity and decreasing development costs dramatically. In this chapter, you will learn what software factories are.

The ultimate goal of this chapter is to show you how to develop a part of a software factory; we will show you how to develop a domain-specific language (DSL) for creating connectable web parts. If you want to succeed in developing such a language, it is essential that you have a solid understanding of the SharePoint web part connection framework. If you do not possess this knowledge already, this chapter will help you to acquire it.

Introducing Software Factories

A *software factory* is a software product line that automates parts of software development. Most discussions about software factories will probably start with a reference to a book called "Software Factories: Assembling Applications with Patterns, Models, Frameworks, and Tools" published by Wiley, 2004 (see the bibliography for more details). This book is rapidly becoming a classic, and if you want to delve deeply into the theory behind software factories we can definitely recommend it. We also advise you to take a look at the web site http://www.softwarefactories.com, which contains general information about software factories.

"Software development is an art." This is a phrase you have probably heard before. It is true, even nowadays; software development is based on the individual skills of software developers. This is sometimes referred to as *heroism*, the developers being the heroes. The developers engage in manual, labor-intensive tasks, just like other craftsmen do. Such a development style is slow and allows much room for mistakes, and the level of software quality is very much dependent on the skills of the individual software developer. As the art of software development matures it must transcend to another level. We have to move toward software industrialization, which is all about assembling software products from components, automating tasks, forming product lines (the steps required to create software) and supply chains (that deliver standard components), and standardizing processes and architectures. The belief that industrialization can be accomplished for the world of software development is based on the premise that software is fundamentally like every other industry.

Although software factories help to industrialize the work of software developers, we do not think this will make being a software developer boring. Software factories help to automate boring tasks, thus giving developers the opportunity to spend a higher percentage of their time on the interesting bits of creating software. You might also wonder if the increasing productivity caused by the use of software factories leads to unemployment amongst developers. We cannot give you a job guarantee, but we do not believe so. As more work is achieved in less time, we expect companies to move to the next generation of a software product sooner, thus becoming more responsive to end-user needs and gaining or keeping a competitive edge. We believe more software will be developed by more-or-less the same amount of developers, rather than more-or-less the same amount of software developed by fewer developers.

Another trend related to software factories is that programming languages tend to become more abstract over time. Nowadays, you can still create programs by typing code, although more and more you will have the opportunity to program by creating visual models graphically. Creating BizTalk orchestrations (Chapter 7 covers BizTalk orchestrations) and workflows created using Windows Workflow Foundation (Chapter 4 covers Windows Workflow Foundation) are excellent examples of this. This is also known as *model-driven development*, a development approach where visual modeling is used to create models to capture information in forms that can be processed easily. The goal of model-driven development does not lie in creating design documentation; the goal lies in creating models that are used to fully or partially automate its implementation. You can think of model-driven development as programming with models.

FLAWS IN UML?

The Unified Modeling Language (UML) has been successful as a language that allows developers, analysts, and architects to create models that are used for design and documentation purposes. However, UML has not been successful as a language that is used widely and effectively in creating models that are used in model-driven development. Or to put it another way, UML has not been successful as a language that is able to help to automate the development of software. This is primarily caused by one of the great strengths of the language: its generality. As it turns out, automation of development requires precise languages, and UML has failed as a language that can be mapped precisely to programming languages such as C#.

Background on Domain-Specific Languages

If you are going to adopt a model-driven development approach and you want to create a model that is suitable for use in a model-driven development environment you need it to be precise and unambiguous. Because of this, a modeling language needs to be closely tied to the problem domain itself (something that does not hold true for UML). Such modeling languages are called *DSLs* or domain-specific languages. DSLs can be textual or graphical, although this chapter only discusses the creation of a graphical DSL. The opposite of a DSL is a *general purpose language* (GPL). General purpose languages are generic and can be applied to any kind of problem domain, whereas DSLs are intended to be used in a very specific problem domain.

Models created in some kind of high-level DSL need to be transformed to some other form before they are really useful. Most often, models will be transformed to either code (that can be compiled into executables) or directly into executables, but it is also possible to use a model and transform it in another lower-level DSL. Different types of model transformation exist:

Vertical: Vertical transformations take some kind of higher-level model and map this model to another lower-level model.

Horizontal refactoring: Horizontal refactoring transformations reorganize a model to improve its design but not its meaning.

Horizontal delocalizing: Horizontal delocalizing transformations optimize a model. A typical example of this type of refactoring is the generation of binary code that is optimized to improve performance. Horizontal delocalizing transformations can also be used to specify a part or aspect of software. This is an essential part of aspect-oriented programming (AOP). For example, AOP allows you to address a part of software (let's say, security concerns), and apply this part to one or more separate software programs.

Oblique: Oblique transformations combine horizontal and vertical transformations.

Typically, modeling languages are declarative, not imperative. Imperative languages focus on the *how* of software execution. Such languages describe which instructions need to be executed and do not bother to describe the desired results of the execution of the software program. Declarative languages focus on the *what* of software execution. Declarative languages describe what the desired results of the execution of the software program are, but do not bother to describe how these results are obtained. DSLs are used to express developer intent and are thus an example of declarative languages.

DSLs are used in model-driven development approaches, where metadata is captured in models to automate software development tasks. Model-driven development has the following features:

- Model-driven development uses DSLs that capture developer intent.

- Model-driven development allows you to create and adapt software via configuration, not coding.

- Tools that support model-driven development make it easy to generate software based on models.

- Tools that support model-driven development make it easy to create and debug models.

Components of a Software Factory

A software solution solves a problem or subproblem in a specific domain and reduces the total cost of software creation. In software factory terms, a *solution* is a production asset that makes software creation cheaper every time the solution is reused. Building software factories and supply chains are used to create software that is similar and yet distinct, using the same practices, processes, tools, and materials, thus providing another level of reuse.

Software factories are software product lines that contain extensible tools, processes, and content using a software factory template based on a software factory schema to automate (parts of) software development. A software factory schema categorizes and summarizes development artifacts that are relevant to a software factory. Examples of such artifacts are configuration files, models, and source code files.

■**Note** A software factory schema does not *contain* development artifacts, it *describes* them.

Software factory schemas also define relationships between the artifacts. Tables are very suitable to represent software factory schemas. If you represent a software factory in a table, every table cell represents a perspective or viewpoint from which you can build a certain aspect of the software. Such tables can be used to create more than one software product. A software factory schema provides a high-level overview of a software product belonging to a certain software product family and describes the artifacts that must be developed to produce a software product in a fully or partially automated way.

The software factory schema represents the entire software development process for producing software that belongs to a certain software family. Software factory schemas contain fixed and variable parts; the fixed parts remain the same for every member of the product family.

To summarize what we have discussed so far, a software factory schema describes the software factory; a software factory template contains the actual assets used to build a software product belonging to a certain software family. DSLs are assets of a software factory template and are used to capture information about some aspect (or viewpoint) of a family of software products. Multiple DSLs are needed to describe a typical business application.

Using DSL Tools

A DSL is a language designed to be useful for a specific task in a fixed problem domain, in contrast to a general-purpose language. DSLs are an important part of software factories, so it is interesting to see what you need to create a DSL. If you want to use DSLs, you will need the following tools:

- Editors for creating and maintaining specifications. For complex languages, graphical editors may be required for editing and validation.

- Language processors for producing implementations from models.

- Debugging tools to debug implementations using the DSL.

- Tools that automate other development tasks using metadata captured by models based on the language, including test generation and execution, instrumentation and measurement, configuration management and deployment.

The first three tools can be found in the new Microsoft DSL Toolkit product that enables users to design graphical DSLs that can be tailored to any problem domain, and to generate code and other artifacts from the languages. The last set of tools belongs to the realm of Visual Studio Team System and will not be discussed in this chapter. The DSL Toolkit consists of the following:

- A project wizard that supports the creation of domain models via a designer and a textual artifact generator. Domain models created with this project wizard can be tested within separate instances of Visual Studio .NET 2005.

- A graphical designer that can be used to define and edit domain models.

- An XML format that is used for describing designer definitions. Designer definitions define the look and feel of a graphical designer hosted in Visual Studio .NET 2005 that is used to create domain models.

- A set of code generators that is able to generate code for a DSL that is defined via a domain model definition and designer definition.

- A framework for defining templates.

Running the project wizard results in the creation of a Visual Studio DSL solution that contains two projects: DomainModel and Designer. The DomainModel project describes the DSL and allows you to visually customize and define this language. The Designer project defines the look and feel of the DSL. After creating a DSL using the DSL Toolkit, you can create a deployment package (.msi file) to distribute your DSL. We will discuss the DSL Toolkit in detail in the section "Creating the Web Part Connection Language" when we start discussing the creation of the Web Part Connection Language, a domain-specific language for creating connectable web parts.

■**Note** The DSL Toolkit and the Guidance Automation Toolkit (GAT) both fall under the Software Factories Initiative umbrella at Microsoft. Basically, GAT is an extension to Visual Studio .NET 2005 that creates rich user experiences. If you want more information about GAT, please refer to Chapter 1. Currently, the integration between the two tools is limited to the shared use of the T4 templating engine (which is discussed later in the chapter in the section "Text Templates"). There are additional plans to integrate both products. For example, it will be possible to run GAT recipes from commands in a model designer that is created using the DSL Toolkit.

Web Part Connections

Since this chapter discusses how to create a graphical DSL for web part connections, it is useful if you are up to speed on connectable web part technology. If you are already there, you can freely skip this section. If not, you will learn the ins and outs of creating connectable web parts here.

The Digital Dashboard Services Component (DDSC) can be considered to be the first version of connectable web parts. The DDSC is a client-side component included first in SharePoint technology in 2001. It provides a standard infrastructure for services such as the following:

Part discovery: A web part discovers another web part on a web part page (or a *dashboard*, as it was called in 2001).

Notification: The notification system allows web parts to respond to external events that occur at the web part page or web part level.

Session state management: The session state management system allows web parts to interchange information and objects within a browser session.

State management: The state management system allows web part pages and web parts to maintain global state and offered access to a state persistence mechanism.

Item retrieval: This allows web parts to retrieve and maintain the state of items.

Although not used as often, the DDSC is still included in SharePoint Products and Technologies 2003. In SharePoint Products and Technologies 2003 the DDSC is renamed to Web Part Services Component (WPSC), a component that plays an important role in creating client-side web part connections. Creating client-side web part connections will be discussed in detail later in the section "Creating a Connectable Web Part."

In a nutshell, connectable web parts are web parts that can communicate with other web parts. There are two ways end-users can connect web parts to each other: via the browser or using FrontPage 2003. Web part connections are useful in many ways; the next list provides an overview of the most common scenarios:

Master/detail: In this scenario, a master web part provides information that allows a detail web part to show further details. For example, a web part provides an overview of all employees. If you click on the name of one of the employees, employee details are shown in another web part.

Parent/child: In this scenario, a parent web part provides an overview of items of some sort; a child web part shows the children of these items. For example, a web part provides an overview of orders. If you click one of the orders, another web part shows all items belonging to this order.

Data entry and filtering: In this scenario, a web part contains some kind of search or filter form. The data entered in this form is used to filter the data that is shown in another web part.

Alternate views: In this scenario, a web part passes data to another web part that displays this data in some new and interesting way. For example, a web part provides an overview of order items; product A is ordered 10 times, product B 20 times. This data is passed to another web part that uses a pie chart to display this information.

Data enhancement: In this scenario, a web part enhances the data shown in another web part. For example, a web part shows an overview of all employees. If you click the name of one of the employees, another web part shows a picture of this employee.

These scenarios all have in common that web parts share information and are able to communicate with each other. The intent, however, is a little bit different in every scenario. To be able to support these scenarios, the `Microsoft.SharePoint.WebPartPages.Communication` namespace contains several interfaces that allow web parts to receive or pass information to other connected web parts on a web part page. The following interface provider/consumer pairs are available for implementing web part connection scenarios:

- Cell interface provider/consumer pair.

- Row interface provider/consumer pair.

- List interface provider/consumer pair.

- Filter interface provider/consumer pair.

- ParamsOut interface provider/consumer pair.

- ParamsIn interface provider/consumer pair.

The Cell Interface Pair

Cell interfaces, which define connectable web part providers and consumers, are used when a web part (the provider) wants to pass a single value to another web part (the consumer). The provider web part needs to implement the ICellProvider interface, and the consumer web part needs to implement the ICellConsumer interface. Cell interfaces are very suitable to implement data enhancement scenarios.

The ICellProvider interface defines the CellProviderInit event. This initialization event can be used to pass information about a cell, such as the cell name and cell display name. For example, a web part implementing the ICellProvider interface contains the following declaration:

```
public event CellProviderInitEventHandler CellProviderInit;
```

The web part can inform web parts implementing the ICellConsumer interface about cell and display names via the following code (the code is taken from the Windows SharePoint Services (WSS) SDK):

```
// If there is a listener, fire the CellProviderInit event.
if (CellProviderInit != null)
{
  // Create the InitEventArgs structure for the CellProviderInit event.
  CellProviderInitEventArgs cellProviderInitArgs = new CellProviderInitEventArgs();

  // Set the FieldName and FieldDisplay values.
  cellProviderInitArgs.FieldName = _cellName;
  cellProviderInitArgs.FieldDisplayName = _cellDisplayName;

  // Fire the CellProviderInit event.
  CellProviderInit(this, cellProviderInitArgs);
}
```

The CellProviderInit event of the ICellProvider interface corresponds to the CellConsumerInit event of the ICellConsumer interface, which is also used to pass initialization information to other connected web parts. This time, the event passes information from the consumer side to the provider side. For example, a web part implementing the ICellConsumer interface contains the following declaration:

```
public event CellConsumerInitEventHandler CellConsumerInit;
```

The web part can inform web parts implementing the ICellProvider interface about cell and display names via the following code (the code is taken from the WSS SDK):

```
// If there is a listener, fire the CellConsumerInit event.
if (CellConsumerInit != null)
{
  // Create the CellConsumerInitEventArgs structure for the CellConsumerInit event.
  CellConsumerInitEventArgs cellConsumerInitArgs = new CellConsumerInitEventArgs();
```

```
  // Set the FieldName and FieldDisplayName values.
  cellConsumerInitArgs.FieldName = _cellName;
  cellConsumerInitArgs.FieldDisplayName = _cellDisplayName;

  // Fire the CellConsumerInit event.
  CellConsumerInit(this, cellConsumerInitArgs);
}
```

The ICellProvider interface also defines the CellReady event, which is used to pass the actual cell value to another web part. For example, an ICellProvider web part might contain the following declaration:

```
public event CellReadyEventHandler CellReady;
```

The following code is taken from the WSS SDK and sends a cell value to another web part:

```
if (CellReady != null)
{
  // Create the CellReadyEventArgs data structure for the CellProviderInit event.
  CellReadyEventArgs cellReadyArgs = new CellReadyEventArgs();

  // If the user clicked the button, then send the value.
  if (_cellClicked)
  {
    // Set the cell to the value of the TextBox text.
    // This is the value that will be sent to the Consumer
    cellReadyArgs.Cell = _cellInput.Text;
  }
  else
  {
    // The user didn't actually click the button
    // so just send an empty string to the consumer.
    cellReadyArgs.Cell = "";
  }

  // Fire the CellReady event.
  // The Consumer will receive the cell value in its CellReady event handler
  CellReady(this, cellReadyArgs);
}
```

At this point we have seen that the ICellProvider interface defines two events: CellProviderInit and CellReady. The CellProviderInit event is used to provide information about a cell; the CellReady event is used to pass the actual cell value. The ICellConsumer interface defines two event handlers that respond to these provider events: the CellProviderInit() and CellReady() event handlers. The following code is taken from the WSS SDK and shows an example implementation of the CellProviderInit() event handler:

```
// The connected provider part(s) will call this method during its
// PartCommunicationInit phase
// to pass initialization information to this consumer Web Part.
// <param name="sender">Reference to the Consumer Web Part</param>
// <param name="cellProviderInitEventArgs">
//   The args passed by the provider Web Part
// </param>
public void CellProviderInit(object sender, CellProviderInitEventArgs ➥
  cellProviderInitEventArgs)
{
  // Encode and store the field display name.
  _connectedField = SPEncode.HtmlEncode(cellProviderInitEventArgs.FieldDisplayName);
}
```

The following code is taken from the WSS SDK and shows an example implementation of the CellReady() event handler:

```
// The connected provider part(s) will call this method during its
// PartCommunicationMain phase
// to pass their primary data to the consumer Web Part.
// <param name="sender">Reference to the provider Web Part</param>
// <param name="cellReadyEventArgs">The args passed by the provider Web Part</param>
public void CellReady(object sender, CellReadyEventArgs cellReadyEventArgs)
{
  // Make sure child controls have been created.
  EnsureChildControls();

  // Set the label text to the value of the cell that was passed by the provider
  //part.
  if(cellReadyEventArgs.Cell != null)
  {
    _cellConsumerTextBox.Text = cellReadyEventArgs.Cell.ToString();
  }
}
```

The Row Interface Pair

The Row interfaces are used when a provider web part wants to pass a row of information to a consumer web part. The provider web part needs to implement the IRowProvider interface; the consumer web part needs to implement the IRowConsumer interface. Row interfaces are very suitable to implement master/detail scenarios.

The IRowProvider interface is probably the most popular interface when it comes to connectable web parts, because the data provided by such provider web parts cannot only be consumed by IRowConsumer web parts, the data can be transformed in ways understandable to a range of other types of consumer web parts as well. Data provided by IRowProvider web parts can be consumed by ICellConsumer, IRowConsumer, IFilterConsumer, and IParametersInConsumer web parts.

The IRowProvider interface defines the `RowProviderInit` event. This initialization event can be used to pass information about a row (field names and field display names) to another web part. The IRowProvider interface also defines a `RowReady` event. The `RowReady` event is used to pass the actual row to another web part. The IRowConsumer interface defines two event handlers that respond to those events: `RowProviderInit()` and `RowReady()`.

The List Interface Pair

The List interfaces are coarser grained than the Cell and Row interfaces. They are used when a provider web part wants to pass an entire list of data (a set of rows) to a consumer web part. The provider web part needs to implement the IListProvider interface; the consumer web part needs to implement the IListConsumer interface. List interfaces are very suitable to implement alternate-view scenarios.

The IListProvider interface defines the `ListProviderInit` event. This initialization event can be used to pass information about a list (field names and optionally field display names) to another web part. The IListProvider interface also defines a `ListReady` event. The `ListReady` event is used to pass the actual list of data to another web part. The IListProvider interface defines another event that allows you to send a part of a list to another web part: the `PartialListReady` event. The IListConsumer interface defines three event handlers that respond to those events: the `ListProviderInit()`, `ListReady()`, and `PartialListReady()` event handlers.

The Filter Interface Pair

The Filter interfaces are used when a provider web part wants to pass filter values to a consumer web part. The provider web part needs to implement the IFilterProvider interface, and the consumer web part needs to implement the IFilterConsumer interface. Filter interfaces are, as the name already implies, very suitable to implement data entry and filtering scenarios.

The IFilterProvider interface defines the `FilterProviderInit` event. This initialization event can be used to pass information about the list of field names and field display names used to filter a list that is shown in a consumer web part.

The IFilterProvider interface defines a couple of events that are used to regulate inter–web part communication. First of all, it defines the `SetFilter` event. This event is used by the provider web part to pass filter values to the consumer web part. The interface also defines the `ClearFilter` event that indicates that the current filter value used in the consumer web part needs to be reset. The `NoFilter` event notifies the consumer web part that no filter will be provided. This event is also used to indicate that the filter value has not changed. The IFilterConsumer interface defines event handlers that respond to those provider events: the `SetFilter()`, `ClearFilter()`, and `NoFilter()` event handlers.

The IFilterConsumer interface defines an event that is identical in purpose to the `FilterProviderInit` event of the IFilterProvider interface; the `FilterConsumerInit` event is used to send information to a provider.

The ParamsOut Interface Pair

Imagine a scenario where you want to pass a property bag containing various values to other web parts. For example, suppose you are building a web part that collects data from end users required to calculate the mortgage of a house. The collecting web part (the provider) can pass a parameter list containing all relevant information to another web part that knows how to perform the calculation. If you want to implement such a scenario, you should implement the ParamsOut interfaces. The provider web part needs to implement the IParamsOutProvider interface; the consumer web part needs to implement the IParamsOutConsumer interface.

There is a big difference between the ParamsOut interfaces and all of the interfaces discussed previously. Whereas the previously discussed interfaces are very flexible and loosely coupled, web parts connected via the ParamsOut interfaces have intimate knowledge about each other.

The IParamsOutProvider interface defines the `ParamsOutProviderInit` event. This initialization event can be used to pass information about the parameters a web part is providing to other connected parts. The `ParametersOutReady` event passes the actual parameters to other web parts. The final event defined within the IParamsOutProvider interface is the `NoParametersOut` event; this event indicates that no new parameters are passed to the consumer web part. Instead, the consumer web part should reuse its existing parameters. The IParamsOutConsumer interface defines event handlers that respond to those provider events: the `ParametersOutProviderInit()`, `ParametersOutReady()`, and `NoParametersOut()` event handlers.

The ParamsIn Interface Pair

The previous section discussed how to pass a property bag from a provider web part to a consumer web part via the ParamsOut interface pair. There is another scenario where parameters are passed from one web part to another; in this scenario one of the web parts implements a ParamsIn interface.

In the previous section, we established that a provider and a consumer web part that both consume ParamsOut interfaces have intimate knowledge about each other (they are tightly bound). If you do not like this and want to be able to pass parameters to unknown consumer web parts that do not have knowledge about the provider web part, you should combine a ParamsOut provider interface with a ParamsIn consumer interface to force an interface mismatch. For example, build a provider web part that implements the IParamsOutProvider interface. Then build a consumer web part that implements the IParamsInConsumer interface. In itself, those interfaces are not compatible, thus causing an interface mismatch. This forces the SharePoint user interface to display a transformation window that allows the person connecting the web parts to choose which values need to be connected to each other. This offers more flexibility and loose coupling.

ParamsIn provider web parts need to implement the IParamsInProvider interface; ParamsIn consumer web parts need to implement the IParamsInConsumer interface. IParamsInProvider web parts can only be connected to IParamsInConsumer web parts. If ParamsIn provider and consumer web parts are connected, the SharePoint user interface will not display the transformer dialog. In such scenarios, the IParamsInConsumer web part is designed with a deeper understanding of the data that will be provided by an IParamsInProvider web part; the web parts are tightly coupled.

The IParamsInProvider interface does not define an initialization event that can be used to pass information about the parameters a web part is providing to other connected parts. The `ParametersInReady` event is responsible for passing the actual parameters to other web parts. The IParamsInProvider interface also defines the `NoParametersIn` event; this event indicates there is no parameter list to be sent to the consumer web part. The IParamsInConsumer interface defines event handlers that respond to those provider events: the `ParametersInReady()` and `NoParametersIn()` event handlers. The IParamsInConsumer interface also defines an event that initializes information that will be passed to the provider web part; it's called `ParametersInConsumerInit`.

What Else Do You Need to Know?

The SharePoint web part connection framework includes transformers that allow a provider and consumer web part to connect to each other, even though they implement different interfaces. The following transformers are available:

- IRowProvider to ICellConsumer

- IRowProvider to IFilterConsumer

- IRowProvider to IParametersInConsumer

- IParametersOutProvider to IParametersInConsumer

You have the option of choosing between two available clients when it comes to creating web part connections: the browser and FrontPage 2003. If you are connecting web parts implementing interfaces that require the use of a transformer, you cannot always use either client. Table 5-1 shows an overview of the available clients for different transformer scenarios.

Table 5-1. *Available Clients in Different Transformer Scenarios*

Transformation	Clients
IRowProvider to ICellConsumer	Browser and FrontPage
IRowProvider to IFilterConsumer	Browser and FrontPage
IRowProvider to IParametersInConsumer	FrontPage
IParametersOutProvider to IParametersInConsumer	FrontPage

Note There are some other less often used ways to create web part connections. You can also create them programmatically by setting the connection ID, hard-coding the connection in the web part by setting the connection ID in the consuming web part (which is useful in testing scenarios), or by defining a web part connection within a site template.

Connectable web parts can have different types of connections: server-side, client-side, and cross-page. Cross-page connections can only be created via FrontPage. If web parts are connected via a server-side connection, communication results in a postback to the server. In client-side connection scenarios, web parts communicate via JavaScript. This is more efficient because it results in less postbacks to the server; the downside is that implementations for client-side connections are more difficult to develop. A cross-page connection is a connection that is made between two web parts that are located on different SharePoint pages. There are only five types of allowable cross-page connections; they are listed in Table 5-2.

Table 5-2. *Cross-Page Connections*

Source Page	Target Page
IRowProvider	IFilterConsumer
IRowProvider	IParametersInConsumer
IFilterProvider	IFilterConsumer
IParametersOutProvider	IParametersInConsumer
IParametersInProvider	IParametersInConsumer

Creating a Connectable Web Part

Creating a connectable web part consists of a number of steps. These steps are quite similar for every type of connectable web part. In this section, we will discuss in detail how to create an ICellConsumer web part. The next steps provide a high-level overview of the process for creating a connectable web part followed by a detailed discussion of each step:

1. Make a reference to the Communication namespace.

2. Inherit from the WebPart base class and implement the ICellConsumer interface.

3. Declare the ICellConsumer event.

4. Implement the EnsureInterfaces() method and call the RegisterInterface() method.

5. Override the CanRunAt() method.

6. Override the PartCommunicationConnect() method.

7. Implement the CellProviderInit() event handler.

8. Implement the CellReady() event handler.

9. Override the PartCommunicationInit() method.

10. Optionally override the GetInitEventArgs() method.

11. For client-side connections, implement the following functions:

    1. PartCommunicationInit()

    2. CellProviderInit()

    3. CellReady()

    4. GetInitEventArgs()

All interfaces related to creating connectable web parts are located within the SharePoint Communication namespace located in the Windows SharePoint Services assembly (Microsoft. SharePoint.dll), so it makes sense to make a reference to it, like so:

```
using Microsoft.SharePoint.WebPartPages.Communication;
```

All web parts inherit from the WebPart base class; cell consumer web parts will also need to implement the ICellConsumer interface. This is shown in the following code:

```
public class ServerSideCellConsumer : WebPart, ICellConsumer
```

You will also need to declare the ICellConsumer event that is used to inform provider web parts of initialization information. This is shown in the following code:

```
public event CellConsumerInitEventHandler CellConsumerInit;
```

The EnsureInterfaces() method is used to indicate which interfaces are supported by the connectable web part. The EnsureInterfaces() method calls the RegisterInterface() method once for each specified interface. The following code shows an example implementation:

```
public override void EnsureInterfaces()
{
  RegisterInterface("MyCellConsumerInterface",  //InterfaceName
  InterfaceTypes.ICellConsumer,  //InterfaceType
  WebPart.LimitOneConnection,  //MaxConnections
  ConnectionRunAt.Server,  //RunAtOptions
  this, //InterfaceObject
  "", //InterfaceClientReference
  "Consume Cell From", //MenuLabel
  "Consumes a single value from another Web Part.");  //Description
}
```

Note Typically, you should set the number of connections to unlimited for provider web parts, and to 1 for consumer web parts. Allowing multiple connections for consumer web parts makes creating them very complex.

The CanRunAt() method needs to be overridden to let the web part connection framework know which types of connections are supported by a web part (server-side, client-side, or both). The following code shows an example implementation:

```
public override ConnectionRunAt CanRunAt()
{
  //This Web Part can run on the server.
  return ConnectionRunAt.Server;
}
```

Next you need to override the PartCommunicationConnect() method. This tells the web part connection framework how a web part is connected (server-side, client-side), to which web part it is connected, and which web part connection interface is used. The following code shows an example implementation:

```
// <param name="interfaceName">Friendly name of the interface ➥
   that is being connected</param>
// <param name="connectedPart">Reference to the other Web Part ➥
   that is being connected to</param>
// <param name="connectedInterfaceName">Friendly name of ➥
   the interface on the other Web Part</param>
// <param name="runAt">Where the interface should execute</param>
public override void PartCommunicationConnect(
  string interfaceName,
  WebPart connectedPart,
  string connectedInterfaceName,
  ConnectionRunAt runAt)
{
  // Keep track of whether the Web Part is connected or not.
  if (interfaceName == "MyCellConsumerInterface")
  {
    _connected = true;
    _connectedWebPartTitle = SPEncode.HtmlEncode(connectedPart.Title);
  }
}
```

After that you need to implement the CellProviderInit() event handler, so you are able to process the initialization information of the provider web part. The next code shows an example implementation:

```
// <param name="sender">Reference to the Consumer Web Part</param>
// <param name="cellProviderInitEventArgs">The args passed by the ➥
   provider Web Part</param>
public void CellProviderInit(object sender
  , CellProviderInitEventArgs cellProviderInitEventArgs)
{
  //Encode and store the field display name.
  _connectedField = SPEncode.HtmlEncode(cellProviderInitEventArgs.FieldDisplayName);
}
```

The CellReady() event handler is used to process data sent by the provider web part. The next code shows an example implementation:

```
// <param name="sender">Reference to the provider Web Part</param>
// <param name="cellReadyEventArgs">The args passed by the provider Web Part</param>
public void CellReady(object sender, CellReadyEventArgs cellReadyEventArgs)
{
  // Make sure child controls have been created.
  EnsureChildControls();
```

```
  // Set the label text to the value of the cell that was passed by the
  // provider part.
  if(cellReadyEventArgs.Cell != null)
  {
    _cellConsumerTextBox.Text = cellReadyEventArgs.Cell.ToString();
  }
}
```

The PartCommunicationInit() method needs to be overridden to fire initialization events, such as CellProviderInit. The next code shows an example implementation:

```
public override void PartCommunicationInit()
{
  // Check if connected.
  if(_connected)
  {
    // If there is a listener, fire the CellConsumerInit event.
    if (CellConsumerInit != null)
    {
      // Create the CellConsumerInitEventArgs structure for the
      // CellConsumerInit event.
      CellConsumerInitEventArgs cellConsumerInitArgs = ➥
        new CellConsumerInitEventArgs();

      // Set the FieldName and FieldDisplayName values.
      cellConsumerInitArgs.FieldName = _cellName;
      cellConsumerInitArgs.FieldDisplayName = _cellDisplayName;

      // Fire the CellConsumerInit event.
      CellConsumerInit(this, cellConsumerInitArgs);
    }
  }
}
```

Connectable web parts use the PartCommunicationMain() method to fire the remaining events that actually pass data to other web parts. A good example of such an event is the CellReady event. ICellConsumer web parts do not send values to other web parts; the following code shows an example implementation taken from an ICellProvider web part:

```
public override void PartCommunicationMain()
{
  // Check if connected.
  if(_connected)
  {
    // If there is a listener, fire the CellReady event.
    if (CellReady != null)
    {
```

```
      // Create the CellReadyEventArgs data structure for
      // the CellProviderInit event.
      CellReadyEventArgs cellReadyArgs = new CellReadyEventArgs();

      // If the user clicked the button, then send the value.
      if (_cellClicked)
      {
        // Set the cell to the value of the TextBox text.
        // This is the value that will be sent to the Consumer
        cellReadyArgs.Cell = _cellInput.Text;
      }
      else
      {
        // The user didn't actually click the button
        // so just send an empty string to the consumer.
        cellReadyArgs.Cell = "";
      }

      // Fire the CellReady event.
      // The Consumer will receive the cell value in its CellReady event handler
      CellReady(this, cellReadyArgs);
    }
  }
}
```

You need to override the GetInitEventArgs() method if the web part needs to participate in transformations. This method supplies the data that is used in the SharePoint transformer user interface. The next code shows an example implementation:

```
// <param name="interfacename">Name of interface on which the Web Part ➥
   Infrastructure is requesting information</param>
public override InitEventArgs GetInitEventArgs(string interfaceName)
{
  // Check if this is my particular cell interface.
  if (interfaceName == "MyCellConsumerInterface")
  {
    // Create the object that will return the initialization arguments.
    CellConsumerInitEventArgs cellConsumerInitArgs = ➥
      new CellConsumerInitEventArgs();

    // Set the FieldName and FieldDisplay name values.
    cellConsumerInitArgs.FieldName = _cellName;
    cellConsumerInitArgs.FieldDisplayName = _cellDisplayName;

    //return the CellConsumerInitEventArgs object.
    return(cellConsumerInitArgs);
  }
```

```
  else
  {
    return(null);
  }
}
```

If you are creating a connectable web part that supports client-side connections, you will need to add a couple of client-side JavaScript functions and render them within the RenderWebPart() method. In the case of an ICellConsumer web part, you will need to implement client-side JavaScript functions that take care of handling the PartCommunicationInit, CellProviderInit, CellReady, and GetInitEventArgs events. In the next example code, the event handlers are implemented in JavaScript functions called myInit(), myCellProviderInit(), myCellReady(), and myGetInitEventArgs().

Client-side functions responsible for handling client-side connections rely heavily on the use of the Web Part Page Services component. This is a client-side JavaScript component that is inserted into a SharePoint web part page by the web part infrastructure that encapsulates the set of services provided to web parts and web part pages. If you want more information about the services provided by the Web Part Page Services component, you can refer back to the beginning of the "Web Part Connections" section earlier in this chapter.

The following code shows how to add client-side code to a web part:

```
protected override void RenderWebPart(HtmlTextWriter output)
{
  // Check for connection interface registration error.
  if (_registrationErrorOccurred)
  {
    output.Write(_registrationErrorMsg);
    return;
  }

  // Render script if connected.
  if(_connected)
  {
    output.Write(ReplaceTokens(
    "<P>\n"
    + "    <B>Consume Cell: </B>\n"
    + "    <INPUT TYPE=\"text\" ID=\"CellValue_WPQ_\"/><br><br>\n"
    + "    Connected to Web Part: <I>" + _connectedWebPartTitle + "</I><br>\n"
    + "    Received from Field: <I><span ID=\"ConnectedField_WPQ_\"></span></I>\n"
    + "</P>\n"

    + "<SCRIPT LANGUAGE='JavaScript'>\n"
    + "<!-- \n"
    + "    var CellConsumerInterface_WPQ_ = new Consumer_WPQ_();\n"

    + "    function Consumer_WPQ_()\n"
    + "    {\n"
    + "        this.PartCommunicationInit = myInit;\n"
```

```
    +  "        this.CellProviderInit = myCellProviderInit;\n"
    +  "        this.CellReady = myCellReady;\n"
    +  "        this.GetInitEventArgs = myGetInitEventArgs;\n"

    +  "        function myInit()\n"
    +  "        {\n"
    +  "           var cellConsumerInitEventArgs = new Object();\n"
    +  "           cellConsumerInitEventArgs.FieldName = \"ConsumerCellName\";\n"
    +  "           cellConsumerInitEventArgs.FieldDisplayName = \"Consume Cell\";\n"
    +  "           WPSC.RaiseConnectionEvent(\"MyCellConsumerInterface_WPQ_\", ➥
                      \"CellConsumerInit\", cellConsumerInitEventArgs);\n"
    +  "        }\n"

    +  "        function myCellProviderInit(sender, cellProviderInitEventArgs)\n"
    +  "        {\n"
    +  "           document.all(\"ConnectedField_WPQ_\").innerText = ➥
                      cellProviderInitEventArgs.FieldDisplayName;\n"
    +  "        }\n"

    +  "        function myCellReady(sender, cellReadyEventArgs)\n"
    +  "        {\n"
    +  "           if(cellReadyEventArgs.Cell != null)\n"
    +  "           {\n"
    +  "              document.all(\"CellValue_WPQ_\").value = ➥
                         cellReadyEventArgs.Cell;\n"
    +  "           }\n"
    +  "        }\n"

    +  "        function myGetInitEventArgs()\n"
    +  "        {\n"
    +  "           var cellConsumerInitEventArgs = new Object();\n"
    +  "           cellConsumerInitEventArgs.FieldName = \"Consume Cell\";\n"
    +  "           cellConsumerInitEventArgs.FieldDisplayName = \"Consume Cell\";\n"
    +  "           return(cellConsumerInitEventArgs);\n"
    +  "        }\n"
    +  "    }\n"
    +  "//-->\n"
    +  "</SCRIPT>\n"));
  }
  else
  {
    //The Web Part isn't connected.
    output.Write(_notConnectedMsg);
  }
}
```

The next code listing shows a complete implementation for an ICellConsumer web part:

```csharp
using System;
using System.ComponentModel;
using System.Web.UI;
using Microsoft.SharePoint.WebPartPages;
using System.Xml.Serialization;
using System.Web.UI.WebControls;
using System.Security;
using Microsoft.SharePoint.Utilities;
using Microsoft.SharePoint.WebPartPages.Communication;

namespace ConnectionCodeSamples
{
  public class ServerSideCellConsumer : WebPart, ICellConsumer
  {
    public event CellConsumerInitEventHandler CellConsumerInit;
    private bool _connected = false;
    private string _connectedWebPartTitle = string.Empty;
    private string _connectedField = string.Empty;
    private string _registrationErrorMsg = "An error has occurred ➥
      trying to register your connection interfaces.";
    private bool _registrationErrorOccurred = false;
    private string _notConnectedMsg = "NOT CONNECTED. To use this Web Part, ➥
      connect it to a server-side Cell Provider Web Part.";
    private string _cellName = "ConsumeCell";
    private string _cellDisplayName = "Consume Cell";
    private TextBox _cellConsumerTextBox;
    private string _connectedWebPartLabel = "Connected to Web Part";
    private string _connectedFieldLabel = "Received from Field";

    public override void EnsureInterfaces()
    {
      try
      {
        RegisterInterface("MyCellConsumerInterface", ➥
          InterfaceTypes.ICellConsumer, WebPart.LimitOneConnection, ➥
          ConnectionRunAt.Server, this, "", "Consume Cell From", ➥
          "Consumes a single value from another Web Part.");
      }
      catch(SecurityException se)
      {
        _registrationErrorOccurred = true;
      }
    }
```

```
public override ConnectionRunAt CanRunAt()
{
  return ConnectionRunAt.Server;
}

public override void PartCommunicationConnect(string interfaceName,
WebPart connectedPart, string connectedInterfaceName, ConnectionRunAt runAt)
{
  if (interfaceName == "MyCellConsumerInterface")
  {
    _connected = true;
    _connectedWebPartTitle = SPEncode.HtmlEncode(connectedPart.Title);
  }
}

public void CellProviderInit(object sender,
CellProviderInitEventArgs cellProviderInitEventArgs)
{
  _connectedField = ➡
    SPEncode.HtmlEncode(cellProviderInitEventArgs.FieldDisplayName);
}

public void CellReady(object sender, CellReadyEventArgs cellReadyEventArgs)
{
  EnsureChildControls();

  if(cellReadyEventArgs.Cell != null)
  {
  _cellConsumerTextBox.Text = cellReadyEventArgs.Cell.ToString();
  }
}

public override void PartCommunicationInit()
{
  if(_connected)
  {
    if (CellConsumerInit != null)
    {
      CellConsumerInitEventArgs cellConsumerInitArgs = ➡
        new CellConsumerInitEventArgs();
      cellConsumerInitArgs.FieldName = _cellName;
      cellConsumerInitArgs.FieldDisplayName = _cellDisplayName;
      CellConsumerInit(this, cellConsumerInitArgs);
    }
  }
}
```

```
public override InitEventArgs GetInitEventArgs(string interfaceName)
{
  if (interfaceName == "MyCellConsumerInterface")
  {
    CellConsumerInitEventArgs cellConsumerInitArgs = ➡
      new CellConsumerInitEventArgs();
    cellConsumerInitArgs.FieldName = _cellName;
    cellConsumerInitArgs.FieldDisplayName = _cellDisplayName;
    return(cellConsumerInitArgs);
  }
  else
  {
    return(null);
  }
}

protected override void RenderWebPart(HtmlTextWriter output)
{
  if (_registrationErrorOccurred)
  {
    output.Write(_registrationErrorMsg);
    return;
  }

  if(_connected)
  {
    output.RenderBeginTag(HtmlTextWriterTag.B);
    output.Write(_cellDisplayName + ": ");
    output.RenderEndTag();

    _cellConsumerTextBox.RenderControl(output);
    output.RenderBeginTag(HtmlTextWriterTag.Br);
    output.RenderEndTag();

    output.Write(_connectedWebPartLabel + ": ");
    output.RenderBeginTag(HtmlTextWriterTag.I);
    output.Write(_connectedWebPartTitle);
    output.RenderEndTag();
    output.Write("<br>");

    output.Write(_connectedFieldLabel + ": ");
    output.RenderBeginTag(HtmlTextWriterTag.I);
    output.Write(_connectedField);
    output.RenderEndTag();
  }
```

```
    else
    {
      output.Write(_notConnectedMsg);
    }
  }

  protected override void CreateChildControls()
  {
    _cellConsumerTextBox = new TextBox();
    _cellConsumerTextBox.ID = "_cellConsumerTextBox";
    Controls.Add(_cellConsumerTextBox);
  }
 }
}
```

Thus, we conclude the section about connectable web parts. After reading this section, you can be confident that you have enough knowledge for creating a web part connections language DSL.

Creating the Web Part Connection Language

In this section we will use the Visual Studio .NET 2005 DSL Toolkit to create a new graphical DSL for creating connectable web parts. We will call this DSL the Web Part Connection Language (WPCL). This section explains in detail how to create the WPCL and how to use it to create connectable web parts.

If you are creating a DSL for Visual Studio .NET 2005 you will need to take a standard series of steps. First, you need to download and install the Visual Studio .NET 2005 DSL Toolkit. The DSL Toolkits enable you to create a graphical DSL. Then, you need to use the DSL Toolkit to create a domain model that describes how the graphical DSL works and how it should be shown within Visual Studio .NET 2005. A standard domain model captures basic validation rules, for example, concept A has a relationship with concept B, but not with concept C. Most of the time, after creating a standard domain model, you will need to add advanced validation rules. After that, you need to create a set of text templates that is responsible for generating code based on a given model of your custom DSL. Most DSL solution development life cycles will conclude with the deployment of the DSL. To this end, you need to create a DSL setup project. You do not need to do this if you are just creating a DSL to use yourself.

We will start with a discussion of the DSL Toolkit, explain how to create a domain model, add advanced validation rules, and create a text template that is able to generate code for connectable web parts based on a WPCL model. We will create another text template that is able to generate code for web part description (.dwp) files, which can be used to import connectable web parts to SharePoint web sites. We will also create a setup project for our custom DSL. Finally, we will show how to use the Web Part Connection Language.

Installation of the DSL Toolkit for Visual Studio .NET 2005

Newer versions of the DSL Toolkit for Visual Studio .NET 2005 are released very regularly. You can check the web site http://msdn.microsoft.com/vstudio/DSLTools/ or go to the Visual Studio

2005 Extensibility Center (http://msdn.microsoft.com/vstudio/extend/) and download the latest release of these tools. The only installation requirement is Visual Studio .NET 2005. Double-click the installation file (VsSDKJune2006.exe) and follow the steps presented to you by the installation wizard.

Note At the time this chapter was written, you needed to join the Visual Studio Industry Partners (VSIP) program before you were allowed to download the software. You can join the program at the Microsoft Visual Studio Developer Center (http://affiliate.vsipmembers.com/).

In this book we have used the June 2006 Community Technology Preview (CTP) release. In earlier releases, the DSL Toolkit installation file was a separate download; nowadays the DSL Toolkit is a part of the Visual Studio 2005 SDK.

The APIs, code generators, and DSL definition format are close to their final form for the release of the first version of the DSL Toolkit, so we do not expect you to have many problems implementing the WPCL in newer versions of the DSL Toolkit. The June 2006 CTP release contains a preview of the DSL Designer that can be used to edit DSL definitions. The preview of the designer still contains bugs and is not as stable as one would like it to be, so if anything, we expect you to have a better developer experience when creating a DSL.

Creating a Domain Model

The purpose of the WPCL is to let developers create connectable web parts in a graphical manner. The WPCL will allow you to drag shapes representing web parts to a designer canvas, connect them to other web parts, and have them implement certain interfaces required for connectable web parts in SharePoint Products and Technologies 2003, such as the ICellConsumer interface (for clarity's sake, we will call those interfaces IConnectable interfaces). The WPCL will validate web part connections for you and is able to generate code based on WPCL models. The WPCL will speed up the development of connectable web parts and reduce chances for making mistakes.

To illustrate what the WPCL can do for you, imagine a plain and simple data enhancement scenario where you want to create an employee web part (called Employee) that implements the IRowProvider interface. Further suppose that you want to create another employee web part (called EmployeePicture) that shows a picture of the employee, based on the employee name chosen in the first web part. The second employee web part will implement the ICellConsumer interface. The two employee web parts will be connected via a server-side connection. In the WPCL, creating these web parts consists of the creation of a WPCL model. Figure 5-1 shows a WPCL model representing the employee scenario.

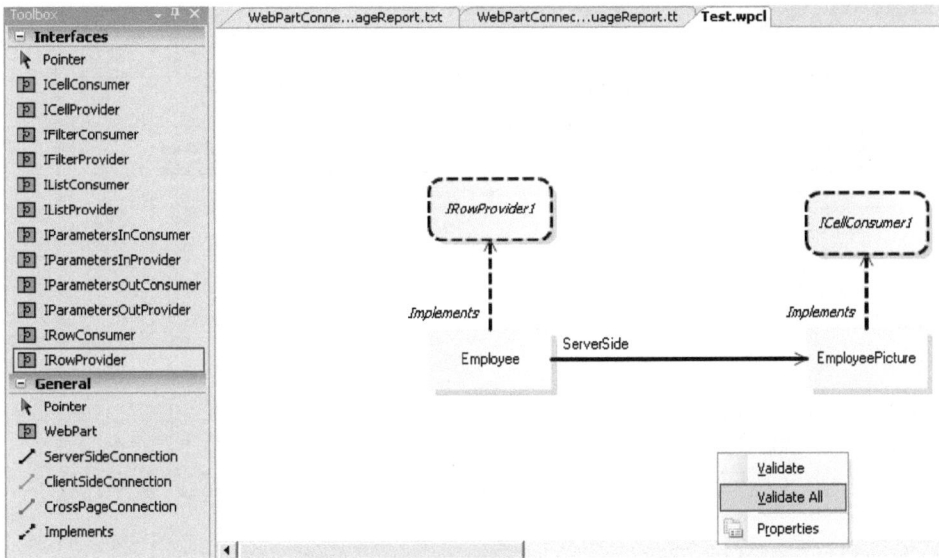

Figure 5-1. *Employee scenario WPCL model*

Choosing a Domain-Specific Language Template

In this section we show how to create the domain model for the WPCL, thus laying the basis for our custom DSL. During the next procedure, you will create a new DSL Designer project used to create DSLs:

1. Start Visual Studio .NET 2005.

2. Choose File ➤ New ➤ Project.

3. On the New Project window, in the Project Types pane, choose Other Project Types ➤ Extensibility.

4. In the Templates pane, under Visual Studio Installed Templates, choose the DSL Designer.

5. Type the following name: **WebPartConnectionLanguage**.

6. Type the following location: **C:\Projects**. At this point, the New Project window should look like Figure 5-2.

7. Click OK. This opens the DSL Designer Wizard.

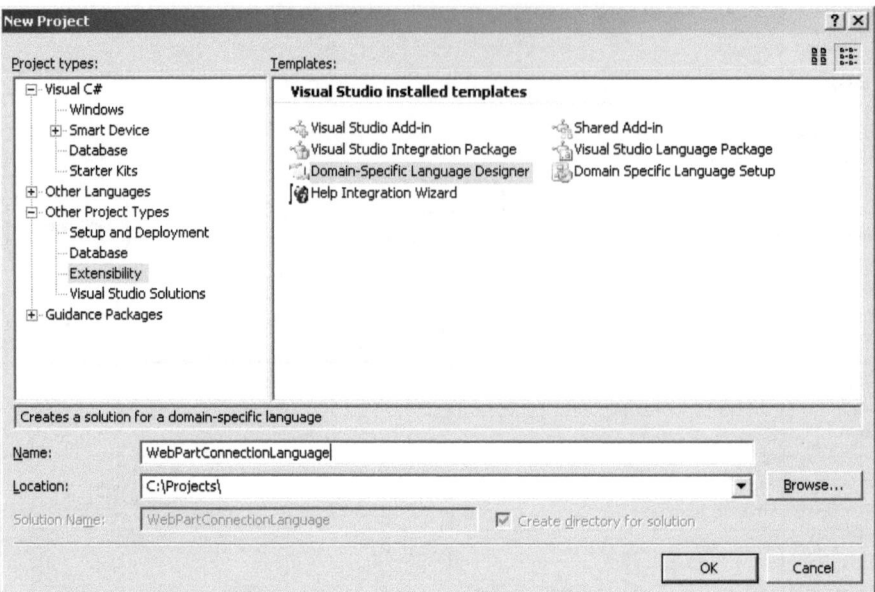

Figure 5-2. *Creating a new DSL*

The first screen of the DSL Designer Wizard lets you choose between several solution templates for DSLs. Solution templates are the starting points for defining custom DSLs. (Figure 5-7 shows the templates that are available out of the box.) The following list contains a description of each of the solution templates:

Class diagrams: Choose this solution template if you want to create UML-like class diagrams. This template includes graphical symbols for classes, interfaces, several types of associations, and generalization and implementation relations. Look at Figure 5-3 to see a DSL that is built using this template.

Component models: Choose this solution template if you want to create basic UML-like component diagrams. This template can be used to create a DSL that uses ports to connect components to other components. Look at Figure 5-4 to see a DSL that is built using this template.

MinimalLanguage: Choose this solution template if the DSL you want to create is very different from any of the other solution templates. This template creates a very basic language consisting of only a box and a line. This is an ideal starting point for creating new and advanced languages. Look at Figure 5-5 to see a DSL that is built using this template.

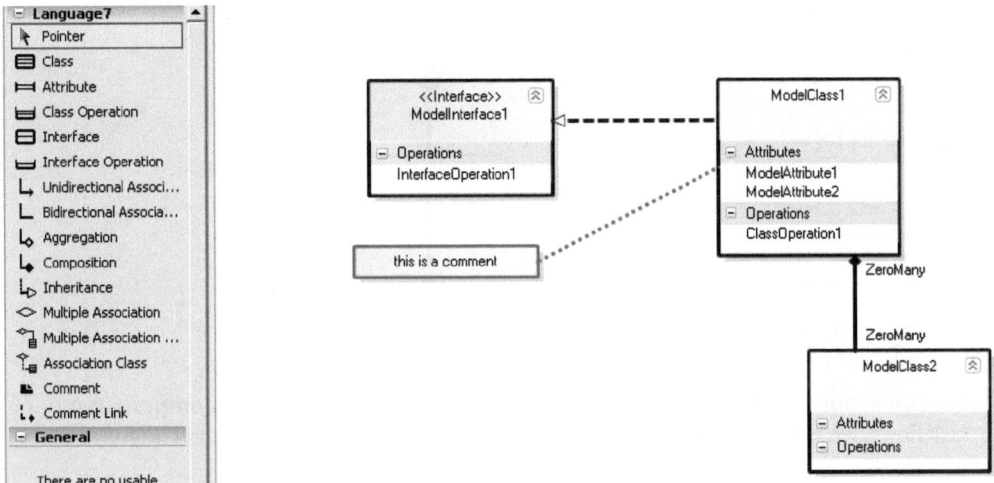

Figure 5-3. *Class diagram template*

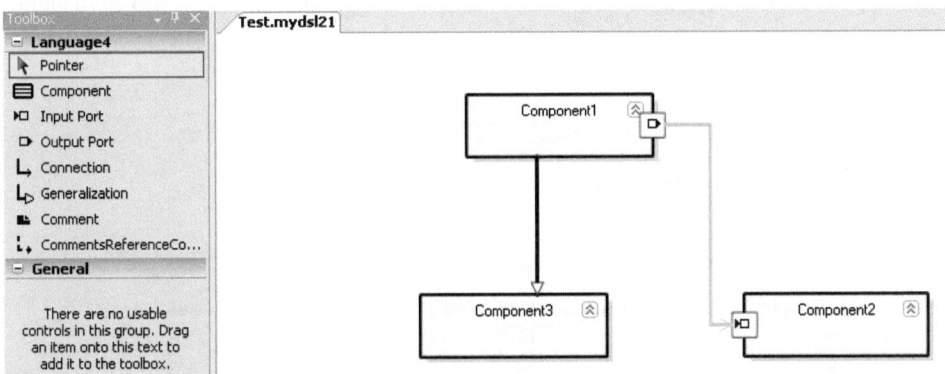

Figure 5-4. *Component model template*

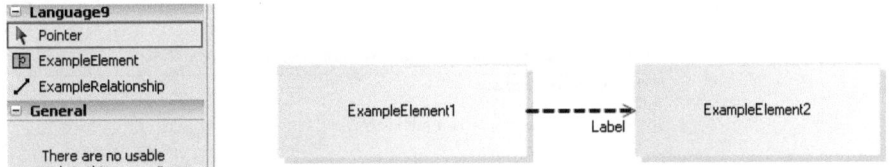

Figure 5-5. *MinimalLanguage template*

Task flow. Choose this solution template if you want to create a language that deals in workflows, states, or sequences. The template helps to create DSLs that resemble UML activity diagrams. Look at Figure 5-6 to see a DSL that is built using this template.

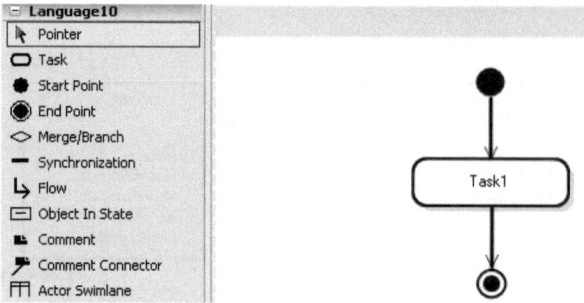

Figure 5-6. *Task flow template*

Since our own DSL, the WPCL, does not look like class diagrams, component models, or task flows, we will start from scratch and build a new DSL using the MinimalLanguage template:

1. Make sure the Solution Settings tab of the DSL Designer Wizard window is selected. Choose the following template: MinimalLanguage.

2. Type the following DSL name: **WebPartConnectionLanguage**. This is shown in Figure 5-7.

3. Click Next.

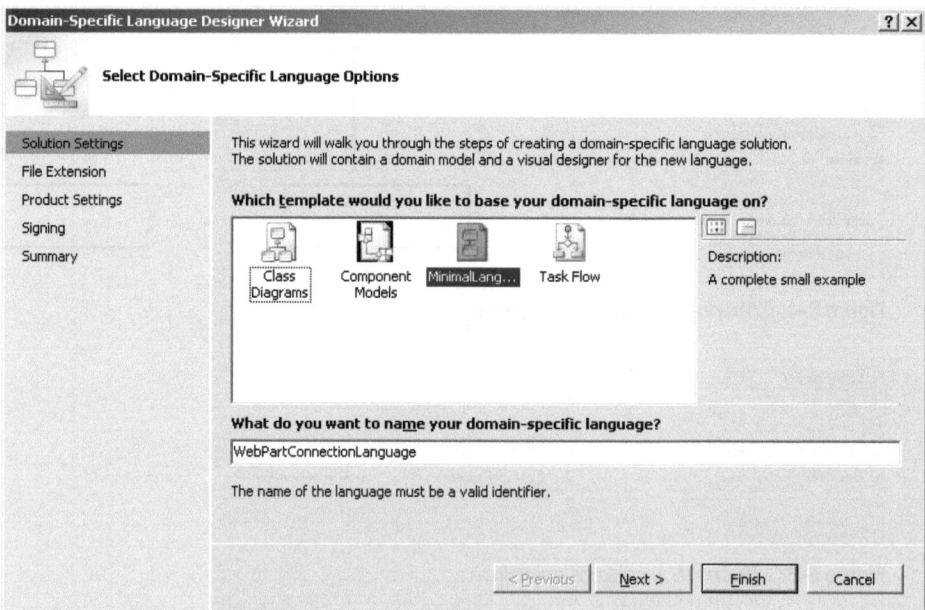

Figure 5-7. *Selecting DSL options*

Configuring the DSL Solution

Once our DSL is created, a new item template is added to Visual Studio .NET 2005 that is associated to our language. Since we are planning to call our DSL the Web Part Connection Language, we will use the following extension: .wpcl. The following procedure explains how to create a new DSL that can generate an item template for creating WPCL models:

1. On the File Extension tab, type the following extension: **wpcl**.

2. If other tools and applications are registered to handle this extension, check the Unregister Domain-Specific Language Tools That Currently Handle This Extension check box. By default, there should be no other registrations.

3. Choose an icon to use for .wpcl model files, or leave the default setting (Default Template Icon). We have chosen to use our own company icon; the window shows a preview of it in Figure 5-8.

4. Click Next.

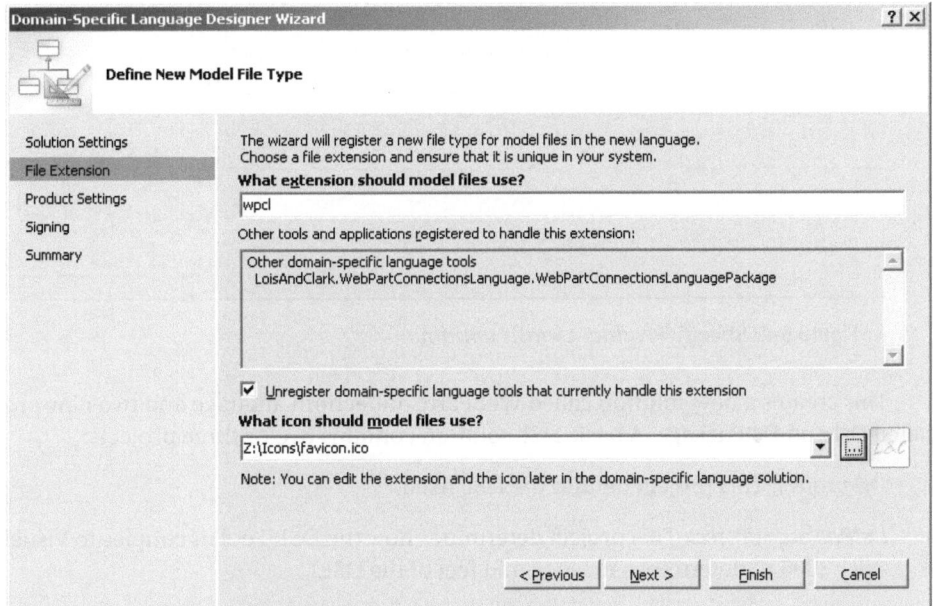

Figure 5-8. *The Define New Model File Type window*

In the next step, you need to define a couple of general product settings: the name of the DSL, the name of the company creating the language, and the default namespace of classes created within the DSL:

1. On the Product Settings tab, type the following product name: **WebPartConnectionLanguage**.

2. Type a company name. We have chosen the name of our own company, Lois and Clark IT Services.

3. Type the following root namespace: **LoisAndClark.WebPartConnectionLanguage**. This is shown in Figure 5-9.

4. At this point we have not reached the end of the wizard yet, but we are satisfied with the settings we have configured so far. So let's skip the strong naming and summary windows and click Finish.

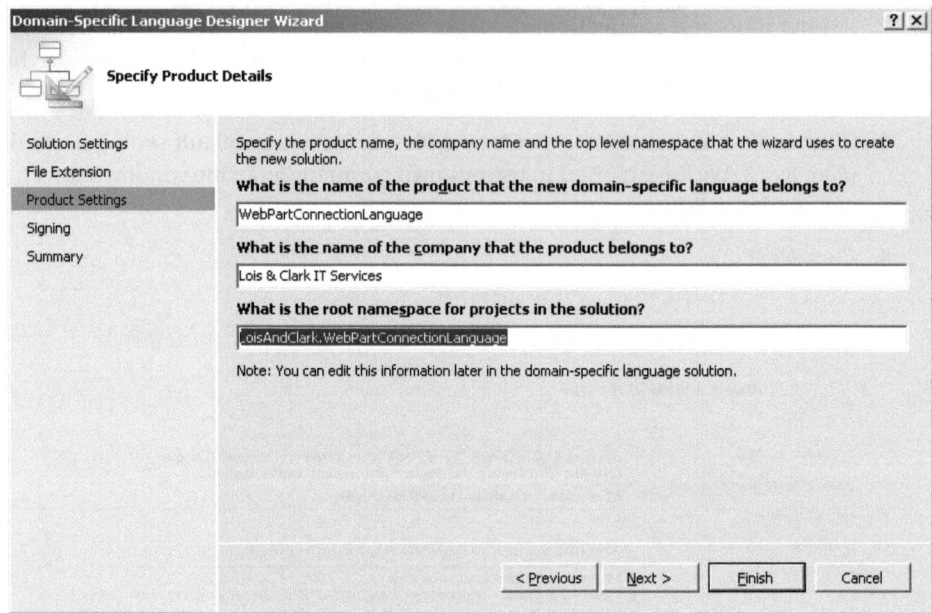

Figure 5-9. *Specify Product Details window*

This creates a new solution called WebPartConnectionLanguage and two new projects called Dsl and DslPackage. A basic DSL solution contains two or three projects:

Dsl project: This project defines the DSL itself.

DslPackage project: This project determines how the DSL Toolkit couples to Visual Studio .NET 2005 (it determines the look and feel of the DSL).

Setup project: Although not created by default, most DSL solutions will also contain a setup project. DSL Setup projects are used to deploy DSL solutions.

The Dsl and DslPackage projects contain text templates that are used to generate code. This code is required to run the DSL. As soon as the new solution is created, automatically all text templates are used to generate the required code for the MinimalLanguage template. Wait until the transformation of all text templates is finished, then make sure that DslDefinition.dsl of the Dsl project is selected. DslDefinition.dsl contains the definition of the domain model, which defines the entities and relationships that exist in any given DSL. The default domain model for our WebPartConnectionLanguage language is shown in Figure 5-10.

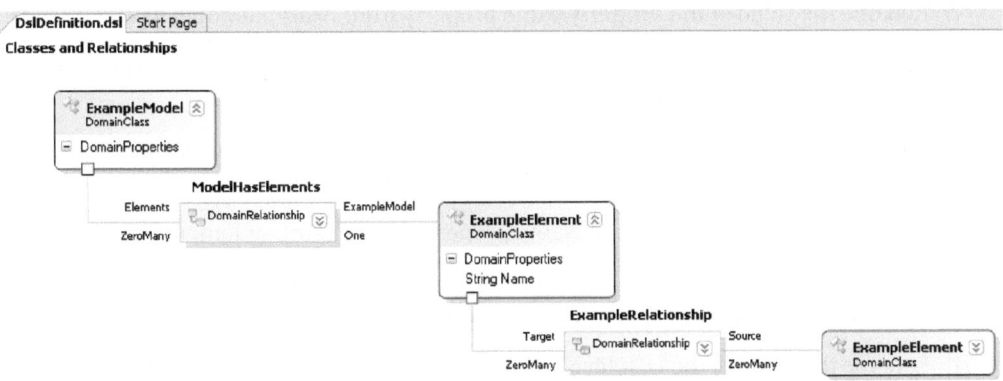

Figure 5-10. *Default domain model*

Adding Support for Web Parts

Figure 5-10 shows the MinimalLanguage template domain model. The domain model starts with the definition of the ExampleModel root domain class which can be found at the upper left corner of Figure 5-10. Root domain classes are the starting point of every DSL. The ExampleModel root domain class has a relationship with the ExampleElement domain class, called the ModelHasElements relationship. This relationship expresses that our WPCL consists of multiple ExampleElement instances that have a Name property. Since the ExampleModel root domain class has no other relationships, our language cannot contain other kinds of domain classes. The ExampleRelationship relationship expresses that ExampleElement instances can be related to each other. Figure 5-5 shows a small program created via the MinimalLanguage.

We will use this domain model and enhance it step-by-step to build our WPCL. First, you will adjust the MinimalLanguage domain model to accommodate the most basic of needs of the WPCL. You will adjust the current model so that our language consists of web parts that can be related to each other via server-side connections:

1. On the Classes and Relationships swimming lane (located on the left of the canvas, as can be seen in Figure 5-10), click the ExampleModel domain class, go to the Properties window and change the value of the Name property to WPCLModel.

2. Right-click the DomainProperties section of the WPCLModel domain class ➤ Add New DomainProperty.

3. Set the name of the new property to the following value: Namespace. This property will be used as the default namespace of web parts that are generated using a WPCL model.

4. Right-click the DomainProperties section of the WPCLModel domain class ➤ Add New DomainProperty.

5. Set the name of the new property to the following value: Assembly. This property will be used as the value for the assembly name when creating web part description files.

6. Click the right side of the ModelHasElements relationship, go to the Properties window, and rename the value of the PropertyDisplayName property from ExampleModel to WPCLModel.

7. Rename the value of the PropertyName property from ExampleModel to WPCLModel.

8. Click the left side of the ModelHasElements relationship, go to the Properties window, and rename the value of the Name property to WPCLModel.

9. Click the ExampleElement domain class, go to the Properties window, and rename the value of the Name property from ExampleElement to WebPart.

10. Rename the value of the DisplayName property from ExampleElement to WebPart.

11. Click the ExampleRelationship relationship, go to the Properties window and rename the value of the Name property from ExampleRelationship to ServerSideConnection.

12. Rename the value of the DisplayName property from ExampleRelationship to ServerSideConnection.

13. Click the right side of the ServerSideConnection relationship, go to the Properties window, and rename the value of the Name property from Target to Consumers.

14. Click the left side of the ServerSideConnection relationship, go to the Properties window, and rename the value of the Name property from Source to Providers.

The Classes and Relationships section of the basic Web Part Connection Language DSL should look like Figure 5-11.

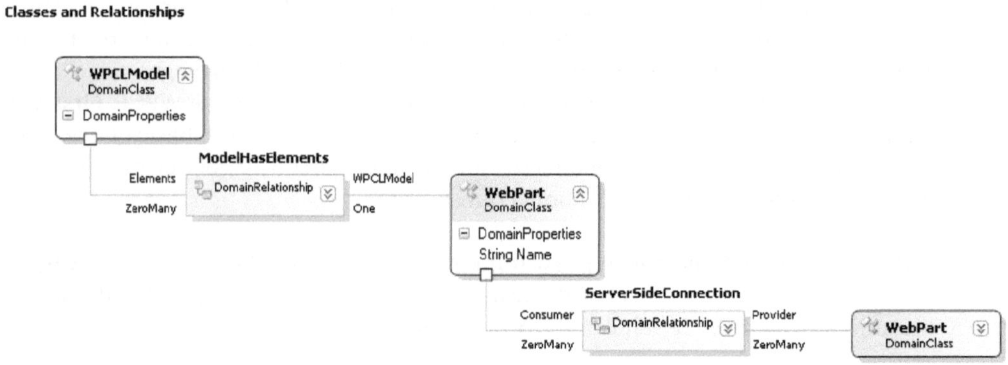

Figure 5-11. *The Classes and Relationships section*

For the benefit of the generation of web part description files, we will also add the ability to define web part titles and descriptions:

1. Click the WebPart domain class.

2. Right-click the DomainProperties section of the WebPart domain class ➤ Add New DomainProperty.

3. Set the name of the new property to the following value: Title. This property will be used as the value for the <Title> element of a web part description file.

4. Right-click the DomainProperties section of the WebPart domain class ➤ Add New DomainProperty.

5. Set the Name of the new property to the following value: Description. This property will be used as the value for the <Description> element of a web part description file.

Creating the Look and Feel for Web Parts in the WPCL

You have defined a logical model of the Web Part Connection Language DSL to indicate that our WPCLModel consists of WebPart domain classes representing web parts.

The WPCL is a graphical language that allows you to create visual models that describe sets of connectable web parts and their relationships. Although the logical part of the domain model that describes web parts is created, we have yet to translate this logic to a user interface that can be shown in Visual Studio .NET 2005. Next, we will define what a web part shape will look like in the WPCL when displayed in Visual Studio .NET 2005 in a WPCL model.

Although not strictly necessary, for consistency reasons we will rename the connector that binds web parts to other web parts to ServerSideConnectionConnector.

1. Go to the right swimming lane called Diagram Elements and click the ExampleShape GeometryShape. Go to the Properties window and rename the value of the Name property from ExampleShape to WebPartShape.

2. Change the InitialHeight property from 0.75 to 0.5.

3. Change the InitialWidth property from 2 to 1.

4. Change the FillColor property to Linen.

5. Click the ExampleConnector connector, go to the Properties window, and rename the value of the Name property from ExampleConnector to ServerSideConnectionConnector.

The Diagram Elements section of your base WPCL DSL should look like Figure 5-12.

Diagram Elements

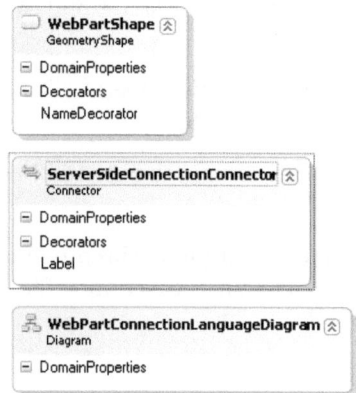

Figure 5-12. *Select domain model diagram elements*

Changing the WPCL Toolbox

If you look back at Figure 5-3, you will see that the toolbox related to class diagram items contains entries for class diagram elements such as Class, Attribute, Class Operation, and Interface. If you compare this to Figure 5-5, you will notice that the toolbox in Figure 5-5 only contains the following elements: ExampleElement and ExampleRelationship. In the next step we will adjust the toolbox for our WPCL so that it contains elements representing web parts and server-side web part connections. This reflects the entities defined in our logical domain model so far:

1. Click the DSL Explorer tab. This hides the Solution Explorer window.

2. Expand Editor ➤ Toolbox Tabs ➤ Toolbox tab. Change the TabText property to General.

3. Expand Tools.

4. Click ExampleElement. ExampleElement is an ElementTool. Change the value of the Name property from ExampleElement to WebPart.

5. Ensure the Order property is set to 0.

6. Click ExampleRelationship. ExampleRelationship is a ConnectionTool. Change the value of the Name property from ExampleRelationship to ServerSideConnection.

7. Set the Order property to 10.

The toolbox definition should look like Figure 5-13.

Figure 5-13. *Changing the toolbox via the DSL Explorer*

Adding Client-Side and Cross-Page Connections

Our WPCL domain model already allows web part server-side connections to be made. As you have learned from the section "Web Part Connections," three types of web-part-to-web-part connections can be made: server-side, client-side, and cross-page connections. In the next steps you will adjust the WPCL domain model so that it also supports client-side and cross-page connections:

1. In the DSL Designer Toolbox pane on the left part of the screen, click Reference Relationship.

2. Click the WebPart DomainClass shape on the designer canvas and drag the cursor out of the shape and back in again. Once you release the left mouse button, a new relationship between the WebPart domain class and itself is created.

3. Click the new relationship and enter the following value for the name property: **ClientSideConnection**.

4. Click the right side of the ClientSideConnection relationship and change the Name property to the following value: ClientSideConsumers.

5. Click the left side of the ClientSideConnection relationship and change the Name property to the following value: ClientSideProviders.

6. Repeat the previous steps to create another WebPart to WebPart relationship called CrossPageConnection. Change the name of the right part of the relationship to CrossPageConsumers, and change the name of the left part of the relationship to CrossPageProviders.

The relationships of the WebPart domain class should look like Figure 5-14.

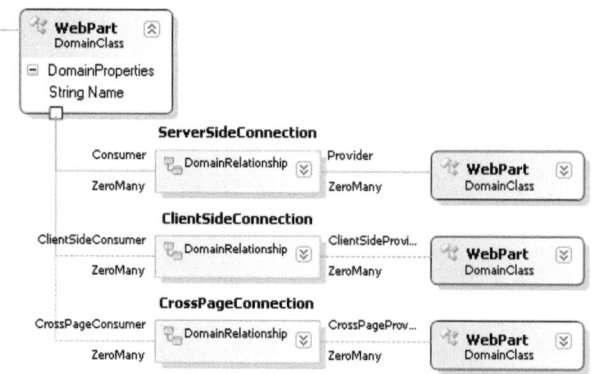

Figure 5-14. *WebPart relationships*

Creating the Look and Feel for Existing Relationships

At this point you have defined the kinds of connections web parts are allowed to have. Since the WPCL is a graphical language, you will also need to define what these relationships will look like when you are starting to create programs written in the WPCL. First, we will create two new icons that will be used to represent client-side and cross-page connections in our WPCL toolbox:

1. Open the Solution Explorer and go to the Resources folder of the Dsl project. Copy ExampleConnectorToolBitmap.bmp (to represent server-side connections) twice, and rename the copies to ClientSideConnectorToolBitmap.bmp and CrossPageConnectorToolBitmap.bmp.

2. If you click them, a simple Colors toolbox appears that helps to customize the images, should you feel the need to. The images will appear later on the toolbox of our WPCL. We have changed the images so that the client-side connection toolbox icon is green and the cross-page connection toolbox icon is red. This can be seen in Figure 5-15 and Figure 5-16.

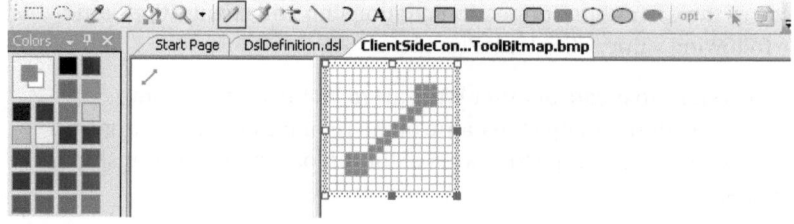

Figure 5-15. *Client-side connection toolbox image*

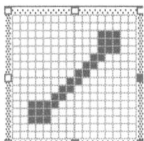

Figure 5-16. *Cross-page connection toolbox image*

Next, you will change the look and feel of the connection shapes that will be used within the WPCL. Basically, server-side connections will be black, client-side connections green, and cross-page connections red. Furthermore, you will add a Label property to all relationships, so developers using the WPCL can annotate them. You will also define that the default names of relationships will be shown at the upper left corner:

1. Double-click DslDefinition.dsl and switch to the DSL Explorer.

2. Expand the Connection Builders node.

3. Select the connection builder called ConnectExampleRelation and change the value of the Name property to ServerSideConnectionBuilder.

4. Examine the list of connection builders as shown in Figure 5-17.

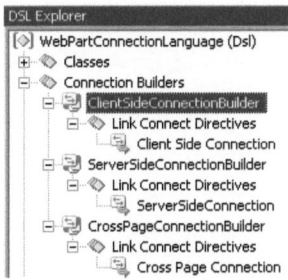

Figure 5-17. *Current list of connection builders*

5. In the DSL Explorer, expand the Connectors node and select ServerSideConnectionConnector.

6. Change the value of the DashStyle property to Solid.

7. Change the value of the DisplayName property to ServerSideConnectionConnector.

8. Change the value of the FixedTooltipText property to ServerSideConnectionConnector.

9. Expand the Decorators node and click Label.

10. Set the value of the DefaultText property to ServerSideConnection.

11. Set the Position property to SourceTop.

12. Right-click the root node WebPartConnectionLanguage (Dsl) ➤ Add New Connector.

13. Repeat the previous step to add another connector.

14. Click Connectors ➤ Connector1.

15. Change the value of the Color property to LimeGreen.

16. Change the value of the Name property to ClientSideConnectionConnector.

17. Change the value of the TargetEndStyle property to EmptyArrow.

18. Right-click ClientSideConnectionConnector ➤ Add New TextDecorator.

19. Change the value of the Name property of the Text Decorator to Label.

20. Set the value of the DefaultText property to ClientSideConnection.

21. Set the Position property to SourceTop.

22. Click Connector 2 and repeat the previous steps. Set the Color property to Red, the Name property to CrossPageConnectionConnector, and the TargetEndStyle property to EmptyArrow. Add a Text Decorator called Label, set its DefaultText property to CrossPageConnection, and set its Position property to SourceTop.

The current list of Connectors is seen in Figure 5-18.

Figure 5-18. *Current list of connectors*

Connector maps are used to relate logical relationships to connector shapes. Next, you will relate the connector shapes you have just created to the logical client-side and cross-page relationships:

1. In the DSL Explorer, expand the Diagram node ➤ Connector Maps.

2. Right-click the Diagram node ➤ Add New ConnectorMap.

3. Repeat the previous step to add another connector map.

4. Select the first ConnectorMap and change the Relationship property to ClientSideConnection.

5. Set the Connector property to ClientSideConnectionConnector.

6. Select the second ConnectorMap and change the Relationship property to CrossPageConnection.

7. Set the Connector property to CrossPageConnectionConnector.

Figure 5-19 shows the current list of connector maps.

Figure 5-19. *Current list of connector maps*

Adding Client-Side and Cross-Page Connections to the Toolbox

The domain model is updated so that all sorts of web part connections are supported. We have also created shapes for the various kinds of connections and bound the logical relationships to these shapes. Next, you need to customize the toolbox so that it contains elements representing client-side and cross-page connections:

1. In the DSL Explorer, open the Editor node ➤ Toolbox Tabs ➤ ToolboxTab ➤ Add New ConnectionTool.

2. Repeat the previous step to add another connection tool.

3. Expand the Tools node and click ConnectionTool1.

4. Set the Name property to ClientSideConnection.

5. Set the value of the Connection Builder property to ClientSideConnectionBuilder.

6. Set the value of the ToolboxIcon to Resources\ClientSideConnectorToolBitmap.bmp.

7. Set the Order property to 20.

8. Click ConnectionTool2.

9. Set the Name property to CrossPageConnection.

10. Set the value of the Connection Builder property to CrossPageConnectionBuilder.

11. Set the value of the ToolboxIcon to Resources\CrossPageConnectorToolBitmap.bmp.

12. Set the Order property to 30.

At this point the Web Part Connection Language Toolbox contains the items shown in Figure 5-20.

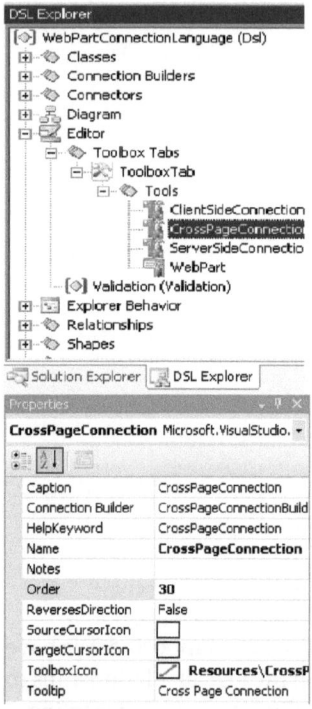

Figure 5-20. *Web Part Connection Language toolbox*

Testing the First Version of the WPCL

Creating a domain model for the very first time is a somewhat abstract activity. It is helpful to build the DSL solution to see what you have accomplished thus far. If you switch to the Solution Explorer and click the Transform All Templates on the Solution Explorer toolbar (shown in Figure 5-21), all text templates in the DSL solution are transformed. The text templates are responsible for creating the code required for creating our WPCL.

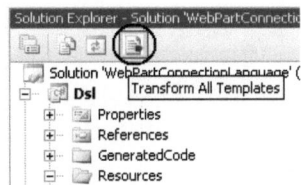

Figure 5-21. *Transform All Templates*

After the transformation is complete, you can build the DSL solution. If you press F5 to start debugging the solution, a new instance of Visual Studio .NET 2005 is started. The new instance of Visual Studio .NET 2005 is a so-called *experimental build*, which means that the new instance uses its own registry hive called the *experimental hive*. This safeguards the original Visual Studio .NET 2005 instance from any changes caused by the experimental instance. You can start Visual Studio .NET 2005 using the experimental registry hive by running the following command from the Visual Studio .NET 2005 command prompt:

```
[drive letter]:\Program Files\Microsoft Visual Studio 8 ➥
\Common7\IDE\devenv /RootSuffix Exp
```

The experimental hive is created upon installation of the Visual Studio .NET 2005 SDK; installation creates a clone of the existing Visual Studio registry hive and makes a new copy in the experimental hive.

The new instance of Visual Studio .NET 2005 shows what the WPCL looks like thus far. If it is not selected by default, double-click the following file: test.wpcl. This is a WPCL item that allows you to work with the WPCL. Figure 5-22 shows a sample diagram created using the base version of the WPCL you have created at this point.

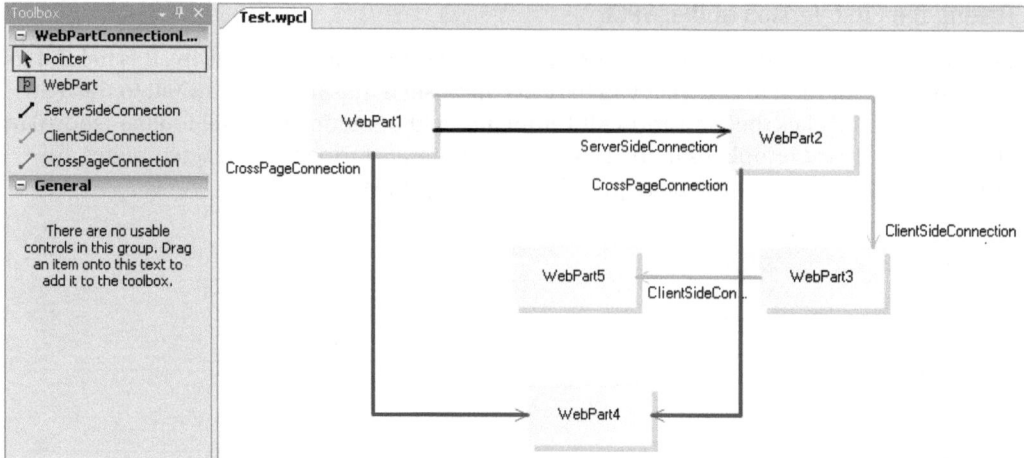

Figure 5-22. *Basic version of WPCL*

Adding IConnectable Interfaces

When building a graphical language that helps to create connectable web parts there is no doubt that web parts and types of web part connections are key parts of such a language. However, until this far, a crucial element of a language for creating connectable web parts is missing: connectable interfaces, such as ICellConsumer, and ICellProvider. In the next part, we will add connectable interfaces to the WPCL.

First of all, the domain model needs to reflect the fact that not only web parts can be added to the WPCLModel root domain class, but interfaces as well. As we do not want to add a relationship between the WPCLModel root domain class and every connectable interface (12 in total), we will create a new domain class called IConnectable (a name we invented ourselves; don't try to find this one in the SharePoint documentation). You will add a relationship between the WPCLModel domain class and the IConnectable domain class called: ModelHasInterfaces. The ModelHasInterfaces relationship expresses the fact that a WPCLModel can contain interfaces. In our domain model, we will make sure that every connectable interface, such as ICellConsumer, inherits from IConnectable. This way, the ModelHasInterfaces relationship applies to every child of IConnectable.

You will also add a new relationship between the WebPart domain class and the IConnectable domain class, called Implements. The Implements relationship expresses the fact that a web part can implement one or more connectable interfaces.

The next procedure adds the possibility to use IConnectable classes within WPCL models:

1. Drag a new Domain Class shape on the designer canvas in the Classes and Relationships swimming lane.

2. Click the new domain class called DomainClass1 and set the value of the Name property to IConnectable.

3. Set the InheritanceModifier property to abstract. This prevents the IConnectable domain class from being used directly in WPCL models.

4. Right-click the DomainProperties section of the IConnectable domain class and choose Add New DomainProperty.

5. Set the name of the new domain property to Name.

6. Set the IsElementName property of the new Name domain property to true.

7. Expand the Xml Serialization Behavior node that is located beneath the WebPartConnectionLanguage (Dsl) root node.

8. Expand the IConnectable ➤ Element Data.

9. Select Name and set its `IsMonikerKey` property to true. A *moniker key* is a domain property that uniquely identifies an object when a model is serialized to a file. For each domain class, you should choose a property that can be set differently for each sibling of the class, typically a name or a serial number. You can mark a property as an `ElementName` to ensure that names are unique; this causes the designer to give a distinct initial value to a property when an instance of a domain class is created. Although not required, often a property that is marked as being a moniker key is also marked as being an element name.

10. In the Toolbox, click Embedding Relationship, then click the WPCLModel domain class and drag the embedding relationship all the way down to the IConnectable domain class.

11. Select the new domain relationship shape and set its Name property to ModelHasInterfaces.

12. Select the right side of the Implements relationship and set the Name property to Interfaces.

13. Drag a new Domain Class shape to the designer canvas and set the Name property to ICellConsumer.

14. In the Toolbox, click Inheritance.

15. Click the ICellConsumer domain class and drag the mouse to the IConnectable domain class. This creates an inheritance relationship where the IConnectable domain class is the parent of the ICellConsumer domain class.

16. Repeat the previous three steps for the following domain classes: ICellProvider, IFilterConsumer, IFilterProvider, IListConsumer, IListProvider, IParametersInConsumer, IParametersInProvider, IParametersOutConsumer, IParametersOutProvider, IRowConsumer, and IRowProvider.

17. In the Toolbox, click Reference Relationship.

18. Click the WebPart domain class and drag the mouse to the IConnectable domain class. This creates a new reference relation between web parts and IConnectable interfaces.

19. Click the new reference relation and choose the following value for the Name property: Implements.

20. Click the right side of the Implements relationship and change the Name property to WebParts.

21. Click the left side of the Implements relationship and change the Name property to IConnectableInterfaces.

Figure 5-23 shows a part of the WPCL definition. As you can see, the IConnectable domain class has several children, such as the ICellConsumer domain class. The ModelHasInterfaces relationship that expresses that a WPCLModel can contain multiple interface domain classes is shown in this figure as well.

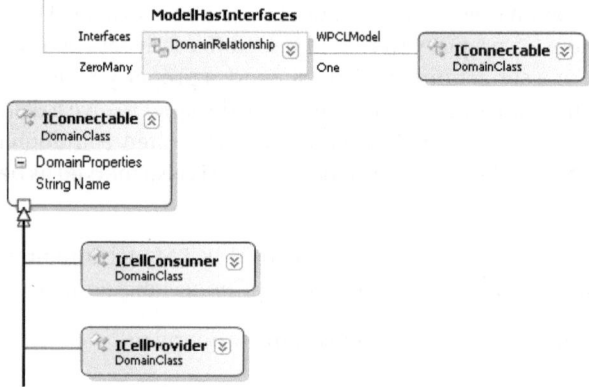

Figure 5-23. *Interfaces of Web Part Connection Language DSL*

Adding Visual Representations for Interface Items

Now that you have created IConnectable interface domain classes for the WPCL, you will need to add interface items in the toolbox as well, thus enabling developers using the WPCL to add interfaces to a WPCL diagram. In this section, you will create a new interface shape, create a new shape that is used to model the Implements relationship, create a new icon that is used in the toolbox to represent the Implements relationship, and create a new toolbox tab that hosts the new toolbox interface elements.

During the next steps, you will add a new interface shape that represents the Implements relationship:

1. Drag a new Geometry Shape to the Diagram Elements swimming lane of the designer canvas.

2. Select the new geometry shape called GeometryShape1, and set the value of the Name property to the following value: InterfaceShape.

3. Set the FillColor property of the InterfaceShape shape to Bisque.

4. Set the Geometry property to RoundedRectangle.

5. Set the InitialHeight property to 0.5.

6. Set the InitialWidth property to 1.

7. Set the OutlineDashStyle to Dash.

8. Switch to the DSL Explorer and expand the Shapes node that is located beneath the WebPartConnectionLanguage (Dsl) root node.

9. Right-click the InterfaceShape shape ➤ Add New TextDecorator.

10. Set the Name property to the following value: NameDecorator.

11. Set the FontStyle property to Italic.

12. Set the Position property to Center.

Next, you will map the newly created interface shape to the IConnectable domain classes. This tells Visual Studio .NET 2005 how to display interfaces in a WPCL model:

1. Expand the Diagram node located beneath the WebPartConnectionLanguage (Dsl) root node.

2. Expand the Shape Maps node and inspect the current ShapeMap located beneath it between the WebPartShape and the WebPart class.

3. Right-click the Diagram node ~ New ShapeMap.

4. Select the new ShapeMap that is located beneath the Shape Maps node.

5. Set the Shape property to InterfaceShape.

6. Set the class Property to ICellConsumer.

7. Repeat the previous four steps to create InterfaceShape mappings to the following classes: ICellProvider, IFilterConsumer, IFilterProvider, IListConsumer, IListProvider, IParametersInConsumer, IParametersInProvider, IParametersOutConsumer, IParametersOutProvider, IRowConsumer, and IRowProvider.

During the next steps, you will create a new shape that represents the Implements relationship in a WPCL model:

1. Right-click the WebPartConnectionLanguage (Dsl) node ➤ Add New Connector.

2. Expand the Connectors node and select the new connector (Connector1).

3. Set the Name property to the following value: ImplementsConnector.

4. Set the DashStyle to Dash.

5. Set the TargetEndStyle property to the following value: EmptyArrow.

6. Right-click the ImplementsConnector node ➤ Add New TextDecorator.

7. Expand the Decorators node and select the new decorator (TextDecorator1).

8. Set the Name property of the text decorator to Label.

9. Set the FontStyle property to Italic.

10. Right-click the Diagram node beneath the WebPartConnectionLanguage (Dsl) root node ➤ Add New ConnectorMap.

11. Expand the Connector Maps node and select the new connector map (ConnectorMap).

12. Set the Relationship property to Implements.

13. Set the Connector property to ImplementsConnector.

Now you will create a toolbox tab to the WPCL toolbox. You will add icons that represent the IConnectable interfaces to this new tab:

1. Expand the Editor node located beneath the WebPartConnectionLanguage (Dsl).

2. Right-click the Expand the Editor node and choose Add New Toolbox Tab.

3. Select the new Toolbox Tab and change the value of the TabText property from Tab2 to Interfaces.

4. Expand the Tools node.

5. Right-click the ToolboxTab node ➤ Add New Element Tool.

6. Select the new Element tool (ElementTool1) that is located under the Tools node.

7. Set the Name property to ICellConsumer.

8. Set the Class property to ICellConsumer.

9. Set the ToolboxIcon property to Resources\ExampleShapeToolBitmap.bmp.

10. Set the Order property to 0. Increase this number by 10 for every new element tool.

11. Repeat the previous six steps for the following classes: ICellProvider, IFilterConsumer, IFilterProvider, IListConsumer, IListProvider, IParametersInConsumer, IParametersInProvider, IParametersOutConsumer, IParametersOutProvider, IRowConsumer, and IRowProvider.

To complete the WPCL toolbox, you will create and add a new icon that represents the Implements relationship:

1. Click Solution Explorer and expand the Resources folder of the Dsl project.

2. Copy ExampleConnectorToolBitmap.bmp and rename the new image to ImplementsConnectorToolBitmap.bmp. We have adjusted the image a little bit so that it looks like Figure 5-24.

3. Double-click DslDefinition.dsl in the Dsl project.

4. Right-click the Diagram node located beneath the WebPartConnectionLanguage (Dsl) root node ➤ Add New ConnectorMap.

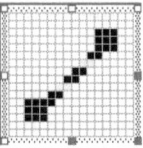

Figure 5-24. *ImplementsConnectorToolBitmap.bmp*

5. Expand the Connector Maps node and select the new connector map (ConnectorMap).

6. Set the Relationship property to Implements.

7. Set the Connector property to ImplementsConnector.

8. Right-click the ToolboxTab node ➤ Add New Connection Tool.

9. Select the new connection tool (ConnectionTool1) and set the Name property to Implements.

10. Set the Connection Builder property to ImplementsBuilder.

11. Set the ToolboxIcon property to Resources\ImplementsConnectorToolBitmap.bmp.

12. Set the Order property to 40.

Making the Interface Shapes Visible on the Canvas

Although you have created interface and interface connector shapes and added elements in the toolbox that represent those elements, if you transform the text templates and build this DSL solution and drag, let's say, an IConsumer interface to the designer canvas, it will not be visible yet. In the next part, you will use the DSL Details window to specify explicit parent elements for every interface domain class. It is only then that the WPCL will function correctly.

■**Note** In this chapter we are using the June 2006 CTP release of the DSL Toolbox. In future versions of the domain model designer it might not be necessary to specify parent elements for the interface domain classes explicitly.

The next procedure visualizes model elements when shown in the designer generated during the compilation of our WPCL domain model:

1. Click View ➤ Other Windows ➤ DSL Details. This opens the DSL Details Window.

2. On the designer canvas that allows you to create WPCL models select the IConsumer domain class.

3. On the DSL Details window, click the Mapping Details tab.

4. On the General Tab, specify the following Parent Element path: ModelHasInterfaces.WPCLModel/!WPCLModel (see Figure 5-25).

5. Click the Decorator Maps tab, check the NameDecorator decorator and choose the following value for the Display property: Name.

6. Repeat the previous four steps for the following domain classes: ICellProvider, IFilterConsumer, IFilterProvider, IListConsumer, IListProvider, IParametersInConsumer, IParametersInProvider, IParametersOutConsumer, IParametersOutProvider, IRowConsumer, and IRowProvider.

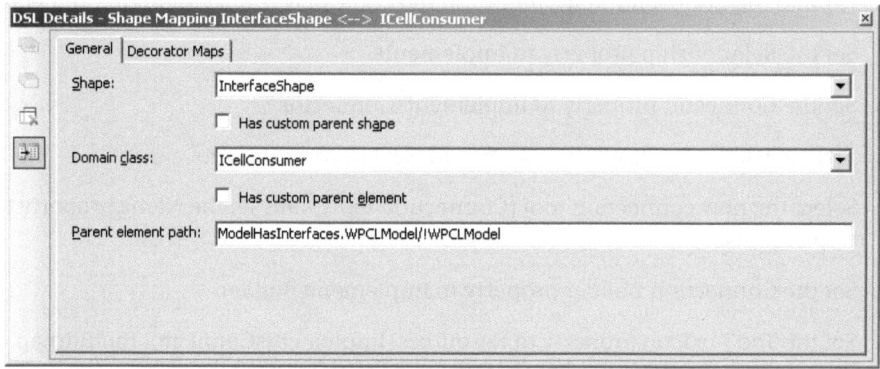

Figure 5-25. *The DSL Details window*

Generating the WPCL

If you transform all text templates and run the solution you can try out the WPCL in a new instance of Visual Studio .NET 2005. Figure 5-26 shows a .wpcl item after creating a model using the WPCL.

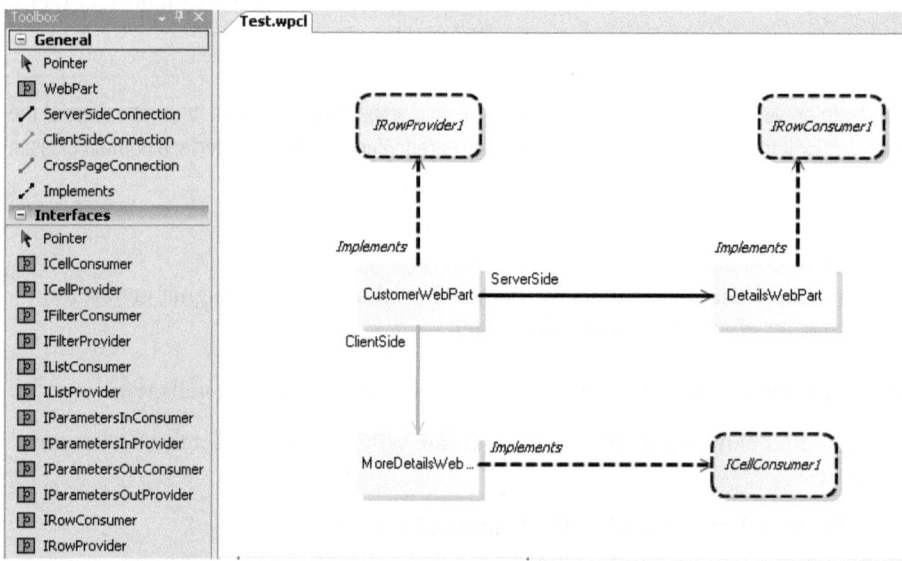

Figure 5-26. *The WPCL*

Validation

The domain model created in the section "Creating a Domain Model" contains basic validation rules. For example, the IListProvider interface is not allowed to have an Implements relationship with another interface. The ability to check for semantic correctness in a domain model will only take you so far. Since the WPCL is governed by a number of additional and advanced validation rules we will need to provide another method of validation.

This is done by adding validation rules in the form of methods of partial classes. The name of a partial class corresponds to the name of the domain model class that you want to validate. The validation framework applies each validation rule to each object in the WPCL model that corresponds to the given domain class or its subclasses. This allows users of our DSL to run validation on WPCL models.

Validation Events

Validation rules can be applied to any domain class in a DSL, including the root model and relationships. You can enable validation for the following events:

Menu: If you enable this option, users can validate a model by right-clicking anywhere in the model.

Save: If you enable this option, users validate a model every time they save it to a file.

Open: If you enable this option, users validate a model every time they open it from a file.

Custom: If you enable this option, you invoke validation from your custom code.

Before you start adding custom validation rules, you should enable validation rules for the Menu, Save, and Open events. You can do this by selecting the DSL Explorer, expanding the Editor node, which is located under the WebPartConnectionLanguage (Dsl) root node, and selecting the Validation (Validation) node. Set the following properties to true: UsesMenu, UsesOpen, and UsesSave. This is shown in Figure 5-27.

Figure 5-27. *Enabling Validation events*

Building a Validation Rule That Always Fails

In this section, you will build a set of validation rules that apply to web parts. To enable this, you will add a new partial class to the Dsl project that has a name that is identical to the WebPart domain class. This partial class will contain a validation method that responds to the following validation events: Open, Save, and Menu. In the first version of this validation method, validation will never succeed. Instead, the LogError() method of the ValidationContext object is called. This method receives three arguments: an error description, an error code, and the current domain object causing the error.

1. Right-click the Dsl project ➤ Add ➤ New Item. This opens the Add New Item – Dsl window.

2. Select the following template: Class.

3. Specifiy the following name: WebPartValidation.cs.

4. Click Add.

5. Double-click WebPartValidation.cs and add the following code:

```
using System;
using System.Collections.Generic;
using System.Text;
using System.Collections.ObjectModel;
using Microsoft.VisualStudio.Modeling.Validation;
```

```
namespace LoisAndClark.WebPartConnectionLanguage
{
  [ValidationState(ValidationState.Enabled)]
  partial class WebPart
  {
    [ValidationMethod(ValidationCategories.Open | ValidationCategories.Save |

      ValidationCategories.Menu)]
    public void ValidateConnections(ValidationContext objContext)
    {
      string strMessage = "My error description";
      objContext.LogError(strMessage, "myerrorcode", this);
    }
  }
}
```

Establishing the Web Part Validation Rules

Now that you have established a validation rule that fails all the time, you are ready to add real validation rules. The first set of validation rules that you will add to the WPCL is that each consumer interface is able to communicate with its corresponding provider interface. This set of validation rules applies to server-side and client-side connections. Table 5-3 shows the basic set of rules of valid web part connections. Please refer back to the section "Web Part Connections" if you need detailed information about this subject.

Table 5-3. *Basic Set of Web Part Connection Validation Rules*

Provider Interface	Consumer Interface
ICellProvider	ICellConsumer
IFilterProvider	IFilterConsumer
IListProvider	IListConsumer
IParametersInProvider	IParametersInConsumer
IParametersOutProvider	IParametersOutConsumer
IRowProvider	IRowConsumer

The second set of validation rules that needs to be added to the WPCL specifies the remaining compatible interfaces. Those interfaces are compatible because the web part connection framework provides transformers that are able to transform the information provided by a web part provider to something that is understandable to a web part consumer. This set of validation rules applies to server-side and client-side connections. Table 5-4 provides an overview of the available web part transformers. You can refer back to the section "Web Part Connections" if you need detailed information about this subject.

Table 5-4. *Web Part Transformers*

Provider Interface	Consumer Interface
IRowProvider	ICellConsumer
IRowProvider	IFilterConsumer
IRowProvider	IParametersInConsumer
IParametersOutProvider	IParametersInConsumer

The last set of validation rules that we will implement in the WPCL concerns validation rules in relation to cross-page connections. Only a limited set of cross-page connections is allowed. Table 5-5 provides an overview of them. Please refer back to the section "Web Part Connections" if you need detailed information about this subject.

Table 5-5. *Allowable Cross-Page Connections*

Provider Interface	Consumer Interface
IRowProvider	IFilterConsumer
IRowProvider	IParametersInConsumer
IFilterProvider	IFilterConsumer
IParametersOutProvider	IParametersInConsumer
IParametersInProvider	IParametersInConsumer

There are other validation rules that we could have implemented, such as a validation rule that prohibits circular references in web part connections. However, we have chosen to include the validation rules discussed earlier in this section and stop there. We have kept the set of validation rules simple but useful. Having said that, it is easy to extend the set of validation rules if you want to.

Implementing Web Part Validation Rules

In pseudocode, the validation process for the WPCL web part domain class looks like this:

1. Establish rules for allowable web part connections (only once).

2. Check the connections for every web part and validate those connections against the rules set established in the first step. Repeat the following steps for every web part:

    1. Determine interfaces implemented by the current web part.

    2. Ensure that the current web part implements at least one interface.

    3. Determine interfaces implemented by server-side connection providers.

4. Validate server-side connection relationships.

5. Determine interfaces implemented by client-side connection providers.

6. Validate client-side connection relationships.

7. Determine interfaces implemented by cross-page connection providers.

8. Validate cross-page connection relationships.

Keep this general structure in mind while we proceed with the explanation of the actual validation code.

Establishing Rules for Allowable Web Part Connections

The validation class uses Dictionary objects to capture the validation rules that apply to web part consumer interfaces. Each web part consumer interface has a corresponding validation rules Dictionary object. For example, the following providers are allowed for a web part implementing the ICellConsumer interface: web parts implementing either the ICellProvider or IRowProvider interfaces. The Dictionary objects are declared as static members to ensure the validation rules are only set up once during the validation process. The rules defined in these Dictionary objects apply to both server-side and client-side connections. The following code shows a part of the code responsible for establishing rules for allowable web part connections:

```
private static Dictionary<string, string> _objCellConsumerRules;
private static void InitValidationRules()
{
  if (_objCellConsumerRules == null)
  {
  // Add valid connections for Cell consumers.
  _objCellConsumerRules = new Dictionary<string, string>();
  _objCellConsumerRules.Add("ProviderToConsumerRule", "ICellProvider");
  _objCellConsumerRules.Add("RowTransformerRule", "IRowProvider");
  ...
  }
}
```

Later, when the validation class tries to validate a web part connection of a WPCL model, we will use these Dictionary objects. We have created a GetValidationRules() factory method that determines which Dictionary object applies to a given web part in a WPCL model that is validated. The factory method returns null if no validation rules can be found for a web part in a WPCL model. The following code listing shows a part of the GetValidationRules() method:

```
// Retrieves validation rules for client-side and server-side connections.
private Dictionary<string, string> GetValidationRules(string strConsumerInterface)
{
  if (strConsumerInterface.Contains("ICellConsumer"))
  {
    return _objCellConsumerRules;
  }
```

```
  else if (strConsumerInterface.Contains("IFilterConsumer"))
  {
    return _objFilterConsumerRules;
  }
…
  return null;
}
```

We have two separate `Dictionary` objects that contain the validation rules for cross-page connections: one for IFilterConsumer consumer web parts, and one for IParametersInConsumer consumer web parts. The initialization of cross-page validation rules is shown in the next code listing:

```
private static Dictionary<string, string> _objFilterCrossPageConsumerRules;
private static Dictionary<string, string> _objParametersInCrossPageConsumerRules;
private static void InitValidationRules()
{
  …
  // Add valid cross-page Filter consumers.
  _objFilterCrossPageConsumerRules = new Dictionary<string,string>();
  _objFilterCrossPageConsumerRules.Add("CrossPageRowRule", ➥
    "IRowProvider");
  _objFilterCrossPageConsumerRules.Add("CrossPageFilterRule", ➥
    "IFilterProvider");

  // Add valid cross-page ParametersIn consumers.
  _objParametersInCrossPageConsumerRules = new Dictionary<string,string>();
  _objParametersInCrossPageConsumerRules.Add("CrossPageRowRule", ➥
    "IRowProvider");
  _objParametersInCrossPageConsumerRules.Add("CrossPageParametersOutRule", ➥
    "IParametersOut");
  _objParametersInCrossPageConsumerRules.Add("CrossPageParametersInRule", ➥
    "IParametersInRule");
}
```

The `GetCrossPageValidationRules()` method is a factory method that determines which `Dictionary` object containing cross-page validation rules applies to a given web part in a WPCL model. The `GetCrossPageValidationRules()` method returns `null` if no validation rules can be found for a web part in a WPCL model. The following code listing shows the `GetCrossPageValidationRules()` method:

```
// Retrieves validation rules for cross-page connections.
private Dictionary<string, string> GetCrossPageValidationRules( ➥
  string strConsumerInterface)
{
  if (strConsumerInterface.Contains("IFilterConsumer"))
  {
    return _objFilterConsumerRules;
  }
```

```
  else if (strConsumerInterface.Contains("IParametersInConsumer"))
  {
    return _objParametersInConsumerRules;
  }

  return null;
}
```

The DisplayValidationErrors() method provides a detailed error message containing information about why validation failed. It does this by checking whether the current web part that is validated implements a consumer interface. If so, it produces a list of provider interfaces that are valid for the web part. The following code listing shows the DisplayValidationErrors() method:

```
private void DisplayValidationErrors(List<string> objConsumers, ➥
  ValidationContext objContext)
{
  string strErrorMessage = String.Format( ➥
    "The following rules apply to domain object {0}:\n", Name);

  foreach (string strConsumerInterface in objConsumers)
  {
    Dictionary<string, string> objRules = GetValidationRules(strConsumerInterface);

    if (objRules == null)
    {
      strErrorMessage += String.Format( ➥
        "Interface {0} is not a valid consumer interface.\n", strConsumerInterface);
    }
    else
    {
      foreach (string strKey in objRules.Keys)
      {
        strErrorMessage += String.Format( ➥
          "Rule {0}: valid provider {1}", strKey, objRules[strKey]) + "\n";
      }
    }
  }

  objContext.LogError(strErrorMessage, "VALIDATION ERROR", this);
}
```

The DisplayCrossPageValidationErrors() method provides a detailed error message containing information about why cross-page validation failed. It does this by listing all valid cross-page connections. The following code listing shows the DisplayCrossPageValidationErrors() method:

```
private void DisplayCrossPageValidationErrors(ValidationContext objContext)
{
  string strErrorMessage = String.Format( ➥
    "Invalid cross-page connection in {0}:\n", Name);
  strErrorMessage += "The following cross-page connections are allowed:\n"
    + "IRowProvider to IFilterConsumer\n"
    + "IRowProvider to IParametersIn\n"
    + "IFilterProvider to IFilterConsumer\n"
    + "IPparametersOutProvider to IParametersInProvider\n"
    + "IParametersInProvider to IParametersInConsumer\n";

  objContext.LogError( ➥
    strErrorMessage, "CROSS-PAGE CONNECTION ERROR", this);
}
```

Validating Client-Side and Server-Side Connections

The next method we will discuss is the ValidateConnection() method. It checks the validity of the web part connections for any given web part in a WPCL model. If a web part does not have any associated web part providers, there are no connections, which is valid. If there are web part providers, the method checks whether the web part provider implements a provider interface that is compatible with the current web part. The following code listing shows the ValidateConnection() method:

```
// Checks if a connection is a valid client-side or server-side connection.
private void ValidateConnection( ➥
  List<string> objConsumers, List<string> ➥
objProviders, ValidationContext objContext)
{
  // It is valid if there are no connections.
  if (objProviders.Count == 0) return;

  bool blnIsValidConnection = false;

  foreach (string strConsumerInterface in objConsumers)
  {
    Dictionary<string, string> objRules = ➥
    GetValidationRules(strConsumerInterface);
    if (objRules == null) continue;

    foreach (string strProviderInterface in objRules.Values)
    {
      if (blnIsValidConnection) break;

      foreach (string strRule in objProviders)
      {
        if (blnIsValidConnection) break;
```

```
      if (strRule.Contains(strProviderInterface))
      {
        blnIsValidConnection = true;
        break;
      }
    }
  }

  if (!blnIsValidConnection) DisplayValidationErrors(objConsumers, objContext);
  }
}
```

Validating Cross-Page Connections

The ValidateCrossPageConnection() method checks the validity of cross-page web part connections for any given web part in a WPCL model. The implementation of this method is very much comparable to the previous ValidateConnection() method. Mind you, the code presented in this chapter is written in a procedural language style. It would have been more elegant to create separate classes containing the validation rules and implement the validation methods using polymorphism. However, we are not trying to teach you object-oriented software construction in this book, so you will have to live with this code. The next code listing shows the implementation of the ValidateCrossPageConnection() method:

```
private void ValidateCrossPageConnection( ➡
  List<string> objConsumers, List<string> ➡
objProviders, ValidationContext objContext)
{
  // It is valid if there are no connections.
  if (objProviders.Count == 0) return;

  bool blnIsValidConnection = false;

  foreach (string strConsumerInterface in objConsumers)
  {
    if (blnIsValidConnection) break;

    Dictionary<string, string> objRules = ➡
    GetCrossPageValidationRules(strConsumerInterface);
    if (objRules == null) continue;

    foreach (string strProviderInterface in objRules.Values)
    {
      if (blnIsValidConnection) break;

      foreach (string strRule in objProviders)
      {
        if (blnIsValidConnection) break;
```

```
        if (strRule.Contains(strProviderInterface))
        {
          blnIsValidConnection = true;
          break;
        }
      }
    }
  }

  if (!blnIsValidConnection) DisplayCrossPageValidationErrors(objContext);
}
```

Checking Connections for Every Web Part

The ValidateConnections() method is the starting point for validating web part connections, because it is annotated with the [ValidationMethod] attribute. This method controls validation the validation process. It starts with the initialization of all validation rules, which is done only once. Then it determines the interfaces implemented by the current web part and checks if any interfaces are implemented at all. A web part that does not implement any interface at all cannot act as a connectable web part; such a situation results in a validation error. After that, the method determines all relationships with server-side web part providers and checks whether those relationships are valid. It does the same thing for client-side web part providers and finally switches to checking the validity of all cross-page relationships. The implementation of the ValidateConnections() method is shown in this code listing:

```
[ValidationMethod(ValidationCategories.Open | ValidationCategories.Save | ➥
  ValidationCategories.Menu)]
public void ValidateConnections(ValidationContext objContext)
{
  InitValidationRules();

  // Determine interfaces implemented by consumer.
  List<string> objConsumerInterfaces = new List<string>();
  foreach (IConnectable objInterface in IConnectableInterfaces)
  {
    objConsumerInterfaces.Add(objInterface.GetType().ToString());
  }

  // Stop the validation process if this web part does not implement any interface.
  if (objConsumerInterfaces.Count == 0)
  {
    string strErrorMessage = String.Format( ➥
      "Web part {0} does not implement any interface", Name);
    objContext.LogError(strErrorMessage, "ERROR", this);
    return;
  }
```

```csharp
// Determine interfaces implemented for each server-side connection provider.
foreach (WebPart objProvider in Providers)
{
  List<string> objProviderInterfaces = new List<string>();
  foreach (IConnectable objInterface in objProvider.IConnectable)
  {
    objProviderInterfaces.Add(objInterface.GetType().ToString());
  }
  ValidateConnection(objConsumerInterfaces, objProviderInterfaces, objContext);
}

// Determine interfaces implemented for each client-side connection provider.
foreach (WebPart objProvider in ClientSideProviders)
{
  List<string> objProviderInterfaces = new List<string>();
  foreach (IConnectable objInterface in objProvider.IConnectable)
  {
    objProviderInterfaces.Add(objInterface.GetType().ToString());
  }
  ValidateConnection(objConsumerInterfaces, objProviderInterfaces, objContext);
}

// Determine interfaces implemented for each cross-page connection provider.
foreach (WebPart objProvider in CrossPageProviders)
{
  List<string> objProviderInterfaces = new List<string>();
  foreach (IConnectable objInterface in objProvider.IConnectable)
  {
    objProviderInterfaces.Add(objInterface.GetType().ToString());
  }
  ValidateCrossPageConnection(objConsumerInterfaces, objProviderInterfaces, ➡
    objContext);
}
}
```

The Web Part Validation Class

The complete code for the web part validation class, the class that implements all web part
connection business rules in the WPCL, is shown in the next code listing. The complete code
can also be downloaded from our web site at http://www.lcbridge.nl/download.

```csharp
using System;
using System.Collections.Generic;
using System.Text;
using System.Diagnostics;
using System.Collections.ObjectModel;
using Microsoft.VisualStudio.Modeling.Validation;
```

```
namespace LoisAndClark.WebPartConnectionLanguage
{
  [ValidationState(ValidationState.Enabled)]
  partial class WebPart
  {
    private static Dictionary<string, string> _objCellConsumerRules;
    private static Dictionary<string, string> _objFilterConsumerRules;
    private static Dictionary<string, string> _objListConsumerRules;
    private static Dictionary<string, string> _objParametersInConsumerRules;
    private static Dictionary<string, string> _objParametersOutConsumerRules;
    private static Dictionary<string, string> _objRowConsumerRules;
    private static Dictionary<string, string> _objFilterCrossPageConsumerRules;
    private static Dictionary<string, string> ➥
      _objParametersInCrossPageConsumerRules;
    private static void InitValidationRules()
    {
      if (_objCellConsumerRules == null)
      {
        // Add valid connections for Cell consumers.
        _objCellConsumerRules = new Dictionary<string, string>();
        _objCellConsumerRules.Add("ProviderToConsumerRule", "ICellProvider");
        _objCellConsumerRules.Add("RowTransformerRule", "IRowProvider");

        // Add valid connections for Filter consumers.
        _objFilterConsumerRules = new Dictionary<string, string>();
        _objFilterConsumerRules.Add("FilterToConsumerRule", "IFilterProvider");
        _objFilterConsumerRules.Add("RowTransformerRule", "IRowProvider");

        // Add valid connections for List consumers.
        _objListConsumerRules = new Dictionary<string, string>();
        _objListConsumerRules.Add("ListToConsumerRule", "IListProvider");

        // Add valid connections for ParametersIn consumers.
        _objParametersInConsumerRules = new Dictionary<string, string>();
        _objParametersInConsumerRules.Add("ParametersInToConsumerRule", ➥
          "IParametersInProvider");
        _objParametersInConsumerRules.Add("RowTransformerRule", "IRowProvider");

        // Add valid connections for ParametersOut consumers.
        _objParametersOutConsumerRules = new Dictionary<string, string>();
        _objParametersOutConsumerRules.Add("ParametersOutToConsumerRule", ➥
          "IParametersOutProvider");
        _objParametersOutConsumerRules.Add("RowTransformerRule", "IRowProvider");

        // Add valid connections for Row consumers.
        _objRowConsumerRules = new Dictionary<string, string>();
        _objRowConsumerRules.Add("RowToConsumerRule", "IRowProvider");
```

```
      // Add valid cross-page Filter consumers.
      _objFilterCrossPageConsumerRules = new Dictionary<string,string>();
      _objFilterCrossPageConsumerRules.Add("CrossPageRowRule", "IRowProvider");
      _objFilterCrossPageConsumerRules.Add("CrossPageFilterRule", ➥
        "IFilterProvider");

      // Add valid cross-page ParametersIn consumers.
      _objParametersInCrossPageConsumerRules = new Dictionary<string,string>();
      _objParametersInCrossPageConsumerRules.Add("CrossPageRowRule", ➥
        "IRowProvider");
      _objParametersInCrossPageConsumerRules.Add( ➥
        "CrossPageParametersOutRule", "IParametersOut");
      _objParametersInCrossPageConsumerRules.Add( ➥
        "CrossPageParametersInRule", "IParametersInRule");
  }
}

// Retrieves validation rules for client-side and server-side connections.
private Dictionary<string, string> GetValidationRules( ➥
  string strConsumerInterface)
{
  if (strConsumerInterface.Contains("ICellConsumer"))
  {
    return _objCellConsumerRules;
  }
  else if (strConsumerInterface.Contains("IFilterConsumer"))
  {
    return _objFilterConsumerRules;
  }
  else if (strConsumerInterface.Contains("IListConsumer"))
  {
    return _objListConsumerRules;
  }
  else if (strConsumerInterface.Contains("IParametersInConsumer"))
  {
    return _objParametersInConsumerRules;
  }
  else if (strConsumerInterface.Contains("IParametersOutConsumer"))
  {
    return _objParametersOutConsumerRules;
  }
  return null;
}

// Retrieves validation rules for cross-page connections.
private Dictionary<string, string> GetCrossPageValidationRules( ➥
  string strConsumerInterface)
```

```
    {
      if (strConsumerInterface.Contains("IFilterConsumer"))
      {
        return _objFilterConsumerRules;
      }
      else if (strConsumerInterface.Contains("IParametersInConsumer"))
      {
        return _objParametersInConsumerRules;
      }
      return null;
    }

    // Checks if a connection is a valid client-side or server-side connection.
    private void ValidateConnection(List<string> objConsumers, ➥
      List<string> objProviders, ValidationContext objContext)
    {
      // It is valid if there are no connections.
      if (objProviders.Count == 0) return;

      bool blnIsValidConnection = false;

      foreach (string strConsumerInterface in objConsumers)
      {
        Dictionary<string, string> objRules = ➥
          GetValidationRules(strConsumerInterface);
        if (objRules == null) continue;

        foreach (string strProviderInterface in objRules.Values)
        {
          if (blnIsValidConnection) break;

          foreach (string strRule in objProviders)
          {
            if (blnIsValidConnection) break;

            if (strRule.Contains(strProviderInterface))
            {
              blnIsValidConnection = true;
              break;
            }
          }
        }
      }

      if (!blnIsValidConnection) DisplayValidationErrors(objConsumers, objContext);
    }
```

```csharp
private void ValidateCrossPageConnection(List<string> objConsumers, ➡
  List<string> objProviders, ValidationContext objContext)
{
  // It is valid if there are no connections.
  if (objProviders.Count == 0) return;

  bool blnIsValidConnection = false;

  foreach (string strConsumerInterface in objConsumers)
  {
    if (blnIsValidConnection) break;

    Dictionary<string, string> objRules = ➡
      GetCrossPageValidationRules(strConsumerInterface);
    if (objRules == null) continue;

    foreach (string strProviderInterface in objRules.Values)
    {
      if (blnIsValidConnection) break;

      foreach (string strRule in objProviders)
      {
        if (blnIsValidConnection) break;

        if (strRule.Contains(strProviderInterface))
        {
          blnIsValidConnection = true;
          break;
        }
      }
    }
  }

  if (!blnIsValidConnection) ➡
    DisplayCrossPageValidationErrors(objContext);
}

private void DisplayValidationErrors(List<string> objConsumers, ➡
  ValidationContext objContext)
{
  string strErrorMessage = String.Format( ➡
    "The following rules apply to domain object {0}:\n", Name);

  foreach (string strConsumerInterface in objConsumers)
  {
    Dictionary<string, string> objRules = ➡
      GetValidationRules(strConsumerInterface);
```

```
      if (objRules == null)
      {
        strErrorMessage += String.Format( ➡
          "Interface {0} is not a valid consumer interface.\n", ➡
          strConsumerInterface);
      }
      else
      {
        foreach (string strKey in objRules.Keys)
        {
          strErrorMessage += String.Format( ➡
            "Rule {0}: valid provider {1}", strKey, objRules[strKey]) + "\n";
        }
      }
    }

    objContext.LogError(strErrorMessage, "VALIDATION ERROR", this);
}

private void DisplayCrossPageValidationErrors(ValidationContext objContext)
{
  string strErrorMessage = String.Format( ➡
    "Invalid cross-page connection in {0}:\n", Name);
  strErrorMessage += "The following cross-page connections are allowed:\n"
    + "IRowProvider to IFilterConsumer\n"
    + "IRowProvider to IParametersIn\n"
    + "IFilterProvider to IFilterConsumer\n"
    + "IPparametersOutProvider to IParametersInProvider\n"
    + "IParametersInProvider to IParametersInConsumer\n";

  objContext.LogError(strErrorMessage, "CROSS-PAGE CONNECTION ERROR", this);
}

[ValidationMethod(ValidationCategories.Open | ValidationCategories.Save | ➡
  ValidationCategories.Menu)]
public void ValidateConnections(ValidationContext objContext)
{
  InitValidationRules();

  // Determine interfaces implemented by consumer.
  List<string> objConsumerInterfaces = new List<string>();
  foreach (IConnectable objInterface in IConnectable)
  {
    objConsumerInterfaces.Add(objInterface.GetType().ToString());
  }

  // Stop the validation process if this web part does not implement any
  // interface.
```

```
    if (objConsumerInterfaces.Count == 0)
    {
      string strErrorMessage = String.Format( ➡
        "Web part {0} does not implement any interface", Name);
      objContext.LogError(strErrorMessage, "ERROR", this);
      return;
    }

    // Determine interfaces implemented for each
    // server-side connection provider.
    foreach (WebPart objProvider in Provider)
    {
      List<string> objProviderInterfaces = new List<string>();
      foreach (IConnectable objInterface in objProvider.IConnectable)
      {
        objProviderInterfaces.Add(objInterface.GetType().ToString());
      }
      ValidateConnection(objConsumerInterfaces, objProviderInterfaces, ➡
        objContext);
    }

    // Determine interfaces implemented for each client-side connection provider.
    foreach (WebPart objProvider in ClientSideProvider)
    {
      List<string> objProviderInterfaces = new List<string>();
      foreach (IConnectable objInterface in objProvider.IConnectable)
      {
        objProviderInterfaces.Add(objInterface.GetType().ToString());
      }
      ValidateConnection(objConsumerInterfaces, objProviderInterfaces, ➡
        objContext);
    }

    // Determine interfaces implemented for each
    // cross-page connection provider.
    foreach (WebPart objProvider in CrossPageProvider)
    {
      List<string> objProviderInterfaces = new List<string>();
      foreach (IConnectable objInterface in objProvider.IConnectable)
      {
        objProviderInterfaces.Add(objInterface.GetType().ToString());
      }
      ValidateCrossPageConnection(objConsumerInterfaces, ➡
        objProviderInterfaces, objContext);
    }
  }
 }
}
```

This gives you the complete code for the set of web part connection validation rules for the WPCL. We will conclude this section with one last tip: if you want to debug the validation code, just use the Visual Studio .NET 2005 editor like you are used to. Press F5 to debug the solution, which opens another instance of Visual Studio .NET 2005. Break mode will be entered once the first breakpoint in the validation code is reached. Previously we specified that validation logic is run every time we open, save, or validate a WPCL model, so each of these events can trigger the start of a debug session.

Text Templates

So far we have created a domain model and validation logic encompassing the rules related to creating web part connections. At this point, the WPCL can be used to validate the design of and relationships between web part connections. Since we also want to generate code for connectable web parts we will take the WPCL one step further in this section; we will use text templates to generate code.

When it comes to generating code there are a couple of limitations in the current version of the DSL Toolbox for Visual Studio .NET 2005. First of all, the current June 2006 CTP release only allows you to generate one file per text template. This is not good; we would like to generate a separate file for every web part that is generated based on a WebPart domain class in a WPCL model. We would also like to generate separate web part description (.dwp) files for our web parts. The June 2006 CTP release does not support this, so we are condemned to a form of copy-and-paste code generation.

As a work-around we will generate a .cs file containing all code for all web parts. Although this works, you will probably want to divide the web part code over several .cs files: one .cs file per web part. We will also generate one .dwp file containing all web part descriptions. A .dwp file containing multiple web part descriptions does not work, so if you want to use .dwp files to import web parts to a SharePoint site, you will have to split up the contents of this file manually. According to members of the DSL team, the version 1.0 release of the DSL Toolbox for Visual Studio .NET 2005 will support the generation of multiple files per text template, so this is a problem that will be solved in the near future.

■Note The code generation techniques demonstrated in this chapter do not include advanced topics such as code regeneration or integration with source versioning systems. If you want to learn more about code generation we advise you to read the book *Code Generation in Microsoft.NET* by Kathleen Dollard.

Text templates contain text blocks that are used to generate text artifacts, such as a C# source code (.cs) file or an HTML file. A text template generates text artifacts based on information supplied by at least one input source, typically a model.

In this section we will create a text template that generates code for connectable web parts based on one input source only: a WPCL model. We will create another text template that generates web part description files based on the same WPCL model. Text templates are files containing a mixture of text blocks and control logic. The control logic is typically used to manipulate the data held within a model. The data generated by the control logic combined with the data in the text blocks are used to produce an output file. A text template looks very similar to a classic ASP page, as you can seen in the next code listing. This template counts the number of elements present in a WPCL model:

```
<#@ template ➡
  inherits=" ➡
  Microsoft.VisualStudio.TextTemplating.VSHost.ModelingTextTransformation" ➡
  debug="true"#>
<#@ output extension=".txt" #>
<#@ WebPartConnectionLanguage ➡
  processor="WebPartConnectionLanguageDirectiveProcessor" ➡
  requires="fileName='Test.wpcl'" #>
The number of elements in my WPCL model:
<#= WPCLModel.Elements.Count #>
```

Templates are transformed via the Text Template Transformation Toolkit, which is included in the DSL Toolkit. The Text Template Transformation Toolkit consists of the following components:

Text Template Transformation Engine: This engine is responsible for processing text templates given to it.

Hosts: A host is the interface between the engine and the user environment. Out of the box, you can use the Visual Studio host or a command-line host.

Directive processors: Directive processors handle directives in text templates. Directives are typically used to provide data from an input source (for example, from a model) to a text template. When using the DSL Toolkit, a directive processor is generated for each DSL, so that text templates can access the models in that language as input sources. The following code is an example of a directive processor that uses a WPCL model as input source:

```
<#@ WebPartConnectionLanguage ➡
  processor="WebPartConnectionLanguageDirectiveProcessor" ➡
  requires="fileName='Test.wpcl'" #>
```

■**Note** The current version of the Text Template Transformation Engine is also called the T4 Text Templating Engine. The T4 engine is used by the DSL Toolkit, but it is also used in the GAT. Chapter 1 discusses the GAT in detail.

Text Template Syntax

A text template can contain a number of block types that can appear in any order:

- Directive

- Text

- Statement

- Expression

- ClassFeature

Directive block types provide instructions to the Text Template Transformation Engine. The syntax for a directive block type looks like this:

```
<#@ DirectiveName [ParameterName = "ParameterValue"]#>
```

There are three types of directives:

- Built-in directives

- Custom directives

- Generated directives

There are five built-in directive block types:

assembly: This directive is equivalent to using the Add Reference feature in Visual Studio .NET 2005. This directive identifies an assembly that is to be referenced, so you are able to use types that are defined within the referenced assembly. The following code shows an example of an assembly directive:

```
<@ assembly name="MyReferencedLibrary.DLL" #>
```

import: This directive is equivalent to the C# using statement. It enables you to refer to types within the text template without providing a fully qualified name. The following code shows an example of an import directive:

```
<#@ import namespace="LoisAndClark.WebPartConnectionLanguage" #>
```

template: This directive allows you to specify general information about the generated transformation class, a temporary class that is compiled and executed to produce generated text. Examples of such information are code language, class inheritance, and the ability to debug. The template directive allows the use of a number of optional parameters:

- language: This parameter identifies which language is used for code inside statement and expression blocks. By default, this parameter is set to C#.

- inherits: This parameter specifies which class should be used as the base class for the generated transformation class. The base class must be derived from the ModelingTextTransformation class located in the Microsoft.VisualStudio. TextTemplating.VSHost namespace.

- culture: This parameter is used when converting expression blocks to text.

- debug: This parameter determines whether debugging is enabled in the generated transformation class. By default, debugging is set to true.

- hostspecific: This parameter is only used in combination with custom hosts. If this parameter is set to true, you are able to access a property called Host within the text template. The Host property allows you to reference the object hosting the engine.

The following code shows a valid example of a template directive:

```
<#@ template ➡
  inherits=" ➡
  Microsoft.VisualStudio.TextTemplating.VSHost.ModelingTextTransformation" ➡
  debug="true"#>
```

output: This directive specifies the extension of the generated text output file. The following code example shows an output directive that specifies a .cs extension for the generated text output file:

```
<#@ output extension=".txt" #>
```

include: This directive is equivalent to the include statement in classic ASP. The include directive processes text from a specified file and includes it literally in the text template currently being processed. The following code shows an example of the include directive:

```
<#@ include file="c:\test.txt" #>
```

Besides the existing built-in directives there are two other types of directives: custom and generated. Custom directives allow you to create directives that are specific to your custom tools. A typical use of custom directives is to load external data for use within a text template. Generated directives allow you to access models for use within a text template. The following code shows an example of a generated directive:

```
<#@ WebPartConnectionLanguage ➡
  processor="WebPartConnectionLanguageDirectiveProcessor" ➡
  requires="fileName='Test.wpcl'" #>
```

The next block type we will discuss is the text block type. A *text block* is a nonprogrammatic text in a text template that is written directly and literally to the output file of the text transformation. The following code shows an example of a text block:

```
The number of elements in my WPCL model:
```

Statement blocks are used to control the flow of processing in the text template. Code statements are delineated using opening (<#) and closing (#>) text template tags and must be written in the language specified in the language parameter of the template directive. The following code shows an example statement block:

```
<#
  for ( int i = 0; i < 10; i++ )
  {
    WriteLine("Hello");
  }
#>
```

Expression blocks are used to add strings to the generated text output. Expression blocks are delineated by using opening (<#=) and closing (#>) text template tags. The following code shows an example expression block:

```
<#= WPCLModel.Elements.Count #>
```

The final block type is the ClassFeature block type. ClassFeature blocks are used to add helper functions to avoid repeating common code. ClassFeature blocks are delineated by using opening (<#=+) and closing (#>) text template tags. The following code shows an example ClassFeature block. The ClassFeature block contains a method that returns the current date and time:

```
<#@ template ➡
  inherits=" ➡
  Microsoft.VisualStudio.TextTemplating.VSHost.ModelingTextTransformation" ➡
  debug="true"#>
<#@ output extension=".txt" #>
<#@ WebPartConnectionLanguage ➡
  processor="WebPartConnectionLanguageDirectiveProcessor" ➡
  requires="fileName='Test.wpcl'" #>

Current date and time: <#= GetDateAndTime() #>

<#+
private string GetDateAndTime()
{
return DateTime.Now.ToString();
}
#>
```

Running this text template results in the creation of a text file called WebPartDescriptions.txt containing the following text:

```
Current date and time: 7/10/2006 11:48:46 AM
```

You can run text templates by adding a new file to a Visual Studio .NET 2005 project, for example: test.tt. Associate the template file to the text template generator tool by clicking test.tt and specifying the following value for the Custom Tool property: TextTemplatingFileGenerator. Now, if you right-click test.tt ➤ Run Custom Tool, the text template is executed. Below the text template file (test.tt), you will find a new file with an extension identical to the one specified in the output directive.

Debugging Text Templates

A text template consists of a mixture of text blocks and control logic used to combine the text blocks with the data held within a model to produce an output file. If you want to debug text templates, first you need to set the debug parameter of the template directive to true. It helps to import the System.Diagnostics namespace using the import directive, as this makes adding breakpoints easier. Then you can add a Debugger.Break() statement in the text template where you want to insert a breakpoint. The Debugger class is located in the System.Diagnostics namespace. The following code shows a valid text template containing a breakpoint:

```
<#@ template ➡
  inherits=" ➡
  Microsoft.VisualStudio.TextTemplating.VSHost.ModelingTextTransformation" ➡
  debug="true"#>
<#@ output extension=".cs" #>
<#@ WebPartConnectionLanguage ➡
  processor="WebPartConnectionLanguageDirectiveProcessor" ➡
  requires="fileName='Test.wpcl'" #>
<#@ import namespace="System.Diagnostics" #>

<# Debugger.Break(); #>
The number of elements in my WPCL model:
<#= WPCLModel.Elements.Count #>
```

As soon as you run the text template, the break statement will execute and you will either be prompted for a debugging session or be taken to the applicable line of code.

Generating Web Part Description Files

Now that you have seen the elements that the text templates are made of, we will go and build actual text templates. We will build two templates: one for creating a file containing web part descriptions for every web part in a WPCL model, the other one for creating a file containing C# template code for all web parts in a WPCL model. We will start with the creation of the web part description text template:

1. Run the WPCL solution file.

2. Right-click the Debug solution in the new instance of Visual Studio .NET 2005 ➤ Add ➤ New Item.

3. Choose the Text File Template and enter the following name: **WebPartDescriptionsTemplate.tt**.

A web part description file (.dwp) in its simplest form has the following format:

```
<?xml version="1.0" encoding="utf-8"?>
<WebPart xmlns="http://schemas.microsoft.com/WebPart/v2" >
  <Title>Title of Web Part</Title>
  <Description>Description of Web Part</Description>
  <Assembly>Assembly</Assembly>
  <TypeName>Namespace.Classname</TypeName>
</WebPart>
```

Web part description files can contain more information, but we will discuss generating web part description files in the most basic form. Creating more elaborate web part descriptions is more of the same work; we will leave such implementations up to you.

To test the text template that we are going to create, we have created a small test WPCL model that is shown in Figure 5-28. Note that the Assembly and Namespace properties of the WPCLModel domain class are set to MyAssembly and MyNamespace.

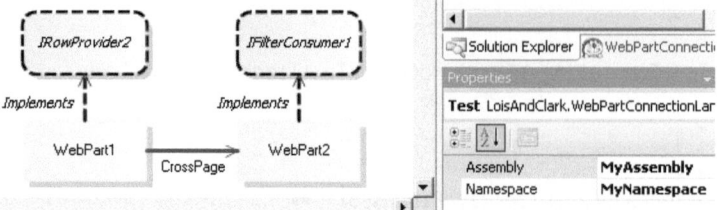

Figure 5-28. *Web part description test WPCL model*

All relevant properties of the web part description test WPCL model are mapped by the web part description text template to generate valid web part description files. The mapping is shown in Table 5-6.

Table 5-6. *Mapping Between Test WPCL Model and Web Part Description Text Template*

Dwp Element	Domain Class	Domain Class Property Name	Property Value
`<Title>`	`WebPart`	`Title`	WebPart1Title and WebPart2Title
`<Description>`	`WebPart`	`Description`	WebPart1Description and WebPart2Description
`<Assembly>`	`WPCLModel`	`Assembly`	MyAssembly
Namespace of `<TypeName>`	`WPCLModel`	`Namespace`	MyNamespace
Classname of `<TypeName>`	`WebPartName`	`Name`	WebPart1

The text template will generate a .dwp file containing all web part descriptions for all web parts in a WPCL model. To do this we will need to traverse the entire Elements collection of the `WPCLModel` domain class. The following code shows the complete code for this text template:

```
<#@ template inherits=" ➡
  Microsoft.VisualStudio.TextTemplating.VSHost.ModelingTextTransformation" ➡
  debug="true"#>
<#@ WebPartConnectionLanguage ➡
  processor="WebPartConnectionLanguageDirectiveProcessor" ➡
  requires="fileName='Test.wpcl'" #>
<#@ output extension=".dwp" #>
<#
foreach (WebPart objWebPart in WPCLModel.Elements )
{
  #>
```

```
<?xml version="1.0" encoding="utf-8"?>
<WebPart xmlns="http://schemas.microsoft.com/WebPart/v2" >
  <Title><#= objWebPart.Title #></Title>
  <Description><#= objWebPart.Description #></Description>
  <Assembly><#= WPCLModel.Assembly #></Assembly>
  <TypeName><#= WPCLModel.Namespace #>.<#= objWebPart.Name #></TypeName>
</WebPart>

<#
}
#>
```

If we run this text template against our test WPCL model, we will get the following result:

```
<?xml version="1.0" encoding="utf-8"?>
<WebPart xmlns="http://schemas.microsoft.com/WebPart/v2" >
  <Title>WebPart1Title</Title>
  <Description>WebPart1Description</Description>
  <Assembly>MyAssembly</Assembly>
  <TypeName>MyNamespace.WebPart1</TypeName>
</WebPart>

<?xml version="1.0" encoding="utf-8"?>
<WebPart xmlns="http://schemas.microsoft.com/WebPart/v2" >
  <Title>WebPart2Title</Title>
  <Description>WebPart2Description</Description>
  <Assembly>MyAssembly</Assembly>
  <TypeName>MyNamespace.WebPart2</TypeName>
</WebPart>
```

Generating Connectable Web Part Code

The next and last template that we will discuss generates code for web parts. The WSS SDK (http://www.microsoft.com/downloads) contains extensive and well-documented templates for every type of connectable web part. When we are building connectable web parts ourselves, we always take these templates as the starting points. So it makes sense to use these templates in our text templates to generate our web parts as well.

First of all, let's create a new text template called WebParts.tt:

1. Run the WPCL solution file.

2. Right-click the Debug solution in the new instance of Visual Studio .NET 2005 ➤ Add ➤ New Item.

3. Choose the Text File Template and enter the following name: **WebPartsTemplate.tt**.

The first part of the template includes a couple of directives that are familiar by now; they are discussed in detail in the section "Text Template Syntax." Then the template imports a couple of namespaces that are used when creating connectable web parts. These are the same for every type of web part. This code listing shows the first part of the WebPartsTemplate template:

```
<#@ template ➥
  inherits=" ➥
  Microsoft.VisualStudio.TextTemplating.VSHost.ModelingTextTransformation" ➥
  debug="true"#>
<#@ WebPartConnectionLanguage ➥
  processor="WebPartConnectionLanguageDirectiveProcessor" ➥
  requires="fileName='Test.wpcl'" #>
<#@ output extension=".cs" #>
using System;
using System.ComponentModel;
using System.Web.UI;
using Microsoft.SharePoint.WebPartPages;
using System.Xml.Serialization;
using System.Web.UI.WebControls;
using System.Security;
using Microsoft.SharePoint.Utilities;
using Microsoft.SharePoint.WebPartPages.Communication;
```

In the WPCL, all web parts in one WPCL model belong to the same namespace. The next part of the template creates the namespace for our web parts:

```
namespace <#= WPCLModel.Namespace #>
{
  ...
}
```

Within the namespace section, you will need to add code in the text template that creates class definitions for all web parts in a WPCL model. This is done by looping through the Elements collection of the WPCLModel object; this collection contains all web parts. All web parts inherit from the WebPart base class. Furthermore, you will need to determine which interfaces are supported by any given web part. We have created a method called GetInterfaces() that loops through the IConnectableInterfaces collection of a web part object and retrieves the correct interface name (based on its type name). This collection contains all interfaces that are supported by a web part. The next code listing shows all code required for creating the core class definitions including base class inheritance and interface implementations:

```
<#
foreach (WebPart objWebPart in WPCLModel.Elements )
{
  #>
  public class <#= objWebPart.Name #> : WebPart<#= GetInterfaces(objWebPart) #>
  {
  }
  <#
}
#>


<#+
```

```
private string GetInterfaces(WebPart objWebPart)
{
  string strInterfaces = String.Empty;

  foreach ( IConnectable objInterface in objWebPart.IConnectable )
  {
    string strTypeName = objInterface.GetType().ToString();
    string[] arrNamespace = strTypeName.Split('.');
    strInterfaces += ", " + arrNamespace[arrNamespace.Length - 1];
  }
  return strInterfaces;
}
#>
```

For every interface supported by the connectable web part, within the class body, we will add the code template taken from the WSS SDK. In this book, we will only show the implementations for the ICellConsumer and ICellProvider interfaces. Otherwise this chapter will simply become too big.

Adding the other interface code templates is straightforward; you just need to add more branches to the switch statement and copy the interface code templates from the WSS SDK.

Every web part has an IConnectableInterfaces collection that contains each of the interfaces which, according to the WPCL model, is supported by the web part. The following code shows how to loop through the IConnectableInterfaces; for every interface a new piece of code will be added to the body of the class. In this code, only the ICellConsumer and ICellProvider interfaces are supported:

```
<#
foreach ( IConnectable objInterface in objWebPart.IConnectableInterfaces )
{
  switch ( objInterface.GetType().ToString() )
  {
    case "LoisAndClark.WebPartConnectionLanguage.ICellConsumer":
#>
ICellConsumer code template
<#
      break;
    case "LoisAndClark.WebPartConnectionLanguage.ICellProvider":
#>
ICellProvider code template
<#
      break;
    default:
      break;
  }
}
#>
```

As it takes too much space to show the entire code listing for the text template, this is all the code we will show. The `ICellConsumer code template...` and `ICellProvider code template texts...` need to be replaced with the actual code templates that can be found in the WSS SDK. You should also note that this text template does not support client-side connectable web parts. An example text template that does contain the template code can be downloaded from our web site at `http://www.lcbridge.nl/download`.

Deploying the Web Part Connection Language

After creating a DSL, you will need to deploy it as well. You can deploy DSL solutions by creating a special Windows Installer package (.msi). In this section, we discuss how to create such a package. If you want more detailed information about this topic, you can refer to the documentation in the Visual Studio 2005 SDK.

In the first step we will export a project template based on the contents of the solution that is opened in the Visual Studio .NET 2005 experimental build. This solution includes our test.wpcl Web Part Connection Language model, and the text templates you have created that are used to generate web part descriptions and code for connectable web parts.

Start the WebPartConnectionLanguage solution. This opens a Visual Studio .NET 2005 experimental build:

1. Choose File ➤ Save All to save all files in the project.

2. Choose File ➤ Export Template. This opens the Export Template Wizard.

3. On the Choose Template Type page, ensure that the Project template option is selected. Click Next.

4. On the Select Template Options page, change the Template name to WPCLDeployment.

5. Enter the following description: **This is the project template for the WPCL.**

6. Clear the Automatically Import the Template into Visual Studio check box.

7. Click Finish.

8. Close the Visual Studio .NET 2005 experimental build.

9. Check that Windows Explorer opens and shows a ZIP file that contains the WPCL project template created by the wizard.

Next, you will add a setup project for DSLs and include the project template that you created in the previous step:

1. In the WebPartConnectionLanguage project, right-click the WebPartConnectionLanguage solution ➤ Add ➤ New ➤ Project.

2. In the left page of the New Project window, under Project types, choose Other Project Types ➤ Extensibility.

3. Under Templates, select the following template: Domain Specific Language Setup.

4. Choose the following name: WPCLDeployment. Click OK.

5. Right-click the Files folder of the WPCLDeploy project ➤ Add ➤ Existing Item.

6. Locate the project template that you created earlier and click Add. This template is called WPCLDeployment.zip.

7. Double-click InstallerDefinition.dslsetup, located in the root folder of the WPCLDeploy project.

8. Locate the `<vsItemTemplates>` section in the InstallerDefinition.dslsetup file; add the new `<vsProjectTemplates>` section shown in the next code listing:

```
...
</vsItemTemplates>
<vsProjectTemplates>
  <vsProjectTemplate localeId="1033" targetDirectories="CSharp" ➥
    templatePath=" ➥
    C:\Projects\WebPartConnectionLanguage\Deploy\Files\WPCLDeployment.zip" />
</vsProjectTemplates>
```

9. Click Transform All Templates on the Solution Explorer toolbar.

10. Right-click the Deploy project ➤ Build.

Now if you click Show All Files on the Project menu, you will see two important files in the bin\Debug folder: DSLToolsRedist.msi and WebPartConnectionLanguage.msi. WebPartConnectionLanguage.msi contains your DSL, and DSLToolsRedist.msi contains the necessary runtime components of the toolkit for DSLs. Copy the entire contents of the bin\Debug folder and paste it to the c:\deployment folder of the computer where you want to deploy the WPCL. Create this folder if it does not exist. The destination computer must have the Visual Studio 2005 SDK installed on it. After that, double-click setup.exe and follow the steps presented in the wizard.

Now you have installed the WPCL successfully, and you can start to use it in Visual Studio .NET 2005:

1. Start Visual Studio .NET 2005. Choose File menu ➤ New ➤ Project.

2. Under Project Types, click the Visual C# node. Under Templates, click WPCLDeployment, and click OK. This is shown in Figure 5-29.

3. A project named WPCLDeployment1 is created.

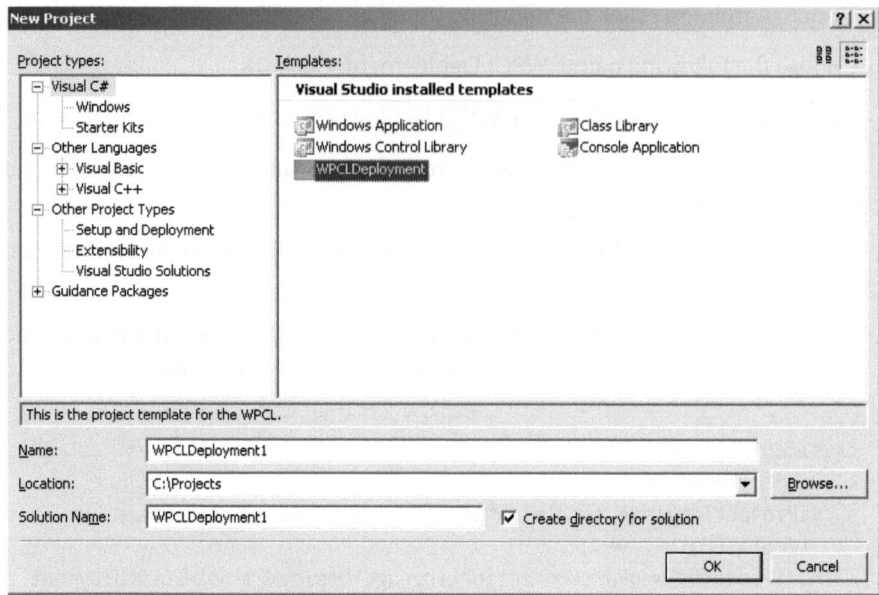

Figure 5-29. *Creating a new WPCL project*

In this project, you can edit test.wpcl or add a new WPCL model. Adding a new WPCL model is shown in Figure 5-30.

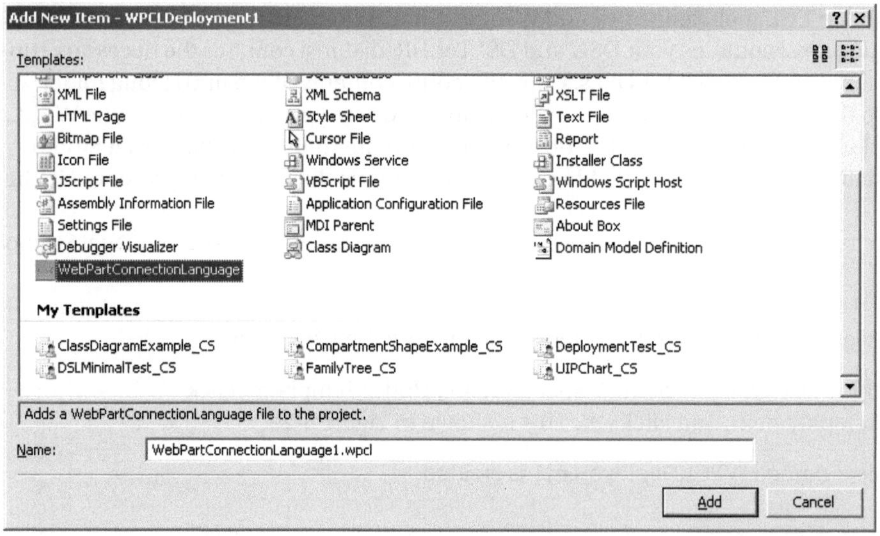

Figure 5-30. *A WPCL item*

If you want to uninstall the WPCL, open Control Panel, and double-click Add or Remove Programs. In the list of installed programs, choose WebPartConnectionLanguage, click Remove, and click OK to confirm.

Using the Web Part Connection Language

We have completed our WPCL, and you have seen how to deploy this DSL to another computer. The current version should help to speed up connectable web part development. This does not mean to say that the language is completely finished, there are a lot of areas where the language can be improved, but there is only so much that can be discussed in a chapter, and this is where we stop.

You should take note of the fact that the current (June 2006 CTP release) version of the DSL Toolkit is limited in some ways. There is no integration yet with versioning systems, and it is not possible to generate more than one file per text template. These limitations require you to take more manual steps when using the WPCL then we would like, but we are certain that at least the one-file-per-text-template limitation will be solved in the near future.

To complete the discussion of the WPCL, we will explore a couple of simple sample scenarios that show how to use the WPCL. First we will show a couple of invalid WPCL models and see what happens when we validate such models. Then we will show a simple scenario where we use a WPCL model to build an ICellProvider web part and an ICellConsumer web part.

In the first sample scenario we will add a web part shape to a WPCL model. As this web part does not implement any IConnectable interface, the WPCL does not accept this as a valid model. Once we validate this model, we will see an error stating that the web part does not implement any interface. This is shown in Figure 5-31.

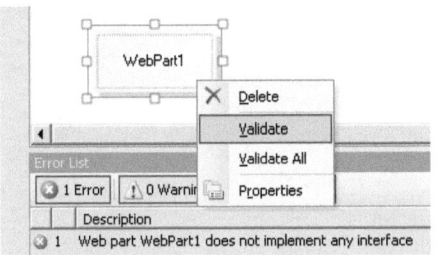

Figure 5-31. *Scenario 1: A single web part*

In the next sample scenario we have created a WPCL model that contains two web parts called MyProducer and MyConsumer. The MyProducer web part implements the IParametersOutProvider interface; the MyConsumer web part implements the ICellConsumer interface. We will also add a server-side connection between those two web parts. As the IParametersOutProvider and ICellConsumer interfaces are incompatible, validation will fail. This is shown in Figure 5-32.

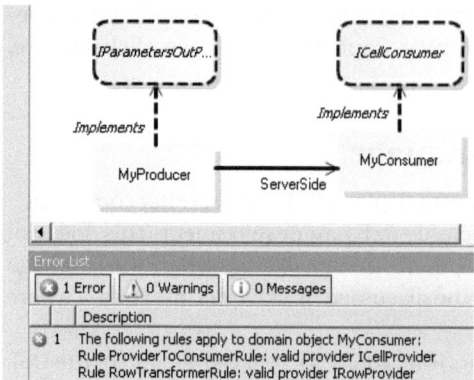

Figure 5-32. *Scenario 2: Invalid provider in server-side connection scenario*

In the third scenario we have created two web parts called MyProducer and MyConsumer. The MyProducer web part implements the IRowProvider interface; the MyConsumer web part implements the ICellConsumer interface. We will also add a cross-page connection between those two web parts. As the IRowProvider and ICellConsumer interfaces are incompatible when used in cross-page connections, validation will fail. This is shown in Figure 5-33.

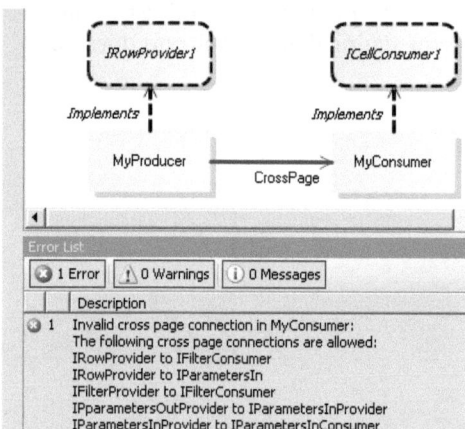

Figure 5-33. *Scenario 3: Invalid provider in cross-page connection scenario*

The final sample scenario that we will discuss is a scenario where we will create two connectable web parts that are compatible to each other. We will create a WPCL model, generate web part descriptions and code, add the code to a web part library, and try the web parts out on a SharePoint site.

First we set the Assembly and Namespace properties of WPCLModel to the following values: TestAssembly and TestNamespace. Our WPCL model contains two web parts: TestProvider and TestConsumer. We set the Title and Description properties of the TestProvider web part to the following values: Our TestProvider, and Test Provider Description. Then, we set the Title and Description properties of the TestConsumer web part to the following values: Our Test Consumer and TestConsumer Description. The TestProvider web part implements the

ICellProvider interface; the TestConsumer web part implements the ICellConsumer interface. The web parts will be connected via a server-side connection. As this is a valid web part connection, the resulting WCPL model is also valid. The WPCL model is shown in Figure 5-34.

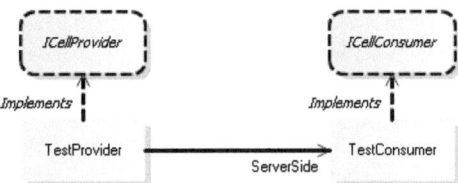

Figure 5-34. *Scenario 4: ICellProvider and ICellConsumer web parts*

During the next steps, we will generate web part description files and web part code based on this WPCL model:

1. If you right-click the WebPartsDescription.tt text template and choose Run Custom Tool, a file called WebPartDescriptionsLanguage.dwp is generated. This file contains the web part descriptions for both the TestProvider and TestConsumer web parts.

2. If you right-click WebPartsTemplate.tt and choose Run Custom Tool, a file called WebPartsTemplate.cs is created. This file contains the default code templates for the TestProvider and TestConsumer web parts.

■**Note** The generated code uses the SharePoint 2003 object model and does not contain any references to .NET 2.0 Framework. Because of this the code can be used in Visual Studio .NET 2003 or Visual Studio .NET 2005 environments.

Now that we have generated the code we will manually add it to a web part library:

1. Open Visual Studio .NET 2003 or 2005 and open a web part library. We will assume the web part library is called TestAssembly. If you want to learn more about creating web parts and web part libraries, refer to Chapter 1.

2. Add two new files to the web part library called TestProvider.dwp and TestConsumer.dwp.

3. Copy the following code, taken from the generated file WebPartDescriptionsLanguage.dwp, and paste it in TestProvider.dwp:

```xml
<?xml version="1.0" encoding="utf-8"?>
<WebPart xmlns="http://schemas.microsoft.com/WebPart/v2" >
  <Title>Our TestProvider</Title>
  <Description>Test Provider Description</Description>
  <Assembly>TestAssembly</Assembly>
  <TypeName>TestProvider</TypeName>
</WebPart>
```

4. Copy the following code, taken from the generated file
WebPartDescriptionsLanguage.dwp, and paste it in TestConsumer.dwp:

```
<?xml version="1.0" encoding="utf-8"?>
<WebPart xmlns="http://schemas.microsoft.com/WebPart/v2" >
  <Title>Our Test Consumer</Title>
  <Description>TestConsumer Description</Description>
  <Assembly>TestAssembly</Assembly>
  <TypeName>TestConsumer</TypeName>
</WebPart>
```

5. Add the generated file called WebPartsTemplate.cs to the web part library. This file contains all code for the connectable web parts. Compile the web part library and copy
MyAssembly.dll to the bin folder of your SharePoint virtual server. By default, this is
[drive letter]:\inetpub\wwwroot\bin.

At this point the web part library is built and ready to be used. Before you can import the
test web parts to a page in a SharePoint site, you will need to add a `<SafeControl>` entry to the
web.config file of the SharePoint virtual server. After that you can add the web parts to a Share-
Point page and connect them to each other as shown in the following steps:

1. Open the web.config file of the root folder of your SharePoint virtual server (by default,
this is [drive letter]:\inetpub\wwwroot), and add the following safe control entry:

```
<SafeControl Assembly="TestAssembly" Namespace="TestNamespace" TypeName="*" />
```

2. Open a SharePoint site, and choose Modify Shared Page ➤ Add Web Parts ➤ Import.

3. Locate the TestProvider.dwp file and choose Upload.

4. Drag the Our TestProvider web part to the Left web part zone.

5. Locate the TestConsumer.dwp file and choose Upload.

6. Drag the Our TestConsumer web part to the Left web part zone.

When added to a SharePoint web part page, the provider and consumer web parts should
look like Figure 5-35.

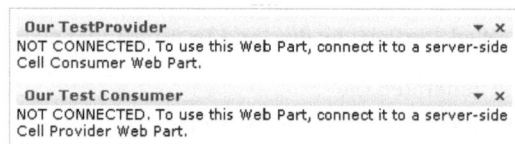

Figure 5-35. *SharePoint web part page including generated test web parts*

If you click the arrow on the Our TestProvider web part ➤ Connections ➤ Provide Cell To ➤ Our Test Consumer, you are connecting both test web parts. The end result will look like Figure 5-36.

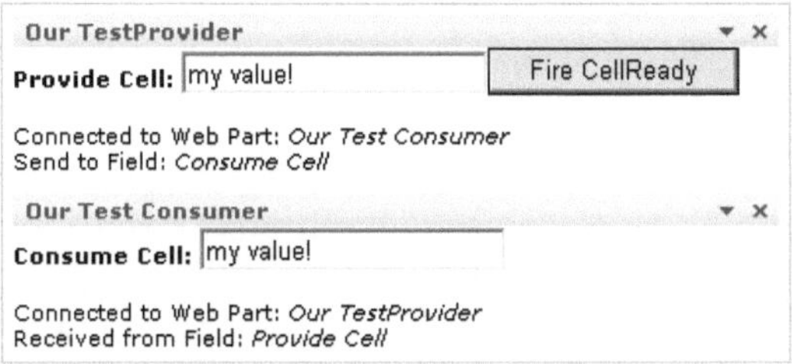

Figure 5-36. *SharePoint web part page including generated connected test web parts*

Now that you have seen how to build the WPCL, deploy it, and use it, we are confident that you will be able to speed up the development of connectable web parts and extend the language to fit any specific needs you might have.

Summary

This chapter showed you how to create a DSL for creating connectable web parts. We have called this language the WPCL. The chapter started with a discussion of software factories, DSLs, and model-driven development. Because our DSL is tied to a very specific problem domain—the creation of connectable web parts—it is essential that you have a good working knowledge of the SharePoint web part connection framework. If you did not have this knowledge, this chapter provided a good overview of this framework. After that, the chapter discussed how to create, deploy, and use the WPCL using the Microsoft DSL Tool.

■ ■ ■

CHAPTER 6

Web Services for Remote Portlets

The primary goal of a portal is to stimulate collaboration and enhance efficiency by offering access to people, content, and application services. Gaining personalized access to information, applications, processes, and people is achieved via a single interface: the portal interface.

When building a portal you need to determine what information your organization needs and where this information comes from. Typically portals obtain information from local or remote data sources such as databases, transaction systems, syndicated content providers, or remote web sites. Portals render and aggregate this information into portal pages.

A *portal page* is a composite of information. Portals typically incorporate the ability to add individual components to a portal page. Such components are often referred to as *portlets*, although in SharePoint terminology we will speak of *web parts* instead.

The Web Services for Remote Portlets (WSRP) protocol is a web services protocol for aggregating content and interactive web applications from remote sources. In this chapter, we will discuss what WSRP is and how this specification can be of help in portal implementations. After that, we will look deeper into the WSRP specification. Also, we explain how to configure a generic WSRP consumer web part in SharePoint and how to build WSRP producers.

Getting to Know WSRP

WSRP is an OASIS (Organization for the Advancement of Structured Information Standards) standard that simplifies the integration of remote content and applications into other applications, most notably portals. The current version of WSRP, version 1.0, was approved in August 2003. WSRP version 2.0 is in the making and will probably be approved at the end of 2006. Check the OASIS web site (http://www.oasis-open.org) if you want an update of the status of WSRP version 2.0.

According to the definition in the WSRP specification, WSRP defines presentation-oriented, interactive web services with a common, well-defined interface and protocol for processing user interactions and for providing presentation fragments. The presentation fragments are suited for mediation and aggregation by portals. WSRP also defines conventions for publishing, finding, and binding such services. WSRP is built on standards such as XML, SOAP, and WSDL. It is not a serious misrepresentation to describe WSRP as a protocol that defines how to send and receive HTML via SOAP, as this is what WSRP currently is used for most often.

A specification closely related to WSRP is Web Services for Interactive Applications (WSIA). If you are looking for information about WSRP, the WSIA specification gets mentioned frequently, so we might as well prepare you for this. Both specifications are standards for presentation-oriented, interactive web services. WSRP and WSIA let you create web services that include presentation and multipage, multistep user interaction. WSRP defines interfaces to include portal-specific features; WSIA focuses on the framework for creating interactive web services.

Another specification that gets mentioned a lot in discussions about WSRP is Sun Microsystem's Java Portlet specification, formerly and better known as the JSR 168 specification. Where WSRP is primarily intended as a communication protocol that allows the reuse of the user interface of a portlet (web part) in one portal within another portal, JSR 168 is a Java specification that lets Java-based portlets work within other JSR 168-compliant portal products (such as Vignette Application Portal, IBM WebSphere Portal, and BEA WebLogic Portal). Via WSRP you can share a centrally hosted portlet; via JSR 168 you can send the portlet code itself and use the portlet in another portal product.

WSIA and JSR 168 do not belong to the topic list of this chapter and are not discussed further, but at least you will be able to discern those specifications from WSRP.

The implementation of the WSRP standard requires the presence of WSRP producers and WSRP consumers. A WSRP producer contains portlets. In general, the WSRP producer implements WSRP-defined web services. To be more specific, there are two kinds of WSRP producers: *complex* and *simple*. A complex producer requires explicit consumer registration, offers more advanced features such as URL rewriting, and has support for a management interface. Simple producers lack these features but do offer support for portal and portlet description, basic portlet and consumer management, and portlet markup.

A WSRP consumer communicates with presentation-oriented web services (WSRP producers). The consumer gathers and aggregates the content and displays it to the end-user. Portals are typical examples of WSRP consumers. Consumers route requests from users to the appropriate WSRP producer, which in turn processes the request and sends results back to the consumer. It is possible that a consumer communicates with multiple producers and aggregates the results to send the final result back to the end user. Such communication is completely opaque: the end-user will never know what communication actually takes place to fulfill a user request.

Approaches for User Interface Reuse

The WSRP specification helps to reuse remote content and/or applications in a portal, but there are alternatives available that do something similar. This section discusses the remote reuse options that are available today:

Image: The image approach is a very easy way to reuse a part of the user interface. All you need to do is add an `<IMG>` tag to a web page and specify the image URL, like so: `<img src="[url]" />`. While image channels are easy to define, they are very limited. The image reuse approach can only be used to display the image in a current browser.

Inline frame: The inline frame approach allows you to include a web page into your own web pages. This is very easy to implement; you only need to include an `<IFRAME>` tag into your web page and provide the URL of the other web page you want to include, like so: `<iframe src="[url]" />`. The problem with this approach is that other web pages might not be very well suited for inline framing. The look and feel of your own portal can be broken if a remote web page incorporates its own navigation system or has a distinct appearance that collides with the style of your own portal. Quite often, remote web pages use JavaScript to prevent inline framing altogether.

Embedded client-side applications: In this approach you will build small client-side applications that will be incorporated in portal pages. At the moment, ActiveX controls, Java applets, and Flash applications are the most popular examples of embedded client-side applications. Embedded client-side applications contain the logic for obtaining content or application services. The user interfaces of such applications tend to be feature-rich and easy to replicate across pages and portals. Developing embedded client-side applications places restrictive demands on clients and are difficult to develop depending on the diversity of environments where the embedded client-side applications will be hosted.

RSS: RSS stands for Real Simple Syndication. The RSS approach allows you to import content that blends in far better than inline framing remote web pages. RSS content is rendered from RSS files. An RSS file contains XML that describes the content and also contains the actual content itself. The RSS specification does not support navigation mechanisms and suppresses control over the look and feel of RSS content. Use of RSS can easily lead to links to external reference points, thus luring the end user away from your portal as an undesirable side effect.

Web proxy/screen scraping: The web proxy or screen scraping approach tries to convert well-formed HTML from remote web pages into XML and render that XML in your portal. This approach allows you to reuse remote web pages that are not even intended for reuse. You can leverage the existing HTML knowledge within an organization to implement this approach. In the web proxy/screen scraping approach you have complete control over layout and behavior.

Having listed the advantages, there are disadvantages as well. Creating implementations like this tends to be very cumbersome and fragile. It is cumbersome because you are consuming remote web pages that are not intended for reuse in this way and that do not have a well-defined communication interface. Consuming such remote web pages is a process of trial and error. Such implementations are fragile because the author of a remote page typically does not know that you are reusing content and certainly cannot be held responsible for breaking your application, so whenever the content author decides to change or move the page it probably will break your application.

Finally, you run the risk of facing legal issues when you are reusing content without the explicit consent of the content author. In situations where a third party knows that you are consuming content or application services and takes responsibility for delivering those services, the web proxy/screen scraping approach is the wrong one. In this case, you should choose an approach that allows parties to agree upon a well-defined interface.

Traditional web service: In this approach a portlet consumes XML and transforms the XML to portal content. For example, the portlet might use XSLT to do the transformation. Nowadays, portlets primarily use web services as the means to obtain XML from remote locations. The use of web services returning XML offers you complete control over layout and behavior as well as well-defined communication interfaces. As a drawback, you need to build logic into portlets consuming web services so that they are able to do something useful with the XML obtained via a web service. To alleviate this drawback, there are products that make consuming web services and creating a user interface very easy, such as FrontPage or the forthcoming Business Data Catalog technology, which is part of Microsoft Office SharePoint Server (MOSS) 2007.

Proprietary remoting: In this approach, you use a proprietary remoting protocol to obtain content or application services. In a Microsoft environment, you can use .NET remoting or DCOM to perform remote communication. Custom channels offer complete control over layout and behavior as well as well-defined communication interfaces. Implementing portlets that use custom remoting are relatively difficult to develop and result in solutions with limited interoperability.

WSRP: WSRP allows a complete interactive channel to be incorporated in other applications (for example, a portal). The maintenance of this interactive channel is managed in a single location. It is very easy to add interactive content or application services to a portal using WSRP. WSRP is ideal for offloading work to a server separate from the portal server. As a drawback, the WSRP specification has not matured yet. Also, it is important to realize that WSRP is not a replacement for traditional web services; WSRP is an addition to them.

Common WSRP Architectures

In this section, we will discuss common usage scenarios for WSRP. Figure 6-1 shows a common pattern for portlets. In this pattern the actual content is delivered via remote web services. Figure 6-1 represents a SharePoint environment where two portlets (Web Part 1 and 2) are imported on a web part page on a SharePoint portal. The portlets consume remote web services and are responsible for implementing the presentation layer.

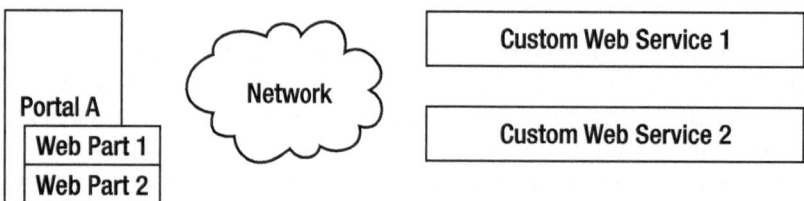

Figure 6-1. *Basic web part architecture*

In this approach the portlets have to be installed physically on the portal server or, in a server farm, on every front end of the portal server. Every portlet that will ever be developed that uses our custom web services 1 and 2 will need to redevelop a presentation layer. In terms of time and cost, this is not optimal.

Figure 6-2 shows how you can solve these problems while making use of WSRP. In this scenario, the business logic is wrapped in the web services Custom Web Service 1 and 2. This part of the solution is identical to the previous approach. The difference is that we will add two web services containing the presentation logic. Those web services are WSRP producers. The portlets (Web Part 1 and 2) that contain the presentation layer are replaced with generic portlets that are able to consume WSRP services.

WSRP interfaces are well-defined. All web services that implement the WSRP standard can be plugged in to a WSRP compliant portal. WSRP compliant portals contain some kind of generic WSRP consumer portlet that is able to communicate with WSRP services. A portal can do more when it comes to WSRP. If the portal contains a WSRP producer as well, the portal can publish any portlet it contains via a WSRP service. This will be completely opaque to the portlet developer. These WSRP services can then be consumed by other WSRP compliant portals.

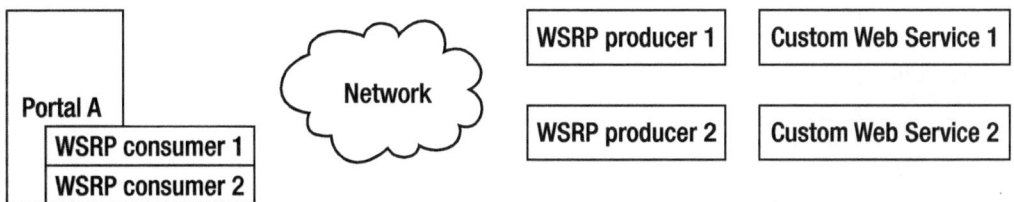

Figure 6-2. *Web services for remote portlets web part architecture*

A typical WSRP architecture looks like Figure 6-3. This picture looks different in Share-Point environments, but we will get to that later. You can see that Portal A is a WSRP producer. Some of these WSRP services are consumed by Portal B, a WSRP-compliant portal that contains a generic WSRP consumer portlet to do so. The portal contains a number of portlets that are made available to other applications via the WSRP producer of Portal B. WSRP consumers, such as Portal C, are able to consume the portlets of Portal B via Portal B WSRP services. Portal C uses its own set of generic WSRP consumer portlets to consume those services. User agents such as browsers consume the markup returned by Portal B.

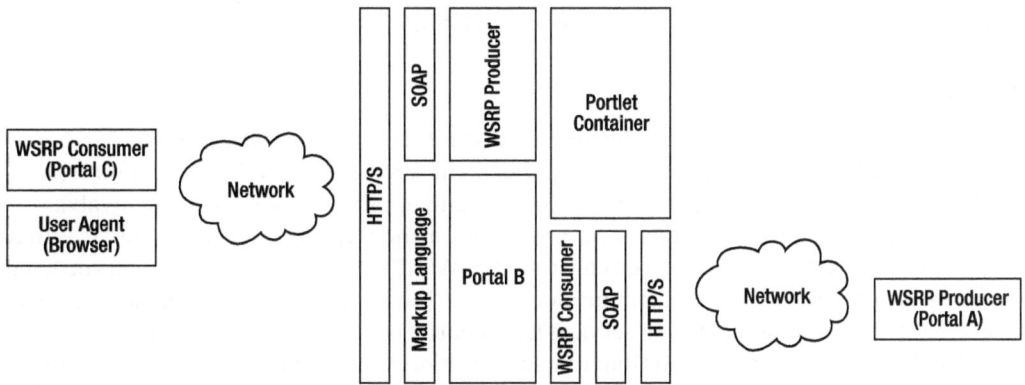

Figure 6-3. *A typical WSRP architecture*

It is very important to keep this typical architecture in mind. Realizing WSRP is created for reusing portlets at the presentation level in other portals is essential in understanding the entire specification.

When it comes to WSRP, Microsoft has a different portal vision compared to portal vendors implementing WSRP producers in their portal products. Within the Microsoft view, a SharePoint portal consolidates all information on a big centralized server. Within this view, there is no need to share the user interface of web parts via WSRP services with other portals. Instead, if you need access to content or application services you should go to the central SharePoint portal. Do not expect a WSRP producer to be included in SharePoint technology anytime soon.

This does not mean to say that WSRP cannot play a role in SharePoint portals. WSRP consumers can be of great help when consolidating content and applications in a central location. This results in an architecture as described in Figure 6-4. Here you see a traditional web service that contains the business layer. The WSRP web service encapsulates the presentation layer. WSRP consumer web parts in various portals are able to consume these services.

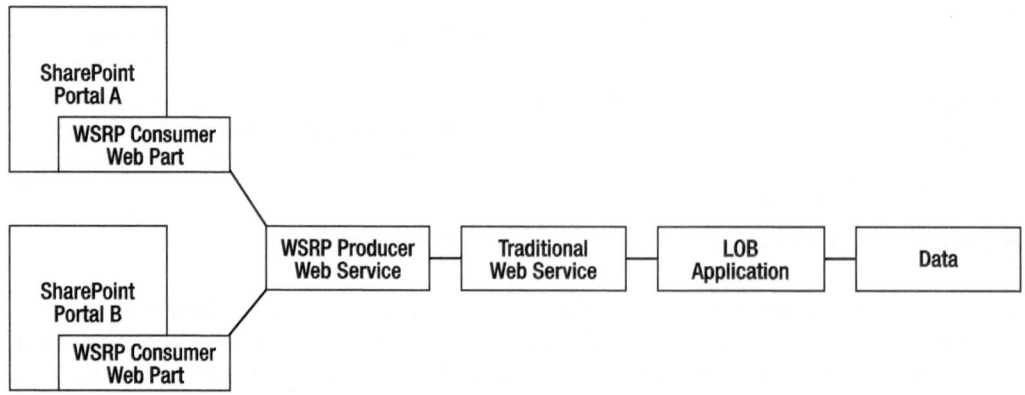

Figure 6-4. *A typical SharePoint WSRP architecture*

WSRP Benefits and Drawbacks

The section "Approaches for User Interface Reuse" talked briefly about the advantages and disadvantages of WSRP, but there is a whole lot more to say about this topic. In this section, we will look in detail at the benefits and drawbacks of WSRP.

Benefits

Let's start with a discussion of the advantages of WSRP. The first advantage of WSRP is that it defines a standard for remote content and application service reuse at the presentation level. Without WSRP, most scenarios of remote content and application service reuse involves custom coding. Because WSRP interfaces are common and well-defined, all web services that implement the WSRP standard can be consumed by WSRP consumers. In a portal, all you need is access to a generic WSRP consumer portlet to do so. Using such a portlet, even nontechnical users are able to incorporate WSRP services into a portal in a plug-and-play fashion.

Another advantage of WSRP is that this specification allows applications to reuse presentation layers, thus saving investments in good user interfaces. Although in principle every kind of application can be a WSRP consumer; the specification is created for use in portals, as portals are the kind of application that aggregate and reuse information.

The next advantage is related to reusing portal content itself. If you are using a portal that includes a WSRP producer, SharePoint Portal Server 2003 not being one of those portals, you can integrate the user interface of your portlets into other portals. Again, this does not require any coding on your part. WSRP allows you to integrate content and applications services in other applications in a fast and easy way while keeping costs low.

If you are consuming a content service you need to determine if the content producer or the content consumer is responsible for the look and feel of the content. An advantage of WSRP in scenarios where content producers are responsible for the look and feel of the content is that it enables content producers to maintain complete control over layout and behavior of their content. This reduces the distribution of update problems frequently faced in other solutions.

WSRP is advantageous in server farm scenarios. WSRP allows content and application services to be hosted in the environment most sensible for its execution (regardless of location or platform), while remaining easy to access by WSRP consumers. This makes WSRP an attractive candidate in distributed computing and load balancing scenarios. This results in flexible, interoperable, and scalable architectures that decouple portal aggregation from portlet execution. A result of this flexibility is that it is easy to switch to new WSRP producers.

WSRP is a standard that can be used in all sorts of environments and scenarios, because it is agnostic to what and how it communicates. As a protocol, WSRP is agnostic to the markup type being communicated between WSRP producers and consumers. WSRP is also agnostic to the protocol that is used for communication. Having said that, a typical WSRP solution uses HTML as the markup type and HTTP as the communication protocol. This fits well into the security infrastructure of most companies. WSRP can be used in all sorts of environments because it builds on standards such as XML, SOAP, and WSDL and is supported by large players in the industry (e.g., BEA, IBM, Microsoft, Oracle, and Sun).

WSRP decouples deployment and delivery of applications. WSRP consumers get to use the latest version of remote content or application services, independent of the location where portlets are physically deployed. Portals are able to consume WSRP services without deploying any additional code on the portal server at all, resulting in a zero-installation effort on the portal. This way, portal developers and administrators get to focus on building and managing a portal; other developer groups can focus on building WSRP-compliant portlets.

WSRP services deliver data and presentation logic. Traditional web services are data-oriented; they contain business logic but lack presentation logic. As a result, every client needs to implement its own piece of presentation logic. Providing presentation logic via a WSRP service makes it easy to dynamically integrate business applications. This way, consumers get the complete package. This does not mean to say that WSRP services replace traditional web services; instead, WSRP services complement traditional web services.

Drawbacks

We have looked at the benefits of WSRP, but there are drawbacks as well. The goal of WSRP is rather ambitious: is it indeed possible to build highly interactive applications that can be exposed in different portal products and offer a unified and secure experience completely opaque to the end user?

The first problem is that application service providers do not have a great incentive for building WSRP producers. For example, if you sell an ERP application that holds mission-critical data, vendors might ask themselves why they would want to expose their services in other portals. This does not sound like a sure way to make money. Until now, major vendors have shown that they do not have any problems creating WSRP consumers for their products. The effort put into creating WSRP producers for their own application services is considerably less. Having said this, it does not stop you from creating your own WSRP producers, which can be used freely in, let's say, an intranet environment.

The next disadvantage is that although interactive, WSRP offers a limited experience compared to full-blown portlets. A normal portlet utilizes programming models such as JavaScript, DOM, and embedded client-side applications. In generic WSRP portlets you have less control over the user interface, using JavaScript is more problematic and some types of interactivity are hard to achieve. For example, Ajax-style development is considerably more complex to do in WSRP scenarios. Within WSRP 1.0 you are allowed to include JavaScript within a markup fragment, but you cannot include JavaScript outside the <body> of the aggregated page. A WSRP portlet cannot use external style sheets provided by a WSRP consumer. Locally running portlets will usually be faster than calling remote WSRP services. Local portlets typically have access to information about the portal server, portal site, and portal pages hosting the portlet and to other portlets as well. In the future, new versions of the WSRP specification will solve at least some of these problems.

Another disadvantage is related to security; there are additional security issues in WSRP scenarios. Because WSRP consumers have little or no control over the contents of markup fragments sent by WSRP producers, unknown code (for example, client-side JavaScript) can be embedded in WSRP responses, which make WSRP consumers vulnerable for script injection attacks. This means you need to have a considerable amount of trust in the WSRP producers you are using. The creators of the WSRP specification thought this would not be a big concern for WSRP consumers, because of inherent client-side JavaScript limitations. Optionally, WSRP responses can contain binary data as well, but it is up to the consumer to decide how to interpret and use this binary data

---

■**Note** In addition to being subject to script injection issues, a WSRP service is exposed to the same security issues as other web services. The WSRP specification will leverage existing and forthcoming web service standards such as WS-Security. Currently, a typical WSRP solution that needs to be secure uses HTTPS and the combination of client and server certificates.

Another problem for the WSRP specification is the question about its usefulness compared to, in some scenarios, the competing and hugely successful technology RSS. RSS can be used for content syndication. It is simple and very popular. Although WSRP provides a richer content delivery mechanism, RSS is already used in a lot of content syndication scenarios, thus limiting the role WSRP can play in those scenarios.

It can be hard to work with WSRP because the WSRP specification is quite complex, although this problem is alleviated by several commercial vendors building WSRP frameworks and tools. For .NET, the only vendor that we know of that is offering a WSRP framework is a company called NetUnity (http://www.netunitysoftware.com).

Another disadvantage of WSRP is related to speed and performance. WSRP introduces additional latency because user interaction is required to be passed through the WSRP consumer to the remote WSRP provider. The WSRP protocol typically uses SOAP over HTTP which brings a considerable amount of overhead. WSRP consumers send two kinds of data to WSRP consumers: form parameters and uploaded data. For HTTP POST requests, this data is sent as multipart requests to the WSRP consumer, which transports the data within a SOAP envelope to the WSRP producer. This takes up additional memory and processing power on the servers hosting WSRP consumers and WSRP producers. A WSRP solution is not optimized for speed and performance.

WSRP can be used to aggregate content from multiple sources. Although WSRP offers mechanisms to standardize the look of this content, those mechanisms are superficial, resulting in a user experience that may not always be optimal. If a WSRP consumer aggregates markup fragments from various producers, you do not have the guarantee that every WSRP producer follows the same style and naming conventions. For example, Form A might contain a Submit button; a comparable Form B might contain a Proceed button. As another example, date formats might be represented in different ways in different forms. Yet another example, field and form validation requirements may differ between forms. WSRP addresses only a part of this problem by specifying a standard set of CSS (Cascading Style Sheets) styles that can be defined by WSRP consumers. Although this enhances consistency, user experience usability issues remain.

A danger of using WSRP producers in a portal is that they invite you to promote portlets at the presentation level only, as this level of reuse is available automatically after creating a portlet. This creates an application that is not really built with reuse in mind or the reuse is at the wrong level. If you refer back to Figure 6-3 you will see that WSRP promotes reuse at the presentation level. If you are building applications that need to be reused, it can be a mistake to offer reuse only at the user-interface level. Always consider whether it makes sense to offer a traditional web service encapsulating business logic as well. Refer back to Figure 6-4 to see a diagram depicting this kind of architecture.

Finally, there are some drawbacks to the maturity of web service standards. The WSRP specification itself does not currently include eventing, security, and caching. Instead, WSRP builds on other web service standards to provide these features. Those standards have not yet matured, which can also be said for WSRP itself.

Delving Deeper into the WSRP Specification

In most situations, developers implementing an architecture involving WSRP will have little or nothing to do with the WSRP specification itself, as this will be abstracted away by a portal or framework. This holds true for the examples discussed later in the chapter in the sections "Configuring a WSRP Consumer for SharePoint 2003 Portals" and "Implementing a WSRP Producer," where we will show how to use a WSRP consumer in SharePoint and build a WSRP producer using a WSRP .NET framework. Nevertheless, it is helpful to gain a better understanding of the underlying WSRP technology. In this section, we will take a closer look at the WSRP specification and discuss the most important aspects of the specification.

WSRP Interfaces

The WSRP specification defines four interfaces:

- Service Description

- Registration

- Markup

- Portlet Management

A WSRP producer may be discovered through discovery mechanisms such as UDDI (Universal Description, Discovery, and Integration) and WSIL (Web Services Inspection Language). The following code shows an example WSRP service WSDL that specifies the locations of services responsible for implementing the four WSRP interfaces:

```
<?xml version="1.0" encoding="UTF-8"?>
<wsdl:definitions targetNamespace="urn:oasis:names:tc:wsrp:v1:wsdl" ➥
  xmlns:bind="urn:oasis:names:tc:wsrp:v1:bind" ➥
  xmlns=http://schemas.xmlsoap.org/wsdl/ ➥
  xmlns:wsdl=http://schemas.xmlsoap.org/wsdl/ ➥
  xmlns:soap="http://schemas.xmlsoap.org/wsdl/soap/">
```

```
  <import namespace="urn:oasis:names:tc:wsrp:v1:bind" ➥
    location="wsrp_v1_bindings.wsdl"/>

  <wsdl:service name="WSRPService">
    <wsdl:port binding="bind:WSRP_v1_Markup_Binding_SOAP" name="WSRPBaseService">
      <soap:address location="http://my.service:8080/WSRPService"/>
    </wsdl:port>
    <wsdl:port binding="bind:WSRP_v1_ServiceDescription_Binding_SOAP" ➥
      name="WSRPServiceDescriptionService">
      <soap:address location="http://my.service:8080/WSRPService"/>
    </wsdl:port>
    <wsdl:port binding="bind:WSRP_v1_Registration_Binding_SOAP" ➥
      name="WSRPRegistrationService">
      <soap:address location="http://my.service:8080/WSRPService"/>
    </wsdl:port>
    <wsdl:port binding="bind:WSRP_v1_PortletManagement_Binding_SOAP" ➥
      name="WSRPPortletManagementService">
      <soap:address location="http://my.service:8080/WSRPService"/>
    </wsdl:port>
  </wsdl:service>
</wsdl:definitions>
```

The Service Description interface is required and provides the means for a consumer to ascertain the capabilities of a WSRP producer and the portlets it has to offer. The Service Description interface defines only a single method called getServiceDescription(). This method is responsible for providing information about the capabilities of a producer in a context-sensitive manner. For example, a consumer may be required to register itself first before it is allowed to discover the full capabilities of a producer.

The following code shows an example of a web service call to the getServiceDescription() method of the Service Description interface:

```
POST /wsrp/wsrp4j/WSRPServiceDescriptionService HTTP/1.0
Content-Type: text/xml; charset=utf-8
Accept: application/soap+xml, application/dime, multipart/related, text/*
User-Agent: Mozilla/4.0 (compatible; MSIE 6.0; ➥
MS Web Services Client Protocol 1.1.4322.2300)
Host: localhost
Cache-Control: no-cache
Pragma: no-cache
SOAPAction: "urn:oasis:names:tc:wsrp:v1:getServiceDescription"
Content-Length: 499

<?xml version="1.0" encoding="UTF-8"?>
<soapenv:Envelope xmlns:soapenv="http://schemas.xmlsoap.org/soap/envelope/" ➥
  xmlns:xsd="http://www.w3.org/2001/XMLSchema" ➥
  xmlns:xsi="http://www.w3.org/2001/XMLSchema-instance">
```

```
<soapenv:Body>
  <getServiceDescription xmlns="urn:oasis:names:tc:wsrp:v1:types">
    <registrationContext>
      <registrationHandle>22.34.152.220_2039571409459_4</registrationHandle>
    </registrationContext>
  </getServiceDescription>
</soapenv:Body>
</soapenv:Envelope>
```

The Registration interface is used to register or deregister a WSRP consumer with a WSRP producer. This interface defines the following methods: register(), modifyRegistration(), and deregister(). The register() method is used to establish a relationship between a consumer and a producer. It returns a handle that is used in all subsequent invocations the consumer makes. Consumers and producers are free to end this relationship anytime. If the consumer ends the relationship, it must call the deregister() method. A producer indicates it wants to end the relationship by informing the consumer via an error message. The modifyRegistration() method is used by the consumer to modify a relationship.

The following code shows an example of a web service call to the register() method of the Registration interface:

```
<soap:Envelope xmlns:soap="http://schemas.xmlsoap.org/soap/envelope/" ➥
  xmlns:xsi="http://www.w3.org/2001/XMLSchema-instance" ➥
  xmlns:xsd="http://www.w3.org/2001/XMLSchema">
  <soap:Body>
    <register xmlns="urn:oasis:names:tc:wsrp:v1:types">
      <consumerName>wsrpConsumer</consumerName>
      <consumerAgent>wsrpConsumer.1.1</consumerAgent>
      <methodGetSupported>false</methodGetSupported>
    </register>
  </soap:Body>
</soap:Envelope>
```

The Markup interface is required and contains operations to request the generation of markup and the processing of interactions with that markup. This interface defines the following methods: getMarkup(), performBlockingInteraction(), initCookie(), and releaseSessions(). The getMarkup() method requests the markup for rendering the current state of a portlet. The performBlockingInteraction() method is used for synchronization purposes. A portlet will receive only one invocation of this method per client interaction and persists some sort of state change. The consumer has to wait for the response before invoking the getMarkup() method on the portlets it is aggregating. This allows the WSRP producer to share state between portlets. The initCookie() method is used in scenarios where the WSRP consumer assists in managing state via cookies and allows the consumer to supply cookies. The releaseSessions() method enables the consumer to inform the producer that it will no longer be using session information. The following code shows an example response from a WSRP producer after a call to the getMarkup() method of the Markup interface:

```
<soapenv:Envelope xmlns:soapenv="http://schemas.xmlsoap.org/soap/envelope/">
  <soapenv:Body>
    <urn:getMarkupResponse xmlns:urn="urn:oasis:names:tc:wsrp:v1:types">
      <urn:markupContext>
        <urn:mimeType>text/html; charset=UTF-8</urn:mimeType>
        <urn:markupString>
          <![CDATA[<form name="searchForm" ➡
          action="http://localhost:7001/consumer/test.portal?_nfpb=true ➡
          &_windowLabel=search_1_1&_pageLabel=test_page_2&wsrp- ➡
          urlType=blockingAction&wsrp-url= ➡
          &wsrp-requiresRewrite=&wsrp-navigationalState=&wsrp-interactionState= ➡
          _action%3D%252FSearch%252Fsearch&wsrp-mode=&wsrp-windowState=" ➡
          method="post">
          <table>
          <tr valign="top">
          <td>First Name:</td>
          <td><input type="text" name=" ➡
          search_1{actionForm.firstName}" value=""></td>
          </tr>
          <tr valign="top">
          <td>Last Name:</td>
          <td><input type="text" name="search_1{actionForm.lastName}" value=""></td>
          </tr>
          </table>
          <br/>
          <input type="submit" value="search">
          </form>]]>
        </urn:markupString>
        <urn:locale>en-US</urn:locale>
        <urn:requiresUrlRewriting>false</urn:requiresUrlRewriting>
      </urn:markupContext>
      <urn:sessionContext>
        <urn:sessionID>
          B9Ml78JJyZNrMbzKnPxfyXZj511LL420BfKZGmLssNGO2DbSJm3y!-1979539005
        </urn:sessionID>
        <urn:expires>3600</urn:expires>
      </urn:sessionContext>
    </urn:getMarkupResponse>
  </soapenv:Body>
</soapenv:Envelope>
```

The Portlet Management interface is used to manage portlets. It can be used for operations such as cloning portlets, destroying portlets, and retrieving portlet definitions. This interface defines the following methods: getPortletDescription(), clonePortlet(), destroyPortlets(), setPortletProperties(), getPortletProperties(), and getPortletPropertyDescription(). The getPortletDescription() method allows the producer to provide information about the portlets it offers in a context-sensitive manner. The clonePortlet() method allows the creation of a new portlet from an existing portlet. The initial state of a cloned portlet will need to be identical to the original portlet. Basically, this is a copy-by-value action that can be used to copy a producer-offered portlet, resulting in a consumer-configured portlet. You can also use the clonePortlet() method to copy previously cloned consumer-configured portlets. Consumer-configured portlets can be discarded by calling the destroyPortlets() method. Portlet properties are metadata-specific to a portlet. The setPortletProperties() method allows the consumer to set portlet properties. The getPortletProperties() method exhibits the opposite behavior: it is used to retrieve portlet metadata. The getPortletPropertyDescription() method is used for discovering portlet properties and information such as type and description about those properties. This information can be used when generating a user interface for editing the portlets configuration.

The following code shows an example of a web service call to the clonePortlet() method of the Portlet Management interface:

```
<soap:Envelope xmlns:soap="http://schemas.xmlsoap.org/soap/envelope/" ➥
  xmlns:xsi="http://www.w3.org/2001/XMLSchema-instance" ➥
  xmlns:xsd="http://www.w3.org/2001/XMLSchema">
  <soap:Body>
    <clonePortlet xmlns="urn:oasis:names:tc:wsrp:v1:types">
      <registrationContext>
        <registrationHandle>AAAUU111yy777…</registrationHandle>
      </registrationContext>
      <portletContext>
        <portletHandle>portlet_1</portletHandle>
      </portletContext>
      <userContext>
        <userContextKey>wsrpConsumer</userContextKey>
      </userContext>
    </clonePortlet>
  </soap:Body>
</soap:Envelope>
```

WSRP State

There are scenarios where you have the need to keep track of the session state of a WSRP portlet. If you find yourself in such a situation, you can choose between the uses of multiple WSRP portlet state types:

- URL state

  - Navigational state

  - Interaction state

- Session state

- Persistent state

The URL WSRP portlet state type can be divided into two subtypes: portlet navigational state and portlet interaction state. Portlets using navigational state let WSRP consumers take care of keeping track of most of the state. The only part of the portlet state that gets pushed to the consumer is navigational state. Portlet navigational state identifies the current view of the portlet. Examples of the use of navigational state are support for page refreshes and bookmarks. Portlets using interaction state let WSRP consumers take care of keeping track of the state but also push interaction state to the consumer. Portlet interaction state identifies what action should be taken by a portlet.

In session state scenarios, a WSRP producer establishes a session and returns some sort of handle (a session ID) which is returned by a consumer on all subsequent invocations of a portlet instance. Session state is transient, can expire, and can be stored on the consumer or producer side. Session state is user- and portlet-specific.

In persistent state scenarios, the state is kept in some type of permanent data store, typically a database, and held for the entire lifetime of a portlet. The WSRP producer is responsible for keeping track of persistent state. Persistent state is typically used to store portlet configuration.

WSRP Portlet Mode

A portlet should render different content and perform different activities based on its state and the operation requested by the end user. The WSRP specification defines a set of modes that reflects common functionality for portal-to-portlet interactions. WSRP defines the following modes:

- wsrp:view

- wsrp:edit

- wsrp:help

- wsrp:preview

- custom consumer modes

The wsrp:view mode will render portlet markup reflecting the current state of a portlet. This mode will include one or more screens that the end user can view, navigate, or even interact with. In wsrp:edit mode, a portlet should provide content and logic that lets a user customize the behavior of a portlet. The wsrp:help mode provides context-sensitive help. If a portlet is in wsrp:preview mode, it should render a preview of the standard content shown in wsrp:view mode. Finally, consumers can declare additional custom modes.

WSRP Window State

Window state is an indicator of the amount of page space that will be assigned to the content generated by a portlet. It is up to the consumer to decide how much information will be rendered eventually. WSRP defines the following Window states:

- wsrp:normal

- wsrp:minimized

- wsrp:maximized

- wsrp:solo

- custom mode

In the `wsrp:normal` Window state the portlet is likely sharing the aggregated page with other portlets. Therefore, the size of its rendered output should be restricted. The `wsrp:minimized` Window state indicates the portlet should not render visible markup. The portlet is free to include nonvisible data such as JavaScript or hidden forms. If a portlet is in `wsrp:maximized` Window state the portlet is likely to be the only portlet being rendered on the aggregated page, or the portlet is assigned more space compared to other portlets on the aggregated page. In this case, a portlet can generate richer content if it wants to. The `wsrp:solo` Window state is comparable to the `wsrp:maximized` Window state. It indicates that the portlet is the only portlet being rendered on the aggregated page, so the portlet is free to generate richer content. Finally, consumers are allowed to declare additional custom Window states.

WSRP Markup URLs

Portlets return markup. Often, a portlet creates URLs that reference the portlet itself. When an end user clicks a link or submits a form, eventually this should result in a new invocation to the portlet. Portlet URLs embedded in a markup fragment often cannot or should not be direct links. For example, you always have the guarantee that the end user has access to the WSRP consumer. However, the WSRP producer may be shielded from the end user. As another example, the WSRP consumer might want to perform additional operations such as enriching the end-user request with context information. In such scenarios, WSRP consumers will need to intercept end-user requests and reroute them to the WSRP producer.

To facilitate interception mechanisms, URLs need to be encoded. The encoding of URLs is a process that is also known as URL rewriting. There are two styles when it comes to URL rewriting:

- Consumer URL rewriting

- Producer URL writing

The consumer URL rewriting style renders the URL in the markup with delimiters that are replaced by the WSRP consumer with real URLs. The disadvantage of this approach is that the result of consumer URL parsing is that the consumer will become more complex and takes up more processing time. The following URL is an example of a consumer URL that is marked with delimiters and fit for consumer URL rewriting:

```
wsrp_rewrite?wsrp_urlType=render&wsrp-mode=help&wsrp-windowState=solo/wsrp_rewrite
```

Consumer portlet URLs start with the following token: `wsrp_rewrite` appended by a question mark (?). The end of such a URL is another token: `wsrp_rewrite` preceded by a forward slash (/). The content of a consumer portlet URL consists of name/value pairs separated by ampersand (&) characters. The names of those pairs consist of a series of well-known portlet URL parameters. The portlet URL parameters specify what the consumer needs to do. Currently, the WSRP specification defines the following portlet URL parameters:

- `wsrp-urlType`

- `wsrp-url`

- `wsrp-requiresRewrite`

- `wsrp-navigationalState`

- `wsrp-interactionState`

- `wsrp-mode`

- `wsrp-windowState`

- `wsrp-fragmentID`

- `wsrp-secureURL`

The `wsrp-urlType` portlet URL parameter must be specified first. This parameter can be set to the following values: `blockingAction`, `render`, and `resource`. If the `wsrp-urlType` parameter is set to `blockingAction` the `performBlockingInteraction()` method is called on the portlet generating the markup. The `performBlockingInteraction()` method is described in section WSRP interfaces. If the `wsrp-urlType` parameter is set to `render` the `getMarkup()` method is called. Finally, if the `wsrp-urlType` parameter is set to `resource`, the WSRP consumer will try to retrieve some sort of resource, possibly in a cached manner, and return it to the end user.

The `wsrp-url` parameter provides the actual URL to a resource. The URL needs to be absolute and URL-escaped (for example, use & instead of &). The `wsrp-requiresRewrite` parameter is a Boolean parameter that tells the WSRP consumer whether it needs to parse a URL for consumer URL rewriting. The `wsrp-navigationalState` parameter defines the navigational state of a portlet. The navigational state is determined by the WSRP consumer and sent to the WSRP producer. The `wsrp-interactionState` parameter contains the interaction state provided by the consumer. The `wsrp-mode` parameter requests a change of portlet mode. Valid values are `wsrp:view`, `wsrp:edit`, `wsrp:help`, `wsrp:preview`, or a custom mode. Portlet modes are discussed in detail in the section "WSRP Portlet Mode" previously in this chapter.

The `wsrp-windowState` requests a change of window state. Valid values are `wsrp:normal`, `wsrp:minimized`, `wsrp:maximized`, `wsrp:solo`, or a custom mode. Window states are discussed in detail in the section "WSRP Window State." The `wsrp-fragmentID` parameter specifies a portion of a URL that navigates to a place within a document. The `wsrp-secureURL` parameter is a Boolean parameter indicating whether a URL needs to be accessed in a secure manner. Setting this parameter to true means that the communication between the end user and the WSRP consumer needs to be secure, and also that the communication between WSRP consumer and WSRP producer needs to be secure.

In the producer URL writing style, URL templates are provided by the WSRP consumer, and known tokens within those templates are replaced by the WSRP producer. In this approach, the consumer passes context information to the producer. The URL template format is completely up to the WSRP consumer, as the consumer is the only party that knows what the final URL should look like. A disadvantage of the producer URL approach is that the resulting markup might be less cacheable by the consumer. The following URL is an example of a producer URL fit for producer URL writing: `http://www.theConsumerPortal.com/site/{wsrp-urlType}?mode={wsrp-mode}&amp;navigationalState={wsrp-navigationalState}&amp;`

A producer URL contains zero or more replacement tokens that are enclosed in curly braces ({ }). Any content outside the curly braces will not be modified by the WSRP producer. As an example, in the previous producer URL the WSRP producer might replace the token `{wsrp-urlType}` with the value `render`. The list of defined portlet URL parameters that can be used as replacement tokens in producer URLs is a superset of the set of consumer URL parameters. All parameters starting from `wsrp-urlType` to `wsrp-secureURL` are supported in producer URLs.

There are also four new parameters that cannot be used as parameters in consumer URLs. These parameters help to establish the correct context; the parameters are `wsrp-portletHandle`, `wsrp-userContextKey`, `wsrp-portletInstanceKey`, and `wsrp-sessionID`. The producer will replace those tokens with actual handles to a portlet, user, portlet instance, and session ID. The values are provided by the consumer itself, originally.

Although the exact template format of a producer URL is up to the consumer, the WSRP specification does define various templates that determine the minimal amount of URL parameters that must be included in a producer URL. The WSRP specification discerns the following templates:

- blockingActionTemplate

- secureBlockingActionTemplate

- renderTemplate

- secureRenderTemplate

- resourceTemplate

- secureResourceTemplate

- defaultTemplate

- secureDefaultTemplate

The blockingActionTemplate template results in a `performBlockingInteraction()` method call. When this template is used, a consumer must include the following replacement tokens: `wsrp-navigationalState`, `wsrp-interactionState`, `wsrp-mode`, and `wsrp-windowState`. The secureBlockingActionTemplate template is identical to the blockingActionTemplate template, but uses secure communication (SSL connections).

The renderTemplate template results in a `getMarkup()` method call. When this template is used, a consumer must include the following replacement tokens: `wsrp-navigationalState`, `wsrp-mode`, and `wsrp-windowState`. The secureRenderTemplate template is identical to the renderTemplate template, but uses secure communication.

The resourceTemplate template fetches a resource. When this template is used a consumer must include the following replacement tokens: `wsrp-url` and `wsrp-requiresRewrite`. The secureResourceTemplate template is identical to the resourceTemplate template, but uses secure communication.

The defaultTemplate template is the default template, a generic template that is used whenever a specialized template is not provided by the consumer. When this template is used, a consumer must include the following replacement tokens: `wsrp-navigationalState`, `wsrp-interactionState`, `wsrp-mode`, and `wsrp-windowState`. The secureDefaultTemplate template is identical to the defaultTemplate template, but uses secure communication.

The following code example shows typical uses of the render, blocking action, and resource producer URL templates within HTML markup:

```
<a href="[render template]">…</a>
<form action="[blocking action template]">…</form>
<img src="[resource template]" />
```

CSS Style Definitions

One of the biggest strengths of the WSRP specification is the ability to create a common look and feel across portlets on an aggregated page. This is done by using a common CSS style sheet for all portlets, and defining a set of standard styles. Portlets must use these CSS style definitions to be able to participate in a uniform display by various consumers. For example, to indicate that a text fragment is in the normal page font, you should use the portlet-font style definition:

```
<div class="portlet-font">A normal text</div>
```

More details about all available style definitions can be found in the OASIS WSRP specification (http://www.oasis.org).

Portlet Cloning

In the introduction of this chapter we state that portals help to gain personalized access to information, applications, processes, and people. To empower this, portals typically contain portlet personalization and customization features. As the WSRP specification is targeted toward portlets, WSRP needs to support the ability to have end users have their own instances of portlets and set their own preferences on those instances. The mechanism that makes this possible is called *portlet cloning* and is done via methods defined in the portlet management interface.

In WSRP, there are two types of portlets: producer-offered portlets and consumer-configured portlets. By default a portlet is a producer-offered portlet. It is not personalized or customized. *Producer-offered portlets* are preconfigured and not modifiable by consumers. Since personalization and customization are important aspects of a portlet, WSRP allows consumers to clone a producer-offered portlet, so that consumers can customize it and change its persistent state. After cloning, the portlet is called a *consumer-configured portlet*.

There are multiple ways to change the persistent state of a consumer-configured portlet. You can clone a portlet explicitly, via the clonePortlet() method defined in the portlet management interface. This method takes the registration context, portlet context, and user context as parameters, and its response returns a new portlet context identifying the new portlet. You can also clone a portlet explicitly; in such scenarios the WSRP consumer creates a portlet clone that is used by a group of end users. This is completely opaque to the end user.

Namespace Encoding

Aggregating multiple portlets from different sources can lead to naming conflicts in portlet elements such as IDs of HTML tags, CSS styles, and JavaScript functions. To create unique names in markup you can use namespaces. WSRP defines two forms of namespace encoding: producer namespacing and consumer namespacing.

When using producer namespacing, the portlet uses a namespace prefix provided by the consumer to prefix elements in a portlet that need to be unique. The following code shows how producer namespacing is used to create a unique namespace for an HTML form called myform:

```
<form name="NS001_myform" …>
```

If a portlet prefixes a portlet element that is intended to be unique with the wsrp_rewrite token, the WSRP consumer will locate them and generate a unique namespace. The following code shows how to use this token to create a unique namespace for an HTML form called myform:

```
<form name="wsrp_rewrite_myform" …>
```

Markup Tag Restrictions

For efficiency reasons, WSRP consumers are not required to validate the markup fragments returned by producers. To allow consumers to safely aggregate multiple portlet markup fragments there are restrictions placed on the set of markup tags that may be returned by portlets. Disallowed tags can break the coherence of an entire aggregated page. Examples of HTML tags that should never be returned by a portlet are <body>, <frame>, <frameset>, <head>, <html>, and <title>.

There are other tags that, according to the HTML specification, should never occur outside the <head> element of a document. However, some user-agent implementations might support otherwise. As a result of this, it is up to the portlet developer to use or refrain from using those tags. Examples of such tags are <base>, <link>, <meta>, and <style>.

Configuring a WSRP Consumer for SharePoint 2003 Portals

In this section we show how to configure a WSRP consumer web part and use it within SharePoint Portal Server 2003. At the time of this writing there was only one generic WSRP consumer web part implementation for SharePoint 2003 that we were aware of. It is called the WSRP consumer web part and is created by members of the SharePoint team as a proof of concept for the forthcoming WSRP consumer web part that will be included in Microsoft Office SharePoint Server 2007.

The WSRP consumer web part for SharePoint 2003 is a part of the WSRP Web Part Toolkit for SharePoint Products and Technologies and can be found on the GotDotNet web site (http://www.gotdotnet.com). The web part is written in .NET 1.1 and, as WSRP is a topic that most often plays a role in portal implementations, we have chosen SharePoint Portal Server 2003 (instead of Windows SharePoint Services 2003) as the platform to demonstrate how to configure the GotDotNet WSRP consumer web part.

As the WSRP consumer web part is just a proof of concept, it will not be supported officially. The web part is a basic implementation of a WSRP consumer and seems to have trouble with communicating with interactive WSRP producers. This is caused by the inability of the web part to deal well with hidden form fields such as the ViewState hidden field. Advanced WSRP consumers are typically created by portal vendors themselves, as some things (such as portlet-to-portlet communication) are just too hard to do if you do not have access to the portal framework. So do not expect an advanced WSRP consumer web part to appear anytime soon on the SharePoint 2003 market or you will probably be disappointed.

The current implementation of the WSRP consumer web part will allow you to consume information-oriented WSRP producers without problems, thus providing an experience comparable to RSS solutions. You do have access to the source code of the WSRP consumer web part, so you can take the web part as far as you want.

The GotDotNet workspace containing the WSRP Web Part Toolkit contains documentation, although, in our opinion, the quality of it is not great, something that can be explained by the fact that the WSRP consumer web part is just a proof of concept. In this section we discuss the minimal amount of configuration you need to perform to get the WSRP consumer web part working. If you need more information about the configuration process, you can refer to the documentation provided on the GotDotNet workspace.

The first part of the configuration consists of adjusting the web.config file to suit the needs of the WSRP consumer web part:

1. Open the web.config file of your SharePoint virtual server (ours is located at [drive letter]:\inetpub\wwwroot).

2. Locate the `<SafeControls>` section and add a new safe control for the web part consumer library:

```
<SafeControl Assembly="WSRPConsumerWebPartLibrary" ➥
Namespace="WSRPConsumerWebPartLibrary" TypeName="*" Safe="True" />
```

3. Locate the `<httpModules>` section and uncomment the following element:

```
<add name="Session" type="System.Web.SessionState.SessionStateModule"/>
```

4. Locate the `<pages>` element and set the `enableSessionState` property to true:

```
<pages enableSessionState="true" enableViewState="true" ➥
enableViewStateMac="true" validateRequest="false" />
```

At this point, you have configured the web.config file for your SharePoint virtual server successfully. Next, you will need to install the WSRP consumer web part and configure it correctly. We will assume you have downloaded the WSRP Web Part Toolkit from the GotDotNet web site successfully. We will configure the WSRP consumer web part so that it will consume a test WSRP service built by NetUnity (http://www.netunitysoftware.com), a company that provides products and services that enable businesses to develop and deploy portal solutions based on WSRP using the Microsoft .NET platform. The NetUnity test WSRP service is a prebuilt WSRP producer and provides an excellent way to test if the WSRP consumer web part is working correctly.

First you need to install the web part. Then you need to configure the WSRP consumer web part. You will also need to configure the WSRP consumer to use the NetUnity test WSRP producer, which is located at the following location: http://wsrp.netunitysoftware.com:80/WSRPTestService/WSRPTestService.asmx.

The following procedure describes how to install the WSRP consumer web part:

1. Go to the WebPartLibrary/deployment folder and copy WSRPConsumerWebPartLibrary.dll to the GAC by dragging it in the [drive letter]:\WINDOWS\assembly folder.

2. Go to the WebPartLibrary/deployment folder and copy WSRPConsumerWebPartLibrary.config in the following folder: [drive letter]:\Inetpub\wwwroot\sites\wsrptest\wpresources\wsrpconsumerwebpartlibrary. WSRPTest is the name of our test SharePoint site, so you might have to replace this name with the name of your SharePoint site.

3. Open WSRPConsumerWebPartLibrary.config.

4. Locate the `<add>` element with the `MarkUpURL` key attribute and let it refer to the test NetUnity WSRP producer, like so:

```
<add key="MarkUpURL" value= ➥
"http://wsrp.netunitysoftware.com:80/WSRPTestService/ ➥
WSRPTestService.asmx" />
```

5. Locate the `<add>` element with the `PortletManagementURL` key attribute and let it refer to the test NetUnity WSRP producer, like so:

```
<add key="PortletManagementURL" ➥
value="http://wsrp.netunitysoftware.com:80/WSRPTestService/ ➥
WSRPTestService.asmx" />
```

6. Locate the `<add>` element with the `RegistrationURL` key attribute and let it refer to the test NetUnity WSRP producer, like so:

```
<add key="RegistrationURL" ➥
value="http://wsrp.netunitysoftware.com:80/WSRPTestService/ ➥
WSRPTestService.asmx" />
```

7. Locate the `<add>` element with the `ServiceDescriptionURL` key attribute and let it refer to the test NetUnity WSRP producer, like so:

```
<add key="ServiceDescriptionURL" ➥
value="http://wsrp.netunitysoftware.com:80/WSRPTestService/ ➥
WSRPTestService.asmx" />
```

8. Open a command prompt and type: **iisreset**.

9. Go to a SharePoint site. In our example we have created a SharePoint site called WSRPTest.

10. Click Modify Shared Page ➤ Add Web Parts ➤ Import.

11. Go to the WebPartLibrary/deployment folder and select WSRPConsumerWebPartEx.dwp. Click Open.

12. Click Upload.

13. Drag the WSRPConsumerWebPart to a web part zone.

You should access the SharePoint site via `http://[server]/sites/[site name]`. If you access the SharePoint site via `http://localhost/sites/[site name]` instead, the WSRP consumer web part will not work. This is a little idiosyncrasy of the WSRP consumer web part implementation; since the source code is made available to you via the GotDotNet web site, you can change the code to support both scenarios if you feel the need to.

The WSRP consumer web part contacts the NetUnity test WSRP producer and displays the HTML retrieved from it, consisting of a news feed. The result of this is seen in Figure 6-5.

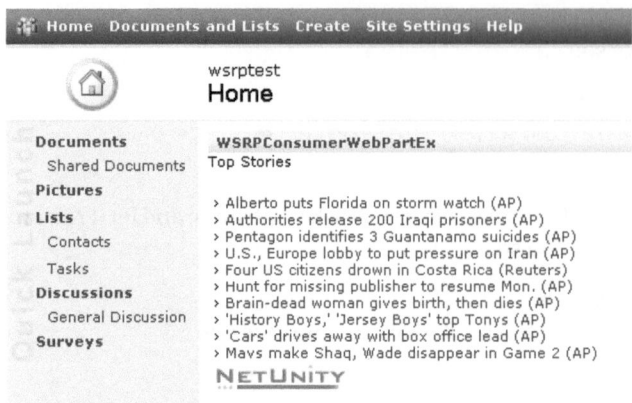

Figure 6-5. *WSRP consumer web part shows Top Stories.*

Implementing a WSRP Producer

In this section, we will show you how to create your own WSRP producer and consume it via the WSRP consumer web part. Not only did the members of the SharePoint development team create the WSRP Web Part Toolkit, they also created a toolkit for creating WSRP producers: the WSRP Web Service Toolkit. If you check out the WSRP Web Service Toolkit on the GotDotNet web site you will find a test WSRP producer called WSRPProducer. There is some documentation that explains how to install and configure the test WSRP producer, so you can choose to adjust this sample when building your own WSRP producers.

However, we will not follow this route here. We will use a commercial WSRP .NET framework created by NetUnity. This framework makes creating WSRP producers really easy. You can sign up for a limited free trial version of the framework at the NetUnity web site. If you are serious about creating WSRP producers, we would advise you not to bother with the GotDotNet WSRP producer sample; the sample is just too rudimentary and the documentation too terse. Instead, use a mature and supported product.

Although we prefer to use this WSRP framework instead of the proof of concept of a WSRP producer provided by the SharePoint team, there does not seem to be a lot of choice when it comes to choosing WSRP .NET frameworks. At the time of this writing, the only framework available was the NetUnity framework which is built on .NET 1.1. By the time you read this, NetUnity will also have released a WSRP .NET framework based on .NET 2.0.

Let's move on to creating a WSRP producer. The first part of creating a WSRP producer is creating an unmanaged virtual directory for it. If you want more information about unmanaged SharePoint paths, you should refer to Chapter 2.

The following procedure explains how to create a WSRP producer:

1. Open Windows Explorer.

2. Add a new folder to [drive letter]:\inetpub\wwwroot called: testwsrpproducer.

3. Click Start ➤ Administrative Tools ➤ SharePoint Central Administration. This opens the Windows SharePoint Services Central Administration page.

4. In the Virtual Server Configuration section, click the Configure virtual server settings link.

5. On the Windows SharePoint Services Virtual Server List page, click the Default Web Site link.

6. On the Windows SharePoint Services Virtual Server Settings page, in the Virtual Server Management section, click the Define Managed Paths link.

7. On the Windows SharePoint Services Define Managed Paths page, in the Add a New Path section, add the following path: testwsrpproducer.

8. Choose the following type: Excluded path.

9. Click OK.

At this point, you have created an unmanaged path for the WSRP producer that you will create next. To be able to create a WSRP producer via this example, you must have requested and downloaded the NetUnity WSRP .NET framework.

First you need to install the WSRP .NET framework, and then you will create a WSRP producer via the WSRP producer template and implement two basic Hello World portlets that can be consumed via the WSRP consumer web part.

The NetUnity WSRP .NET framework can be installed on Windows XP Professional, Windows 2000, or Windows 2003, and can be used with either a SQL Server 2000 or Oracle 8.7x or higher database. Take the following steps to create the WSRP producer:

1. Double click the NetUnity WSRP .NET Framework 1.5.1.2.msi file. This starts the WSRP .NET Framework 1.5.1.2 Setup Wizard. Follow the instructions.

2. Start Visual Studio .NET 2003.

3. Choose File ➤ New ➤ Project.

4. In the New Project window, in the Templates section, choose the WSRP producer template.

5. Enter the following location: `http://localhost/testwsrpproducer`.

6. Click OK.

Now you have created a WSRP producer: Producer1.asmx. It is very easy to create a WSRP producer using the NetUnity WSRP framework, all you need to do is create a new web service that inherits from the `NetUnity.WSRP.Producer` class. The following code shows a working WSRP producer:

```
using System;
using System.Collections;
using System.ComponentModel;
using System.Data;
using System.Diagnostics;
using System.Web;
using System.Web.Services;
```

```
using NetUnity.WSRP;

namespace testwsrpproducer
{
  [WebService(Namespace=@"urn:TODO Enter Web Service Namespace")]
  [System.Web.Services.Protocols.SoapDocumentService(RoutingStyle= ➥
    System.Web.Services.Protocols.SoapServiceRoutingStyle.RequestElement)]
  [RequiresRegistration(true)]
  public class Producer1 : NetUnity.WSRP.Producer
  {
    public Producer1()
    {
      InitializeComponent();
    }

    #region Component Designer generated code
    ...
    #endregion
  }
}
```

This is all the code we need for our WSRP producer example. Next we will create two portlets. Later, the SharePoint WSRP consumer web part will reuse the user interface of those portlets by accessing the WSRP producer. Although our example WSRP producer contains no custom code at all, by default, a NetUnity WSRP producer is able to find all portlets in the same assembly via reflection. So when a WSRP consumer calls the getServiceDescription() method described in the WSRP interfaces section, the metadata for all portlets in the producer assembly will be returned. You can override this behavior via configuration of the web.config file of a WSRP Producer project and allow a restriction of portlets or allow the producer to search other assemblies for portlets.

In the next steps, you will create two test portlets:

1. Right-click the TestWSRPProducer project and choose Add ➤ Add New Item.

2. In the Templates section, choose the WSRP Portlet and enter the following name: **TestPortlet.cs**.

3. Click Open.

4. Locate the OnRenderView() method and add the following code:

   ```
   Response.Write("<B>Hello</B>, world!");
   ```

   The complete code for TestPortlet.cs looks like this:

   ```
   using System;
   using System.Web.UI;
   using NetUnity.WSRP;
   ```

```
namespace testwsrpproducer
{
  [OfferedHandle("aeaecac5-73af-4ea0-aa2e-ead87f793660")]
  [Title("TODO: Enter Portlet Title")]
  [DisplayName("TODO: Enter Portlet Display Name")]
  [Modes(PortletMode.View, PortletMode.Edit, PortletMode.Help, ➥
  PortletMode.Preview)]
  [WindowStates(WindowState.Maximized, WindowState.Minimized, ➥
    WindowState.Normal, WindowState.Solo)]
  public class TestPortlet : NetUnity.WSRP.Portlet
  {
    protected override void OnRenderView()
    {
      Response.Write("<B>Hello</B>, world!");
    }

    protected override void OnRenderEdit()
    {
      //TODO: Add code to render the edit view
    }

    protected override void OnRenderHelp()
    {
      //TODO: Add code to render portlet help text
    }

    protected override void OnRenderPreview()
    {
      //TODO: Add code to render the portlet in preview mode
    }

    protected override void OnAction()
    {
      //TODO: Add code to handle blocking action (no rendering)
    }

    protected override void OnGetResource()
    {
      //TODO: Add code to return resource using Producer.Context property
    }
  }
}
```

5. Right-click the TestWSRPProducer project and choose Add ➤ Add New Item.

6. In the Templates section, choose the WSRP Portlet and enter the following name:
AnotherPortlet.cs.

7. Click Open.

8. Locate the `OnRenderView()` method and add the following code:

```
Response.Write("<I>Hello</I>, from my second portlet!");
```

9. Compile the project.

At this point, you have successfully created a WSRP producer that can be consumed so you can reuse the user interface of two test portlets. As you may have noticed, creating portlets and building HTML programmatically is very similar to creating web parts. In the next procedure, you will configure the WSRP consumer web part so it knows which WSRP producer to consume and which portlet to reuse:

1. Go to [drive letter]:\Inetpub\wwwroot\sites\[sharepoint site]\wpresources\ wsrpconsumerwebpartlibrary.

2. Open WSRPConsumerWebPartLibrary.config in a text editor such as Notepad.

3. Locate the MarkUpURL, PortletManagementURL, RegistrationURL, and ServiceDescriptionURL application settings and let them refer to the Producer1 WSRP producer, like so (replace [server] with your own server name):

```
<add key="MarkUpURL" value="http://[server]:80/testwsrpproducer/ ➥
Producer1.asmx" />
<add key="PortletManagementURL" ➥
  value="http:// [server]:80/testwsrpproducer/Producer1.asmx" />
<add key="RegistrationURL" ➥
  value="http:// [server]:80/testwsrpproducer/Producer1.asmx" />
<add key="ServiceDescriptionURL" ➥
  value="http:// [server]:80/testwsrpproducer/Producer1.asmx" />
```

4. Locate the SelectedPortlet application setting and set it to reuse the user interface of the first portlet, like so:

```
<add key="SelectedPortlet" value="0" />
```

The WSRP consumer web part is configured correctly. By default, directory security is enabled on a SharePoint virtual server. In this example, we will allow anonymous users to access the WSRP producer:

1. Open a command prompt and type `inetmgr`. This opens the Internet Information Services (IIS) Manager.

2. Expand the [server] (local computer) node.

3. Expand the Web Sites node.

4. Expand the Default Web Site node.

5. Right-click the TestWSRPProducer virtual directory and choose Properties. This opens the TestWSRPProducer Properties window.

6. Click the Directory Security tab.

7. Click Edit.

8. Click Enable Anonymous Access.

9. Clear Integrated Windows Authentication.

10. Click OK twice.

11. Open a command prompt and type: **iisreset**.

If you open a browser and navigate to the SharePoint site containing the WSRP consumer web part you can see what the user interface of the first portlet looks like. The result is shown in Figure 6-6.

Figure 6-6. *Hello World from a portlet*

In the next steps, you will change the WSRP consumer web part configuration so that it displays the user interface of the second portlet. The primary reason we discuss how to display the second portlet is because it might not be obvious that the specific portlet returned by a WSRP producer and displayed by the WSRP consumer web part is controlled by the web part configuration file.

1. Go to [drive letter]:\Inetpub\wwwroot\sites\wsrptest\wpresources\ wsrpconsumerwebpartlibrary.

2. Open WSRPConsumerWebPartLibrary.config in a text editor such as Notepad.

3. Locate the SelectedPortlet application setting and set it to reuse the user interface of the second portlet, like so:

```
<add key="SelectedPortlet" value="1" />
```

If you open a browser and navigate to the SharePoint site containing the WSRP consumer web part you can see what the user interface of the second portlet looks like. The result is seen in Figure 6-7.

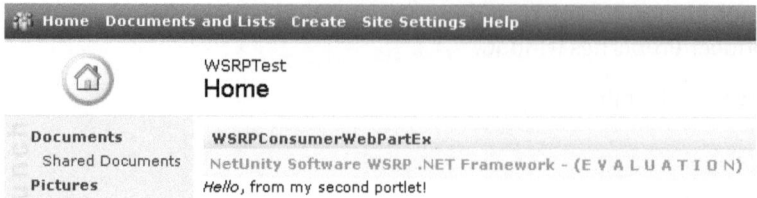

Figure 6-7. *Hello from the second portlet*

Summary

In this chapter, you learned what Web Services for Remote Portlets is. You learned about approaches for remote content and application service reuse. We looked at common architectures for solutions incorporating WSRP. Then we discussed the advantages and disadvantages of WSRP. We discussed in greater detail the WSRP specification, taking a closer look at all the important aspects. You also learned how to configure a generic WSRP consumer web part for SharePoint 2003. Finally, you saw how to create a WSRP producer using the NetUnity WSRP framework.

CHAPTER 7

■■■

InfoPath

When talking about SharePoint 2003 Products and Technologies and Office 2003, the conversation will most definitely include InfoPath 2003. This product is a rich client desktop application in the Office system that teams and organizations can use to collect data in an efficient way. With InfoPath 2003, you can create rich and dynamic forms and publish them so users can fill them out and submit them. The fact that InfoPath has native XML support makes it very easy to share information in organizations. In this chapter, we discuss the basic principles of creating InfoPath forms and the connection between InfoPath 2003 and SharePoint 2003 products and technologies.

We will discuss a workaround that enables you to add more than one InfoPath template to a SharePoint *form library*. Form libraries are used to store XML-based business forms, such as InfoPath forms. By default, form libraries are associated to a default template.

This chapter also discusses how to access data that is stored in a SharePoint list from within an InfoPath form. After that, we show you how to update and save InfoPath forms programmatically in a SharePoint form library.

If you have a need for automated collection and distribution of InfoPath forms, BizTalk Server 2006 can help you out. This chapter goes into detail about using the BizTalk Server 2006 Windows SharePoint Services adapter.

InfoPath Walkthrough

On our development computer we have InfoPath 2003 with Office 2003 Service Pack 2.0 installed. However, if all you have is InfoPath 2003 with InfoPath Service Pack 1.0 you will be able to follow the examples.

The first thing you need to find out when starting to work with InfoPath is how to design and develop an InfoPath form. The easiest way to start is by creating a form based on an existing template. You can do this by opening InfoPath and clicking Design a Form on the Fill Out a Form task pane. In the Design a Form task pane, click Customize a Sample.

InfoPath has a number of default templates that you can customize any way you want (see Figure 7-1). For this example, we will use the Performance Review template. You can choose a template by going to the Customize a Sample Dialog window and selecting the template you want to use.

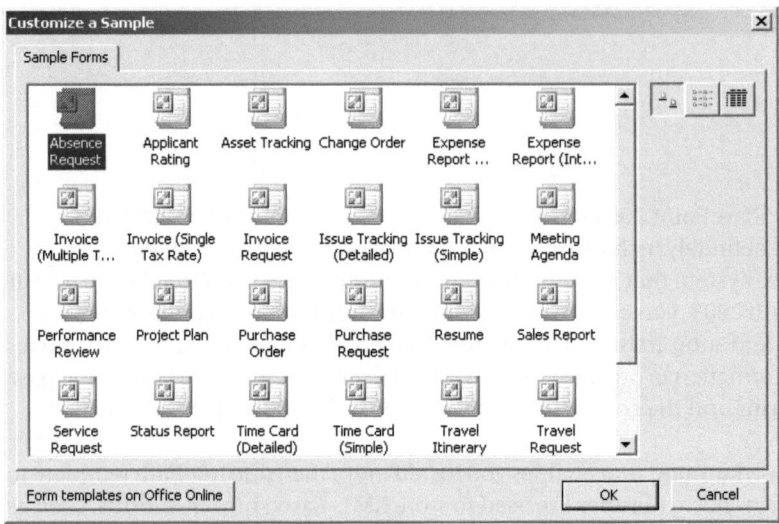

Figure 7-1. *An overview of sample forms in InfoPath*

InfoPath runs in either design mode or published mode. Design mode lets developers set up the form structure, as well as the look and feel of the form. Published mode shows the way users will see the form. By default, our sample form will open in design mode as you can see in Figure 7-2.

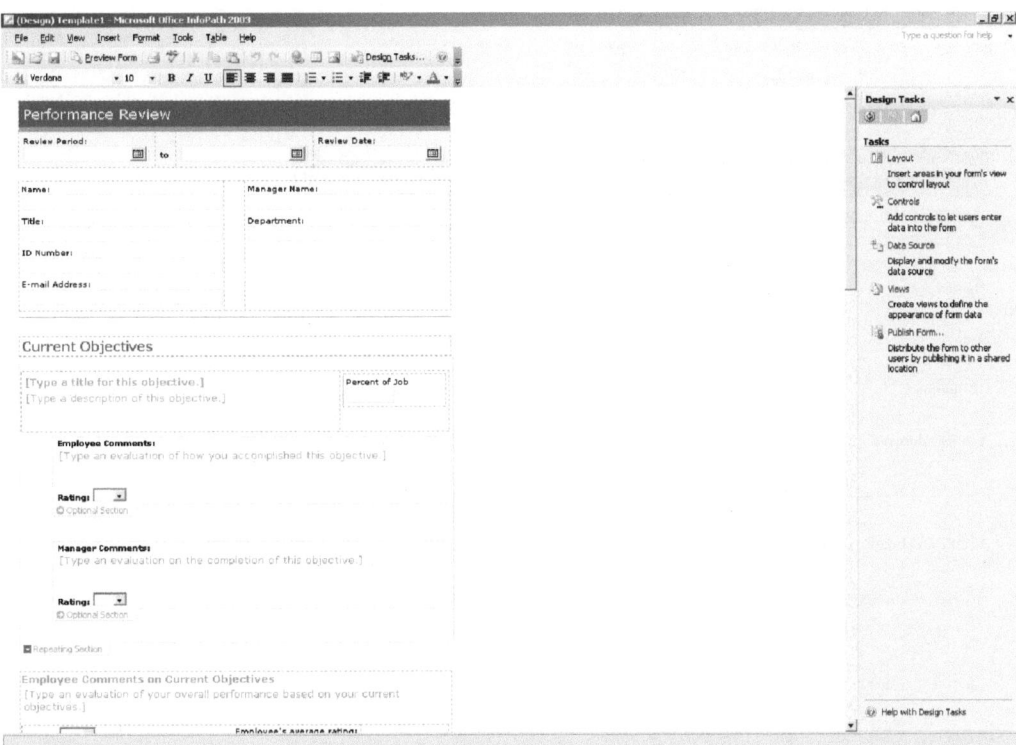

Figure 7-2. *The Performance Review sample form opened in design mode*

When you look at the Performance Review sample form, you will notice that InfoPath has taken care of the layout of the form and puts several different controls on the form. In the Design Tasks task pane, you will see a couple of tasks to help you design your form. The Layout task is meant to create the form layout. For example, you can use the Layout task for adding a table. The Controls task will let you add controls so users can easily fill out the form. Examples of such controls are the text box and drop-down list controls. The Data Source task displays the data sources that are available and bindable to the controls you have added to the form. The Views task will let you create one or multiple views of the same InfoPath form. Views let you create a manager's view, a print view, or any other kind of view. The last task, Publish, is also the last step you will take in the form creation process. Before you publish your form, you can preview how it will look when published (see Figure 7-3), via the Preview Form button, which is located on the toolbar of InfoPath.

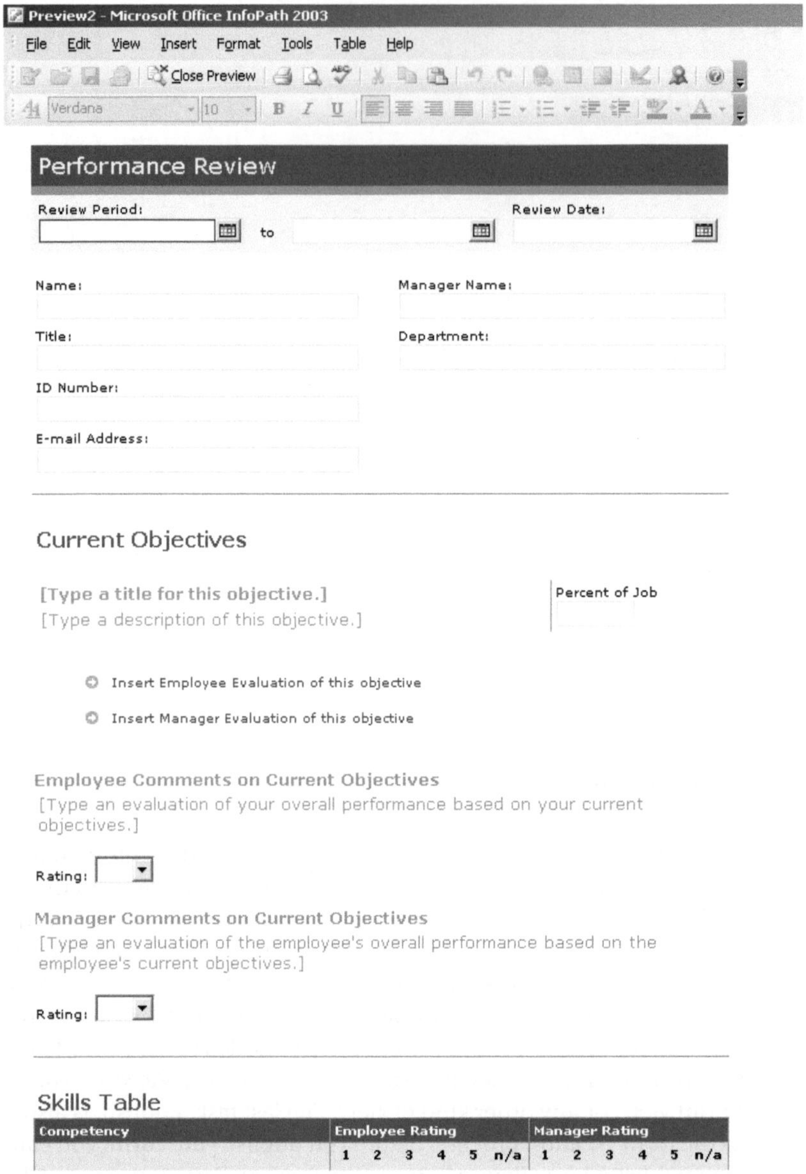

Figure 7-3. *The Performance Review sample form opened in preview mode*

Finally, you want to publish your form somewhere where users can easily find it to fill it out. The form library, which is available in SharePoint Portal Server 2003 and in Windows SharePoint Services 2003, is a recommended place to store and distribute your InfoPath forms. The other places where you can publish your form are shared folders and web folders. In this example, we will publish our Performance Review form to a SharePoint form library.

To publish a form, choose File from the toolbar and click Publish. This will bring up the Publishing Wizard dialog window. Click Next on the welcome screen. In the second step of the publishing wizard you can choose where you want to publish your form, as shown in Figure 7-4.

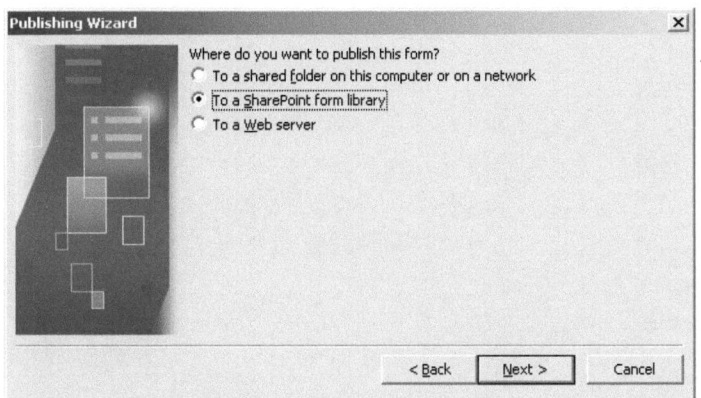

Figure 7-4. *The Publishing Wizard window shows the different places to publish an InfoPath form.*

Choose to publish the form to a SharePoint form library and click Next. In the next step of the Publishing Wizard you have to decide whether you want to create a new form library or modify an existing one. If you want to publish a form to an existing form library, you are going to overwrite the existing one and possibly lose data; this is not a recommended option. Therefore, choose to create a new SharePoint form library and click Next again.

The next thing to do is to enter the URL of the SharePoint site you want to use. This can be either the URL of a SharePoint site or the URL of a SharePoint Portal Server area. You have to give the form library a name (we will call it Reviews) and a description. Users who go to the form library will see this name and description. The publishing wizard wants you to determine which form data elements you want to be visible as columns in the SharePoint form library, as you can see in Figure 7-5.

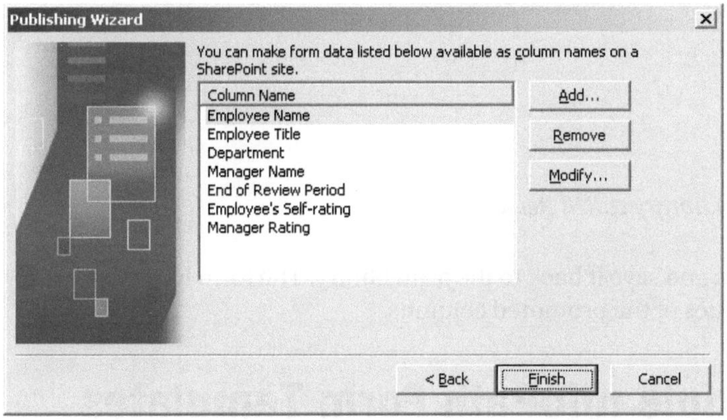

Figure 7-5. *Choose the columns in the SharePoint form library.*

To add a column you have to click Add. This will display the Select a Field or Group dialog window. Here you can select which field you want to promote to a SharePoint form library column (see Figure 7-6).

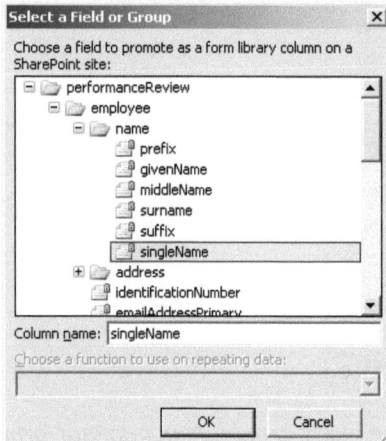

Figure 7-6. *Choose which fields you want to promote.*

The last step of the publishing wizard gives you the opportunity to notify users via e-mail that you have published a form in a SharePoint form library. Once you have published the InfoPath form you can browse to the Reviews form library on the SharePoint site (see Figure 7-7). The form library shows a Fill Out This Form link; when you click this link, InfoPath will start and show you the form in published mode.

Figure 7-7. *The SharePoint form library called Reviews*

A user can fill out the form and save it back to the form library. The form library will show all filled-out forms and the values of the promoted columns.

Supporting Multiple InfoPath Form Templates

SharePoint form libraries do not allow you to publish more than one InfoPath form template per library. This can be hard to work with because it is quite feasible that organizations want to publish more than one template per library. Suppose you have created a new and improved version of an existing InfoPath form template. Chances are you also want to be able to support the old template because there are still old filled-out forms in the form library. One solution would be to create another form library for the new form template but this could confuse your users.

This section shows how to publish more than one form template in a SharePoint form library. The first thing to do is to create an InfoPath form. You have already created the Performance Review form and published it in a form library called Reviews.

The next thing to do is to create a different InfoPath form. This time we will use the sample form called Travel Request. You should not publish this form template. Instead, save it on your local hard disk. You can save the form template by clicking File ➤ Save on the toolbar. You must click Save again in the Microsoft Office InfoPath dialog window. Do not forget to give the template a different name than the first form template because you do not want to overwrite that one. The default name given by the SharePoint form library to a form template is template.xsn. Name the second template template_version2.xsn.

Go to the location on your hard disk where you saved the second template and rename the file extension to .cab. You can do this because the form template is actually a compressed package of files. This way you can edit the files, which are located inside the template. You have to edit the manifest.xsf file. Manifest.xsf is a file that contains every element that makes up the form. You can edit manifest.xsf by opening the file in Notepad (or any other text editor). The first element in the manifest.xsf file is called <xsf:xDocumentClass>. This element contains an attribute called publishUrl. You have to remove this attribute and its value. You have to place all items back in the .cab file and rename the extension to .xsn.

After that, you have to copy this new template into the SharePoint form library. To do this you have to go to the SharePoint form library and click Explorer View. This will give you a Windows Explorer view of the form library (see Figure 7-8). Copy the second template, template_version2.xsn, into the forms folder.

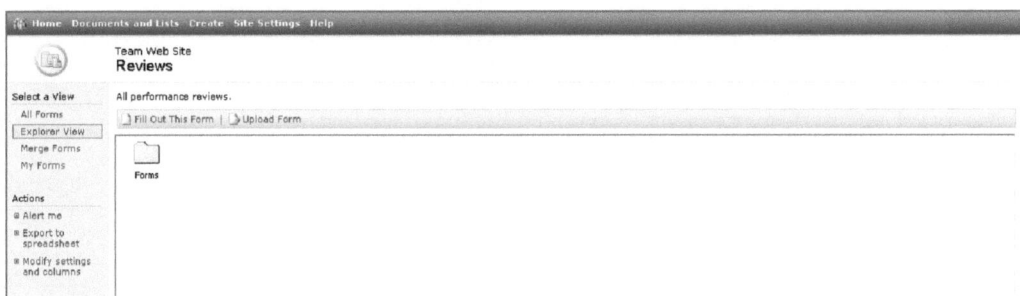

Figure 7-8. *Explorer view of the form library*

The forms in the form template based on the old template will still work. The next thing to do is to make the new template the default template when filling out a form. To accomplish this, follow these steps:

1. Click Modify Settings and Columns.

2. Click Change General Settings.

3. Change the name of the form template to the name of the new form template.

This way you can still open your old filled-out forms and use the new template for the new forms.

Data Binding with InfoPath

Besides publishing a form in a SharePoint form library there are other ways to use SharePoint and InfoPath together. You can access data that is stored in a SharePoint list within an InfoPath form. Form libraries and document libraries are special kinds of SharePoint lists. Data stored in a SharePoint list can be accessed via the SharePoint library or list data connection or via the SharePoint Lists web service.

Sometimes you want to use data listed in a SharePoint site. For example, imagine a list of users or e-mail addresses that you would like to use in an InfoPath form. We will show you how to make a drop-down list in an InfoPath form populated by a SharePoint list. The SharePoint list we are going to use for this example will contain a couple of e-mail addresses. We have made a custom list called Email and added a couple of e-mail addresses in the Title column.

We are going to work with the Performance Request form template that we saved in the Reviews form library. To edit the template go to the SharePoint form library and click Modify Settings and Columns. On the Customize Form Library page, you can click Edit Template to open the form template in design mode in InfoPath, as you can see in Figure 7-9.

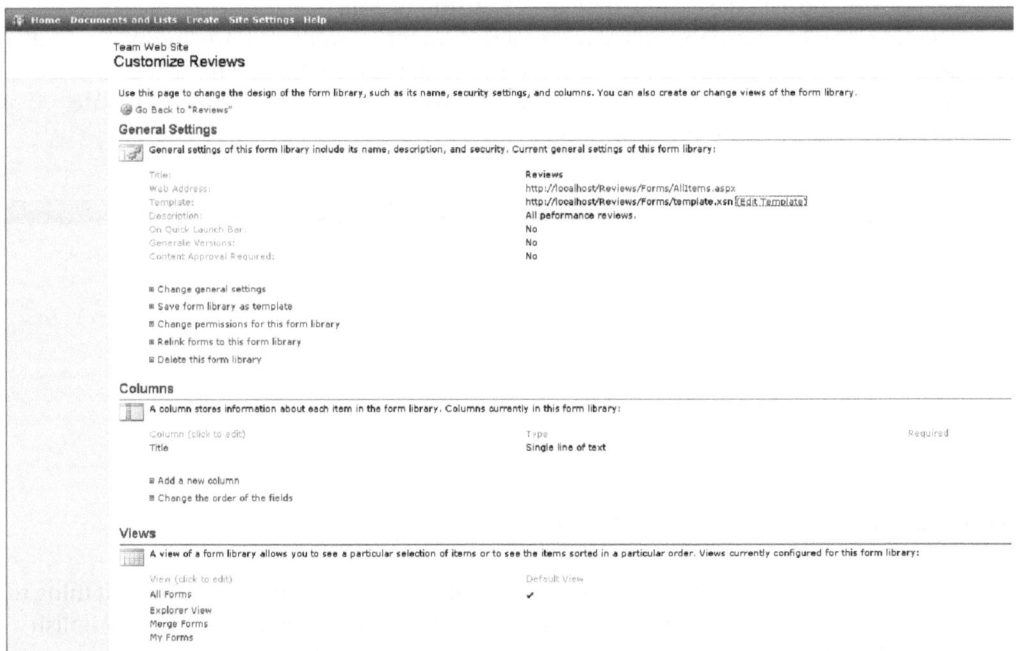

Figure 7-9. *The Customize Form Library page*

This will start InfoPath and open the form in design mode. Click Data Connections from the Tools menu. This option will only be available if you have installed Office 2003 Service Pack 1 or higher or InfoPath 2003 Service Pack 1. In the Data Connections dialog window, click Add. Then you have to specify whether you want to receive or submit data. Choose to receive data from a SharePoint list.

The next step is to enter the URL of your SharePoint site. The Data Connection Wizard page, shown in Figure 7-10, shows all the lists and libraries that are available for providing an XML representation of the content of a list or a library.

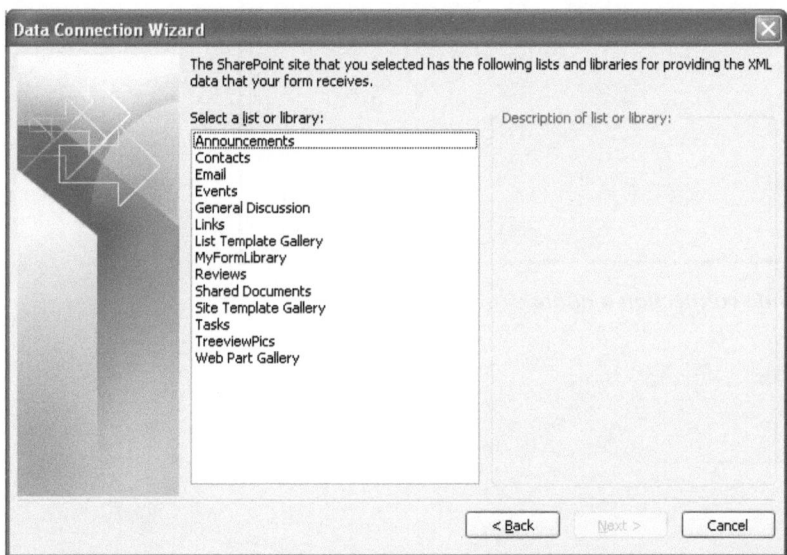

Figure 7-10. *Data Connection Wizard page where you can select the list you want to use*

Select the Email list and click Next. The following step gives you a list of all the columns that can be selected for use. Select the ID and Title columns. Call the data connection Email-Conn and click Finish (see Figure 7-11). This page has a check box that enables automatic data retrieval in the InfoPath form. If the content of the source SharePoint list is changed, the Info-Path form will detect this and display the latest changes in the form.

At this point, the Email data connection is hooked up to the Email list but not to the user interface of the form. To do this you need to go back to the InfoPath form template and bind the EmailConn data connection to the e-mail field of the employee, which is just a text box. Right-click the text box, click Change To, and choose Drop-Down List Box. Right-click again and choose Drop-Down List Box Properties. This will bring up the Drop-Down List Box Properties dialog window (see Figure 7-12).

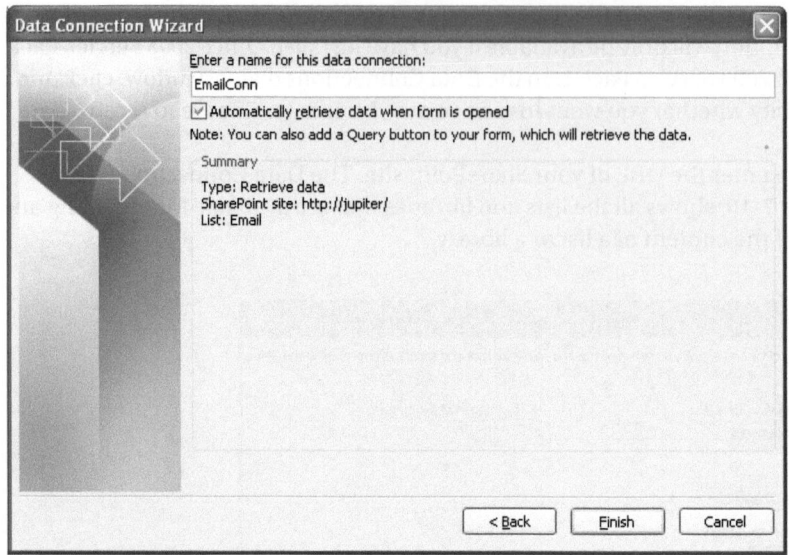

Figure 7-11. *Give your data connection a name.*

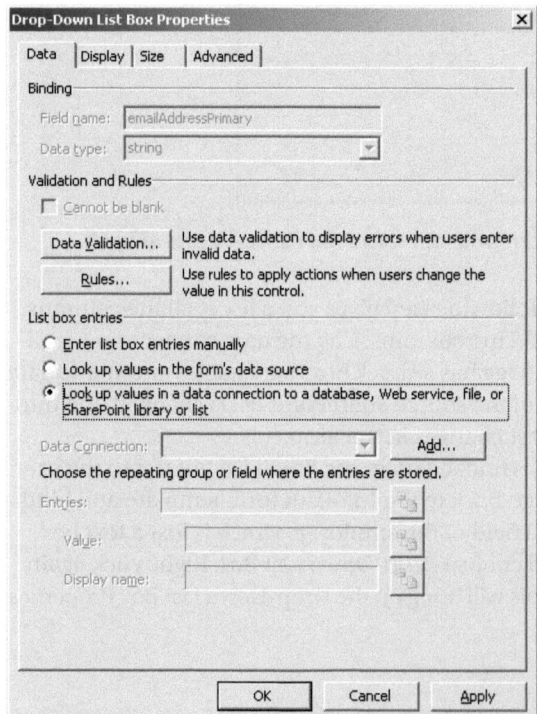

Figure 7-12. *The Drop-Down List Box Properties dialog window*

In the section List Box Entries of the Drop-Down List Box Properties dialog window; select the Look Up Values in a Data Connection option. Set the data connection to the EmailConn data connection, click the button at the right of the Entries field, and select the Title attribute. When previewing the customized form, you will see the content of the SharePoint list in a drop-down list in the InfoPath form (see Figure 7-13).

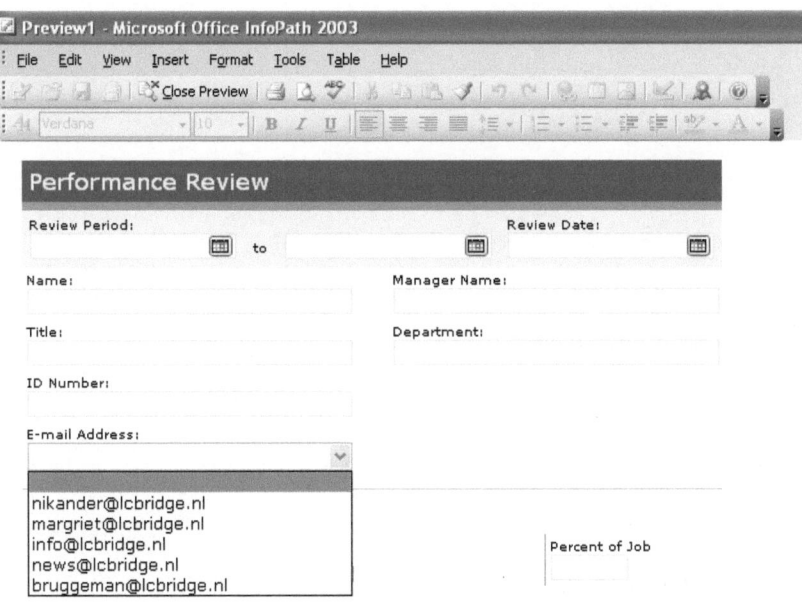

Figure 7-13. *Preview of the customized form template*

Updating and Saving an InfoPath Form Programmatically

In the next example, we will show you how to update an InfoPath form programmatically and save it back to a SharePoint form library. If you want to try out the code, you should create a SharePoint site called InfoPath and create a new InfoPath form without using one of the sample forms. Figure 7-14 shows what our form looks like in design mode. As you can see, the form is rather simple; it contains only a couple of text boxes.

By default, the text boxes will get a name that starts with field and then a sequential number. If you want a friendlier name you can rename a text box by right-clicking the text field and choosing Text Box Properties. In the Text Box Properties pop-up window you can change the Field Name, shown in Figure 7-15.

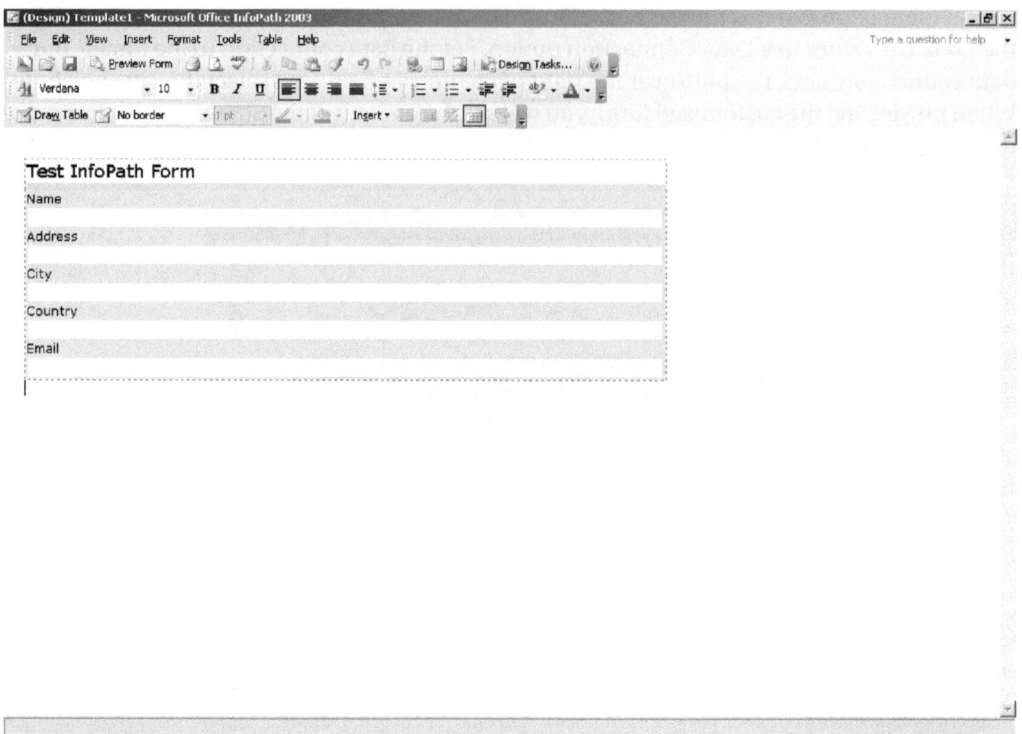

Figure 7-14. *Infopath form in Infopath design mode*

Figure 7-15. *Text Box Properties pop-up window*

Publish the test InfoPath form in a newly created SharePoint form library called TestFormLib. Create an empty form in this form library based on the new template and call it TestA.xml. You can see this in Figure 7-16.

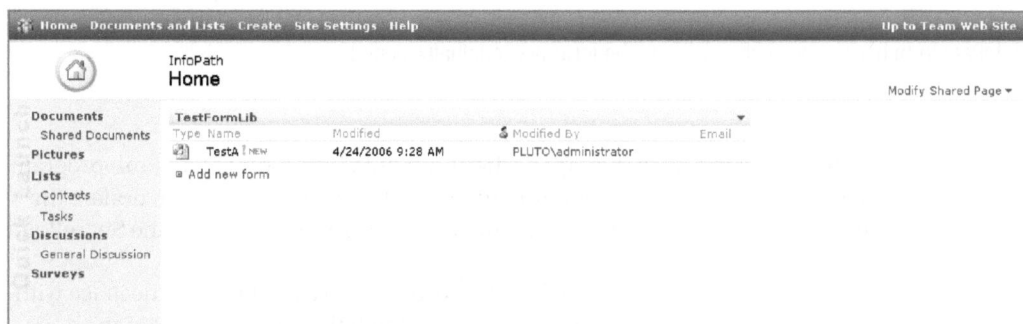

Figure 7-16. *Sharepoint form library with a test form*

Open the InfoPath form (TestA.xml) in Notepad to see the XML contents. The `<mso-infoPathSolution>` InfoPath processing instruction contains attributes that describe the solution version, the version of InfoPath used to create the form, the processing instruction version, and the location and name of the InfoPath template (`href`). The `href` attribute represents the URL of the document template; this is also known as the *template pointer location*. The following code shows the XML contents of the InfoPath form:

```
<?xml version="1.0" encoding="UTF-8"?>
<?mso-infoPathSolution solutionVersion="1.0.0.2" productVersion="11.0.6565" ➥
PIVersion="1.0.0.0" href=http://pluto/InfoPath/TestFormLib/Forms/template.xsn ➥
name="urn:schemas-microsoft-com:office:infopath:TestFormLib: ➥
-myXSD-2006-04-24T07 -25-59" ?>
<?mso-application progid="InfoPath.Document"?>
<my:TestInfoPath xmlns:xsi=http://www.w3.org/2001/XMLSchema-instance ➥
xmlns:my="http://schemas.microsoft.com/office/infopath/2003/myXSD/2006-04 ➥
24T07:25:59" xmlns:xd=http://schemas.microsoft.com/office/infopath/2003 ➥
xml:lang="en-us">
  <my:Name></my:Name>
  <my:Address></my:Address>
  <my:City></my:City>
  <my:Country></my:Country>
  <my:Email></my:Email>
</my:TestInfoPath>
```

Note InfoPath supports the W3C XML Signature standard (XMLDSIG). If you are using XMLDSIG, the XML data of an InfoPath form is secured; changing the XML data of an InfoPath form that is digitally signed invalidates the digital signature, which will be detected by InfoPath once InfoPath attempts to load or otherwise consume the data. XMLDSIG digital signatures are most commonly used to ascertain that the XML data underlying the InfoPath form has not been altered since the form was originally signed.

Next, you will create a web part that opens the empty InfoPath form (TestA.xml) programmatically. Then you are going to read the InfoPath form into an XML document, update the value of the e-mail field, and save the XML document as a new InfoPath form to the SharePoint form library.

Because InfoPath uses namespaces in the XML, you need to associate a namespace with the prefix you are using in your XPath query in order to match the correct nodes in the document. You can do this by making use of the XmlNamespaceManager class:

```
using System;
using System.IO;
using System.Collections.Generic;
using System.Text;
using System.Xml;
using System.Web.UI;
using System.Web.UI.HtmlControls;
using System.Web.UI.WebControls;
using Microsoft.SharePoint.WebPartPages;
using Microsoft.SharePoint;

namespace LoisAndClark.WPLibrary
{
  public class MyWP : WebPart
  {
    protected override void CreateChildControls()
    {
      SPWeb objSite = new SPSite(@"http://pluto/InfoPath/default.aspx").OpenWeb();
      objSite.AllowUnsafeUpdates = true;
      SPFile objFile = objSite.Folders["TestFormLib"].Files["TestA.xml"];

      MemoryStream objMemoryStream = new MemoryStream(objFile.OpenBinary());
      XmlTextReader objXmlReader = new XmlTextReader(objMemoryStream);
      XmlDocument objXmlDocument = new XmlDocument();
      objXmlDocument.Load(objXmlReader);
      objXmlReader.Close();
      objMemoryStream.Close();

      XmlElement objRootElement = objXmlDocument.DocumentElement;
```

```
    XmlNamespaceManager objNamespaceManager = ➡
    new XmlNamespaceManager(objXmlDocument.NameTable);
    objNamespaceManager.AddNamespace("my", "http://schemas.microsoft.com ➡
    /office/infopath/2003/myXSD/2006-04-24T07:25:59");
    XmlNode objNode = objXmlDocument.SelectSingleNode("//my:Email", ➡
    objNamespaceManager);
    objNode.InnerXml = "info@lcbridge.nl";

    ASCIIEncoding encoding = new ASCIIEncoding();
    objFile = objSite.Folders["TestFormLib"].Files.Add("TestA-edited.xml", ➡
    (encoding.GetBytes(objXmlDocument.OuterXml)), true);
  }
 }
}
```

Figure 7-17 shows the programmatically created InfoPath form in a SharePoint form library.

Figure 7-17. *The programmatically created InfoPath form*

Using a Submit Button

InfoPath 2003 allows you to submit form data to a web service or a SharePoint form library or as an e-mail attachment. We will show you how to submit a form to a SharePoint form library via a Submit button.

For this example, create an Absence Request form. Do this by using the Absence Request sample form and publish the form to a new form library called AbsenceRequests. After that, you have to edit the form template. You can do this by going to the form library, clicking Modify Settings and Columns and clicking Edit Template.

Create a secondary data connection to the AbsenceRequests form library (Tools ➤ Data Connections ➤ Add). The InfoPath form will use this data connection to submit data. Choose that you want to submit the data to a form library and enter the URL and the name of the form library. In our case, the URL looks like this: http://pluto/AbsenceRequests. You have to provide a unique file name for each form that the user submits. This file name can contain a formula and you can use fields that are available in the form (see Figure 7-18 and Figure 7-19).

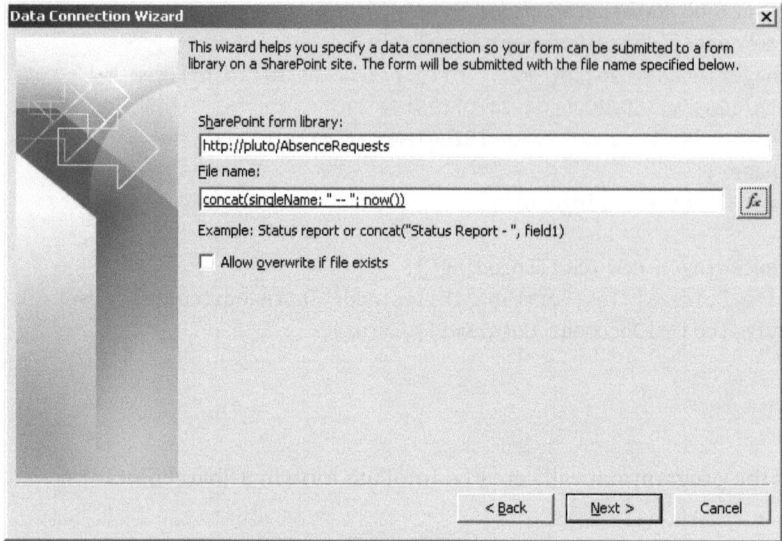

Figure 7-18. *The Data Connection Wizard page*

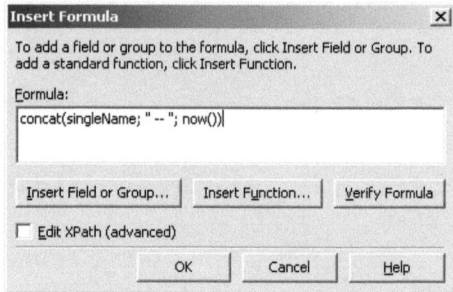

Figure 7-19. *Insert Formula page*

Use the following formula to generate a file name: concat(singleName; " -- "; now()). The formula uses the name of the employee concatenated with the current date and time. Now you need to configure the Submit command for the InfoPath form template. You can do this by going to Tools ➤ Submitting Form. This will open the Submitting Forms dialog window as you can see in Figure 7-20.

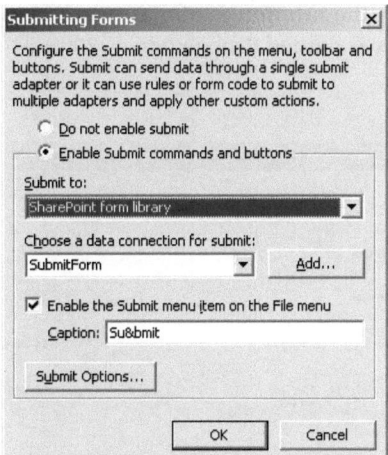

Figure 7-20. *Submitting Forms dialog window*

Click the radio button to enable the Submit commands and buttons and choose to submit the data to a SharePoint form library. Choose the new data connection called SubmitForm and click the button Submit Options. This will open a new dialog box, shown in Figure 7-21, where you can specify what to do after the user submits the form. For example, you can choose to create a new blank form for the user. In addition, you can specify success and failure messages, which the user will see in a pop-up window after clicking the Submit button.

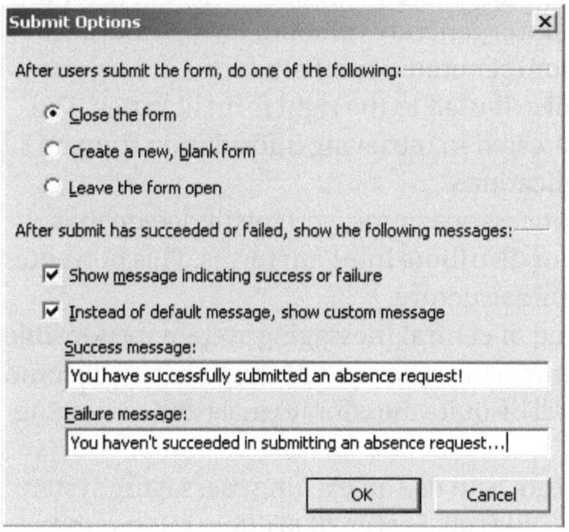

Figure 7-21. *Submit Options dialog window*

When you go to the SharePoint form library you will see the submitted InfoPath forms and their generated names. One of the forms in our form library is named Bruggeman — 2006-04-25T15_28_09, as you can see in Figure 7-22.

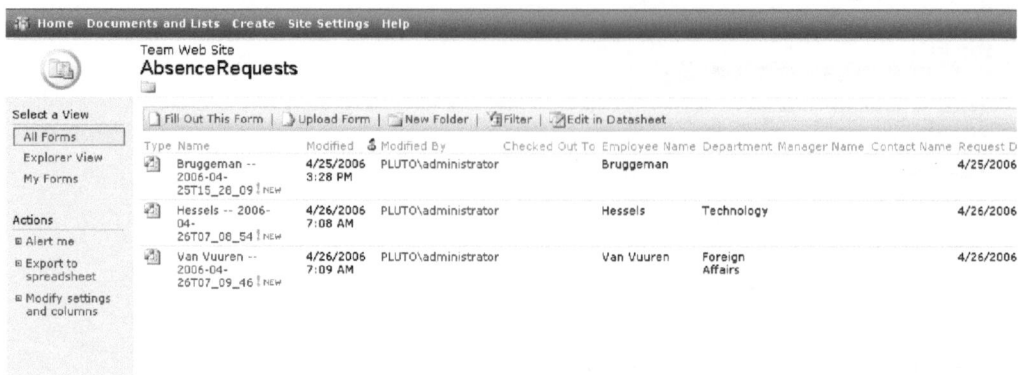

Figure 7-22. *SharePoint form library with submitted form*

Integration Between InfoPath, SharePoint, and BizTalk Server 2006

If InfoPath forms are used regularly in your company, you might find the need to collect or redistribute them automatically. Because InfoPath data is stored in XML, it is possible for any application to grab content from any kind of data store, generate InfoPath forms, and store those forms in a SharePoint form library. Application-generated InfoPath forms are a great example of forms that need to be collected and redistributed to the right form libraries. The other way round is also possible; you might be interested in retrieving information from an InfoPath form and storing pieces of it in other applications.

In such application-to-application business process scenarios, you might decide that every application involved contains logic to collect or distribute InfoPath forms. This promotes code duplication and adds complexity to your IT infrastructure.

So instead, you might decide to build some kind of central messaging system responsible for all collection and redistribution of InfoPath forms. This is better, although there will come a time, rather sooner than later, that you will find it will be quite the effort to make the messaging system robust, scalable, and easy to monitor.

The final option, and probably the best way to go, is to use an existing messaging system. This is where BizTalk Server 2006 enters the picture. BizTalk Server 2006 offers integration capabilities with SharePoint 2003 products and technologies via the Windows SharePoint Services adapter.

In this section, we will show you how to use the Windows SharePoint Services adapter to store or retrieve InfoPath forms in and from SharePoint. Normally, you would use the Windows SharePoint Services adapter to transport InfoPath forms from an application to SharePoint or vice versa. You could also use the Windows SharePoint Services adapter to collect or redistribute data within SharePoint. If the data you are retrieving from another application is not an InfoPath form, BizTalk Server 2006 can be used to transform the data to the required InfoPath form format, although you will have to tell BizTalk how to perform this transformation.

Note In human-oriented workflow scenarios, we do not recommend BizTalk Server 2006. The primary focus of BizTalk Server lies in facilitating process-driven workflows, where messages are exchanged between applications. Since BizTalk Server 2004, BizTalk Server contains Human Workflow Services (HWS), which is aimed at facilitating human-oriented workflows. Unfortunately, HWS has become deprecated technology. It will be supported for the next couple of years, but you have to realize no additional features have been added to the product since its release. Instead, use Windows Workflow Foundation, which is covered in Chapter 4.

Message Processing Overview

To understand how the integration between BizTalk Server 2006 and SharePoint 2003 products and technologies works, you will have to take a closer look at the way BizTalk Server 2006 processes messages. Figure 7-23 shows the message-processing architecture.

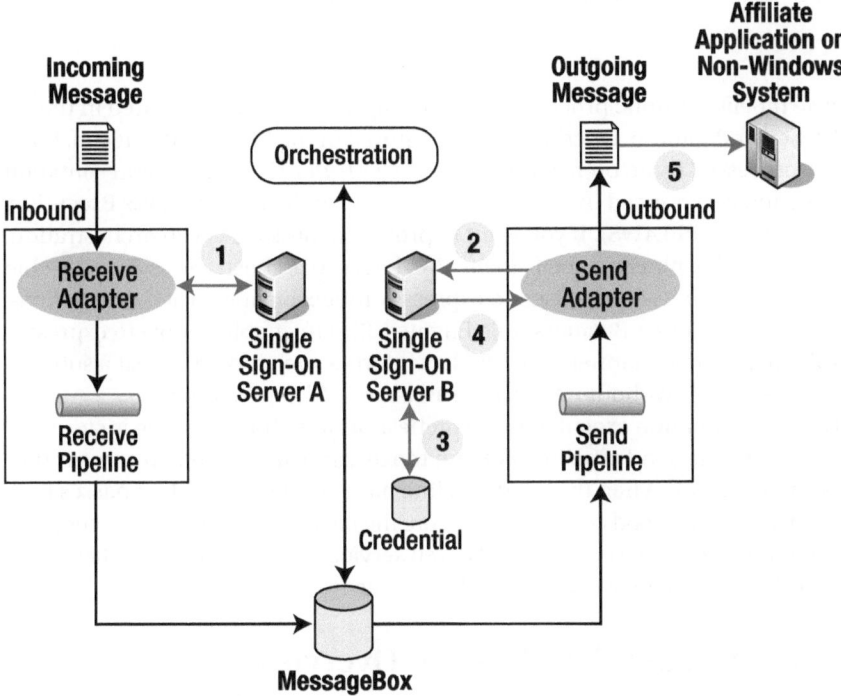

Figure 7-23. *Message processing overview*

BizTalk Server 2006 receives messages in some way via some channel. For example, a message might be delivered via FTP or e-mail. If you want to support this, you will need to create an FTP or e-mail channel that is able to handle such messages. Messages might be posted to a channel manually by an end user or automatically by another application. A BizTalk Receive Adapter picks up the message from the channel. For instance, imagine some application is posting a message to a Microsoft Message Queuing (MSMQ) queue. An MSMQ queue supports transactions and is able to store messages in a reliable way. The BizTalk MSMQ Receive Adapter picks up this message. The adapter passes the message to the receive pipeline. Pipelines consist of one or several components where every component in the pipeline decides if its message-processing wants to do something with the message. For instance, the receive pipeline can validate or transform the message.

■**Note** Architecturally, a pipeline is an implementation of the Chain of Responsibility design pattern. A *design pattern* is a proven architecture for solving some type of problem. The Chain of Responsibility pattern tries to avoid coupling the sender of a request to its receiver by giving more than one object a chance to handle the request. If you want to learn more about the Chain of Responsibility pattern or design patterns in general, we recommend the book *Design Patterns: Elements of Reusable Object-Oriented Software* by Erich Gamma, Richard Helm, Ralph Johnson, and John Vlissides. This is the classic work about this topic.

After the receive pipeline is done processing the message, the message is stored in the MessageBox, a SQL Server database. Once a message is stored in the MessageBox it can, but does not have to, be processed by an orchestration. An *orchestration* is an XML representation of a business process and is expressed in an XML language called Business Process Execution Language for Web Services (BPEL4WS). If you want to process a message via an orchestration, the result message of a receive pipeline needs to be XML because orchestrations are only able to work with XML. Orchestrations can be used to express complex business rules and optionally interact with the BizTalk Server Business Rule Engine (BRE) to enable people to express simple business rules in a simple manner. The BRE lets information workers adjust a subset of the total set of business rules without needing the assistance of IT personnel.

The result of any manipulation executed by an orchestration or business rule is stored in the MessageBox database. The Send pipeline picks up the message and is able to convert the message to any required format. When the Send pipeline has completed its job, it passes the message to the Send adapter. The Send adapter makes sure the message arrives at some endpoint via some channel. For instance, if you want to call a web service of a third-party application, the BizTalk Server SOAP send adapter makes sure the message gets there.

Windows SharePoint Services Adapter Overview

The Windows SharePoint Services adapter is an optional component of BizTalk Server 2006. It consists of two parts: a send adapter and a receive adapter. Basically, the Windows SharePoint Services receive part of the adapter is able to pick up messages from SharePoint; the Windows SharePoint Services send part of the adapter is able to send messages to SharePoint. To be precise, the Windows SharePoint Services adapter can do the following:

- Receive messages from Windows SharePoint Services document libraries and form libraries, optionally filtered by SharePoint views.

- Send messages to document libraries, form libraries, and SharePoint lists.

- Promote message properties.

Note If you are using BizTalk Server 2004 you can download a Windows SharePoint Services adapter for it at http://www.gotdotnet.com/. This adapter has fewer features than the one for BizTalk Server 2006, but is a viable alternative if you need to access SharePoint via BizTalk Server 2004. Go to http://blogs.msdn.com/ahamza/ for a detailed comparison of the two adapters.

The Windows SharePoint Services adapter architecture consists of three important components: the SharePoint adapter web service, the Windows SharePoint Services receive adapter, and the Windows SharePoint Services send adapter.

Although Windows SharePoint Services offers a rich web service interface, the interface is not very friendly when it comes to managing documents. For instance, it won't let you upload a document and set its properties at the same time.

Note If you want to upload a document and set its properties at the same time, use FrontPage RPC over HTTP.

To get around this problem the BizTalk team created its own SharePoint adapter web service called BTSharePointAdapterWS. The BTSharePointAdapterWS web service uses the Windows SharePoint Services object model, and it can be used to upload and set properties of batches of files. The Windows SharePoint Services send adapter and receive adapter use this web service to communicate with Windows SharePoint Services.

The Windows SharePoint Services receive adapter uses a polling mechanism to retrieve messages from SharePoint. This is less efficient when compared to an event-driven architecture, but it is also far easier to manage. If the BizTalk Server Windows SharePoint Services receive adapter used the Windows SharePoint Services event model instead, all document and form libraries would have to be reconfigured so they would refer to event-handling assemblies. The current Windows SharePoint Services adapter architecture is very nonintrusive; Windows SharePoint Services sites do not have to be aware of the fact that BizTalk Server 2006 is using them.

The Windows SharePoint Services adapter uses Windows SharePoint Services versioning to provide transaction support. Whenever a receive adapter retrieves a document from Windows SharePoint Services it checks out the document before it is inserted in the BizTalk Server MessageBox database to prevent conflicts caused by duplicate insertions. The Windows SharePoint Services receive adapter performs destructive reads, which makes it possible to retrieve a document from a folder in a document library, process it in BizTalk Server 2006, and publish it back to the same document library folder.

Working with the Windows SharePoint Services Adapter

If you want to try out the examples in this section you will need to have access to a computer with BizTalk Server 2006, Visual Studio .NET 2005, InfoPath 2003, and Windows SharePoint Services 2003 installed on it. The examples in this section will demonstrate how to retrieve messages from Windows SharePoint Services document libraries and form libraries. We will also show how to filter messages via SharePoint views. In addition, we will discuss how to send messages to document libraries, form libraries, and SharePoint lists, and how to promote message properties.

Creating an XSD Schema

In the first part of this section, you will create an XSD schema that describes the message format. You will use a BizTalk Server project to create the schema. The BizTalk schema editor helps to create XSD schemas in a developer-friendly way. The XSD schema will be used later as the basis for an InfoPath form. Follow the next procedure to create a BizTalk project and an XSD schema describing the message format:

1. Start Visual Studio .NET 2005 and choose File ➤ New ➤ Project ➤ BizTalk Projects ➤ Empty BizTalk Server Project, as shown in Figure 7-24.

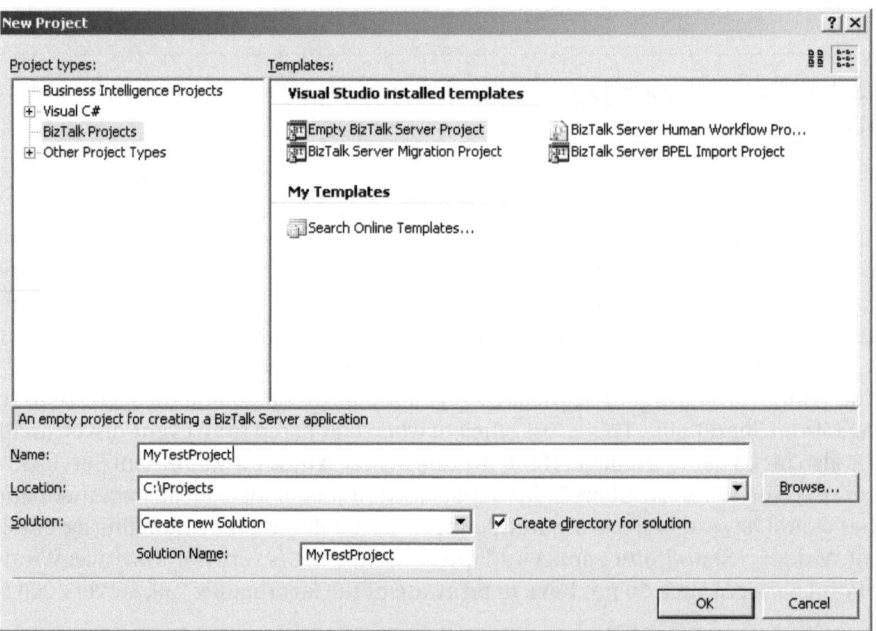

Figure 7-24. *Creating an empty BizTalk project*

2. Right-click the MyTestProject project and choose Add ➤ New Item ➤ Schema Files ➤ Schema. Enter the name **StatusReport.xsd**.

3. Rename the root element to StatusReport by selecting it, then right-click the root element and choose Rename.

4. Right-click the StatusReport root element ➤ Insert Schema Node ➤ Child Field Element and call this item Date. Select the Properties window and set the Base Data Type of the Date child field element to xs:dateTime.

5. Right-click the StatusReport root element ➤ Insert Schema Node ➤ Child Field Element and call this item Name. Select the Properties window and set the Base Data Type of the Name child field element to xs:string.

6. Right-click the StatusReport root element ➤ Insert Schema Node ➤ Child Field Element and call this item EmailAddress. Select the properties Window and set the Base Data Type of the EmailAddress child field element to xs:string.

7. Right-click the StatusReport root element ➤ Insert Schema Node ➤ Child Field Element and call this item Project. Select the properties Window and set the Base Data Type of the Project child field element to xs:string.

8. Right-click the StatusReport root element ➤ Insert Schema Node ➤ Child Field Element, and call this item ManagerName. Select the properties Window and set the Base Data Type of the ManagerName child field element to xs:string.

9. Right-click the StatusReport root element ➤ Insert Schema Node ➤ Child Field Element, and call this item BillingCode. Select the Properties window and set the Base Data Type of the BillingCode child field element to xs:string.

10. Right-click the StatusReport root element ➤ Insert Schema Node ➤ Child Field Element, and call this item Department. Select the Properties window and set the Base Data Type of the Department child field element to xs:string.

11. Right-click the StatusReport root element ➤ Insert Schema Node ➤ Child Field Element, and call this item Summary. Select the Properties window and set the Base Data Type of the Summary child field element to xs:string.

Figure 7-25 shows the way the StatusReport.xsd schema looks in the BizTalk 2006 development environment.

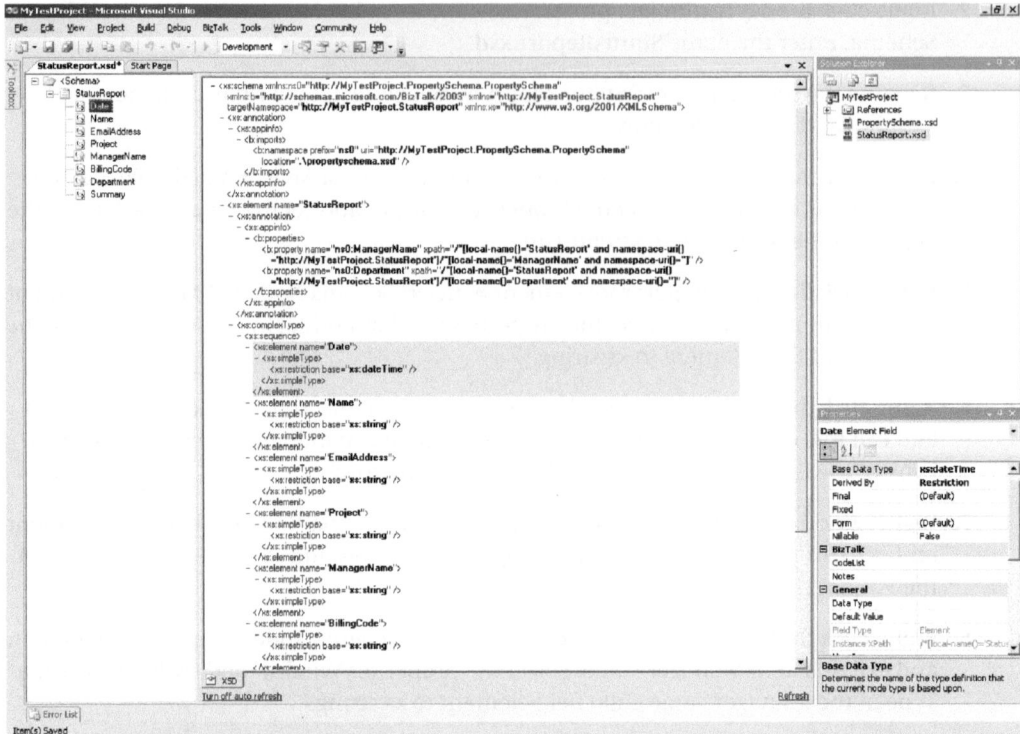

Figure 7-25. *StatusReport schema*

Creating an Orchestration

Next you will create a simple orchestration that receives a message via a logical receive port that will be bound to a physical receive port later. The physical receive port will be connected to a SharePoint document library so that the Windows SharePoint Services adapter knows where to retrieve messages. Normally an orchestration would process the message. However, for this example you will just pass the message to a logical send port. The send port will be connected to a SharePoint document library (via a physical send port) so that the Windows SharePoint Services adapter knows where to send the messages.

1. Right-click the project MyTestProject ➤ Add ➤ New Item ➤ Orchestration Files ➤ Biztalk Orchestration, and name the orchestration MyTestOrchestration.odx.

2. Open the Toolbox window and drag a Receive shape to the orchestration surface in the Drop a Shape from the Toolbox Here area.

3. Drag a Send shape from the Toolbox below the Receive shape on the orchestration surface.

4. Drag a Port shape from the Toolbox to the upper left Port Surface. This starts the Port Configuration Wizard. Click Next on the welcome screen.

5. On the Port Properties window of the Port Configuration Wizard, enter the name **TestReceivePort**. Click Next.

6. On the Select a Port Type window of the Port Configuration Wizard, choose Create a New Port Type. Type the name **TestReceivePortType** as the Port Type Name. Make sure the Communication Pattern is set to One-Way. Make sure the Access Restrictions are set to Public — No Limit. Click Next.

7. On the Port Binding window of the Port Configuration Wizard go to Port Direction of Communication and select I'll Always Be Receiving Messages on This Port. Go to Port Binding and select Specify Later. Click Next.

8. Click Finish on the Completing the Port Wizard page.

At this point, you have successfully configured a receive port. Now you are ready to configure a send port:

1. Drag a Port shape from the Toolbox to the right Port Surface. This starts a new instance of the Port Configuration Wizard. Click Next.

2. On the Port Properties window, enter the following name: **TestSendPort**. Click Next.

3. On the Select a Port Type window, select the following port type to be used for this port: Create a New Port Type. Enter the following Port Type Name: **SendPortType**. Make sure the communication pattern is set to One-Way. Set Access Restrictions to Public—No Limit.

4. On the Port Binding window, choose the following Port Direction of Communication: I'll Always Be Receiving Messages on This Port. Choose the following Port Binding: Specify Later. Click Next.

5. On the Completing the Port Wizard window, click Finish.

Now you have also configured a send port. Specify which message types can be handled by the MyTestOrchestration orchestration:

1. Go to the Orchestration View window ➤ Messages ➤ New Message.

2. Go to the Properties window and name the Identifier property StatusReportMessage.

3. Choose Message Type ➤ Schemas ➤ MyTestProject.StatusReport.

4. Go back to the orchestration design surface and select the Receive_1 Receive shape. Set its Activate property to True in the Properties window. Set its Message property to StatusReportMessage.

5. Select the Send_1 Send shape on the orchestration design surface. Set its Message property to StatusReportMessage.

The orchestration is almost ready. Drag a line from the TestReceivePort port shape to the Receive_1 Receive shape by keeping the left mouse button pressed. Then drag a line from the

Send_1 Send shape to the TestSendPort Send port. The StatusReport orchestration should look like Figure 7-26.

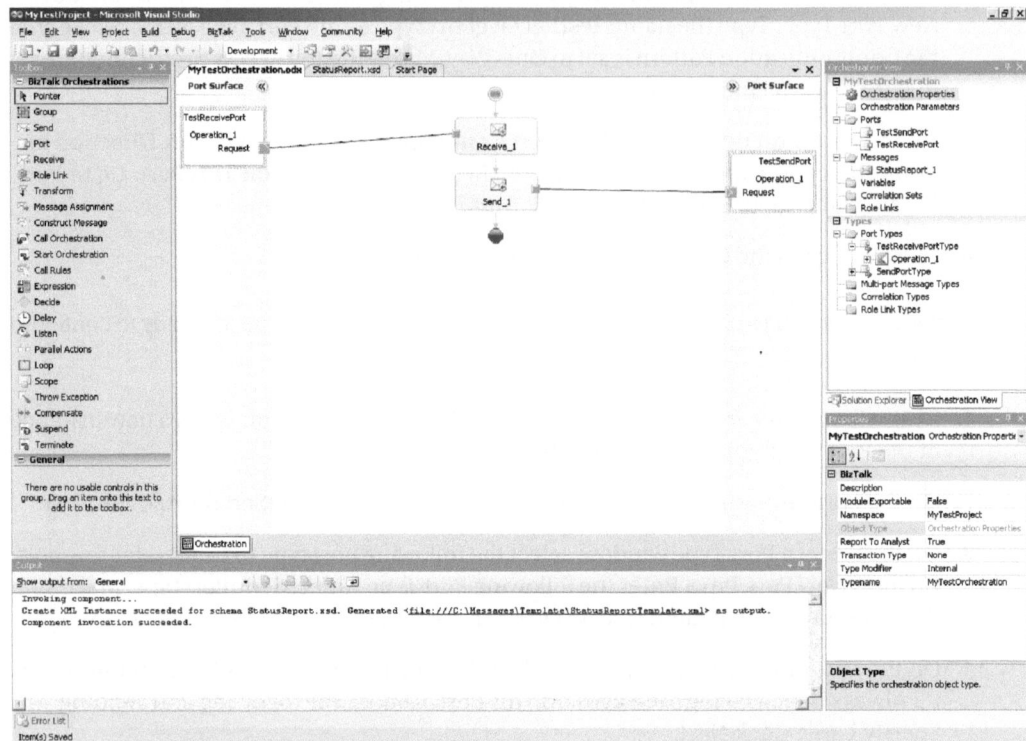

Figure 7-26. *StatusReport orchestration*

BizTalk orchestrations are compiled into .NET assemblies that are ultimately added to the GAC. In order to be able to do so, the MyTestProject project needs to be strong named.

Unfortunately in BizTalk 2006 projects you do not have the ability to create strong-named key files directly via the Visual Studio .NET 2005 user interface. In the following steps, you will strong name the MyTestProject project:

1. Open a Visual Studio 2005 command prompt and generate a strong name key file manually by typing: **sn –k c:\MyKey.snk**.

2. Go to the Solution Explorer ➤ Properties ➤ Common Properties ➤ Assembly ➤ Assembly Key File and enter the path to the strong-name key file: **c:\MyKey.snk**.

3. Click Apply.

4. Select Configuration Properties ➤ Deployment, and set Redeploy to True. Click OK.

5. Build the MyTestProject project. After that, right-click the MyTestProject project and choose Deploy. You should see a status message indicating the deploy succeeded.

In the test orchestration, you have defined two logical ports: a send and a receive port. In time, the logical BizTalk ports will be bound to physical BizTalk ports. We will connect the physical ports to actual locations in SharePoint sites.

Before we can bind physical ports to locations in SharePoint sites, we need to create two document libraries. First, we need to define a SharePoint document library that we will call Source. This document library will be connected to a BizTalk receive port. This document library will contain messages that will be picked up by the Windows SharePoint Services receive adapter. Second, we need to define a SharePoint document library that we will call Destination. This document library will be connected to a BizTalk send port. The Windows SharePoint Services send adapter will send all messages to this document library.

In the next step, you will create the Destination and Source document libraries and set the security settings of those libraries in such a way that the Windows SharePoint Services adapter will be able to read from and write to those document libraries. On our computer, we have used the local administrator account as our BizTalk service account. You will need to add the BizTalk service account to the SharePoint Enabled Hosts group that is created during the installation of BizTalk Server 2006. Only members of the SharePoint Enabled Hosts are allowed to call the BTSharePointAdapterWS adapter Web service. This web service executes under the identity of the BizTalk service account. Because of that, you also need to add the SharePoint Enabled Hosts group to the SharePoint Site Group of the SharePoint site where the document libraries are located.

After adding the BizTalk service account to the SharePoint Enabled Hosts group, the BizTalkServerApplication host instance needs to be restarted because group membership will only take place after you log off and log in again. Failing to do this will lead to "HTTP 401 — unauthorized errors" at a later stage.

Tip The Windows Event Viewer is a valuable aid when troubleshooting BizTalk solutions.

The next procedure explains how to add the BizTalk service account to the SharePoint Enabled Hosts group:

1. Go to Start ➤ Administrative Tools ➤ Computer Management.

2. Expand Local Users and Groups. Go to Groups. Locate the SharePoint Enabled Hosts group and double-click it. Click Add. Add the BizTalk service account to the group. In our example, this is the Pluto\Administrator account.

3. Go to the BizTalk Server 2006 Administration Console ➤ Platform Settings ➤ Host Instances and right-click BizTalkServerApplication ➤ Restart. Now the new security settings will be in effect.

4. Add two document libraries to a top-level SharePoint site called Test and call them Source and Destination.

5. On the Test SharePoint site, go to Site Settings ➤ Go to Site Administration (under the Administration section) ➤ Manage Site Groups (on the Top-Level Administration page).

6. On the Manage Site Groups page, click the Contributor link.

7. On the Members of Contributor page, click Add Members.

8. On the Add Users: Team Web Site page add the [domain name]\SharePoint Enabled Hosts group. Click Next. Click Finish.

In the following steps, you will create a physical BizTalk send port that will be connected to the Destination document library of our SharePoint site called Test:

1. Open the BizTalk Server 2006 Administration Console via Start ➤ All Programs ➤ Microsoft BizTalk Server 2006 ➤ BizTalk Server Administration.

2. Expand BizTalk Server 2006 Administration ➤ BizTalk Group [ServerName: BizTalkMgmtDb] ➤ Applications ➤ BizTalk Application 1.

3. Right-click Send Ports ➤ New ➤ Static One-Way Send Port.

4. Right-click the Send Ports node under the BizTalk Application 1 node and choose New ➤ Static One-Way Send Port. This opens the SendPort 1 — Send Port Properties screen.

5. On the SendPort1 — Send Port Properties window type the name **WSSSendPort**.

6. In the Transport section, choose the following Type: Windows SharePoint Services.

7. Choose the following Send Handler: BizTalkServerApplication.

8. Choose the following Send Pipeline: PassThruTransmit. This can be seen in the WSSSendPort — Send Port Properties window in Figure 7-27.

9. Click Configure. On the Windows SharePoint Services Transport Properties window in the General section, choose the following SharePoint Site URL: `http://localhost/sites/Test`.

10. In the General section, choose the following Destination Folder URL: Destination.

11. In the General section, choose the following Filename: %MessageID%.xml. This can be seen in Figure 7-28.

12. Click OK twice.

CHAPTER 7 ■ INFOPATH

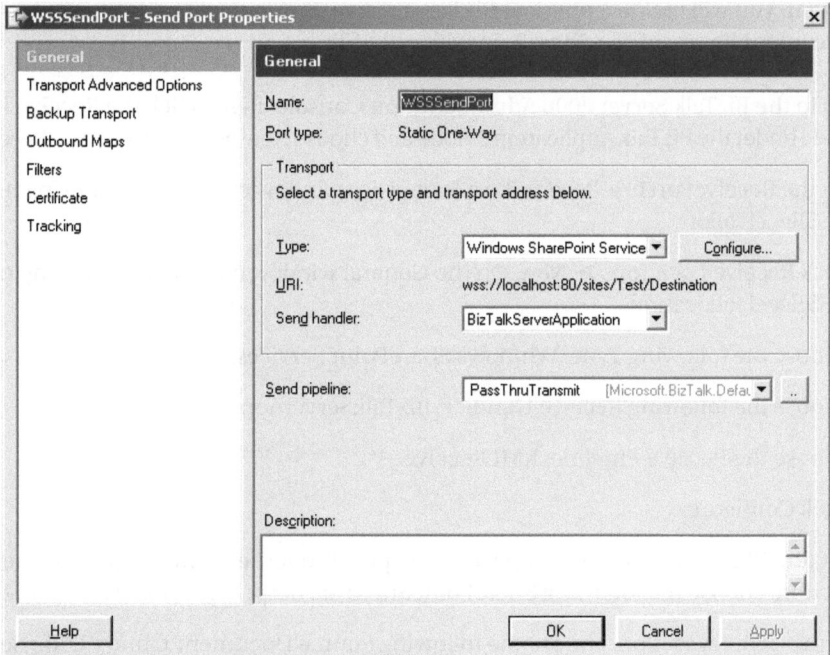

Figure 7-27. *Send Port Properties window*

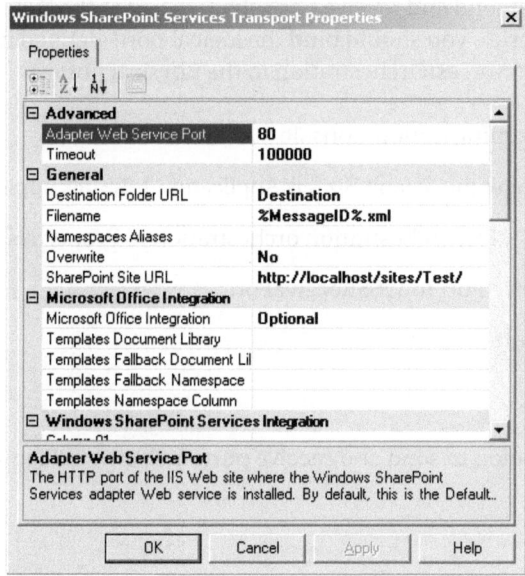

Figure 7-28. *Windows SharePoint Services Transport Properties window*

After that, you will create a physical BizTalk receive port that will be connected to the Source document library of our SharePoint site called Test:

1. Go to the BizTalk Server 2006 Administration Console. Right-click the Receive Ports node under the BizTalk Application 1 node and choose New ➤ Static One-Way Receive Port.

2. On the ReceivePort1 — Receive Port Properties window choose the following name: WSSReceivePort.

3. Click Receive Locations ➤ New. On the General window choose the following name: WSSReceiveLocation.

4. Choose the following Type: Windows SharePoint Services.

5. Choose the following Receive Handler: BizTalkServerApplication.

6. Choose the Receive Pipeline: XMLReceive.

7. Click Configure.

8. On the Windows SharePoint Services Transport Properties window in the General section, choose the following SharePoint Site URL: http://localhost/sites/Test.

9. In the General section, choose the following Source Document Library URL: Source.

10. Click OK three times.

Now that you have created physical send and receive ports that are tied to the Destination and Source SharePoint document libraries, you should bind the logical ports defined in our test orchestration called MyTestProject.MyTestOrchestration to the physical ports:

1. Go to the BizTalk Server 2006 Administration Console.

2. Click the Orchestrations node under the default BizTalk Application 1 BizTalk application.

3. Right-click the MyTestProject.MyTestOrchestration orchestration ➤ Properties.

4. Click Bindings and set the Receive Port to WSSReceivePort.

5. Set the Send Port to WSSSendPort.

6. Click OK.

The result of binding the orchestration to send and receive ports is shown in Figure 7-29.

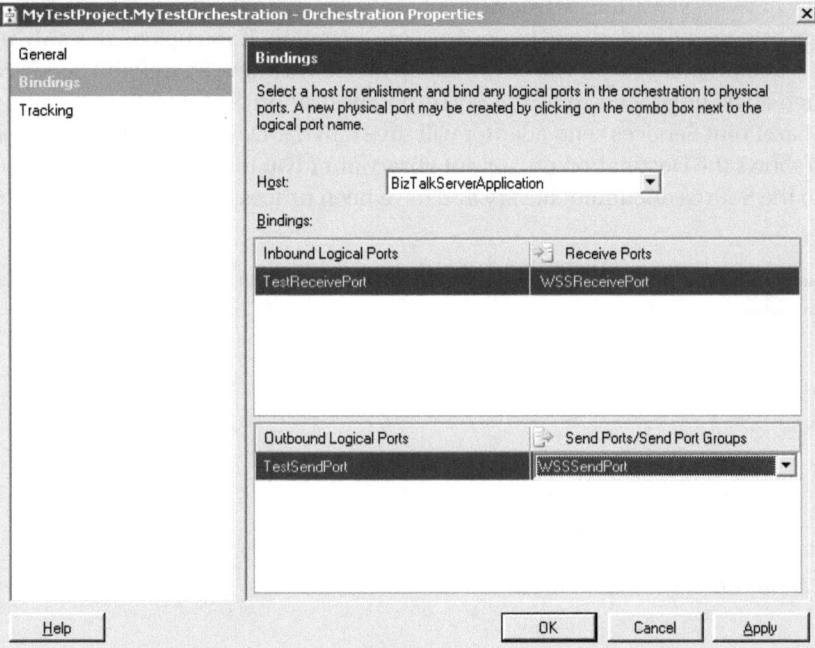

Figure 7-29. *Orchestration properties*

All you have to do now is start the orchestration, as shown in the following steps, and wait until new messages are placed in the Source document library.

1. Open Console Root ➤ BizTalk Server 2006 Administration ➤ BizTalk Group [Server name:BizTalkMgmtDb] ➤ Applications. On the Applications pane, right-click BizTalk Application 1 and choose Start to start the application.

   The orchestration will start performing its task as soon as new messages arrive in the Source document library, although it will not respond to any kind of message. It looks for XML messages that adhere to our ReportStatus.xsd schema. In order to test the orchestration, you need to create an XML message that is compliant with this schema. The BizTalk Server 2006 Visual Studio .NET 2005 add-in makes it easy to do this. It allows you to generate an XML file based on a given XSD schema.

2. Open the BizTalk MyTestProject project in Visual Studio .NET 2005 and locate StatusReport.xsd.

3. Right-click StatusReport ➤ Properties.

4. Choose the following Output Instance Filename (under the General section): C:\Message\Template\StatusReportTemplate.xml. Click OK.

5. Right-click ReportStatus.xsd ➤ Generate Instance.

You now have access to an XML document that adheres to the ReportStatus XSD schema. This message type can be understood by your test orchestration. If you upload this XML message to the Source document library it will be picked up by the Windows SharePoint Services receive adapter. Then it will be processed by the MyTestOrchestration orchestration. Finally, the Windows SharePoint Services send adapter will save it in the Destination document library. Figure 7-30 shows the Destination document library after two test XML messages have been uploaded to the Source document library and have been processed by the orchestration.

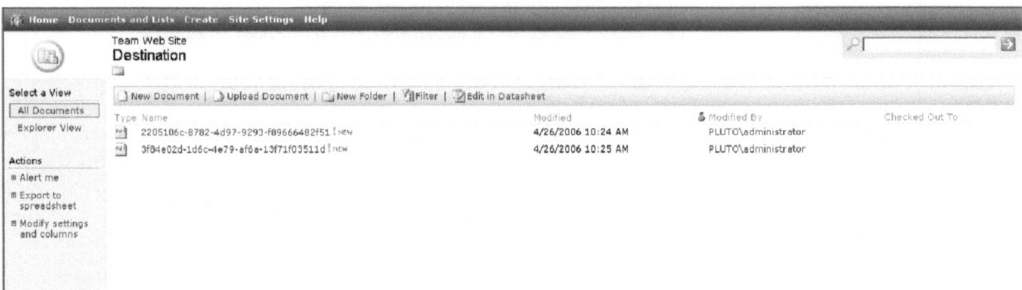

Figure 7-30. *Destination document library*

Form Libraries

It is possible to bind the physical send and receive ports to form libraries instead of document libraries. This is most useful if you create an InfoPath form template and associate it with a form library. In the next part, you will create an InfoPath form template that is based on the ReportStatus.xsd schema that was created earlier. Then you will associate the InfoPath form template to a SharePoint form library called ReportSource. After that you will use InfoPath to add test data to the ReportSource form library. To show that the Windows SharePoint Services adapter is able to filter messages based on SharePoint views you will also add a custom view to the SharePoint form library. The next procedure explains how to create an InfoPath form and publish it to a SharePoint form library:

1. Start InfoPath 2003.

2. Choose Design a Form. This is located under the Design a Form section on the right task pane.

3. Choose New from Data Source in section Design a New Form.

4. The Data Source Setup Wizard is started. Choose the following type of data source you want to use for your form: XML Schema or XML data file. Click Next.

5. Enter the following location for the XML data file or XML schema: [**path to your ReportStatus.xsd schema**]. In our case this is: C:\Projects\MyTestProject\MyTestProject\ReportStatus.xsd. Click Finish.

6. Drag all StatusReport elements (Date, Name, EmailAddress, Project, ManagerName, BillingCode, Department, and Summary) to the InfoPath form. After doing some layout work, the InfoPath form might look like Figure 7-31.

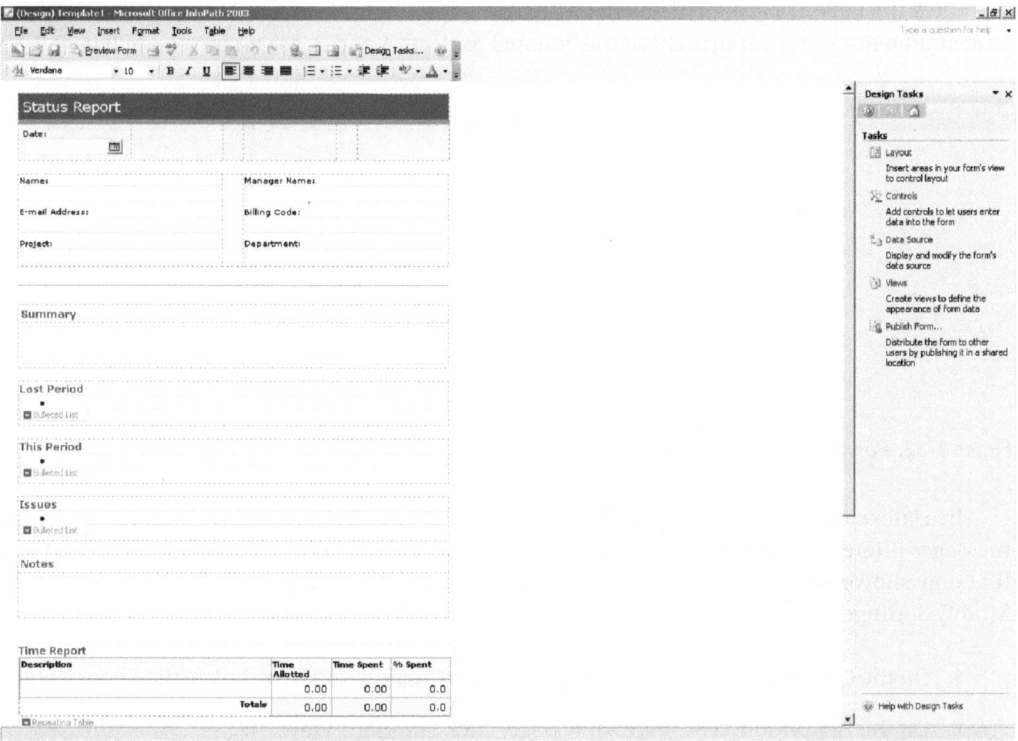

Figure 7-31. *Status Report InfoPath template*

7. Publish the InfoPath template to a SharePoint form library by choosing File ➤ Publish.

8. This starts the Publishing Wizard. On the first screen click Next.

9. Choose to publish InfoPath Form to a SharePoint Form Library on the next screen. Click Next.

10. Choose the Create a New Form Library (Recommended) option ➤ Next.

11. Enter the location of the SharePoint site where you want to publish the InfoPath form. For our example, we will use a test SharePoint site located at the following location: http://pluto/sites/test/.

12. Type the following name for the form library: **ReportSource**. Type the following description: **ReportSource Description** ➤ Next.

13. Click Add, and add the following fields: Name, Project, ManagerName, Department. This ensures all fields will be promoted as form library columns on the SharePoint site. Click Finish.

14. Check the Open This Form from Its Published Location option ➤ Close.

15. Close InfoPath.

Click the Fill out This Form link to create some test data. We created some InfoPath forms that contain test status reports about the fictional projects A and B, as can be seen in Figure 7-32.

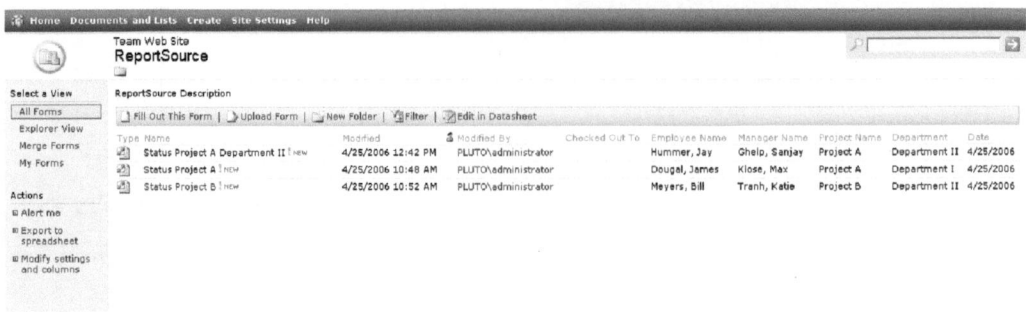

Figure 7-32. *Form library with test data*

In a later stage, you will define the Windows SharePoint Services receive adapter to pick up messages filtered by a SharePoint view. You will create a SharePoint view called Project A View that only shows projects with the Project A project name. Go to ReportSource Form Library ➤ Modify Settings and Columns.

1. On the Customize ReportSource page, click the Create a New View link in the Views section.

2. On the ReportSource: Create View page, click Standard View.

3. Choose the following View name: Project A View.

4. Go to the Filter section. Click the Show Items Only When the Following Is True radio button.

5. Choose the following: Show the Items When Column Value. Set its value to Project.

6. Choose the following comparison value: Is Equal To.

7. In the empty TextBox, type **Project A**.

8. Click OK.

9. On the Customize ReportSource page, click the Go Back to ReportSource link.

10. Click the ProjectView link in the Select a View section in the upper left of the page. Check that the view shows all the forms related to Project A. This can be seen in Figure 7-33.

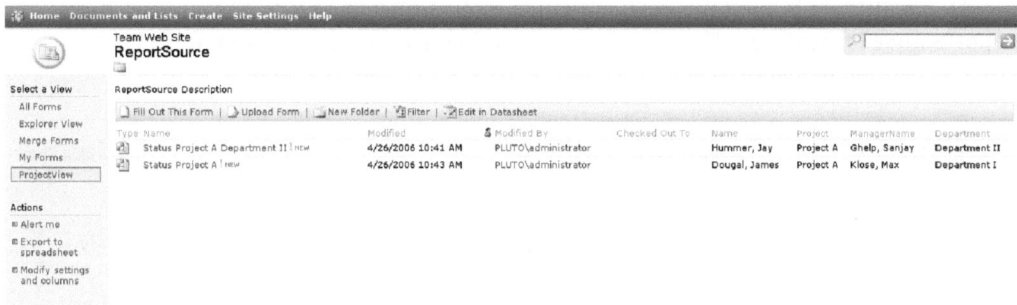

Figure 7-33. *ProjectView view*

At this point you have created a source form library that can be used by the Windows SharePoint Services receive adapter to retrieve InfoPath forms. The InfoPath forms will be processed by your test orchestration and eventually they will be published to another form library. Next you will create a form library called ReportDestination. The Windows SharePoint Services send adapter will use this form library as the end point to send its messages. The next procedure explains how to create the ReportDestination form library:

1. Click the Create link ➤ Form Library.

2. On the New Form Library page, enter the following name: **ReportDestination**.

3. Keep the other default values and click Create.

During the following steps, you will reconfigure the physical BizTalk send and receive ports to the ReportDestination and ReportSource form libraries. You will also configure the Windows SharePoint Services receive adapter in such a manner that it will only retrieve Info-Path forms that can be seen in the ProjectView SharePoint view:

1. Go back to the BizTalk Server 2006 Administration Console. Locate the Send Ports node under BizTalk Application 1. Right-click the WSSSendPort Send Port ➤ Properties ➤ Configure.

2. On the Windows SharePoint Services Transport Properties window, in the General section, change the Destination Folder URL to ReportDestination. Click OK twice.

3. Go to the Receive Ports node. Right-click WSSReceivePort Receive Port ➤ Properties ➤ Receive Locations ➤ Properties ➤ Configure.

4. On the Windows SharePoint Services Transport Properties window, locate the General section. Change the Source Document Library URL to ReportSource.

5. Specify the following View name: ProjectView.

6. Click OK three times.

7. Stop and start BizTalk Application 1.

After a little while, all forms related to the project Project A will disappear from the ReportSource form library. They should reappear in the ReportDestination form library. This can be seen in Figure 7-34.

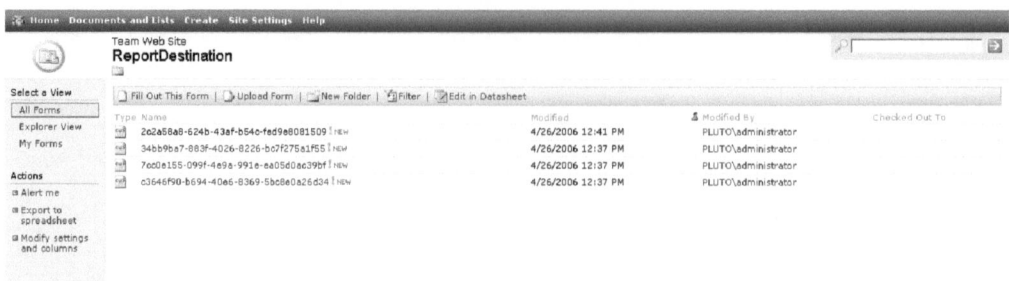

Figure 7-34. *ReportDestination form library*

Property Promotion

You can take InfoPath form properties and copy their values to the metadata of SharePoint libraries. This is known as *property promotion*.

If you did not associate an InfoPath form library to the ReportSource form library, you will notice that the InfoPath forms in this library consist of regular XML with a schema compliant with the ReportStatus.xsd schema. If you did define a template, InfoPath will be opened when you click the InfoPath forms in the destination document library.

The following XML shows an example of the XML data found in our ReportDestination form library. Please notice that the namespace of this XML is http://MyTestProject.ReportStatus.

```
<ns1:ReportStatus xmlns:ns1="http://MyTestProject.ReportStatus" ➥
xmlns:b="http://schemas.microsoft.com/BizTalk/2003" ➥
xmlns:ns0="http://MyTestProject.PropertySchema.PropertySchema">
  <Date />
  <Name>Richter, Gumball</Name>
  <EmailAddress>info@lcbridge.nl</EmailAddress>
  <Project>Project A</Project>
  <ManagerName>Vuuren van, Casey</ManagerName>
  <BillingCode />
  <Department>Department I</Department>
  <Summary />
</ns1:ReportStatus>
```

Take a look at Figure 7-35. If you look at the Windows SharePoint Services Integration section, you will see a number of columns, such as Column 01 and Column 02. Columns refer to the name of a SharePoint library property. Column values contain XPath expressions that refer to the internal structure of an XML message. The result of the XPath expression will become the value of the library property.

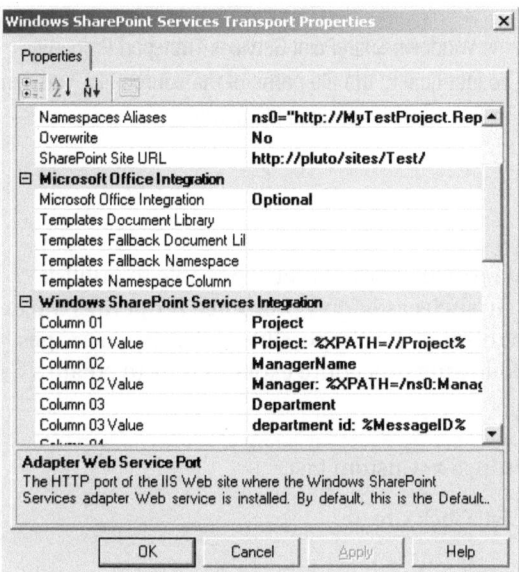

Figure 7-35. *Property Promotion*

For example, if you want to retrieve the value of the Project element use //Project. // as a shortcut for descendant-or-self, which retrieves all nodes with the name Project located somewhere in the XML document. So if you want to promote the value of the <Project> element in the XML document to a library property called MyProperty, you would need to set Column 01 to MyProperty and set Column 01 Value to %XPATH=//Project%.

If you do not want to use the descendant-or-self shortcut, you can also use explicit XPath expressions. Since our XML contains a namespace, http://MyTestProject.ReportStatus, you will have to define the namespace alias in the General section of the Windows SharePoint Services Transport Properties.

Enter the following value for Namespace Aliases: **ns0="http://TestWindows SharePoint ServicesAdapterProject.RequestSchema"**.

This enables you to define XPath queries such as the following: %XPATH=/ns0:MyParent/MyChild/MyGrandChild%.

If you want to define multiple namespaces, you can do it by separating them with a comma. You can also use literal values in column values, or combine XPath expressions and literal values. You could add the following column value: My title: %XPATH=/ns0:Request/Item/Name%'.

It is also possible to use predefined macros. For example, a %MessageID% macro is replaced at run time by a GUID. If you want, you can combine literal values with XPath expressions and macros. For example, you could define the following Filename property in the Windows SharePoint Services Transport Properties screen: MyFilename %XPATH=//Project%%MessageID%.xml.

■Note If you leave the `Filename` property empty on the Windows SharePoint Services Transport Properties screen, the file name on the destination end point will be identical to the file name of the source file. You can also use the %FileName% and %Extension% macros to re-create the original file name.

SharePoint List

You can send InfoPath forms to document and form libraries. It is also possible to publish messages to Windows SharePoint Services lists. In such cases, only promoted properties will be published to the list; the message itself is not published. It is impossible to receive messages from a Windows SharePoint Services list. The following procedure explains how to create a SharePoint list and send InfoPath forms to it:

1. Go to the Test SharePoint site ➤ Site Settings ➤ Custom List.

2. Type the following name: **DestinationList**. Click Create.

3. Click Modify Settings and Solumns.

4. On the Customize DestinationList page, click the Add a New Column link.

5. Add the following columns: Name, Project Name, Manager, and Department. All columns have the same column type: Single Line of Text.

6. Click Go Back to DestinationList. The SharePoint list should look like Figure 7-36.

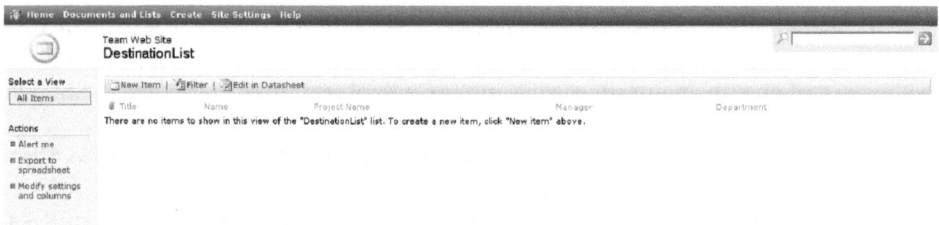

Figure 7-36. *DestinationList SharePoint list*

7. Go back to the BizTalk Server 2006 Administration Console. Go to Send Ports and double-click WSSSendPort Send Port ➤ Configure.

8. Change the SharePoint Site URL to `http://pluto/sites/Test/Lists`.

9. Change the Destination Folder URL to DestinationList.

10. Change the Filename to Filename – %FileName%.%Extension%.

11. Copy the transport properties as seen in Figure 7-37. Click OK twice.

12. Stop and Start BizTalk Application 1.

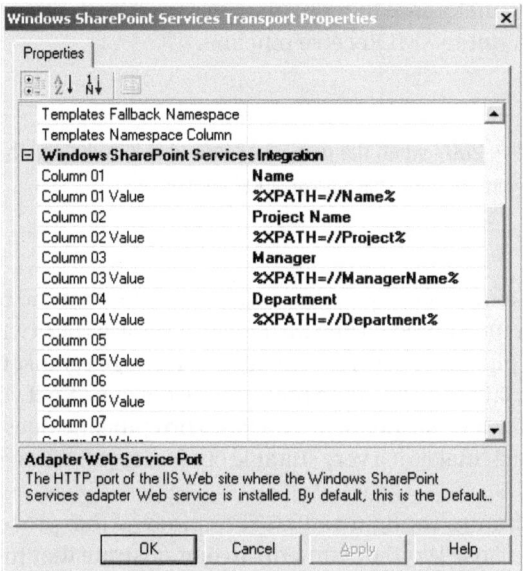

Figure 7-37. *SharePoint list transport properties*

If everything goes well, the SharePoint list DestinationList looks like Figure 7-38.

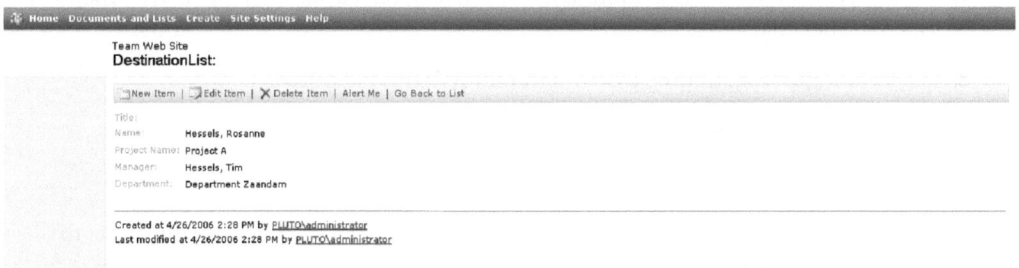

Figure 7-38. *DestinationList list item*

Moving Binary Content

All the examples related to the Windows SharePoint Services adapter you have seen so far involve InfoPath forms. We want to show that you can also use BizTalk Server 2006 to move other types of content, such as Word documents. Orchestrations only handle XML messages, so it is impossible to implement a complex business process in an orchestration and apply that to binary content. However, it is possible to send a message via BizTalk Server 2006 without using orchestrations.

In such a scenario, messages will be processed by the receive and the send ports without the intervention of any orchestration. You can define a filter on a send port that subscribes the send port to messages that originate from a given location. In our example, we will configure the send port in such a way that it will process all messages originating from the Source document library (created earlier). We will use a Word document to demonstrate this technique. Since a

Word document is not XML you need to make sure that the pipelines used by the receive and send ports are set to PassThru pipeline, not to XMLReceive pipeline.

■**Note** Word documents will be XML in Office 2007 when the new .docx format is introduced. This will make working with Word documents, SharePoint, and BizTalk Server 2006 very easy.

The XML pipeline checks whether a message type is known. This means that the pipeline checks that an XSD schema is defined for the message. The XML pipeline will also check whether a message contains valid XML. The XML pipeline does not validate the message against the XSD schema itself. If the pipeline validation fails, it will lead to message suspension. So if you use the XML pipeline, all Word documents will be suspended. The PassThru pipeline does not perform any validation whatsoever, which makes it a very suitable choice for processing binary messages such as Word documents.

The following procedure explains how to configure a PassThru pipeline that processes binary messages. In this example, we will use Word documents to demonstrate that the PassThru pipeline works:

1. Go back to the BizTalk Server 2006 Administration Console, right-click BizTalk Application 1, and choose Stop.

2. Go to Receive Locations. Double-click WSSReceiveLocation ➤ Set Receive Pipeline to PassThruReceive.

3. Click Configure. Set Source Document Library URL to Source.

4. Set the View name to Empty.

5. Click OK twice.

6. Go to Send Ports ➤ WSSSendPort ➤ Properties. Ensure the Send pipeline is set to PassThruTransmit.

7. Click Configure. Change the SharePoint site URL to `http://pluto/sites/Test/`.

8. Set the Destination Folder URL to Destination. Click OK.

9. Set Namespace Aliases to Empty.

10. Make sure the Windows SharePoint Services Integration section is entirely empty.

11. Click the Filters tab. Add the `WSS.InListName` property. Choose the `==` operator. Choose the following value: Source. Click OK.

12. Go to BizTalk Application 1 and choose Start. This time press the Options button. Make sure the following four check boxes are checked: Enlist and Start All Send Ports; Enable All Receive Locations; Start All Associated Host Instances; and Resume Suspended Instances. Make sure Enlist and Start All Orchestrations is not checked. Click Start.

13. Upload a test document to the Source document library.

The result of using BizTalk Server 2006 to route a Word document from the Source document library to the Destination document library is shown in Figure 7-39.

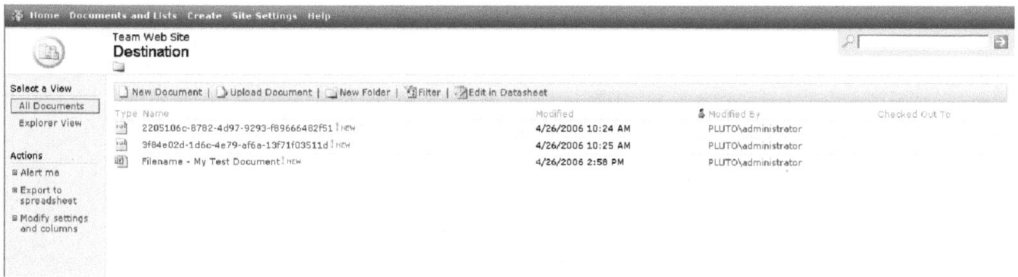

Figure 7-39. *Destination document library*

Summary

This chapter discussed the connection between InfoPath 2003 and SharePoint Product and Technologies 2003. Firstly, we discussed the basics of creating InfoPath forms. Then we discussed the connection between InfoPath and SharePoint. We showed you how to access data stored in a SharePoint list from within an InfoPath form. Next we showed how to create or update an InfoPath form programmatically in a SharePoint form library and how to submit data from an InfoPath form to a SharePoint form library. Finally, we went into detail discussing how to use the combination of InfoPath, BizTalk Server 2006, and SharePoint Product and Technologies 2003.

■ ■ ■

CHAPTER 8

Impersonation and Elevation

This chapter shows you all you need to know about doing impersonation, elevation, and delegation for SharePoint Products and Technologies. Assuming another user context is widely known as *impersonation*, although we prefer to use the term in a narrower sense to be able to specify more precisely what kind of impersonation scenario we are talking about. We will discern two types of user identity assumption: impersonation and elevation, which differ only in their intent.

LogonUser

Every web part is executed under a given identity. In most cases, this will be the identity of the current logged-on user. There are times when a web part needs to be able to assume another user context in order to do the work it is intended to do.

A web part *impersonates* when it does something on behalf of someone else. For example, user A checks in a document on behalf of user B. This is especially useful in workflow scenarios. Normally speaking, changing identities is only a temporary situation. A web part *elevates* when it does something that the current user is not allowed to do. In those types of scenarios, a superaccount is used to perform the required actions.

Elevation is particularly useful for *roll-up type web parts*: web parts that provide overviews of some sort. You can also discern two types of impersonation based on scope: we talk about impersonation when a server process impersonates the client security context on its local system; we talk about delegation when the server process impersonates the client security context on a remote system.

Our first impersonation example shows how to check out a file on behalf of a different user using the LogonUser Win32 API call. If you want to try out the code, you should create a test SharePoint site called ImpersonationAndElevation with unique security permissions, and add a user to it called Author A. Add the account to the ImpersonationAndElevation SharePoint site and grant the Author A account contributor rights, as shown in Figure 8-1.

You should also create a test document called Test document.doc and upload it to the Shared Documents document library (see Figure 8-2). Enable versioning on the Shared Documents document library.

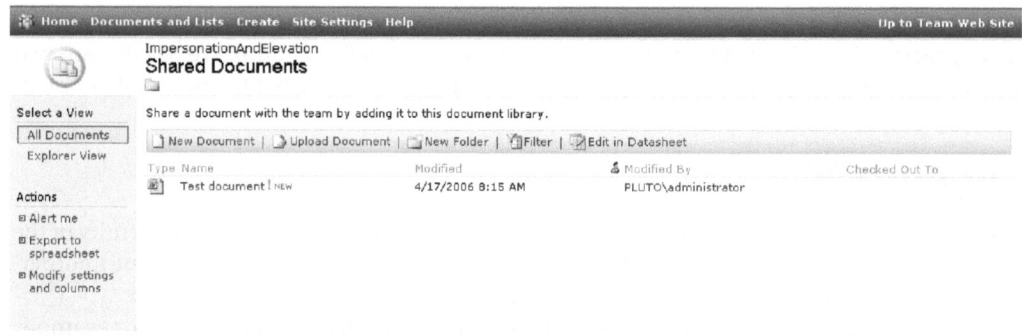

Figure 8-1. *The Manage Users page from the ImpersonationAndElevation site*

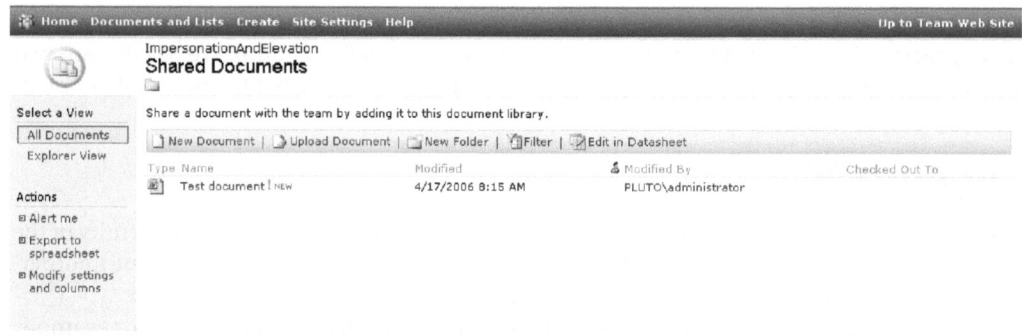

Figure 8-2. *The Shared Documents document library*

Then create a web part called Impersonator. Chapter 1 explains how to create web parts in Visual Studio.NET 2005. The purpose of this web part will be to check out the test document and check it back in again adding a check-in comment containing the current file version.

Since this web part will need more security permissions than what's contained by the default security permission set granted by SharePoint, the easiest solution is to set the trust level in the <trust> element in the web.config file of the root web folder to Full, like so:

```
<trust level="Full" originUrl="" processRequestInApplicationTrust="false" />
```

This is not exactly the best-recommended security practice. If you need a reminder why setting the trust level to Full is not a good idea, try out the following code in a web part that reboots the server. Make sure the trust level in the web.config file is set to Full:

```
using System;
using System.Collections.Generic;
using System.Text;
using System.Web.UI;
using Microsoft.SharePoint.WebPartPages;
using System.Runtime.InteropServices;
```

```
namespace LoisAndClark.ImpersonationAndElevation
{
  public class Impersonator : WebPart
  {
    private const uint REBOOT = 2;

    [DllImport("user32.dll", SetLastError = true)]
    static extern bool ExitWindowsEx(uint uFlags, uint uReason);

    protected override void CreateChildControls()
    {
      try
      {
        ExitWindowsEx(REBOOT, 1);
      }
      catch (Exception err)
      {
        Controls.Add(new LiteralControl(err.Message));
      }
    }
  }
}
```

Having noted that setting the trust level to Full is a risk liability in production environments, setting the trust level to Full is great for experimenting with code and for trying out the examples in this book. If you prefer creating custom policy files, you should ensure the following permissions are present in your policy file to execute the impersonation code sample:

```
<IPermission class="AspNetHostingPermission" version="1" Level="Minimal" />
<IPermission class="EnvironmentPermission" version="1" Unrestricted="true"/>
<IPermission class="SecurityPermission" version="1" ➥
Flags="Execution,UnmanagedCode,ControlPrincipal, ➥
ControlAppDomain, ControlEvidence" />
<IPermission class="WebPartPermission" version="1" Connections="True" />
<IPermission class="SharePointPermission" version="1" ObjectModel="True" ➥
UnsafeSaveOnGet="True" />
```

The code retrieves the current site collection from the current SharePoint context and gets the ImpersonationAndElevation SharePoint site from this site collection. By default, you are not allowed to check out and check in files in SharePoint in HTTP GET requests. To get around that, our code sample allows unsafe updates on the ImpersonationAndElevation SPWeb instance. An instance of SPFile associated to the test document can be retrieved from the ImpersonationAndElevation SPWeb instance. Finally, the code outputs some information to the screen by adding the information to a LiteralControl. The code responsible for checking out and checking in the test document looks like this:

```
SPSite objSiteCollection = SPControl.GetContextSite(Context);
SPWeb objSite = objSiteCollection.AllWebs["ImpersonationAndElevation"];
objSite.AllowUnsafeUpdates = true;
SPFile objFile = objSite.GetFile("Shared Documents/Test Document.doc");
objFile.CheckOut();
SPUser objUser = objFile.CheckedOutBy;
objFile.CheckIn("check-in version: " + objFile.UIVersion);
Controls.Add(new LiteralControl(objFile.Name + " checked out by: " + objUser.Name));
```

Figure 8-3 shows the version history, which can be used to check the result of performing a programmatic checkout and check-in of the test document. As you can see, the user administrator created the document.

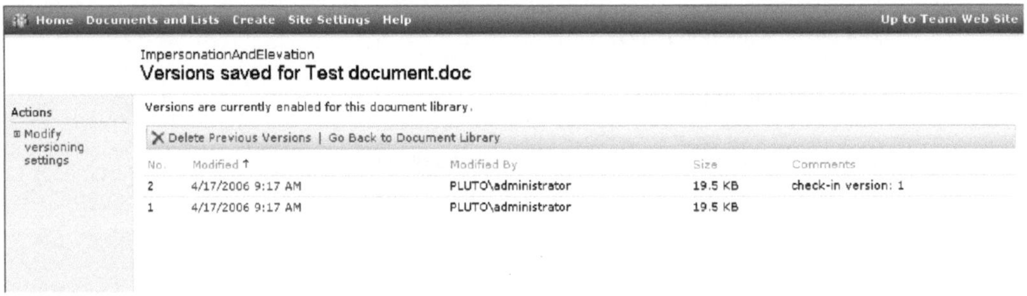

Figure 8-3. *Version history of the test document*

We have added the test web part to the home page of the ImpersonationAndElevation SharePoint site and accessed the page by logging in as administrator. As a result, you can see that the administrator account is also the account used when modifying the test document programmatically. The complete code listing looks like this:

```
using System;
using System.Collections.Generic;
using System.Text;
using System.Web.UI;
using System.Web.UI.HtmlControls;
using System.Web.UI.WebControls;
using Microsoft.SharePoint;
using Microsoft.SharePoint.WebPartPages;
using Microsoft.SharePoint.WebControls;

namespace LoisAndClark.ImpersonationAndElevation
{
  public class Impersonator : WebPart
  {
    protected override void CreateChildControls()
    {
      try
      {
        SPSite objSiteCollection = SPControl.GetContextSite(Context);
```

```
      SPWeb objSite = objSiteCollection.AllWebs["ImpersonationAndElevation"];
      objSite.AllowUnsafeUpdates = true;

      SPFile objFile = objSite.GetFile("Shared Documents/Test Document.doc");
      objFile.CheckOut();

      SPUser objUser = objFile.CheckedOutBy;

      objFile.CheckIn("check-in version: " + objFile.UIVersion);

      Controls.Add(new LiteralControl(objFile.Name + " checked out by: " + ➥
      objUser.Name));
    }
    catch (Exception err)
    {
      Controls.Add(new LiteralControl(err.Message));
    }
  }
 }
}
```

Now we are ready to show how to impersonate the Author A account. Again, we will access the home page, logging in as administrator, but this time we will check out and check in the file using the Author A account. To make it easier to concentrate on the impersonation part of the code, copy the code concerning the document modification to a new private method called CheckInAndOut() in the web part.

The impersonation code makes a Win32 API call to the LogonUser function to impersonate the Author A user account. To do this you will need to import two dlls: advapi.dll and kernel32.dll. This can be done via the [DllImport] attribute which can be found in the System.Runtime. InteropServices namespace. Add the import statements to the web part class:

```
[DllImport("advapi32.dll", SetLastError = true)]
static extern bool LogonUser(
  string principal,
  string authority,
  string password,
  LogonTypes logonType,
  LogonProviders logonProvider,
  out IntPtr token);

[DllImport("kernel32.dll", SetLastError = true)]
static extern bool CloseHandle(IntPtr handle);
```

Advapi32.dll contains the LogonUser() function, which attempts to log on a user to a local computer. The most important arguments that need to be passed to this function are a user-name, domain, and password. The function returns a Boolean value indicating whether the logon is successful. A handle is passed (by reference). This handle is very important because it can be used to create a new windows identity.

You might have noticed the advapi32.dll uses the LogonTypes and LogonProviders types. These types are enumerations that can be used as arguments for the LogonUser() function. You will need to add the following code to your web part class:

```
enum LogonTypes : uint
{
  Interactive = 2,
  Network,
  Batch,
  Service,
  NetworkCleartext = 8,
  NewCredentials
}

enum LogonProviders : uint
{
  Default = 0, // default
  WinNT35,
  WinNT40, // uses NTLM
  WinNT50 // negotiates Kerberos or NTLM
}
```

Kernel32.dll contains the CloseHandle() function that closes an open object handle. This function is used to close the handle that is the result of the LogonUser() call.

The WindowsIdentity class in the System.Security.Principal namespace represents a Windows user. It can be useful to retrieve the current Windows identity by calling the GetCurrent() method of the WindowsIdentity class so you are able to restore the original user context later. If you call the advapi32.dll LogonUser() function, you will obtain a token that can be used to create a new Windows identity. In our example this will be the Author A account. If you now call the Impersonate() method of this Windows identity object, a WindowsImpersonationContext object is returned that impersonates the user represented by the WindowsIdentity object. Calling the CheckInAndOut() method will modify the test document within the context of the Author A user account. Calling the Undo() method of the WindowsImpersonationContext object reverts the user context and then you need to clean up the open object handle (the token) by calling the Kernel32.dll CloseHandle() function. The code looks like this:

```
// you could use this one later if you need the original user context
objOrgIdentity = WindowsIdentity.GetCurrent();
bool blnReturn = LogonUser(@"authorA", "pluto", "a", LogonTypes.Interactive, ➡
LogonProviders.Default, out objToken);
objIdentity = new WindowsIdentity(objToken);
objUserContext = objIdentity.Impersonate();
CheckInAndOut(); // modify document
objUserContext.Undo(); // revert user context
CloseHandle(objToken);
```

The complete code listing looks like this:

```
using System;
using System.Collections.Generic;
using System.Text;
using System.Web.UI;
using System.Web.UI.HtmlControls;
using System.Web.UI.WebControls;
using Microsoft.SharePoint;
using Microsoft.SharePoint.WebPartPages;
using Microsoft.SharePoint.WebControls;
using System.Runtime.InteropServices;
using System.Security.Principal;

namespace LoisAndClark.ImpersonationAndElevation
{
  public class Impersonator : WebPart
  {
    [DllImport("advapi32.dll", SetLastError = true)]
    static extern bool LogonUser(
      string principal,
      string authority,
      string password,
      LogonTypes logonType,
      LogonProviders logonProvider,
      out IntPtr token);

    [DllImport("kernel32.dll", SetLastError = true)]
    static extern bool CloseHandle(IntPtr handle);

    enum LogonTypes : uint
    {
      Interactive = 2,
      Network,
      Batch,
      Service,
      NetworkCleartext = 8,
      NewCredentials
    }

    enum LogonProviders : uint
    {
      Default = 0, // default
      WinNT35,
      WinNT40, // uses NTLM
      WinNT50 // negotiates Kerberos or NTLM
    }
```

```
protected override void CreateChildControls()
{
  try
  {
    WindowsImpersonationContext objUserContext;
    IntPtr objToken;
    WindowsIdentity objOrgIdentity;
    WindowsIdentity objIdentity;

    bool blnReturn = LogonUser(@"authorA", "pluto", "a", LogonTypes.Interactive,
    LogonProviders.Default,
    out objToken);

    string strValue = String.Empty;

    if (blnReturn)
    {
      objOrgIdentity = WindowsIdentity.GetCurrent();
      objIdentity = new WindowsIdentity(objToken);
      objUserContext = objIdentity.Impersonate();

      CheckInAndOut();

      strValue += "Identity name after impersonation: " + " " + ➥
      objIdentity.Name + "<br/>";
      objUserContext.Undo();
      strValue += "Identity name when impersonation is undone: " + ➥
      objOrgIdentity.Name;

      CloseHandle(objToken);
    }
    else
    {
      strValue = "Logon failed!";
    }
  }
  catch (Exception err)
  {
    Controls.Add(new LiteralControl(err.Message));
  }
}

private void CheckInAndOut()
{
  SPSite objSiteCollection = SPControl.GetContextSite(Context);
  SPWeb objSite = objSiteCollection.AllWebs["ImpersonationAndElevation"];
  objSite.AllowUnsafeUpdates = true;
```

```
      SPFile objFile = objSite.GetFile("Shared Documents/Test Document.doc");
      objFile.CheckOut();
      SPUser objUser = objFile.CheckedOutBy;
      objFile.CheckIn("check-in version: " + objFile.UIVersion);
      Controls.Add(new LiteralControl(objFile.Name + " checked out by: " + ➡
      objUser.Name));
    }
  }
}
```

Encrypting Sensitive Data via DPAPI

In the previous example, the user credentials are stored in the code. It is unsafe to store passwords in plain text in code. This can be avoided by saving the credentials in a configuration file and encrypting the sensitive areas using DPAPI. The *DP* in DPAPI stands for *data protection*. It's an API provided by the operating system since Windows 2000. In .NET 2.0, working with DPAPI becomes significantly easier via the new `ProtectedData` class that is located in the `System.Security.Cryptography` namespace.

The `ProtectedData` class allows you to encrypt or decrypt data. The `Protect()` method of this class encrypts data. The first argument of this method expects a byte array containing data. Optionally, as the second parameter, you can pass an entropy parameter which is a random value designed to make deciphering more difficult. You could define a unique entropy per application to prevent other applications from being able to decrypt your sensitive data, although the use of the entropy parameter raises the question of how to manage the entropy information in a secure fashion. If you do not want to use the entropy parameter, you can pass the value `null`. The last parameter of the `Protect()` method allows you to specify the DataProtectionScope. This can be set to CurrentUser or LocalMachine mode. If you use CurrentUser, only the current user will be able to decrypt the information; in LocalMachine mode every process on the machine will be able to decrypt it. For server scenarios in which SharePoint web parts decrypt sensitive information, setting the mode to LocalMachine makes a lot of sense, because there will be no untrusted logins to the server. Client applications should always use CurrentUser mode. The following code shows how to encrypt and decrypt information:

```
string strValue = "secret password";
byte[] arrSecret = Encoding.Unicode.GetBytes(strValue);
byte[] arrEntropy = {0, 1, 2};
byte[] arrEncryptedData = ProtectedData.Protect(arrSecret, arrEntropy, ➡
DataProtectionScope.LocalMachine);
byte[] orgData = ProtectedData.Unprotect(arrEncryptedData, arrEntropy, ➡
DataProtectionScope.LocalMachine);
string strSecret = Encoding.Unicode.GetString(orgData);
```

If you want to try out this code in a web part, make sure the following namespaces are imported:

```
using System.Text;
using System.Security.Cryptography;
```

Using the SecureString Class

In the previous code sample, we show how to decrypt data and store it in a string. At this point, within the string, the data is not encrypted anymore. If storing sensitive unencrypted data in memory is something that worries you, you should use the SecureString class in the System. Security namespace instead. The value of an instance of SecureString is automatically encrypted. The following code shows how to place data in a SecureString object and how to get it out of there:

```
string strValue = "secret password";
SecureString strSecureSecret = new SecureString();
char[] charValue = Encoding.Unicode.GetChars(Encoding.Unicode.GetBytes(strValue));
for (int i = 0; i < charValue.Length; i++)
{
  strSecureSecret.AppendChar(charValue[i]);
}
IntPtr objPointer = Marshal.SecureStringToBSTR(strSecureSecret);
string strNormalString = Marshal.PtrToStringUni(objPointer);
```

If you want to try out this code in a web part, make sure the following namespaces are imported:

```
using System.Security;
using System.Runtime.InteropServices;
```

Storing Sensitive Information in an Encrypted Way

At this point, we have shown you how to use DPAPI to encrypt and decrypt data. If you want a safe way to store data in memory you can use SecureString. However, our goal is to show you how to store sensitive information in an encrypted way in a config file and we have not yet reached that goal.

Suppose you want to store the password for user Author A in a .config file. You would create an <add> element under the <appSettings> configuration section, like so:

```
<appSettings>
  <add key="AuthorA" value="a" />
</appSettings>
```

You could add this manually by opening the web.config file. You could also add this information manually via a more advanced user interface by opening the web site properties of the SharePoint web site in Internet Information Services, clicking the ASP.NET tab, and clicking the Edit Configuration button. You will find the Application settings under the General tab. Finally, you can also add application settings programmatically and take care of the encryption of sensitive data at the same time. We will demonstrate the last approach.

You can use the WebConfigurationManager in the System.Web.Configuration namespace to retrieve the SharePoint web.config file. The OpenWebConfiguration() method of the WebConfigurationManager class returns a Configuration object. The Configuration object provides access to the AppSettings in the web.config file via its AppSettings property which returns an AppSettingsSection object. You can add application settings via the Add() method of the AppSettingsSection object. Via the ProtectSection() method of the ConfigurationSection class you can determine whether the content of a given configuration section should be encrypted, and, if so, what data protection provider should be used to encrypt the data. In the following code example, we use the DataProtectionConfigurationProvider, which uses DPAPI:

```
string strUser = "AuthorA";
string strPassword = "a";
Configuration objConfig = ➥
WebConfigurationManager.OpenWebConfiguration(Context.Request.ApplicationPath);
AppSettingsSection objAppSettings = objConfig.AppSettings;
objAppSettings.Settings.Add(strUser, strPassword);
objAppSettings.SectionInformation.ProtectSection ➥
("DataProtectionConfigurationProvider");
objConfig.Save();
```

If you want to try out this code in a web part you should add a reference to the system. configuration.dll. You should also have write permission on the configuration file. Make sure the following namespaces are imported:

```
using System.Configuration;
using System.Web.Configuration;
```

The AppSettings section now looks like this:

```
<appSettings configProtectionProvider="DataProtectionConfigurationProvider">
  <EncryptedData>
    <CipherData>
      <CipherValue>AQAAANCM …deleted stuff…fnKLBAw==</CipherValue>
    </CipherData>
  </EncryptedData>
</appSettings>
```

As you can see, no sensitive data is stored in plain text anymore.

You do not have to do anything special to retrieve encrypted data from the SharePoint web.config file. Just do this:

```
string strSetting = WebConfigurationManager.AppSettings["AuthorA"];
```

If you want to go back to a web.config file without encrypted data, use the following line of code:

```
objAppSettings.SectionInformation.UnprotectSection();
```

Single Sign-On

In the previous section, you saw how to encrypt sensitive data. Instead of encrypting data, you could also use SharePoint Single Sign-On (SSO) to store user credentials in the Single Sign-On database. The Single Sign-On database is also called the *credential-mapping database* and it keeps the information safe and encrypted. A drawback to this approach is that you will need to use SharePoint Portal Server 2003, because SharePoint Single Sign-On is a part of this product. Because SharePoint Portal Server 2003 has no support for the .NET 2.0 Framework, the example code is written using Visual Studio.NET 2003, whereas the rest of the examples in this chapter are written with Visual Studio.NET 2005.

We are assuming you have access to a server with SharePoint Portal Server installed and Single Sign-On enabled on it. The Microsoft TechNet web site contains a sample chapter taken from the Microsoft SharePoint Products and Technologies 2003 Resource Kit called "Single Sign-On in SharePoint Portal Server 2003." It contains a detailed description of Single-Sign-On and discusses how to configure this technology. The information can be found at the following location: `http://www.microsoft.com/technet/prodtechnol/sppt/reskit/c2661881x.mspx`.

The first thing you need to do is go to the Manage Enterprise Application Definitions page (SharePoint Portal Server Central Administration ➤ Manage Single Sign-On) as shown in Figure 8-4.

Figure 8-4. *Manage Single Sign-On page*

You should add an Enterprise Application Definition called SuperAccount, which defines the different parts of information that form the credential information you are interested in. In our example, all we need is a username and a password. You should set the display type to Mask so the password is not shown onscreen in plain text later on. Choose the Individual account type in situations where every user has access to another system. For example, suppose a user logs in on the portal and needs information extracted from SAP enterprise software within the portal.

It would be a drag if users would need to type their credentials repeatedly. This is the type of scenario where the Individual account type makes sense. In impersonation scenarios you should choose Group as the account type because you want to define one impersonation account for a group of users. The administrator manages this impersonation account, not the end user. Figure 8-5 shows the Edit Enterprise Application Definition page.

In the next step, you need to tie the credential information template, the Enterprise Application Definition, to a group account name. This is done on the Manage Account Information for Enterprise Application Definition page (SharePoint Portal Server Administration ➤ Manage Single Sign-On). For our example we created a group called MyApplication. Every member of this group will be allowed to use web parts that need to elevate user privileges temporarily. This is shown in Figure 8-6.

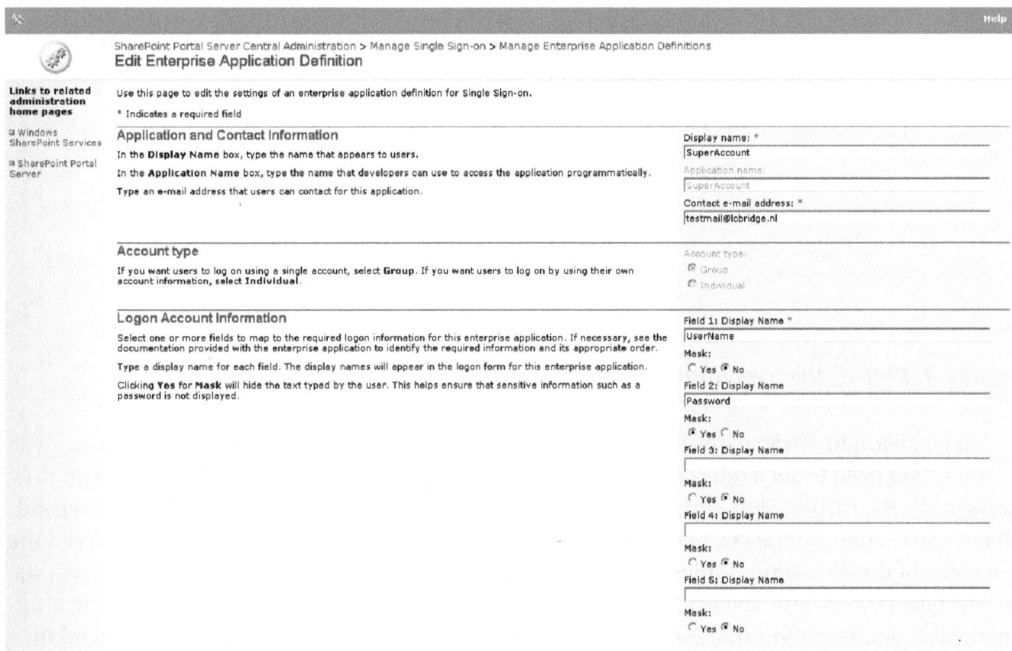

Figure 8-5. *The Edit Enterprise Application Definition page*

Figure 8-6. *The Manage Account Information for an Enterprise Application Definition page*

On the Provide [Enterprise Application Definition name] page (SharePoint Portal Server Administration ➤ Manage Single Sign-On ➤ Manage Account Information) you can define the credentials of the superaccount that is used for impersonation. As defined earlier, this information consists of a username and password. This is shown in Figure 8-7.

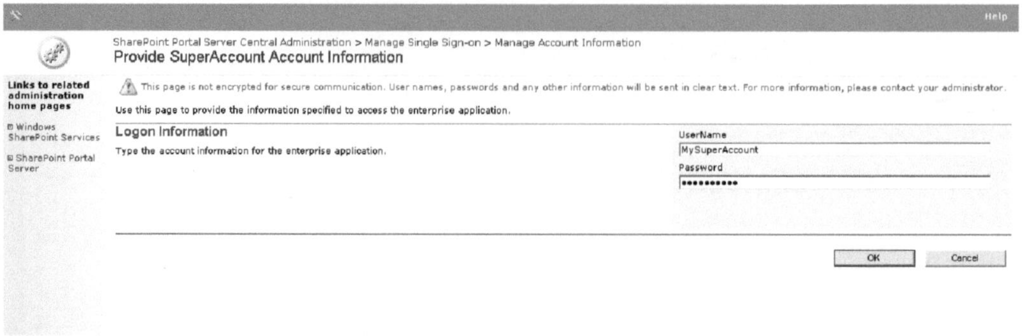

Figure 8-7. *Provide the credentials of the impersonation account.*

If you want to retrieve this information from the Single Sign-On service from within a web part you will need to set a reference to Microsoft.SharePoint.SingleSignOn.dll. The Credentials class in the `Microsoft.SharePoint.SingleSignOn` namespace has a `GetCredentials()` method that retrieves the superaccount credentials defined earlier. This method is, in our view, not the best part of the SharePoint object model. Although the method is called `GetCredentials()` its return type is `void`. The first argument of the method expects an unsigned integer as the argument. The documentation says this flag is reserved for internal use. Apparently you need to pass it the value of 1, but the reason is a mystery. Then you need to pass the application name, which is the name of the Enterprise Application Definition. Finally, you need to pass a string array by reference, which is filled by the `GetCredentials()` method, with all the credential information the Single Sign-On service can find. The code looks like this:

```
string[] strCredentialData = null;
Credentials.GetCredentials(1, "SuperAccount", ref strCredentialData);
string strUserName = strCredentialData[0];
string strPassword = strCredentialData[1];
```

This is the complete code listing:

```
using System;
using System.ComponentModel;
using System.Web.UI;
using System.Web.UI.WebControls;
using System.Xml.Serialization;
using Microsoft.SharePoint;
using Microsoft.SharePoint.Utilities;
using Microsoft.SharePoint.WebPartPages;
using Microsoft.SharePoint.Portal.SingleSignon;

namespace LoisAndClark.TestSSO
{
  /// <summary>
  /// Description for SSO.
  /// </summary>
  [DefaultProperty("Text"),
```

```
    ToolboxData("<{0}:SSO runat=server></{0}:SSO>"),
    XmlRoot(Namespace="TestSSO")]
  public class SSO : Microsoft.SharePoint.WebPartPages.WebPart
  {
    private const string defaultText = "";

    private string text = defaultText;

    [Browsable(true),
      Category("Miscellaneous"),
      DefaultValue(defaultText),
      WebPartStorage(Storage.Personal),
      FriendlyName("Text"),
      Description("Text Property")]
    public string Text
    {
      get
      {
        return text;
      }

      set
      {
        text = value;
      }
    }


    /// <summary>
    /// Render this Web Part to the output parameter specified.
    /// </summary>
    /// <param name="output"> The HTML writer to write out to </param>
    protected override void RenderWebPart(HtmlTextWriter output)
    {
      try
      {
        string[] strCredentialData = null;
        Credentials.GetCredentials(1, "SuperAccount", ref strCredentialData);
        string strUserName = strCredentialData[0];
        string strPassword = strCredentialData[1];
        output.Write("username: " + strUserName + " password: " + strPassword);
      }
      catch (Exception err)
      {
        output.Write("error: " + err.Message);
      }
    }
  }
}
```

RevertToSelf

You have seen how to store encrypted information in configuration files and how to store credentials in the Single Sign-On database. In elevation scenarios where you want to perform actions that require more privileges than the current user has, an easier and more elegant solution is available. This solution is called *credentialless impersonation*. In this approach, a call is made to the Win32 API RevertToSelf function that terminates the impersonation of a client application.

A SharePoint user context is itself an impersonated identity. SharePoint uses Internet Information Server 6, and Internet Information Server 6 uses application pool identities as the context in which worker processes are run. If you call the advapi32.dll RevertToSelf() function you will end the current user impersonation—the effect being that you revert from a current user context (say, Author A) to the original identity, which is the application pool identity.

The credentials of the application pool identity are stored safely in the Internet Information Services metabase. This trait makes the application pool identity account an ideal candidate for use in elevation scenarios. If you dump the current context and revert to the application pool's security context it is possible to perform actions that require an extensive set of privileges while avoiding storing credentials in code.

If you have installed SharePoint (either Windows SharePoint Services or SharePoint Portal Server) using an existing SQL Server instance, you get to choose the application pool identity. This account needs to be a local administrator and will become administrator of the SharePoint content database.

This is not the case if you install SharePoint using Windows Microsoft SQL Server 200 Desktop Engine (WMSDE), which is the license-free version of SQL Server. In this scenario, the predefined NT AUTHORITY\NETWORK SERVICE account will be used as the security account for the application pool. By default, the Network Service account will not be a member of the SharePoint administration group and it is not a local administrator either. The use of the WMSDE is highly unlikely if you are using SharePoint Portal Server, but it is a far more feasible solution if you are using Windows SharePoint Services which comes free with the Windows Server 2003 operating system.

In elevation scenarios you will probably want to use some kind of superaccount that has at least SharePoint admin rights. You can go to the Internet Information Services manager and change the application pool identity or go to the SharePoint Central Administration pages and extend the permissions of the Network Service account. You can do the latter by clicking the Set SharePoint Administration Group link directly under the Security Configuration section. If you set NT AUTHORITY\NETWORK SERVICE as the group account name you will be granted sufficient rights to execute the example described in this section.

To demonstrate the credentialless impersonation solution, you can use the Author A account again. Our next example uses the SharePoint object model to display the URL and server ID of the current virtual server. You need to be an administrator to be able to do this, otherwise you will get an "access denied" error.

The code retrieves the current site collection and opens the virtual server for this site collection via the SPVirtualServer class. Next, the code retrieves a couple of properties from the virtual server object. Normally if a user such as Author A tries to retrieve those properties, unhandled "access denied" errors cause authentication dialog boxes to pop up repeatedly, but the code suppresses this by setting the CatchAccessDeniedException property of the virtual server object to false. The code looks like this:

```
string strValue = String.Empty;
SPSite objSite = SPControl.GetContextSite(Context);
SPGlobalAdmin objAdmin = new SPGlobalAdmin();
SPVirtualServer objServer = objAdmin.OpenVirtualServer(new Uri(objSite.Url));
objServer.CatchAccessDeniedException = false;
strValue += objServer.Url + " virtual server id: " + objServer.VirtualServerId;
```

If you open a browser by right-clicking it, choose the Run As option and log in with the Author A account and you will see that access will be denied. This is shown in Figure 8-8. If you forget to set the CatchAccessDeniedException to false, you will have a lot more opportunity to notice this.

Figure 8-8. *'Access is denied' error in the web part*

At this point you can use the RevertToSelf() Win32 API call to illustrate elevation. All you need to do is to import the Advapi32.dll into the web part class:

```
[DllImport("advapi32.dll")]
static extern bool RevertToSelf();
```

It is advisable to store the current user context in a WindowsIdentity object so that you are able to elevate privileges temporarily. Then you can execute the code that absolutely needs to have an extensive set of privileges and go back to the original user context. This way you are limiting security risks associated with user elevation. The following code listing shows how to do this:

```
WindowsIdentity objOriginalUser = WindowsIdentity.GetCurrent();
RevertToSelf();
ShowVirtualServerInfo(); // reads virtual server info
WindowsImpersonationContext objContext = objOriginalUser.Impersonate();
```

The complete code listing looks like this:

```
using System;
using System.Collections.Generic;
using System.Text;
using System.Web.UI;
using System.Web.UI.HtmlControls;
using System.Web.UI.WebControls;
```

```csharp
using Microsoft.SharePoint;
using Microsoft.SharePoint.WebPartPages;
using Microsoft.SharePoint.WebControls;
using Microsoft.SharePoint.Administration;
using System.Runtime.InteropServices;
using System.Security.Principal;

namespace  LoisAndClark.ImpersonationAndElevation
{
  public class Impersonator : WebPart
  {
    [DllImport("advapi32.dll", SetLastError = true)]
    static extern bool RevertToSelf();

    protected override void CreateChildControls()
    {
      try
      {
        string strValue = String.Empty;

        WindowsIdentity objOriginalUser = WindowsIdentity.GetCurrent();
        RevertToSelf();
        strValue += "application pool identity name: " + ➥
        WindowsIdentity.GetCurrent().Name + "<br/>";
        strValue += ShowVirtualServerInfo();
        WindowsImpersonationContext objContext = objOriginalUser.Impersonate();
        strValue += "original user name: " + WindowsIdentity.GetCurrent().Name;

        Controls.Add(new LiteralControl(strValue));
      }
      catch (Exception err)
      {
        Controls.Add(new LiteralControl(err.Message));
      }
    }

    private string ShowVirtualServerInfo()
    {
      SPSite objSite = SPControl.GetContextSite(Context);
      SPGlobalAdmin objAdmin = new SPGlobalAdmin();
      SPVirtualServer objServer = objAdmin.OpenVirtualServer(new Uri(objSite.Url));
      objServer.CatchAccessDeniedException = false;

      return "url: " + objServer.Url + " virtual server id: " ➥
      + objServer.VirtualServerId + "<br/><br/>";
    }
  }
}
```

Creating a New AppDomain

There are times when the impersonation methods discussed previously do not work—when calling the SharePoint object model fails if you are not an administrator. The following code sample retrieves the current SharePoint site and shows the collection of site groups of which the current user is a member:

```
string strValue = String.Empty;
RevertToSelf();
SPWeb objCurrentWeb = SPControl.GetContextWeb(Context);
foreach (SPRole objRole in objCurrentWeb.CurrentUser.Roles)
{
  strValue += "Role: " + objRole.Name + "<br/>";
}
```

This code fails unless you are an administrator. As it turns out, there are situations when the SharePoint object model will always validate its actions against the original user context of the request, for example Author A, even after explicitly impersonating to another user context. In such cases impersonation via the LogonUser() and RevertToSelf() functions is useless. This is a bug, and as another downside this behavior is not discussed in the SharePoint documentation, which makes a trial-and-error strategy the only way to find out if impersonation succeeds.

Luckily, there is a way around this, although it is more complicated compared to the previous impersonation strategies. This new strategy consists of a number of steps:

1. Impersonate by calling either the LogonUser() or RevertToSelf() function.

2. Create a new application domain.

3. Execute any actions that need an extensive set of privileges within the new application domain.

4. Marshal back any results.

5. Unload the application domain.

6. Finally, resume the original identity.

We've discussed calling the LogonUser() and RevertToSelf() functions extensively in previous sections of this chapter. To understand the rest of the steps you need to understand a couple of things about AppDomains.

AppDomains are very similar to operating system processes in that they form the fundamental scope for execution of code and ownership of resources. There is a big difference, however; operating system processes are abstractions created by the operating system, and AppDomains are abstractions created by the CLR. Any AppDomain resides in exactly one operating system process, whereas one operating system process can host multiple AppDomains. Objects always reside in exactly one AppDomain, and object references must always refer to objects within the same AppDomain.

It is quite easy to create and destroy AppDomains programmatically by calling the following:

```
AppDomain objAppChild = AppDomain.CreateDomain("MyChild");
AppDomain.UnLoad(objAppChild);
```

You can load and execute code in a freshly created AppDomain and retrieve the results. The following code shows how to do that:

```
Object obj = objMyAppDomain.CreateInstanceAndUnwrap("MyAssembly", "MyType");
MyClass obj2 = (MyClass) obj;
String strValue = obj2.DoSomething();
```

We will get to the Unwrap bit later, but let's first look at the obj2.DoSomething() call. It's impossible to make an object reference refer to objects that reside in other AppDomains, so how does this work?

If you want to transfer an object reference to another AppDomain it has to be marshaled. Not every type you will create can be marshaled. If you create your own class, by default it will be a *remote-unaware* type, which means it cannot be marshaled to another AppDomain. If you mark a type as being [Serializable] it is called an *unbound* type. Unbound types will be marshaled by value; the CLR will hand a disconnected clone to the receiving AppDomain. Then there is a third type: the *AppDomain-bound type*. In this scenario the type is marshaled by reference; the CLR will give the receiving AppDomain a proxy object that forwards all calls back to the original object, which resides in the source AppDomain.

AppDomain-bound types derive from System.MarshalByRefObject, either directly or indirectly. For our example, we have created an AppDomain-bound class called RoleManager that performs some operations using the SharePoint administration object model. Its definition looks like this:

```
using System;
using System.Collections.Generic;
using System.Text;
using Microsoft.SharePoint;
using Microsoft.SharePoint.Administration;

namespace LoisAndClark.ImpersonationAndElevation
{
  public class RoleManager: MarshalByRefObject
  {
    public string GetSomeValue()
    {
      string strReturn = String.Empty;

      SPSite objSite = new SPSite("http://pluto");
      SPGlobalAdmin objAdmin = new SPGlobalAdmin();
      SPVirtualServer objServer = objAdmin.OpenVirtualServer(new Uri(objSite.Url));
      objServer.CatchAccessDeniedException = false;
      strReturn += "url: " + objServer.Url + " server id: " + ➥
      objServer.VirtualServerId;

      return strReturn;
    }
  }
}
```

Previously, you saw a call to the CreateInstanceAndUnwrap() method. This method does two important things: it calls the CreateInstance() and Unwrap() methods. Take a look at the following piece of code, which is semantically identical to a call to the CreateInstanceAndUnwrap() method:

```
ObjectHandle objHandle = objMyAppDomain.CreateInstance("MyAssembly", "MyType")
Object objProxy = objHandle.Unwrap();
```

The CreateInstance() method returns an object handle, not a real object reference. The type is not loaded into the AppDomain until Unwrap() is called. This is efficient in scenarios where two new child AppDomains are created. The parent AppDomain could pass an object handle to an object in AppDomain child1 to AppDomain child2 without requiring the type of the object to be loaded in the parent AppDomain. However, this does mean that you will need to call the Unwrap() method before actually using an object.

So where will the CLR look when it tries to load the assembly when calling CreateInstance? It is possible to deploy your assembly in the GAC, or you could specify other locations during the setup of an AppDomain. Every AppDomain has a SetupInformation property that exposes data that controls the behavior of the assembly resolver that is responsible for deciding from which locations assemblies are loaded. In our example we will just copy this information from the current AppDomain:

```
AppDomainSetup objAppDomainSetup = AppDomain.CurrentDomain.SetupInformation;
```

This makes it possible to deploy our assembly in the [drive letter]:\inetpub\wwwroot\bin folder. There is one catch: you need to do this before the AppDomain is created, otherwise you cannot change the AppDomainSetup information for the AppDomain anymore.

We also need to provide our new AppDomain with evidence information. Evidence contains information about the identity of an assembly. This information is important if a system administrator needs to grant permissions based on the executing assembly's identity. There are two different kinds of evidence information: *origin-based* and *content-based*. Origin-based evidence provides information about the location where the assembly is coming from (for example, an application directory or the GAC). Origin-based evidence is unrelated to the content of the assembly. Content-based evidence examines the content of the assembly. For example, the presence of a strong name is important content-based evidence information. In our example, we will copy the evidence information from the current AppDomain:

```
Evidence objEvidence = AppDomain.CurrentDomain.Evidence;
```

The following code creates a new application domain and sets it up with the right information. Then it creates another class that performs some code that uses the SharePoint administration object model and requires administrator privileges. This class is executed in the new application domain. The result is marshaled back to the originating assembly:

```
RevertToSelf();
AppDomainSetup objAppDomainSetup = AppDomain.CurrentDomain.SetupInformation;
Evidence objEvidence = AppDomain.CurrentDomain.Evidence;
AppDomain objMyAppDomain = AppDomain.CreateDomain("MyAppDomain", objEvidence, ➥
objAppDomainSetup);
```

```
ObjectHandle objHandle = objMyAppDomain.CreateInstance ➥
(Assembly.GetExecutingAssembly(). ➥
GetName().FullName, typeof(RoleManager).FullName);

Object objProxy = objHandle.Unwrap();
RoleManager  objClass = (RoleManager) objProxy;
string strValue = objClass.GetSomeValue();
AppDomain.Unload(objMyAppDomain);
```

Here we have created a new AppDomain to perform high-privileged work for us. The complete code listing looks like this:

```
// RoleManager.cs

using System;
using System.Collections.Generic;
using System.Text;
using Microsoft.SharePoint;
using Microsoft.SharePoint.Administration;

namespace LoisAndClark.ImpersonationAndElevation
{
  class RoleManager : MarshalByRefObject
  {
  public string GetSomeValue()
    {
      string strReturn = String.Empty;

      SPSite objSite = new SPSite("http://pluto");
      SPGlobalAdmin objAdmin = new SPGlobalAdmin();
      SPVirtualServer objServer = objAdmin.OpenVirtualServer(new Uri(objSite.Url));
      objServer.CatchAccessDeniedException = false;
      strReturn += "url: " + objServer.Url + " server id: " + ➥
      objServer.VirtualServerId;

      return strReturn;
    }
  }
}


// Impersonator.cs

using System;
using System.Collections.Generic;
using System.Text;
using System.Web.UI;
using Microsoft.SharePoint.WebPartPages;
```

```csharp
using System.Reflection;
using System.Security.Policy;
using System.Security.Principal;
using System.Runtime.InteropServices;
using System.Runtime.Remoting;

namespace LoisAndClark.ImpersonationAndElevation
{
  public class Impersonator : WebPart
  {
    [DllImport("advapi32.dll", SetLastError = true)]
    static extern bool RevertToSelf();

    protected override void CreateChildControls()
    {
      try
      {
        string strValue = String.Empty;
        RevertToSelf();
        AppDomainSetup objAppDomainSetup = AppDomain.CurrentDomain.SetupInformation;

        Evidence objEvidence = AppDomain.CurrentDomain.Evidence;

        AppDomain objMyAppDomain = AppDomain.CreateDomain ➡
        ("MyAppDomain", objEvidence, objAppDomainSetup);

        try
        {
          strValue += objMyAppDomain.SetupInformation.ApplicationBase;
          strValue += " probe: " + ➡
          objMyAppDomain.SetupInformation.PrivateBinPathProbe;
          strValue += " private bin: " + ➡
          objMyAppDomain.SetupInformation.PrivateBinPath;
          ObjectHandle objHandle = ➡
          objMyAppDomain.CreateInstance( ➡
          Assembly.GetExecutingAssembly().GetName().FullName, ➡
          typeof(RoleManager).FullName);

          Object objProxy = objHandle.Unwrap();
          RoleManager objClass = (RoleManager) objProxy;
          strValue += "<br/><br/>" + objClass.GetSomeValue();
        }
        catch (Exception err)
        {
          strValue += err.Message;
        }
```

```
        finally
        {
          AppDomain.Unload(objMyAppDomain);
        }

        Controls.Add(new LiteralControl(strValue));
      }
      catch (Exception err)
      {
        Controls.Add(new LiteralControl(err.Message));
      }
    }
  }
}
```

Enterprise Services COM+ Component

You have seen different ways to impersonate users in code. The LogonUser() and RevertToSelf() functions do the trick in the same AppDomain as the original code initiating the impersonation. You can also create a new AppDomain programmatically and have the code that requires more privileges execute there. We can go one step further and execute the high-privileged code in another process. If you wrap the code in a COM+ component, you can take advantage of the component services offered by Enterprise Services, which provides a set of services that are able to tie separate data stores, such as SQL Server, Oracle, and message queues, together in a single transaction. Enterprise Services provides services such as loosely coupled events, queued components, and object pooling, increasing the scalability of applications. One of those services is the possibility to specify the account under which the COM+ component will run. This makes impersonation for COM+ components a breeze. In this section, you will see how to do this.

■**Note** In the future, Enterprise Services will be replaced by Windows Communication Foundation (WCF), which is a part of the .NET Framework 3.0 Runtime Components. More information about the .NET Framework 3.0 Runtime Components can be found in Chapter 4.

In an earlier example discussed in the section "Creating a New AppDomain" we tried to retrieve a collection of site groups of which the user is a member. We have modified that example a little bit so you can pass the URL of the site collection and the username as arguments. The code looks like this:

```
public string GetUserRoles(string strUrl, string strUserName)
{
  string strResult = String.Empty;
  using (SPSite objSiteCollection = ➡
  new SPSite(strUrl))
  {
    using ( SPWeb objSite = ➡
    objSiteCollection.OpenWeb() )
    {
      SPUser objUser = objSite.Users[strUserName];
      foreach (SPRole objRole in objUser.Roles)
      {
        strResult += objRole.Name + ", ";
      }
    }
  }

  return strResult;
}
```

Create a new class library project and call it EnterpriseServicesComponent. Add a new class called RoleManager.cs to the project and add the GetUserRoles() method to it. You will need to set a reference to the Microsoft.SharePoint.dll and import the Microsoft.SharePoint namespace in order for the code to work. The default location for the Microsoft.SharePoint.dll is [drive letter]:\Program Files\Common Files\Microsoft Shared\Web Server Extensions\60\ISAPI\Microsoft.SharePoint.dll.

The Component Services MMC snap-in lets you define the identity under which the COM+ component runs, as shown by the following method:

```
public string GetCurrentUserName()
{
  return WindowsIdentity.GetCurrent().Name;
}
```

Import the System.Security.Principal namespace and add this method to the RoleManager class as well.

If you want to create a COM+ component, you will need to add a reference to System.EnterpriseServices.dll. Every COM+ component class inherits from the System.EnterpriseServices.ServicedComponent class, which is the base class for all classes using COM+ services. You will also need to add a public constructor for any COM+ component class. The code for this class looks like this:

```csharp
using System;
using System.Collections.Generic;
using System.Text;
using System.EnterpriseServices;
using System.Runtime.InteropServices;
using Microsoft.SharePoint;
using System.Security.Principal;

namespace LoisAndClark.EnterpriseServicesComponent
{
  public class RoleManager : ServicedComponent
  {
    public RoleManager()
    {
    }

    public string GetCurrentUserName()
    {
      return WindowsIdentity.GetCurrent().Name;
    }

    public string GetUserRoles(string strUrl, string strUserName)
    {
      string strResult = String.Empty;
      using (SPSite objSiteCollection = new SPSite(strUrl))
      {
        using (SPWeb objSite = objSiteCollection.OpenWeb())
        {
          SPUser objUser = objSite.Users[strUserName];
          foreach (SPRole objRole in objUser.Roles)
          {
            strResult += objRole.Name + ", ";
          }
        }
      }

      return strResult;
    }
  }
}
```

If you want to register a .NET library, it needs to be strong named. Right-click the Enter-priseServicesComponent project and choose Properties. Click Signing and check Sign the Assembly. Create a new strong-name key file and call it MyKey.snk. This is shown in Figure 8-9.

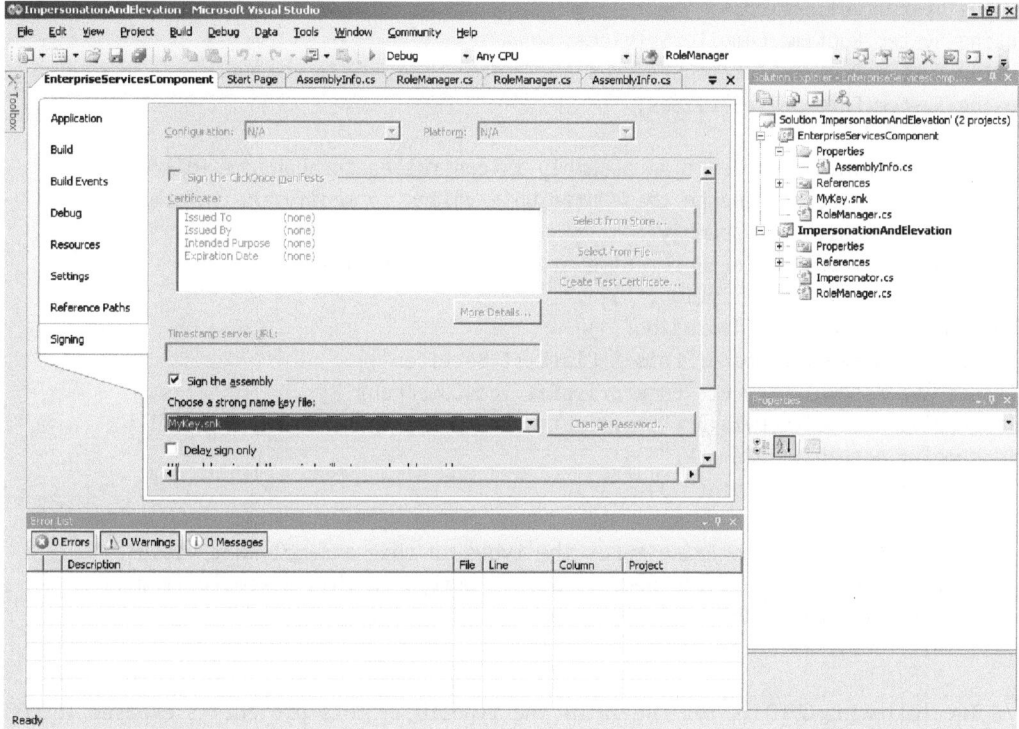

Figure 8-9. *Strong-name key file*

The COM+ component is almost finished; you just need to add some metadata to AssemblyInfo.cs. The metadata is used as input for the configuration of the COM+ application that occurs at installation time. You need to define an application name that becomes the name for the COM+ application and optionally add a description. You also need to specify the activation mode, which is either library or server. Because you want the COM+ component to run in its own process (so you can specify an identity for it), you should choose server. Library mode causes the COM+ component to run in the client process. After choosing the activation mode, choose whether you want to specify restricted access control policies. In this example everybody is allowed to access the COM+ component, so do not bother to specify access control policies. The metadata looks like this:

```
[assembly: ApplicationName("RoleManager ES component")]
[assembly: Description("An example of doing impersonation within a COM+ ➥
application built in .NET")]
[assembly: ApplicationActivation(ActivationOption.Server)]
[assembly: ApplicationAccessControl(false)]
```

Locate the ComVisible attribute in AssemblyInfo.cs and set it to true, like this:

```
[assembly: ComVisible(true)]
```

The presence of this attribute is new in Visual Studio.NET 2005. If it is set to false the COM+ component will not register. By now, the AssemblyInfo.cs file should look a lot like this:

```
using System.Reflection;
using System.Runtime.CompilerServices;
using System.Runtime.InteropServices;
using System.EnterpriseServices;

// General Information about an assembly is controlled through the following
// set of attributes. Change these attribute values to modify the information
// associated with an assembly.
[assembly: AssemblyTitle("EnterpriseServicesComponent")]
[assembly: AssemblyDescription("")]
[assembly: AssemblyConfiguration("")]
[assembly: AssemblyCompany("Lois & Clark IT Services")]
[assembly: AssemblyProduct("EnterpriseServicesComponent")]
[assembly: AssemblyCopyright("Copyright © Lois & Clark IT Services 2006")]
[assembly: AssemblyTrademark("")]
[assembly: AssemblyCulture("")]

// Setting ComVisible to false makes the types in this assembly not visible
// to COM components.  If you need to access a type in this assembly from
// COM, set the ComVisible attribute to true on that type.
[assembly: ComVisible(true)]

// The following GUID is for the ID of the typelib if this project is exposed to COM
[assembly: Guid("821781a6-54e8-425e-ba93-98d378d20b10")]

// Version information for an assembly consists of the following four values:
//
//      Major Version
//      Minor Version
//      Build Number
//      Revision
//
// You can specify all the values or you can default the Revision and Build Numbers
// by using the '*' as shown below:
[assembly: AssemblyVersion("1.0.0.0")]
[assembly: AssemblyFileVersion("1.0.0.0")]
[assembly: ApplicationName("RoleManager ES component")]
[assembly: Description("An example of doing impersonation within a COM+ ➡
application built in .NET")]
[assembly: ApplicationActivation(ActivationOption.Server)]
[assembly: ApplicationAccessControl(false)]
```

Next, you need to install the COM+ component. Open a Visual Studio command prompt, navigate to the folder that contains the EnterpriseServicesComponent.dll and type **regsvcs EnterpriseServicesComponent.dll**. This starts the installation of the COM+ component. You can unregister the component via regsvcs -u EnterpriseServicesComponent.dll. Go to Control Panel ➤ Administrative Tools ➤ Component Services to start the Component Services MMC snap-in. Open Component Services ➤ Computers ➤ My Computer ➤ COM+ Applications, and find the RoleManager ES component COM+ application. Right-click the application, choose Properties, and click the Identity tab. Here you can specify the identity under which the COM+ component runs, which is shown in Figure 8-10. Choose This User and specify the credentials of your administrator account. If you switch identities, you need to restart the COM+ application. You can do this by right-clicking the application and selecting Shutdown and then Start.

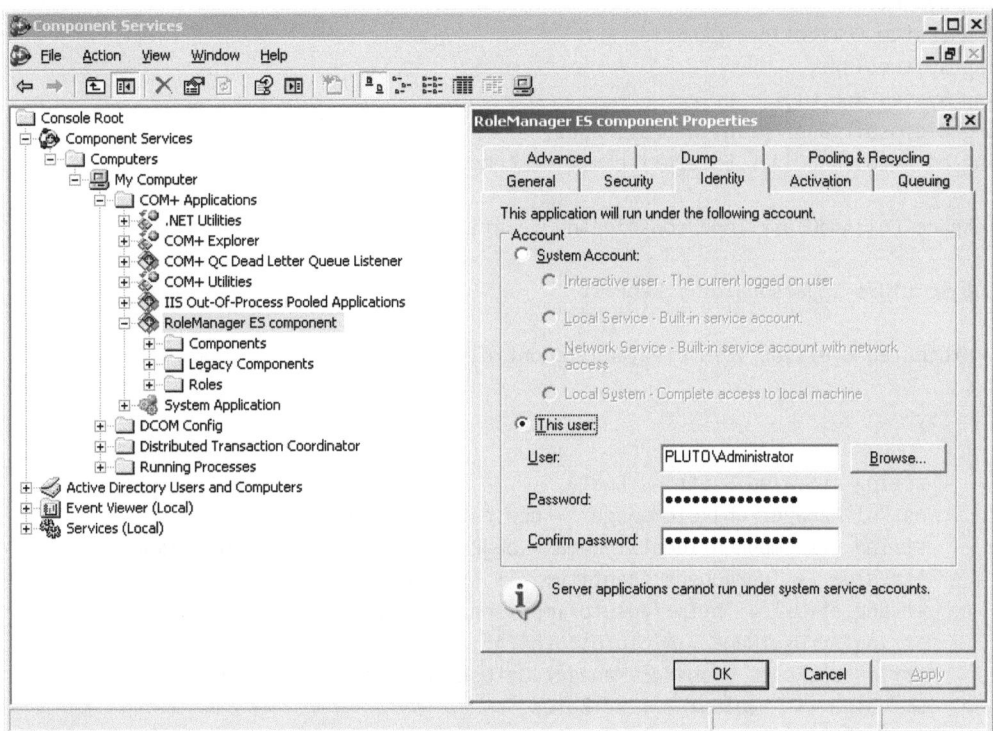

Figure 8-10. *The Identity tab of the RoleManager ES component*

If you want to call the COM+ component from a web part, the web part library must reference the .NET assembly directly and add a reference to System.EnterpriseServices.dll as well. At run time, the web part will not call the .NET assembly, but instead it communicates with the COM+ component. The code creates an instance of the COM+ component class RoleManager and calls the GetCurrentUserName() method to establish the identity of the COM+ application, to check the identity of the COM+ component. After that the client asks the COM+ component to return the roles for a given user. The COM+ component calls the GetUserRoles() method running under its own identity. This way you can even provide readers with an overview of the roles they belong to. The code looks like this:

```
es.RoleManager objRoleManager = new es.RoleManager();
string strComponentIdentityName = objRoleManager.GetCurrentUserName();
string strUrl = "http://pluto/ImpersonationAndElevation/";
string strUserName = @"pluto\AuthorA";
string strRoles = objRoleManager.GetUserRoles(strUrl, strUserName);
```

You should make sure the COM+ component namespace is imported. We used a namespace alias because our web part library already contained a class called RoleManager:

```
using es = EnterpriseServicesComponent;
```

The complete code listing for the web part calling the COM+ component looks like this:

```csharp
using System;
using System.Collections.Generic;
using System.Text;
using System.Web.UI;
using Microsoft.SharePoint.WebPartPages;
using es = LoisAndClark.EnterpriseServicesComponent;

namespace LoisAndClark.ImpersonationAndElevation
{
  public class Impersonator : WebPart
  {
    protected override void CreateChildControls()
    {
      try
      {
        string strValue = String.Empty;
        es.RoleManager objRoleManager = new es.RoleManager();
        string strComponentIdentityName = objRoleManager.GetCurrentUserName();
        strValue += "component identity: " + strComponentIdentityName;
        string strUrl = "http://pluto/ImpersonationAndElevation/";
        string strUserName = @"pluto\AuthorA";
        string strRoles = objRoleManager.GetUserRoles(strUrl, strUserName);
        strValue += " roles: " + strRoles;
        Controls.Add(new LiteralControl(strValue));
      }
      catch (Exception err)
      {
        Controls.Add(new LiteralControl(err.Message));
      }
    }
  }
}
```

Queued Components

There's one last topic left to make the discussion about impersonation complete: how to handle impersonation in asynchronous scenarios. Processing data asynchronously makes a lot of sense if you are handling large messages, a lot of small messages, or messages that take a lot of time to process because of the presence of complex business rules. In such cases it does not make sense for a client (for instance, a web part) to wait until message processing has completed, because the end user will have better things to do with his time than stare at a computer screen for a long time. To implement asynchronous scenarios we will use Enterprise Services queued components.

In this section we will retrieve list data in a web part and call a queued component that processes the list data asynchronously and updates the SharePoint list where the data came from. We will pretend the list data processing involves the appliance of complicated business rules that take quite a long time. Because queued components are hosted within Enterprise Services, we can define the identity under which the queued component runs, thus solving impersonation problems.

Make a custom list called MyTestList if you want to try out the example described in this section. Add three columns to the list called Column1, Column2, and Column3. Add some random test data to the list. Figure 8-11 shows our MyTestList custom list. You also need to have access to a SharePoint server running Enterprise Services and MSMQ.

Figure 8-11. *The MyTestList custom list*

The following code retrieves the list MyTestList from the ImpersonationAndElevation SharePoint site. There is a special factor to consider here. We want the web part to call the queued component and pass the list data as an argument. Parameter types of queued component methods must implement the IPersistStream COM+ interface. This means it is not enough if a .NET type is serializable. As a workaround, we retrieve the list data in a DataTable that still cannot be passed as an argument to a queued component method. However, if we add the DataTable to a DataSet and store the DataSet XML in a string we are where we want to be. .NET strings can be passed directly to queued component methods, so we can use the DataSet XML in a string to call queued component methods. The following code retrieves a collection of lists in a DataTable and converts the DataTable to a string so that it can be passed to a queued component:

```
string strUrl = "http://pluto/ImpersonationAndElevation";
SPSite objSiteCollection = new SPSite(strUrl);
SPWeb objSite = objSiteCollection.OpenWeb();
SPList objTestList = objSite.Lists["MyTestList"];
DataTable dtTestList = objTestList.Items.GetDataTable();
objSite.Close();
objSiteCollection.Close();
```

```
DataSet dsData = new DataSet();
dsData.Tables.Add(dtTestList);
string strListData = dsData.GetXml();
… Some code which calls queued component
```

At this point we are ready to call the queued component. We haven't talked about the queued component yet, but it suffices to know that it contains a class called Processor, which contains a ProcessListData() method, which is able to process the list data. The Processor class implements the IProcessor interface that defines the ProcessListData method. The instantiation of a queued component looks like this:

```
string strUri = "queue:/new:MyQueuedComponent.Processor";
IProcessor objQueuedComponent = (IProcessor) Marshal.BindToMoniker(strUri);
objQueuedComponent.ProcessListData(strListData);
Marshal.ReleaseComObject(objQueuedComponent);
```

What happens after the call to the ProcessListData() method is that the information that is sent to the method is stored in an MSMQ queue. When the server is ready to do some processing, it will retrieve a message from the queue and instantiate the MyQueuedComponent.Processor class. Therefore, the message might be processed more or less immediately if the server is free. If the server is busy, it might take an hour until the message is processed. The important point here is that the message will be processed eventually, thus providing a robust architecture.

Let us take a look at the queued component. Create a new project using the class library template. You should add a reference to the System.EnterpriseServices assembly. You will always have to specify at least one interface for the queued component and add the [InterfaceQueuing] attribute of the System.EnterpriseServices namespace to it, which enables queuing support for the interface. Clients can only communicate with queued components through these interfaces. In our example we created an interface called IProcessor that looks like this:

```
[InterfaceQueuing(Enabled = true)]
public interface IProcessor
{
  void ProcessListData(string strListData);
}
```

A queued component class always inherits from the ServicedComponent class, the base class for all classes using COM+ services. The queued component class must also implement the IProcessor interface defined earlier. You will need to decorate the class with the [InterfaceQueuing] attribute to indicate that the class supports the IProcessor interface. In Visual Studio.NET 2003, classes are public by default; this is not the case anymore in Visual Studio.NET 2005. Queued component classes need to be available outside the confines of the assembly containing the component classes, so make sure the queued component class is public. By the way, the same holds true when creating the IProcessor interface; the interface should be public too. As we have learned ourselves, it is an easy mistake to make.

It is hard to debug a queued component. You will have to attach to the process in which a queued component is executed manually. However, since the component is called asynchronously you do not have exact control over when a method is called and you will have to guess the right time to attach to the process. The best way to debug a queued component is to create an adapter class that performs the actual work for the queued component. Then your test harness can reference the queued component project and instantiate the adapter class that should implement the same interfaces as the queued component class. It is impossible to instantiate the queued component class yourself because it needs the Enterprise Services context.

To sum up, our queued component class inherits from the ServicedComponent class, implements the IProcessor interface, and does not perform any work. The only thing the queued component class should do is call the adapter that we have called ProcessorAdapter and let that class take care of the actual work. The code looks like this:

```
using System;
using System.Collections.Generic;
using System.Text;
using System.EnterpriseServices;

namespace LoisAndClark.MyQueuedComponent
{
  [InterfaceQueuing(Interface = "IProcessor")]
  public class Processor : ServicedComponent, IProcessor
  {
    public void ProcessListData(string strListData)
    {
      ProcessorAdapter objAdapter = new ProcessorAdapter();
      objAdapter.ProcessListData(strListData);
    }
  }
}
```

The processor adapter class performs the actual work. We have added the processor adapter class to make debugging easy. The processor adapter class should implement all the interfaces that are supported by the queued component class, which means our ProcessorAdapter class has a ProcessListData() method as well, because it implements the IProcessor interface. The only argument of the ProcessListData() method is a string that contains list data in the form of XML. As you may remember, the reason we pass list data in a string is that we need to pass an argument type that supports the IPersist COM+ interface. So the first thing our ProcessListData() method does is convert the string data to a form that is easier to deal with: a DataSet. After that, the method obtains a reference to the MyTestList custom list. Then it loops through the list data and executes complicated business logic. In our example, we add the current date and time to Column1 and Column3 of the MyTestList custom list. The ProcessorAdapter class looks like this:

```csharp
using System;
using System.Collections.Generic;
using System.Text;
using Microsoft.SharePoint;
using System.Data;
using System.IO;

namespace LoisAndClark.MyQueuedComponent
{
  public class ProcessorAdapter : IProcessor
  {
    public void ProcessListData(string strListData)
    {
      StringReader objReader = new StringReader(strListData);
      DataSet dsListData = new DataSet();
      dsListData.ReadXml(objReader);
      DataTable dtListData = dsListData.Tables[0];

      string strUrl = "http://pluto/ImpersonationAndElevation";
      SPSite objSiteCollection = new SPSite(strUrl);
      SPWeb objSite = objSiteCollection.OpenWeb();
      SPList objTestList = objSite.Lists["MyTestList"];
      for (int i = 0; i < dtListData.Rows.Count; i++)
      {
        int intID = Convert.ToInt32(dtListData.Rows[i]["ID"]);
        SPListItem objListItem = objTestList.GetItemById(intID);
        objListItem["Column1"] = "1 " + DateTime.Now;
        objListItem["Column2"] = dtListData.Rows[i]["Column2"];
        objListItem["Column3"] = objListItem["Column3"] = "3 " + DateTime.Now;
        objListItem.Update();
      }
    }
  }
}
```

You should strong name the MyQueuedComponent assembly. The section "Enterprise Services COM+ Component" earlier in this chapter describes how to do this. Add the following metadata to AssemblyInfo.cs:

```csharp
[assembly: ApplicationName("MyQueuedComponent")]
[assembly: ApplicationActivation(ActivationOption.Server)]
[assembly: ApplicationQueuing(Enabled = true, ➡
QueueListenerEnabled = true, MaxListenerThreads = 5)]
[assembly: ApplicationAccessControl(false)]
```

The most interesting option here is the maximum number of concurrent instances of your queued component. Instances of the queued component are created as needed (if there are no messages left in the queue there will only be one thread running, the queue listener). The valid range for this value is 0 to 1000. By default, this number is 16 multiplied by the number of CPUs in the server.

The ApplicationAccessControl attribute is optional. This attribute can be used to configure all settings on the hosting COM+ application security tab. If you omit this attribute, you will get the following warning upon assembly registration: "The assembly does not declare an ApplicationAccessControl attribute." Application security will be enabled by default. Setting access control to false allows everybody to access our queued component.

Ensure that the [ComVisible] attribute in AssemblyInfo.cs is set to true, otherwise the registration of the queued component will fail.

Now the MyQueuedComponent assembly can be registered in Enterprise Services. Open a Visual Studio command and navigate to the directory that contains the MyQueuedComponent assembly. Type **regsvcs MyQueuedComponent.dll** at the command line to register the assembly.

At this point a COM+ application called MyQueuedComponent and a couple of MSMQ queues are created: MyQueuedComponent, MyQueuedComponent_0 to MyQueuedComponent_4, and MyQueuedComponent_deadqueue. All calls to a queued component are actually stored in a message queue. As soon as the queued component is ready to do some processing, the message is picked up from the MyQueuedComponent queue and processed by the queued component. Figure 8-12 shows the MyQueuedComponent queue already containing messages waiting to be processed.

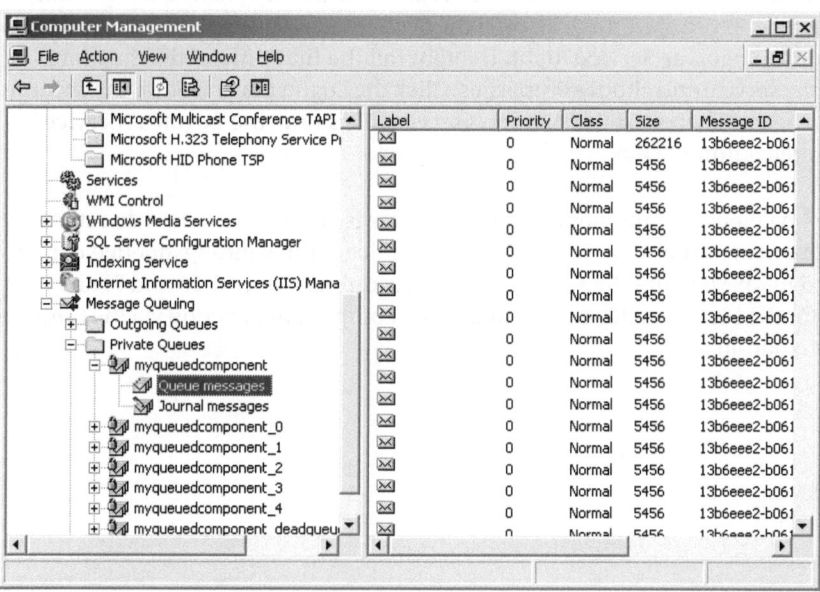

Figure 8-12. *The MyQueuedComponent queue*

If the processing of this message fails, the message is placed in the next queue in line. This process repeats itself until the message is processed successfully or until the message is placed in the dead message queue. After the first attempt, it takes 1 minute before the same message is processed again. The second retry takes a wait time of 2 minutes. The wait time increases until the fifth and final retry attempt, which takes place 16 minutes after the previous (fourth) attempt.

Now that the MyQueuedComponent COM+ application is created, you need to do some additional configuration. Go to Control Panel ➤ Administrative Tools ➤ Component Services. Open the Component Services node, then open the My Computer node, and, finally, open the COM+ Applications folder. The MyQueuedComponent COM+ application should be listed.

The next steps describe how to configure our COM+ application:

1. Right-click Properties. Go to the Queuing tab, and make sure the Queued check box and the Listen check box are checked.

2. Go to the Activation tab and ensure that the Server Application radio button is checked.

3. Check the Run Application as NT Service button. Click the Set up New Service button and click Create. A Windows service for the MyQueuedComponent queued component will be created automatically.

4. Go to the Identity tab. Choose an account with sufficient SharePoint permissions to update the SharePoint list data. On our server, we chose the administrator account as the identity under which the queued component runs.

5. Type **services.msc** from the command prompt and find the MyQueuedComponent Windows service. Try to start the service. If the account used by the Windows service is not granted the Logon as Service Right, it might fail the first time. If this happens, right-click the service and choose Properties. Click the Logon tab and enter the account information again. Then start the Windows service. This time the Logon as Service Right is granted automatically.

As soon as the MyQueuedComponent Windows service is started, messages directed to our queued component are processed. If the Windows service is not running, queued component calls are stored in MSMQ until the service is up and running. Figure 8-13 and Figure 8-14 show how to monitor the MyQueuedComponent queued component in action via the Component Services MMC snap-in.

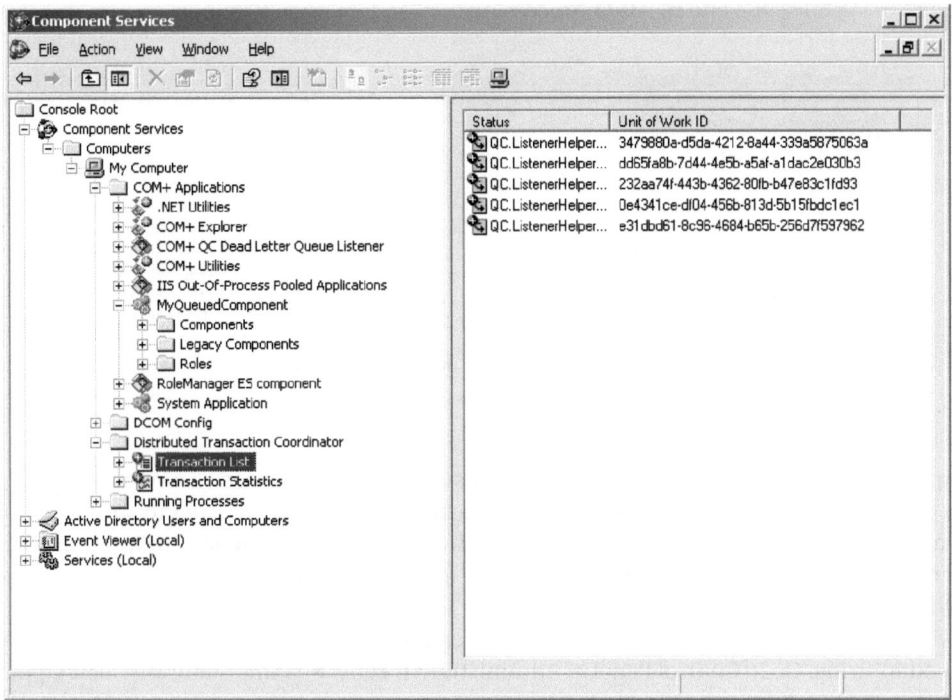

Figure 8-13. *Transaction list*

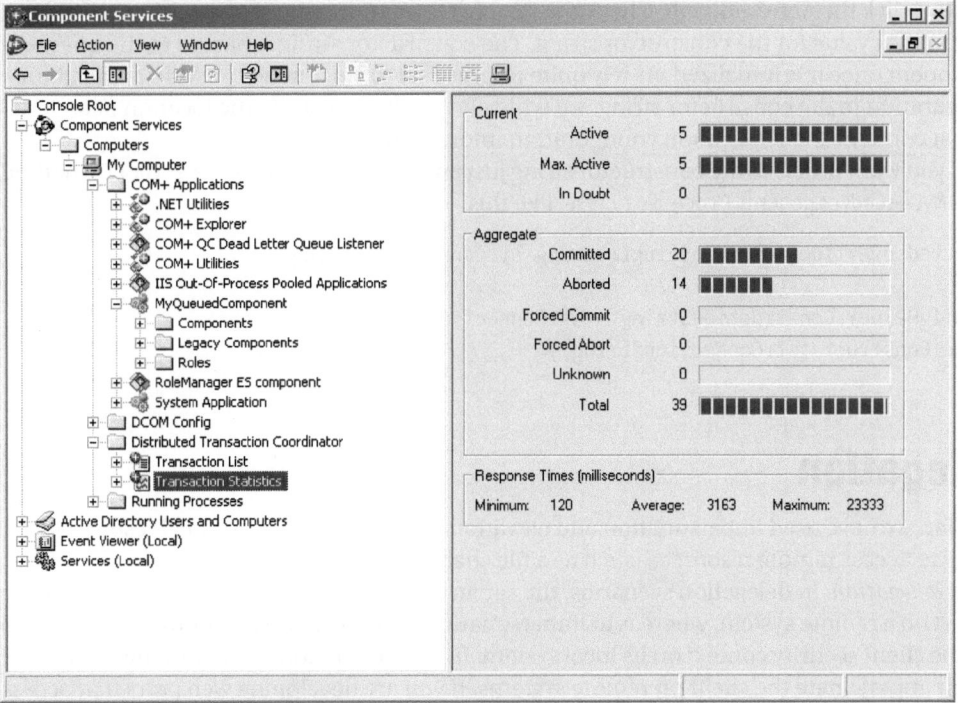

Figure 8-14. *Transaction statistics*

Figure 8-15 shows the end result of processing the list data asynchronously.

Figure 8-15. *The MyQueuedComponent queue*

A queued component is a library (.dll). Once installed and configured as a Windows service the queued component will be loaded into a host. This makes it harder to specify an application configuration file, as the app.config of the host is used. A queued component is hosted by dllhost.exe. By default, dllhost.exe can be found on the following location: C:\WINDOWS\System32\dllhost.exe.

If you want to specify application settings, you can use an Enterprise Service component construction string. Go to Control Panel ➤ Administrative Tools ➤ Component Services. Open the Component Services node, then open the My Computer node, and open the COM+ Applications folder. The MyQueuedComponent COM+ application should be listed. Open this node as well, and, finally, open MyQueuedComponent.Processor. Right-click the queued component and click the Activation tab. Check the Enable Object Construction check box. Now you can specify a value for the constructor string. The constructor string is passed to the queued component once it is initialized. As it is quite impractical to store an entire XML application configuration in the constructor string, we typically use this to specify the location of an XML file that contains the application configuration information.

If you want to access the constructor string just add an override of the Construct() method to the MyQueuedComponent.Processor class, like this:

```
protected override void Construct(string strConnectionString)
{
  ConfigHelper.ConstructionString = strConnectionString;
  base.Construct (strConnectionString);
}
```

Delegation

Thus far, we have used impersonation and elevation techniques to access local resources. Trying to access remote resources (such as a file share) by assuming another user context is called *delegation*. In delegation scenarios, the server process impersonates the client security context on a remote system, whereas in impersonation scenarios the server process impersonates the client security context on its local system. In impersonation scenarios, the server cannot impersonate the client on remote systems. If you are developing web parts that access remote resources you must take a couple of additional steps before you are able to support delegation. This section guides you through these steps.

If you want to get delegation working, the presence of Active Directory is a requirement. You will need to set up your network to use the Kerberos authentication protocol (which requires Active Directory). You will also need to set up the computers and accounts on your network as trusted for delegation.

In the first step, you will enable Kerberos authentication on your SharePoint server. The Kerberos protocol is based on ticketing; users provide a valid username and password to an authentication server which hands the user a ticket that can be used on the network to request other network services.

If you want to enable Kerberos authentication on a SharePoint virtual server, you should do the following:

1. Determine the virtual server ID number of your SharePoint virtual server. By default, this is 1. One way to retrieve the correct virtual server ID is to use the IIS Metabase Explorer, which can be downloaded from http://www.download.com. The IIS Metabase Explorer is shown in Figure 8-16.

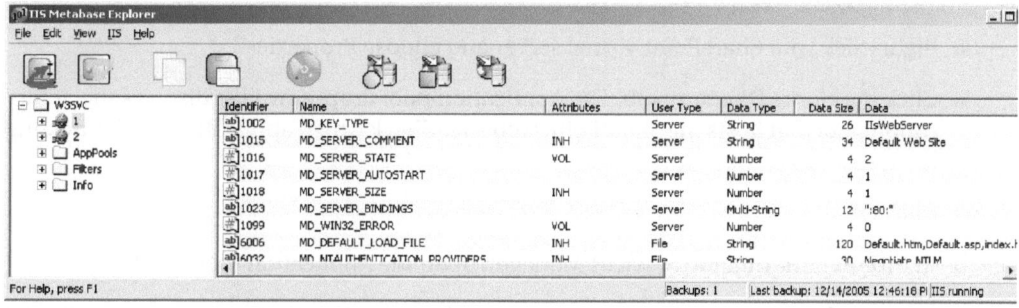

Figure 8-16. *The IIS Metabase Explorer*

2. On the SharePoint server, open a new command prompt.

3. Go to the following location: [drive letter]:\inetpub\adminscripts.

4. You can use the adsutil.vbs utility (located in the adminscripts folder) to retrieve information about a given virtual server. If you want to check out which form of authentication is enabled use the following command:

```
cscript adsutil.vbs get w3svc/1/root/NTAuthenticationProviders
```

5. The default authentication model is NTLM. This is a secure protocol that is based on encrypting usernames and passwords before sending them over the network. If you have not set the authentication provider before, the previous command will return the following message: "the parameter "NTAuthenticationProviders" is not set at this node."

6. To enable Kerberos authentication, issue the following command:

```
cscript adsutil.vbs set w3svc/1/root/NTAuthenticationProviders "Negotiate,NTLM"
```

7. Restart IIS by typing **iisreset** on a command prompt.

Tip If you want to switch back and only allow NTLM authentication on the virtual server, issue the following command: `cscript adsutil.vbs set w3svc/1/root/NTAuthenticationProviders "NTLM"`.

In the next step, we will check that the application pool hosting the SharePoint web site is using the NT Authority\NetworkService identity. Built-in accounts such as the NetworkService account are automatically configured to work with Kerberos authentication. If you are using a domain user account, you will have to specify a service principal name (SPN) for it. There are two kinds of principal names: *user principal names* and *service principal names.* A user principal name is associated to a specific user. A service principal name is the name by which a client uniquely identifies an instance of a service and authorizes the client to use a particular service.

The following steps describe how to specify an identity for a given application pool:

1. Open Internet Information Services Manager.

2. Open the [server name] (local computer) node.

3. Open the Web Sites node.

4. Right-click your SharePoint virtual server and choose Properties.

5. Click the Home Directory tab. The Application pool drop-down list displays the application pool that hosts the SharePoint web site. Check which application pool is hosting the web site.

6. Click OK.

7. In Internet Information Services Manager, open the Application Pools node.

8. Right-click the name of the application pool that is hosting the SharePoint web site and choose Properties.

9. Click the Identity tab.

If the security account is not one of the predefined accounts, use the setspn.exe tool to set a service principal name for it. The setspn.exe tool is a command-line utility that allows you to read, modify, and delete service principal names for an Active Directory property. Setspn.exe is a part of the Support Tools pack located in the Support folder on the Windows Server 2003 CD.

If you want to set a service principal name for an account type, the command in a command prompt (the parameter indicates that a service principal name needs to be added for this account for a given computer) is the following:

```
Setspn -a HTTP/[server] [domain name]\[user name]
```

Note More information about the setspn.exe tool can be found on the Microsoft TechNet web site (`http://www.microsoft.com/technet`) in the article "Configuring Constrained Delegation for Kerberos (IIS 6.0)."

Next, you need to configure the SharePoint server so that it is trusted for delegation:

1. Click Start ➤ Administrative Tools ➤ Start Active Directory Users and Computers.

2. In the left pane, expand the Domain node.

3. Click the Computers node.

4. In the right pane, right-click the name of the SharePoint server, and then click Properties.

5. Click the General tab.

6. Select the Trust Computer for Delegation check box, and click OK.

If the application pool identity is configured to use a domain account instead of a predefined account, or if you are using impersonation techniques to run the process under a domain account, you need to configure that the account is trusted for delegation before you can use Kerberos authentication, as shown in the following procedure:

1. If it is not opened yet, click Start ➤ Administrative Tools ➤ Start Active Directory Users and Computers.

2. In the left pane, expand the Domain node.

3. In the left pane, click the Users node.

4. In the right pane, right-click the name of the user account and choose Properties.

5. Click the Account tab ➤ Account Options. Click to select the Account Is Trusted for Delegation check box. Then click OK.

6. Close Active Directory Users and Computers.

Summary

You have concluded the tour on impersonation and elevation for SharePoint Products and Technologies. You saw how to use the LogonUser() Win32 API function to impersonate user accounts. Then you saw how to store user credentials in a safe and encrypted way in configuration files and the Single Sign-On database. You saw how to avoid storing credentials via credentialless impersonation. You learned that because of bugs in the SharePoint object model, impersonation sometimes fails when using the LogonUser() and RevertToSelf() Win32 API functions, and you learned how to work around that by creating a new AppDomain or using Enterprise Service COM+ components. Then we discussed how to use impersonation in asynchronous scenarios. Finally, you learned what delegation is and how to enable it on a SharePoint server. As far as we are concerned, you are ready to impersonate.

Bibliography

Andrew, Paul; Conard, James; Woodgate, Scott; Flanders, Jon; Hatoun, George; Hilerio, Israel; Indurkar, Pravin; Pilarinos, Dennis; and Willis, Jurgen. *Presenting Windows Workflow Foundation, Beta Edition.* Indianapolis, IN: Sams Publishing, 2006.

Banerjee, Ashish; Corera, Aravind; Greenvoss, Zach; Krowczyk, Andrew; Nagel, Christian; Peiris, Chris; Thangarathinam, Thiru; and Maiani, Brad. *Professional C# Web Services: Building .NET Web Services with ASP.NET and .NET Remoting.* Hoboken, NJ: Wrox Press, 2001.

Beyer, Derek. *C# COM+ Programming.* New York, NY: John Wiley & Sons Inc., 2001.

Bleeker, Todd. "Even Better Impersonation." http://mindsharpblogs.com/todd, 2006.

Bock, Jason. *Visual Basic 6 Win32 API Tutorial.* Hoboken, NJ: Wrox Press, 1998.

Box, Don, and Sells, Chris. *Essential .NET, Volume I: The Common Language Runtime.* Boston, MA: Addison-Wesley, 2002.

Bruggeman, Margriet, and Bruggeman, Nikander. "Creating Enterprise Services Queued Components in C#." http://www.lcbridge.nl/vision/2006/queuedcomponents.htm, 2006.

Bruggeman, Margriet, and Bruggeman, Nikander. "Id, Ego, and Superego." http://www.lcbridge.nl/vision/impersonation.htm, 2005.

Duynstee, Teun. "Reporting over SharePoint Lists with MS Reporting Services." http://www.teuntostring.net/blog/2005/09/reporting-over-sharepoint-lists-with.html, 2005.

English, Bill, et al. *Microsoft SharePoint Products and Technologies Resource Kit.* Redmond, WA: Microsoft Press, 2004.

Esposito, Dino. *Introducing Microsoft ASP.NET 2.0.* Redmond, WA: Microsoft Press, 2004.

Greenfield, Jack; Short, Keith; Cook, Steve; and Kent, Stuart. *Software Factories.* New York, NY: John Wiley & Sons Inc., 2004.

Halstead, Patrick; Mandava-Teredesai, Vani; and Blain, Matthew. *Developing Solutions with Microsoft InfoPath.* Redmond, WA: Microsoft Press, 2004.

Hild, Ed. "Deliver SQL Server Reports to SharePoint to Enhance Team Collaboration." http://msdn.microsoft.com/msdnmag/issues/06/03/ReportingServices/, 2006.

Howard, Michael, and LeBlanc, David C. *Writing Secure Code, Second Edition.* Redmond, WA: Microsoft Press, 2002.

Lachev, Teo. "Create Reports from Any Data Source Using SQL Server Reporting Services Custom Data Extensions." http://www.devx.com/dbzone/Article/31336/0, 2006.

LaMacchia, Brian A.; Lange, Sebastian; Lyons, Matthew; Martin, Rudi; and Price, Kevin T. *.NET Framework Security.* Upper Saddle River, NJ: Pearson Education, 2002.

Landrum, Rodney, and Voytek II, Walter J. *Pro SQL Server 2005 Reporting Services.* Berkeley, CA: Apress, 2006.

Londner, Raphael. "SharePoint Impersonation Using COM+ Components." `http://blogs.microsoft.fr/rlondner/articles/7089.aspx`, 2006.

Lowy, Juval. *Programming .NET Components, Second Edition.* Sebastopol, CA: O'Reilly Media, 2005.

Prather, Maurice. "Advanced Coding Technique: Using AppDomains to Get Past OM Limitations." `http://www.bluedoglimited.com/SharePointThoughts/ViewPost.aspx?ID=7`, 2005.

Willer, Bob. *MCAD/MCSD Self-Paced Training Kit: Developing XML Web Services and Server Components with Microsoft Visual Basic.NET and Visual C#.NET.* Redmond, WA: Microsoft Press, 2003.

Index

You Need the Companion eBook

Your purchase of this book entitles you to buy the companion PDF-version eBook for only $10. Take the weightless companion with you anywhere.

We believe this Apress title will prove so indispensable that you'll want to carry it with you everywhere, which is why we are offering the companion eBook (in PDF format) for $10 to customers who purchase this book now. Convenient and fully searchable, the PDF version of any content-rich, page-heavy Apress book makes a valuable addition to your programming library. You can easily find and copy code—or perform examples by quickly toggling between instructions and the application. Even simultaneously tackling a donut, diet soda, and complex code becomes simplified with hands-free eBooks!

Once you purchase your book, getting the $10 companion eBook is simple:

❶ Visit **www.apress.com/promo/tendollars/**.

❷ Complete a basic registration form to receive a randomly generated question about this title.

❸ Answer the question correctly in 60 seconds, and you will receive a promotional code to redeem for the $10.00 eBook.

2560 Ninth Street • Suite 219 • Berkeley, CA 94710

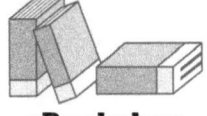
eBookshop

Offer valid through 5/27/07.